THEORIES OF MYTH

*From Ancient Israel and Greece
to Freud, Jung, Campbell,
and Lévi-Strauss*

Series Editor
ROBERT A. SEGAL
University of Lancaster

A GARLAND SERIES

SERIES CONTENTS

VOLUME

6

STRUCTURALISM IN MYTH

LÉVI-STRAUSS, BARTHES,
DUMÉZIL, AND PROPP

Edited with introductions by

ROBERT A. SEGAL
University of Lancaster

GARLAND PUBLISHING, Inc.
New York & London
1996

Library of Congress Cataloging-in-Publication Data

Structuralism in myth : Lévi-Strauss, Barthes, Dumézil, and
   Propp / edited with introductions by Robert A. Segal.
      p.   cm. — (Theories of myth ; v. 6)
   Includes bibliographical references.
   ISBN 0-8153-2260-7 (alk. paper)
   1. Myth.   2. Myth—Study and teaching—History—20th
century—Sources.   3. Folklore—Structural analysis.
4. Structuralism.   I. Segal, Robert Alan.   II. Series: Theories
of myth ; 6.
BL304.S77   1996
291.1'3'07—dc20   95-41491
                                                           CIP

Printed on acid-free, 250-year-life paper
Manufactured in the United States of America

CONTENTS

SERIES INTRODUCTION

The modern study of myth is already more than a hundred years old and is the work of many disciplines. This six-volume collection of 113 essays brings together both classic and contemporary analyses of myth from the disciplines that have contributed most to its study: psychology, anthropology, folklore, philosophy, religious studies, and literature. Because myth has been analyzed for so long by specialists in so many fields, knowledge of the range of sources and access to them are difficult to secure. The present collection provides a comprehensive and systematic selection of the most important writings on myth.

All of the essays in this collection are theoretical. All are concerned with myth per se, not with a single myth or set of myths. Many of the essays make explicit claims about myth generally. Others use individual myths to make or to test those claims. Most of the essayists are proponents of the theories they employ. Some are critics.

By no means has each of the disciplines considered here developed a single, unified theory of myth. Multiple, competing theories have arisen within disciplines as well as across them. The leading theories from each discipline are represented in the collection.

Theories of myth are never theories of myth alone. Myth always falls under a larger rubric such as the mind, culture, knowledge, religion, ritual, symbolism, and narrative. The rubric reflects the discipline from which the theory is derived. For example, psychological theories see myth as an expression of the mind. Anthropological theories view myth as an instance of culture. Literary theories regard myth as a variety of narrative. Within a discipline, theories differ about the nature of myth because they differ about the nature of the rubric involved. At the same time, theorists qualify as theorists of myth only when they single out myth for the application of the larger rubric. Writings that completely subsume myth under its larger rubric—discussing only religion or symbolism, for example—fail to qualify as writings on myth.

Theories of myth purport to answer one or more of the fundamental questions about myth: what is its origin, what is its function, what is its subject matter? Theories differ, first, in the answers they give to these questions. For most theorists, myth originates and functions to satisfy a need, but that need can be for anything—for example, for food, information, hope, or God. The need can be on the part of individuals or on the part of the community. Similarly, the subject matter, or referent, of myth can be anything. It can be the literal, apparent subject matter—for example, gods or the physical world—or a symbolic one—for example, human beings or society.

Theories differ even more basically in the questions they seek to answer. Few theories claim to answer all three of the major questions about myth. Some theories focus on the origin of myth, others on the function, still others on the subject matter. The answer a theory gives to one question doubtless shapes the answer it gives to another, but most theories concentrate on only one or two of the questions. Writings that merely describe or categorize myths fail to qualify as theories, as do writings that are skeptical of any universal claims about myths.

Still more basically, theories differ in the definition of myth. By some definitions myth can be a sheer belief or conviction—for example, the American "myth" of the frontier or of the self-made man. By other definitions myth must be a story. By some definitions the agents in a story can be humans or even animals. By others the agents must be either gods or extraordinary humans such as heroes. Theories employ definitions that reflect the disciplines from which they come. For example, theories from literature assume myth to be a story. Theories from religious studies assume the agents in myth to be gods or other superhuman figures.

Theorizing about myth is as old as the Presocratics. But only since the development of the social sciences in the last half of the nineteenth century has the theorizing become scientific. Some social scientific theories may find counterparts in earlier ones (see Burton Feldman and Robert D. Richardson's introduction to *The Rise of Modern Mythology* [Bloomington: Indiana University Press, 1972]), but social scientific theorizing still differs in kind from earlier theorizing. Where earlier theorizing was largely speculative and philosophical in nature, social scientific theorizing is far more empirical. The anthropologist John Beattie best sums up the differences, which apply to all of the social sciences and to the study of more than myth:

> Thus it was the reports of eighteenth- and nineteenth-century missionaries and travellers in Africa, North America,

the Pacific and elsewhere that provided the raw material upon which the first anthropological works, written in the second half of the last century, were based. Before then, of course, there had been plenty of conjecturing about human institutions and their origins; to say nothing of earlier times, in the eighteenth century Hume, Adam Smith and Ferguson in Britain, and Montesquieu, Condorcet and others on the Continent, had written about primitive institutions. But although their speculations were often brilliant, these thinkers were not empirical scientists; their conclusions were not based on any kind of evidence which could be tested; rather, they were for the most part implicit in their own cultures. They were really philosophers and historians of Europe, not anthropologists. (*Other Cultures* [New York: Free Press, 1964], 5–6)

By no means do all of the theories represented in this collection come from the social sciences. But even theories from philosophy, religious studies, and literature reflect strongly the impact of these fields.

The first four volumes in this collection are organized by disciplines. The selections in each volume typify the nature of the theorizing in the discipline. By far the most influential psychological theories of myth have been Freudian and Jungian. Anthropological theories have proved both more numerous and more disparate, with no one theory dominating the field. Folklorists have been particularly concerned with distinguishing myth from other verbal genres. Many theories of myth from philosophy and especially from religious studies grow out of attempts to decipher the classics and the Bible. Literary critics have understandably been preoccupied with both the similarities and the differences between myth and literature.

The final two volumes of the collection are grouped by theories rather than by disciplines. While the number of essays written on any major theory would readily fill a volume, the number written on the myth-ritualist theory and more recently on structuralism has been so large as to necessitate individual volumes about them. The burgeoning of writing on these theories stems in part from the array of disciplines that have adopted the theories. The myth-ritualist theory originated in the fields of classics and biblical studies but soon spread to the study of myth everywhere and, even more, to the study of secular literature. As a theory of myth, structuralism began in anthropology but has since been incorporated by many other fields.

Space does not permit inclusion in this collection of any essays that survey the field of theories of myth. Some useful surveys in

English are the following:

Campbell, Joseph. "The Historical Development of Mythology," *Daedalus* 88 (Spring 1959): 234–54.

Cohen, Percy S. "Theories of Myth," *Man*, n.s., 4 (September 1969): 337–53.

Dorson, Richard M. "Theories of Myth and the Folklorist," *Daedalus* 88 (Spring 1959): 280–90.

———. "Current Folklore Theories," *Current Anthropology* 4 (February 1963): 93–112.

Eliade, Mircea. "Myth," *Encyclopaedia Britannica*, 14th ed. (1970), vol. 15, 1132–40.

———. "Myth in the Nineteenth and Twentieth Centuries," in *Dictionary of the History of Ideas*, ed. Philip P. Wiener (New York: Scribner, 1973–74), vol. 3, 307–18.

Farnell, L. R. "The Value and the Methods of Mythologic Study," *Proceedings of the British Academy* (1919–20): 37–51.

Fischer, J. L. "The Sociopsychological Analysis of Folktales," *Current Anthropology* 4 (June 1963): 235–73, 292–95.

Georges, Robert A. "Prologue" to *Studies on Mythology*, ed. Georges (Homewood, IL: Dorsey, 1968), 1–14.

Halpern, Ben. "'Myth' and 'Ideology' in Modern Usage," *History and Theory* 1 (1961): 129–49.

Herskovits, Melville J. and Frances S. *Dahomean Narrative* (Evanston, IL: Northwestern University Press, 1958), 80–122.

Kaines, J. "The Interpretation of Mythology," *Anthropologia* 1 (1873–75): 465–75.

Kluckhohn, Clyde. "Recurrent Themes in Myths and Mythmaking," *Daedalus* 88 (Spring 1959): 268–79.

Larson, Gerald James. "Introduction: The Study of Mythology and Comparative Mythology," in *Myth in Indo-European Antiquity*, ed. Larson (Berkeley: University of California Press, 1974), 1–16.

MacIntyre, Alasdair. "Myth," *Encyclopedia of Philosophy* (1968), vol. 5, 434–37.

Maranda, Elli Köngäs. "Five Interpretations of a Melanesian Myth," *Journal of American Folklore* 86 (January-March 1973): 3–13.

Patterson, John L. "Mythology and Its Interpretation," *Poet Lore* 37 (Winter 1926): 607–15.

Puhvel, Jaan. *Comparative Mythology* (Baltimore: Johns Hopkins University Press, 1987), 7–20.

Reinach, Solomon. "The Growth of Mythological Study," *Quarterly Review* 215 (October 1911): 423–41.

Rogerson, J. W. "Slippery Words: V. Myth," *Expository Times* 90 (October 1978): 10–14.

Segal, Robert A. "In Defense of Mythology: The History of Modern Theories of Myth," *Annals of Scholarship* 1 (Winter 1980): 3–49.

Simon, Ulrich. "A Key to All Mythologies?" *Church Quarterly Review* 117 (1956): 251–61.

INTRODUCTION

Beginning in the 1950s, the anthropologist Claude Lévi-Strauss first applied to myths structuralist principles from linguistics. For Lévi-Strauss, myth is the expression of the form, or structure, of the mind. Not the content but the structure of myth is for him primary. The plot of myth, which literary critics stress, Lévi-Strauss dismisses as superficial. The plot progresses from beginning to end. By contrast, the structure is a series of restatements of the relationships among key elements in a myth. The dialectical structure of myth constitutes a series of attempts to resolve deeply felt contradictions in experience, contradictions that arise from the way the mind thinks. Myth does not so much resolve contradictions as temper them and thereby make them more tolerable.

By now, structuralists have analyzed myths from around the world. The most important development of the theory—a development intended to counter the chief criticism of the theory—has been to place myth in its cultural context. It is classicists most of all who have rooted myth in the nature of society and not merely in the nature of the mind.

This volume contains selections not only from Lévi-Strauss, his followers, and his critics but also from Roland Barthes, Georges Dumézil, and Vladimir Propp. These three theorists have also been labeled "structuralist" but have worked independently of Lévi-Strauss.

Myth Today

What is a myth, today? I shall give at the outset a first, very simple answer, which is perfectly consistent with etymology: *myth is a type of speech.*[1]

Myth is a type of speech

Of course, it is not *any* type: language needs special conditions in order to become myth: we shall see them in a minute. But what must be firmly established at the start is that myth is a system of communication, that it is a message. This allows one to perceive that myth cannot possibly be an object, a concept, or an idea; it is a mode of signification, a form. Later, we shall have to assign to this form historical limits, conditions of use, and reintroduce society into it: we must nevertheless first describe it as a form.

It can be seen that to purport to discriminate among mythical objects according to their substance would be entirely illusory: since myth is a type of speech, everything can be a myth provided it is conveyed by a discourse. Myth is not defined by the object of its message, but by the way in which it utters this message: there are formal limits to myth, there are no 'substantial' ones. Everything, then, can be a myth? Yes, I believe this, for the universe is infinitely fertile in suggestions. Every object in the world can pass from a closed, silent existence to an oral state, open to appropriation by society, for there is no law, whether natural or not, which forbids talking about things. A tree is a tree. Yes, of course. But a tree as expressed by Minou Drouet is no longer quite a tree, it is a tree which is decorated, adapted to a certain type of consumption, laden with literary self-indulgence, revolt, images, in short with a type of social *usage* which is added to pure matter.

[1] Innumerable other meanings of the word 'myth' can be cited against this. But I have tried to define things, not words.

Naturally, everything is not expressed at the same time: some objects become the prey of mythical speech for a while, then they disappear, others take their place and attain the status of myth. Are there objects which are *inevitably* a source of suggestiveness, as Baudelaire suggested about Woman? Certainly not: one can conceive of very ancient myths, but there are no eternal ones; for it is human history which converts reality into speech, and it alone rules the life and the death of mythical language. Ancient or not, mythology can only have an historical foundation, for myth is a type of speech chosen by history: it cannot possibly evolve from the 'nature' of things.

Speech of this kind is a message. It is therefore by no means confined to oral speech. It can consist of modes of writing or of representations; not only written discourse, but also photography, cinema, reporting, sport, shows, publicity, all these can serve as a support to mythical speech. Myth can be defined neither by its object nor by its material, for any material can arbitrarily be endowed with meaning: the arrow which is brought in order to signify a challenge is also a kind of speech. True, as far as perception is concerned, writing and pictures, for instance, do not call upon the same type of consciousness; and even with pictures, one can use many kinds of reading: a diagram lends itself to signification more than a drawing, a copy more than an original, and a caricature more than a portrait. But this is the point: we are no longer dealing here with a theoretical mode of representation: we are dealing with *this* particular image, which is given for *this* particular signification. Mythical speech is made of a material which has *already* been worked on so as to make it suitable for communication: it is because all the materials of myth (whether pictorial or written) presuppose a signifying consciousness, that one can reason about them while discounting their substance. This substance is not unimportant: pictures, to be sure, are more imperative than writing, they impose meaning at one stroke, without analysing or diluting it. But this is no longer a constitutive difference. Pictures become a kind of writing as soon as they are meaningful: like writing, they call for a *lexis*.

We shall therefore take *language, discourse, speech,* etc., to

2

mean any significant unit or synthesis, whether verbal or visual: a photograph will be a kind of speech for us in the same way as a newspaper article; even objects will become speech, if they mean something. This generic way of conceiving language is in fact justified by the very history of writing: long before the invention of our alphabet, objects like the Inca *quipu*, or drawings, as in pictographs, have been accepted as speech. This does not mean that one must treat mythical speech like language; myth in fact belongs to the province of a general science, coextensive with linguistics, which is *semiology*.

Myth as a semiological system

For mythology, since it is the study of a type of speech, is but one fragment of this vast science of signs which Saussure postulated some forty years ago under the name of *semiology*. Semiology has not yet come into being. But since Saussure himself, and sometimes independently of him, a whole section of contemporary research has constantly been referred to the problem of meaning: psycho-analysis, structuralism, eidetic psychology, some new types of literary criticism of which Bachelard has given the first examples, are no longer concerned with facts except inasmuch as they are endowed with significance. Now to postulate a signification is to have recourse to semiology. I do not mean that semiology could account for all these aspects of research equally well: they have different contents. But they have a common status: they are all sciences dealing with values. They are not content with meeting the facts: they define and explore them as tokens for something else.

Semiology is a science of forms, since it studies significations apart from their content. I should like to say one word about the necessity and the limits of such a formal science. The necessity is that which applies in the case of any exact language. Zhdanov made fun of Alexandrov the philosopher, who spoke of *'the spherical structure of our planet.'* *'It was thought until now'*, Zhdanov said, *'that form alone could be spherical.'* Zhdanov was right: one cannot speak about structures in terms of forms, and

III

3

vice versa. It may well be that on the plane of 'life', there is but a totality where structures and forms cannot be separated. But science has no use for the ineffable: it must speak about 'life' if it wants to transform it. Against a certain quixotism of synthesis, quite platonic incidentally, all criticism must consent to the *ascesis*, to the artifice of analysis; and in analysis, it must match method and language. Less terrorized by the spectre of 'formalism', historical criticism might have been less sterile; it would have understood that the specific study of forms does not in any way contradict the necessary principles of totality and History. On the contrary: the more a system is specifically defined in its forms, the more amenable it is to historical criticism. To parody a well-known saying, I shall say that a little formalism turns one away from History, but that a lot brings one back to it. Is there a better example of total criticism than the description of saintliness, at once formal and historical, semiological and ideological, in Sartre's *Saint-Genet*? The danger, on the contrary, is to consider forms as ambiguous objects, half-form and half-substance, to endow form with a substance of form, as was done, for instance, by Zhdanovian realism. Semiology, once its limits are settled, is not a metaphysical trap: it is a science among others, necessary but not sufficient. The important thing is to see that the unity of an explanation cannot be based on the amputation of one or other of its approaches, but, as Engels said, on the dialectical co-ordination of the particular sciences it makes use of. This is the case with mythology: it is a part both of semiology inasmuch as it is a formal science, and of ideology inasmuch as it is an historical science: it studies ideas-in-form.[2]

Let me therefore restate that any semiology postulates a relation between two terms, a signifier and a signified. This relation concerns objects which belong to different categories, and this is why it is not one of equality but one of equivalence. We

[2] The development of publicity, of a national press, of radio, of illustrated news, not to speak of the survival of a myriad rites of communication which rule social appearances makes the development of a semiological science more urgent than ever. In a single day, how many really non-signifying fields do we cross? Very few, sometimes none. Here I am, before the sea; it is true that it bears no message. But on the beach, what material for semiology! Flags, slogans, signals, sign-boards, clothes, suntan even, which are so many messages to me.

112

4

must here be on our guard for despite common parlance which simply says that the signifier *expresses* the signified, we are dealing, in any semiological system, not with two, but with three different terms. For what we grasp is not at all one term after the other, but the correlation which unites them: there are, therefore, the signifier, the signified and the sign, which is the associative total of the first two terms. Take a bunch of roses: I use it to *signify* my passion. Do we have here, then, only a signifier and a signified, the roses and my passion? Not even that: to put it accurately, there are here only 'passionified' roses. But on the plane of analysis, we do have three terms; for these roses weighted with passion perfectly and correctly allow themselves to be decomposed into roses and passion: the former and the latter existed before uniting and forming this third object, which is the sign. It is as true to say that on the plane of experience I cannot dissociate the roses from the message they carry, as to say that on the plane of analysis I cannot confuse the roses as signifier and the roses as sign: the signifier is empty, the sign is full, it is a meaning. Or take a black pebble: I can make it signify in several ways, it is a mere signifier; but if I weigh it with a definite signified (a death sentence, for instance, in an anonymous vote), it will become a sign. Naturally, there are between the signifier, the signified and the sign, functional implications (such as that of the part to the whole) which are so close that to analyse them may seem futile; but we shall see in a moment that this distinction has a capital importance for the study of myth as semiological schema.

Naturally these three terms are purely formal, and different contents can be given to them. Here are a few examples: for Saussure, who worked on a particular but methodologically exemplary semiological system—the language or *langue*—the signified is the concept, the signifier is the acoustic image (which is mental) and the relation between concept and image is the sign (the word, for instance), which is a concrete entity.[3] For Freud, as is well known, the human psyche is a stratification of tokens or

[3] The notion of *word* is one of the most controversial in linguistics. I keep it here for the sake of simplicity.

representatives. One term (I refrain from giving it any precedence) is constituted by the manifest meaning of behaviour, another, by its latent or real meaning (it is, for instance, the substratum of the dream); as for the third term, it is here also a correlation of the first two: it is the dream itself in its totality, the parapraxis (a mistake in speech or behaviour) or the neurosis, conceived as compromises, as economies effected thanks to the joining of a form (the first term) and an intentional function (the second term). We can see here how necessary it is to distinguish the sign from the signifier: a dream, to Freud, is no more its manifest datum than its latent content: it is the functional union of these two terms. In Sartrean criticism, finally (I shall keep to these three well-known examples), the signified is constituted by the original crisis in the subject (the separation from his mother for Baudelaire, the naming of the theft for Genet); Literature as discourse forms the signifier; and the relation between crisis and discourse defines the work, which is a signification. Of course, this tri-dimensional pattern, however constant in its form, is actualized in different ways: one cannot therefore say too often that semiology can have its unity only at the level of forms, not contents; its field is limited, it knows only one operation: reading, or deciphering.

In myth, we find again the tri-dimensional pattern which I have just described: the signifier, the signified and the sign. But myth is a peculiar system, in that it is constructed from a semio-logical chain which existed before it: it *is a second-order semio-logical system*. That which is a sign (namely the associative total of a concept and an image) in the first system, becomes a mere signifier in the second. We must here recall that the materials of mythical speech (the language itself, photography, painting, posters, rituals, objects, etc.), however different at the start, are reduced to a pure signifying function as soon as they are caught by myth. Myth sees in them only the same raw material; their unity is that they all come down to the status of a mere language. Whether it deals with alphabetical or pictorial writing, myth wants to see in them only a sum of signs, a global sign, the final term of a first semiological chain. And it is precisely this final term which will become the first term of the greater system which it builds and of which it is only a part. Everything happens as if myth shifted the formal system of the first significations sideways. As this lateral shift is essential for the analysis of myth, I shall represent it in the following way, it being understood, of course, that the spatialization of the pattern is here only a metaphor:

Language	1. Signifier	2. Signified	
MYTH	3. Sign I SIGNIFIER		II SIGNIFIED
	III SIGN		

It can be seen that in myth there are two semiological systems, one of which is staggered in relation to the other: a linguistic system, the language (or the modes of representation which are assimilated to it), which I shall call the *language-object*, because it is the language which myth gets hold of in order to build its own system; and myth itself, which I shall call *metalanguage*, because it is a second language, *in which* one speaks about the first. When he reflects on a metalanguage, the semiologist no longer needs to ask himself questions about the composition of the language-object, he no longer has to take into account the details of the linguistic schema; he will only need to know its total term, or global sign, and only inasmuch as this term lends itself to myth. This is why the semiologist is entitled to treat in the same way writing and pictures: what he retains from them is the fact that they are both *signs*, that they both reach the threshold of myth endowed with the same signifying function, that they constitute, one just as much as the other, a language-object.

It is now time to give one or two examples of mythical speech. I shall borrow the first from an observation by Valéry.[4] I am a pupil in the second form in a French *lycée*. I open my Latin grammar, and I read a sentence, borrowed from Aesop or Phaedrus: *quia ego nominor leo*. I stop and think. There is something ambiguous about this statement: on the one hand, the

[4] *Tel Quel*, II, p. 191.

words in it do have a simple meaning: *because my name is lion.*
And on the other hand, the sentence is evidently there in order to
signify something else to me. Inasmuch as it is addressed to me,
a pupil in the second form, it tells me clearly: I am a grammatical
example meant to illustrate the rule about the agreement of the
predicate. I am even forced to realize that the sentence in no way
signifies its meaning to me, that it tries very little to tell me
something about the lion and what sort of name he has; its true
and fundamental signification is to impose itself on me as the
presence of a certain agreement of the predicate. I conclude that
I am faced with a particular, greater, semiological system, since
it is co-extensive with the language: there is, indeed, a signifier,
but this signifier is itself formed by a sum of signs, it is in itself a
first semiological system (*my name is lion*). Thereafter, the formal
pattern is correctly unfolded: there is a signified (*I am a grammatical example*) and there is a global signification, which is
none other than the correlation of the signifier and the signified;
for neither the naming of the lion nor the grammatical example
are given separately.

And here is now another example: I am at the barber's, and a
copy of *Paris-Match* is offered to me. On the cover, a young
Negro in a French uniform is saluting, with his eyes uplifted,
probably fixed on a fold of the tricolour. All this is the *meaning*
of the picture. But, whether naively or not, I see very well what it
signifies to me: that France is a great Empire, that all her sons,
without any colour discrimination, faithfully serve under her
flag, and that there is no better answer to the detractors of an
alleged colonialism than the zeal shown by this Negro in serving
his so-called oppressors. I am therefore again faced with a
greater semiological system: there is a signifier, itself already
formed with a previous system (*a black soldier is giving the
French salute*); there is a signified (it is here a purposeful mixture
of Frenchness and militariness); finally, there is a presence of the
signified through the signifier.

Before tackling the analysis of each term of the mythical
system, one must agree on terminology. We now know that the
signifier can be looked at, in myth, from two points of view: as the

final term of the linguistic system, or as the first term of the mythical system. We therefore need two names. On the plane of language, that is, as the final term of the first system, I shall call the signifier: *meaning* (*my name is lion, a Negro is giving the French salute*); on the plane of myth, I shall call it: *form*. In the case of the signified, no ambiguity is possible: we shall retain the name *concept*. The third term is the correlation of the first two: in the linguistic system, it is the *sign*; but it is not possible to use this word again without ambiguity, since in myth (and this is the chief peculiarity of the latter), the signifier is already formed by the *signs* of the language. I shall call the third term of myth the *signification*. This word is here all the better justified since myth has in fact a double function: it points out and it notifies, it makes us understand something and it imposes it on us.

The form and the concept

The signifier of myth presents itself in an ambiguous way: it is at the same time meaning and form, full on one side and empty on the other. As meaning, the signifier already postulates a reading, I grasp it through my eyes, it has a sensory reality (unlike the linguistic signifier, which is purely mental), there is a richness in it: the naming of the lion, the Negro's salute are credible wholes, they have at their disposal a sufficient rationality. As a total of linguistic signs, the meaning of the myth has its own value, it belongs to a history, that of the lion or that of the Negro: in the meaning, a signification is already built, and could very well be self-sufficient if myth did not take hold of it and did not turn it suddenly into an empty, parasitical form. The meaning is *already* complete, it postulates a kind of knowledge, a past, a memory, a comparative order of facts, ideas, decisions.

When it becomes form, the meaning leaves its contingency behind; it empties itself, it becomes impoverished, history evaporates, only the letter remains. There is here a paradoxical permutation in the reading operations, an abnormal regression from meaning to form, from the linguistic sign to the mythical signifier. If one encloses *quia ego nominor leo* in a purely linguistic system, the clause finds again there a fullness, a richness, a

117

9

history: I am an animal, a lion, I live in a certain country, I have just been hunting, they would have me share my prey with a heifer, a cow and a goat; but being the stronger, I award myself all the shares for various reasons, the last of which is quite simply that *my name is lion*. But as the form of the myth, the clause hardly retains anything of this long story. The meaning contained a whole system of values: a history, a geography, a morality, a zoology, a Literature. The form has put all this richness at a distance: its newly acquired penury calls for a signification to fill it. The story of the lion must recede a great deal in order to make room for the grammatical example, one must put the biography of the Negro in parentheses if one wants to free the picture, and prepare it to receive its signified.

But the essential point in all this is that the form does not suppress the meaning, it only impoverishes it, it puts it at a distance, it holds it at one's disposal. One believes that the meaning is going to die, but it is a death with reprieve; the meaning loses its value, but keeps its life, from which the form of the myth will draw its nourishment. The meaning will be for the form like an instantaneous reserve of history, a tamed richness, which it is possible to call and dismiss in a sort of rapid alternation: the form must constantly be able to be rooted again in the meaning and to get there what nature it needs for its nutriment; above all, it must be able to hide there. It is this constant game of hide-and-seek between the meaning and the form which defines myth. The form of myth is not a symbol: the Negro who salutes is not the symbol of the French Empire: he has too much presence, he appears as a rich, fully experienced, spontaneous, innocent, *indisputable* image. But at the same time this presence is tamed, put at a distance, made almost transparent; it recedes a little, it becomes the accomplice of a concept which comes to it fully armed, French imperiality: once made use of, it becomes artificial.

Let us now look at the signified: this history which drains out of the form will be wholly absorbed by the concept. As for the latter, it is determined, it is at once historical and intentional; it is the motivation which causes the myth to be uttered. Gram-

118

10

matical exemplarity, French imperiality, are the very drives behind the myth. The concept reconstitutes a chain of causes and effects, motives and intentions. Unlike the form, the concept is in no way abstract: it is filled with a situation. Through the concept, it is a whole new history which is implanted in the myth. Into the naming of the lion, first drained of its contingency, the grammatical example will attract my whole existence: Time, which caused me to be born at a certain period when Latin grammar is taught; History, which sets me apart, through a whole mechanism of social segregation, from the children who do not learn Latin; paedagogic tradition, which caused this example to be chosen from Aesop or Phaedrus; my own linguistic habits, which see the agreement of the predicate as a fact worthy of notice and illustration. The same goes for the Negro-giving-the-salute: as form, its meaning is shallow, isolated, impoverished; as the concept of French imperiality, here it is again tied to the totality of the world: to the general History of France, to its colonial adventures, to its present difficulties. Truth to tell, what is invested in the concept is less reality than a certain knowledge of reality; in passing from the meaning to the form, the image loses some knowledge: the better to receive the knowledge in the concept. In actual fact, the knowledge contained in a mythical concept is confused, made of yielding, shapeless associations. One must firmly stress this open character of the concept; it is not at all an abstract, purified essence; it is a formless, unstable, nebulous condensation, whose unity and coherence are above all due to its function.

In this sense, we can say that the fundamental character of the mythical concept is to be *appropriated*: grammatical exemplarity very precisely concerns a given form of pupils, French imperiality must appeal to such and such group of readers and not another. The concept closely corresponds to a function, it is defined as a tendency. This cannot fail to recall the signified in another semiological system, Freudianism. In Freud, the second term of the system is the latent meaning (the content) of the dream, of the parapraxis, of the neurosis. Now Freud does remark that the second-order meaning of behaviour is its real meaning, that which is appropriate to a complete situation, including its deeper level; it is, just like the mythical concept, the very intention of behaviour.

A signified can have several signifiers: this is indeed the case in linguistics and psycho-analysis. It is also the case in the mythical concept: it has at its disposal an unlimited mass of signifiers: I can find a thousand Latin sentences to actualize for me the agreement of the predicate, I can find a thousand images which signify to me French imperiality. This means that *quantitively*, the concept is much poorer than the signifier, it often does nothing but re-present itself. Poverty and richness are in reverse proportion in the form and the concept: to the qualitative poverty of the form, which is the repository of a rarefied meaning, there corresponds the richness of the concept which is open to the whole of History; and to the quantitative abundance of the forms there corresponds a small number of concepts. This repetition of the concept through different forms is precious to the mythologist, it allows him to decipher the myth: it is the insistence of a kind of behaviour which reveals its intention. This confirms that there is no regular ratio between the volume of the signified and that of the signifier. In language, this ratio is proportionate, it hardly exceeds the word, or at least the concrete unit. In myth, on the contrary, the concept can spread over a very large expanse of signifier. For instance, a whole book may be the signifier of a single concept; and conversely, a minute form (a word, a gesture, even incidental, so long as it is noticed) can serve as signifier to a concept filled with a very rich history. Although unusual in language, this disproportion between signifier and signified is not specific to myth: in Freud, for instance, the parapraxis is a signifier whose thinness is out of proportion to the real meaning which it betrays.

As I said, there is no fixity in mythical concepts: they can come into being, alter, disintegrate, disappear completely. And it is precisely because they are historical that history can very easily suppress them. This instability forces the mythologist to use a terminology adapted to it, and about which I should now like to say a word, because it often is a cause for irony: I mean neologism. The concept is a constituting element of myth: if I want to decipher myths, I must somehow be able to name concepts. The dictionary supplies me with a few: Goodness, Kindness, Wholeness, Humaneness, etc. But by definition, since it is the dictionary which gives them to me, these particular concepts are not historical. Now what I need most often is ephemeral concepts, in connection with limited contingencies: neologism is then inevitable. China is one thing, the idea which a French petit-bourgeois could have of it not so long ago is another: for this peculiar mixture of bells, rickshaws and opium-dens, no other word possible but *Sininess*.[5] Unlovely? One should at least get some consolation from the fact that conceptual neologisms are never arbitrary: they are built according to a highly sensible proportional rule.

The signification

In semiology, the third term is nothing but the association of the first two, as we saw. It is the only one which is allowed to be seen in a full and satisfactory way, the only one which is consumed in actual fact. I have called it: the signification. We can see that the signification is the myth itself, just as the Saussurean sign is the word (or more accurately the concrete unit). But before listing the characters of the signification, one must reflect a little on the way in which it is prepared, that is, on the modes of correlation of the mythical concept and the mythical form.

First we must note that in myth, the first two terms are perfectly manifest (unlike what happens in other semiological systems): one of them is not 'hidden' behind the other, they are both given *here* (and not one here and the other there). However paradoxical it may seem, *myth hides nothing*: its function is to distort, not to make disappear. There is no latency of the concept in relation to the form: there is no need of an unconscious in order to explain myth. Of course, one is dealing with two different types of manifestation: form has a literal, immediate presence; moreover, it is extended. This stems—this cannot be repeated too often—from the nature of the mythical signifier,

[5] Or perhaps *Sinity*? Just as if Latin/latinity = Basque/x, x = Basquity.

which is already linguistic: since it is constituted by a meaning which is already outlined, it can appear only through a given substance (whereas in language, the signifier remains mental). In the case of oral myth, this extension is linear (*for my name is lion*); in that of visual myth, it is multi-dimensional (in the centre, the Negro's uniform, at the top, the blackness of his face, on the left, the military salute, etc.). The elements of the form therefore are related as to place and proximity: the mode of presence of the form is spatial. The concept, on the contrary, appears in global fashion, it is a kind of nebula, the condensation, more or less hazy, of a certain knowledge. Its elements are linked by associative relations: it is supported not by an extension but by a depth (although this metaphor is perhaps still too spatial): its mode of presence is memorial.

The relation which unites the concept of the myth to its meaning is essentially a relation of *deformation*. We find here again a certain formal analogy with a complex semiological system such as that of the various types of psycho-analysis. Just as for Freud the manifest meaning of behaviour is distorted by its latent meaning, in myth the meaning is distorted by the concept. Of course, this distortion is possible only because the form of the myth is already constituted by a linguistic meaning. In a simple system like the language, the signified cannot distort anything at all because the signifier, being empty, arbitrary, offers no resistance to it. But here, everything is different: the signifier has, so to speak, two aspects: one full, which is the meaning (the history of the lion, of the Negro soldier), one empty, which is the form (*for my name is lion*; *Negro-French-soldier-saluting-the-tricolour*). What the concept distorts is of course what is full, the meaning: the lion and the Negro are deprived of their history, changed into gestures. What Latin exemplarity distorts is the naming of the lion, in all its contingency; and what French imperiality obscures is also a primary language, a factual discourse which was telling me about the salute of a Negro in uniform. But this distortion is not an obliteration: the lion and the Negro remain here, the concept needs them; they are half-amputated, they are deprived of memory, not of existence: they are at once stubborn, silently rooted there, and garrulous, a speech wholly at the service of the concept. The concept, literally, deforms, but does not abolish the meaning; a word can perfectly render this contradiction: it alienates it.

What must always be remembered is that myth is a double system; there occurs in it a sort of ubiquity: its point of departure is constituted by the arrival of a meaning. To keep a spatial metaphor, the approximative character of which I have already stressed, I shall say that the signification of the myth is constituted by a sort of constantly moving turnstile which presents alternately the meaning of the signifier and its form, a language-object and a metalanguage, a purely signifying and a purely imagining consciousness. This alternation is, so to speak, gathered up in the concept, which uses it like an ambiguous signifier, at once intellective and imaginary, arbitrary and natural.

I do not wish to prejudge the moral implications of such a mechanism, but I shall not exceed the limits of an objective analysis if I point out that the ubiquity of the signifier in myth exactly reproduces the physique of the *alibi* (which is, as one realizes, a spatial term): in the alibi too, there is a place which is full and one which is empty, linked by a relation of negative identity ('I am not where you think I am; I am where you think I am not'). But the ordinary alibi (for the police, for instance) has an end; reality stops the turnstile revolving at a certain point. Myth is a *value*, truth is no guarantee for it; nothing prevents it from being a perpetual alibi: it is enough that its signifier has two sides for it always to have an 'elsewhere' at its disposal. The meaning is always there to *present* the form; the form is always there to *outdistance* the meaning. And there never is any contradiction, conflict, or split between the meaning and the form: they are never at the same place. In the same way, if I am in a car and I look at the scenery through the window, I can at will focus on the scenery or on the window-pane. At one moment I grasp the presence of the glass and the distance of the landscape; at another, on the contrary, the transparence of the glass and the depth of the landscape; but the result of this alternation is constant: the glass is at once present and empty to me, and the

123

landscape unreal and full. The same thing occurs in the mythical signifier: its form is empty but present, its meaning absent but full. To wonder at this contradiction I must voluntarily interrupt this turnstile of form and meaning, I must focus on each separately, and apply to myth a static method of deciphering, in short, I must go against its own dynamics: to sum up, I must pass from the state of reader to that of mythologist.

And it is again this duplicity of the signifier which determines the characters of the signification. We now know that myth is a type of speech defined by its intention (*I am a grammatical example*) much more than by its literal sense (*my name is lion*); and that in spite of this, its intention is somehow frozen, purified, eternalized, *made absent* by this literal sense (*The French Empire? It's just a fact: look at this good Negro who salutes like one of our own boys*). This constituent ambiguity of mythical speech has two consequences for the signification, which henceforth appears both like a notification and like a statement of fact.

Myth has an imperative, buttonholing character: stemming from an historical concept, directly springing from contingency (a Latin class, a threatened Empire), it is *I* whom it has come to seek. It is turned towards me, I am subjected to its intentional force, it summons me to receive its expansive ambiguity. If, for instance, I take a walk in Spain, in the Basque country,[6] I may well notice in the houses an architectural unity, a common style, which leads me to acknowledge the Basque house as a definite ethnic product. However, I do not feel personally concerned, nor, so to speak, attacked by this unitary style: I see only too well that it was here before me, without me. It is a complex product which has its determinations at the level of a very wide history: it does not call out to me, it does not provoke me into naming it, except if I think of inserting it into a vast picture of rural habitat. But if I am in the Paris region and I catch a glimpse, at the end of the rue Gambetta or the rue Jean-Jaurès, of a natty white chalet with red tiles, dark brown half-timbering, an asymmetrical roof and a wattle-and-daub front, I feel as if I were personally

---

[6] I say 'in Spain' because, in France, petit-bourgeois advancement has caused a whole 'mythical' architecture of the Basque chalet to flourish.

124

receiving an imperious injunction to name this object a Basque chalet: or even better, to see it as the very essence of *basquity*. This is because the concept appears to me in all its appropriative nature: it comes and seeks me out in order to oblige me to acknowledge the body of intentions which have motivated it and arranged it there as the signal of an individual history, as a confidence and a complicity: it is a real call, which the owners of the chalet send out to me. And this call, in order to be more imperious, has agreed to all manner of impoverishments: all that justified the Basque house on the plane of technology—the barn, the outside stairs, the dove-cote, etc.—has been dropped; there remains only a brief order, not to be disputed. And the adhomination is so frank that I feel this chalet has just been created on the spot, *for me*, like a magical object springing up in my present life without any trace of the history which has caused it.

For this interpellant speech is at the same time a frozen speech: at the moment of reaching me, it suspends itself, turns away and assumes the look of a generality: it stiffens, it makes itself look neutral and innocent. The appropriation of the concept is suddenly driven away once more by the literalness of the meaning. This is a kind of *arrest*, in both the physical and the legal sense of the term: French imperiality condemns the saluting Negro to be nothing more than an instrumental signifier, the Negro suddenly hails me in the name of French imperiality; but at the same moment the Negro's salute thickens, becomes vitrified, freezes into an eternal reference meant to *establish* French imperiality. On the surface of language something has stopped moving: the use of the signification is here, hiding behind the fact, and conferring on it a notifying look; but at the same time, the fact paralyses the intention, gives it something like a malaise producing immobility: in order to make it innocent, it freezes it. This is because myth is speech *stolen and restored*. Only, speech which is restored is no longer quite that which was stolen: when it was brought back, it was not put exactly in its place. It is this brief act of larceny, this moment taken for a surreptitious faking, which gives mythical speech its benumbed look.

One last element of the signification remains to be examined:

125

17

its motivation. We know that in a language, the sign is arbitrary: nothing compels the acoustic image *tree* 'naturally' to mean the concept *tree*: the sign, here, is unmotivated. Yet this arbitrariness has limits, which come from the associative relations of the word: the language can produce a whole fragment of the sign by analogy with other signs (for instance one says *aimable* in French, and not *amable*, by analogy with *aime*). The mythical signification, on the other hand, is never arbitrary; it is always in part motivated, and unavoidably contains some analogy. For Latin exemplarity to meet the naming of the lion, there must be an analogy, which is the agreement of the predicate; for French imperiality to get hold of the saluting Negro, there must be identity between the Negro's salute and that of the French soldier. Motivation is necessary to the very duplicity of myth: myth plays on the analogy between meaning and form, there is no myth without motivated form.[7] In order to grasp the power of motivation in myth, it is enough to reflect for a moment on an extreme case. I have here before me a collection of objects so lacking in order that I can find no *meaning* in it; it would seem that here, deprived of any previous meaning, the form could not root its analogy in anything, and that myth is impossible. But what the form can always give one to read is disorder itself: it can give a signification to the absurd, make the absurd itself a myth. This is what happens when commonsense mythifies surrealism, for instance. Even the absence of motivation does not embarrass myth; for this absence will itself be sufficiently objectified to become legible: and finally, the absence of motivation will become a second-order motivation, and myth will be re-established.

Motivation is unavoidable. It is none the less very fragmentary.

[7] From the point of view of ethics, what is disturbing in myth is precisely that its form is motivated. For if there is a 'health' of language, it is the arbitrariness of the sign which is its grounding. What is sickening in myth is its resort to a false nature, its superabundance of significant forms, as in these objects which decorate their usefulness with a natural appearance. The will to weigh the signification with the full guarantee of nature causes a kind of nausea: myth is too rich, and what is in excess is precisely its motivation. This nausea is like the one I feel before the arts which refuse to choose between *physis* and *anti-physis*, using the first as an ideal and the second as an economy. Ethically, there is a kind of baseness in hedging one's bets.

126

To start with, it is not 'natural': it is history which supplies its analogies to the form. Then, the analogy between the meaning and the concept is never anything but partial: the form drops many analogous features and keeps only a few: it keeps the sloping roof, the visible beams in the Basque chalet, it abandons the stairs, the barn, the weathered look, etc. One must even go further: a *complete* image would exclude myth, or at least would compel it to seize only its very completeness. This is just what happens in the case of bad painting, which is wholly based on the myth of what is 'filled out' and 'finished' (it is the opposite and symmetrical case of the myth of the absurd: here, the form mythifies an 'absence', there, a surplus). But in general myth prefers to work with poor, incomplete images, where the meaning is already relieved of its fat, and ready for a signification, such as caricatures, pastiches, symbols, etc. Finally, the motivation is chosen among other possible ones: I can very well give to French imperiality many other signifiers beside a Negro's salute: a French general pins a decoration on a one-armed Senegalese, a nun hands a cup of tea to a bed-ridden Arab, a white school-master teaches attentive piccaninnies: the press undertakes every day to demonstrate that the store of mythical signifiers is inexhaustible.

The nature of the mythical signification can in fact be well conveyed by one particular simile: it is neither more nor less arbitrary than an ideograph. Myth is a pure ideographic system, where the forms are still motivated by the concept which they represent while not yet, by a long way, covering the sum of its possibilities for representation. And just as, historically, ideographs have gradually left the concept and have become associated with the sound, thus growing less and less motivated, the worn out state of a myth can be recognized by the arbitrariness of its signification: the whole of Molière is seen in a doctor's ruff.

Reading and deciphering myth

How is a myth received? We must here once more come back

127

19

to the duplicity of its signifier, which is at once meaning and form. I can produce three different types of reading by focusing on the one, or the other, or both at the same time.[8]

1. If I focus on an empty signifier, I let the concept fill the form of the myth without ambiguity, and I find myself before a simple system, where the signification becomes literal again: the Negro who salutes is an *example* of French imperiality, he is a *symbol* for it. This type of focusing is, for instance, that of the producer of myths, of the journalist who starts with a concept and seeks a form for it.[9]

2. If I focus on a full signifier, in which I clearly distinguish the meaning and the form, and consequently the distortion which the one imposes on the other, I undo the signification of the myth, and I receive the latter as an imposture: the saluting Negro becomes the *alibi* of French imperiality. This type of focusing is that of the mythologist: he deciphers the myth, he understands a distortion.

3. Finally, if I focus on the mythical signifier as on an inextricable whole made of meaning and form, I receive an ambiguous signification: I respond to the constituting mechanism of myth, to its own dynamics, I become a reader of myths. The saluting Negro is no longer an example or a symbol, still less an alibi: he is the very *presence* of French imperiality.

The first two types of focusing are static, analytical; they destroy the myth, either by making its intention obvious, or by unmasking it: the former is cynical, the latter demystifying. The third type of focusing is dynamic, it consumes the myth according to the very ends built into its structure: the reader lives the myth as a story at once true and unreal.

If one wishes to connect a mythical schema to a general history, to explain how it corresponds to the interests of a definite society, in short, to pass from semiology to ideology, it is obviously at the

---

[8] The freedom in choosing what one focuses on is a problem which does not belong to the province of semiology: it depends on the concrete situation of the subject.

[9] We receive the naming of the lion as a pure *example* of Latin grammar because we are, *as grown-ups*, in a creative position in relation to it. I shall come back later to the value of the context in this mythical schema.

level of the third type of focusing that one must place oneself: it is the reader of myths himself who must reveal their essential function. How does he receive this particular myth *today*? If he receives it in an innocent fashion, what is the point of proposing it to him? And if he reads it using his powers of reflection, like the mythologist, does it matter which alibi is presented? If the reader does not see French imperiality in the saluting Negro, it was not worth weighing the latter with it; and if he sees it, the myth is nothing more than a political proposition, honestly expressed. In one word, either the intention of the myth is too obscure to be efficacious, or it is too clear to be believed. In either case, where is the ambiguity?

This is but a false dilemma. Myth hides nothing and flaunts nothing: it distorts; myth is neither a lie nor a confession: it is an inflexion. Placed before the dilemma which I mentioned a moment ago, myth finds a third way out. Threatened with disappearance if it yields to either of the first two types of focusing, it gets out of this tight spot thanks to a compromise — it *is* this compromise. Entrusted with 'glossing over' an intentional concept, myth encounters nothing but betrayal in language, for language can only obliterate the concept if it hides it, or unmask it if it formulates it. The elaboration of a second-order semiological system will enable myth to escape this dilemma: driven to having either to unveil or to liquidate the concept, it will *naturalize* it.

We reach here the very principle of myth: it transforms history into nature. We now understand why, *in the eyes of the myth-consumer*, the intention, the adhomination of the concept can remain manifest without however appearing to have an interest in the matter: what causes mythical speech to be uttered is perfectly explicit, but it is immediately frozen into something natural; it is not read as a motive, but as a reason. If I read the Negro-saluting as symbol pure and simple of imperiality, I must renounce the reality of the picture, it discredits itself in my eyes when it becomes an instrument. Conversely, if I decipher the Negro's salute as an alibi of coloniality, I shatter the myth even more surely by the obviousness of its motivation. But for the myth-reader, the outcome is quite different: everything happens

129

21

as if the picture *naturally* conjured up the concept, as if the signifier *gave a foundation* to the signified: the myth exists from the precise moment when French imperiality achieves the natural state: myth is speech justified *in excess*.

Here is a new example which will help understand clearly how the myth-reader is led to rationalize the signified by means of the signifier. We are in the month of July, I read a big headline in *France-Soir*: THE FALL IN PRICES: FIRST INDICATIONS. VEGETABLES: PRICE DROP BEGINS. Let us quickly sketch the semiological schema: the example being a sentence, the first system is purely linguistic. The signifier of the second system is composed here of a certain number of accidents, some lexical (the words: *first, begins, the* [fall]), some typographical (enormous headlines where the reader usually sees news of world importance). The signified or concept is what must be called by a barbarous but unavoidable neologism: *governmentality*, the Government presented by the national press as the Essence of efficacy. The signification of the myth follows clearly from this: fruit and vegetable prices are falling *because* the government has so decided. Now it so happens in this case (and this is on the whole fairly rare) that the newspaper itself has, two lines below, allowed one to see through the myth which it had just elaborated — whether this is due to self-assurance or honesty. It adds (in small type, it is true): 'The fall in prices is helped by the return of seasonal abundance.' This example is instructive for two reasons. Firstly it conspicuously shows that myth essentially aims at causing an immediate impression—it does not matter if one is later allowed to see through the myth, its action is assumed to be stronger than the rational explanations which may later belie it. This means that the reading of a myth is exhausted at one stroke. I cast a quick glance at my neighbour's *France-Soir*: I cull only a *meaning* there, but I read a true signification; I *receive* the presence of governmental action in the fall in fruit and vegetable prices. That is all, and that is enough. A more attentive reading of the myth will in no way increase its power or its ineffectiveness: a myth is at the same time imperfectible and unquestionable; time or knowledge will not make it better or worse.

130

22

Secondly, the naturalization of the concept, which I have just identified as the essential function of myth, is here exemplary. In a first (exclusively linguistic) system, causality would be, literally, natural: fruit and vegetable prices fall because they are in season. In the second (mythical) system, causality is artificial, false; but it creeps, so to speak, through the back door of Nature. This is why myth is experienced as innocent speech: not because its intentions are hidden — if they were hidden, they could not be efficacious — but because they are naturalized.

In fact, what allows the reader to consume myth innocently is that he does not see it as a semiological system but as an inductive one. Where there is only an equivalence, he sees a kind of causal process: the signifier and the signified have, in his eyes, a natural relationship. This confusion can be expressed otherwise: any semiological system is a system of values; now the myth-consumer takes the signification for a system of facts: myth is read as a factual system, whereas it is but a semiological system.

Myth as stolen language

What is characteristic of myth? To transform a meaning into form. In other words, myth is always a language-robbery. I rob the Negro who is saluting, the white and brown chalet, the seasonal fall in fruit prices, not to make them into examples or symbols, but to naturalize through them the Empire, my taste for Basque things, the Government. Are all primary languages a prey for myth? Is there no meaning which can resist this capture with which form threatens it? In fact, nothing can be safe from myth, myth can develop its second-order schema from any meaning and, as we saw, start from the very lack of meaning. But all languages do not resist equally well.

Articulated language, which is most often robbed by myth, offers little resistance. It contains in itself some mythical dispositions, the outline of a sign-structure meant to manifest the intention which led to its being used: it is what could be called the *expressiveness* of language. The imperative or the subjunctive mode, for instance, are the form of a particular signified, different

131

from the meaning: the signified is here my will or my request. This is why some linguists have defined the indicative, for instance, as a zero state or degree, compared to the subjunctive or the imperative. Now in a fully constituted myth, the meaning is never at zero degree, and this is why the concept can distort it, naturalize it. We must remember once again that the privation of meaning is in no way a zero degree: this is why myth can perfectly well get hold of it, give it for instance the signification of the absurd, of surrealism, etc. At bottom, it would only be the zero degree which could resist myth.

Language lends itself to myth in another way: it is very rare that it imposes at the outset a full meaning which it is impossible to distort. This comes from the abstractness of its concept: the concept of *tree* is vague, it lends itself to multiple contingencies. True, a language always has at its disposal a whole appropriating organization (*this* tree, *the* tree *which*, etc.). But there always remains, around the final meaning, a halo of virtualities where other possible meanings are floating: the meaning can almost always be *interpreted*. One could say that a language offers to myth an open-work meaning. Myth can easily insinuate itself into it, and swell there: it is a robbery by colonization (for instance: *the* fall in prices has started. But what fall? That due to the season or that due to the government? the signification becomes here a parasite of the article, in spite of the latter being definite).

When the meaning is too full for myth to be able to invade it, myth goes around it, and carries it away bodily. This is what happens to mathematical language. In itself, it cannot be distorted, it has taken all possible precautions against *interpretation*: no parasitical signification can worm itself into it. And this is why, precisely, myth takes it away en bloc; it takes a certain mathematical formula ($E = mc^2$), and makes of this unalterable meaning the pure signifier of mathematicity. We can see that what is here robbed by myth is something which resists, something pure. Myth can reach everything, corrupt everything, and even the very act of refusing oneself to it. So that the more the language-object resists at first, the greater its final prostitution;

whoever here resists completely yields completely: Einstein on one side, *Paris-Match* on the other. One can give a temporal image of this conflict: mathematical language is a *finished* language, which derives its very perfection from this acceptance of death. Myth, on the contrary, is a language which does not want to die: it wrests from the meanings which give it its sustenance an insidious, degraded survival, it provokes in them an artificial reprieve in which it settles comfortably, it turns them into speaking corpses.

Here is another language which resists myth as much as it can: our poetic language. Contemporary poetry[10] is *a regressive semiological system*. Whereas myth aims at an ultra-signification, at the amplification of a first system, poetry, on the contrary, attempts to regain an infra-signification, a pre-semiological state of language; in short, it tries to transform the sign back into meaning: its ideal, ultimately, would be to reach not the meaning of words, but the meaning of things themselves.[11] This is why it clouds the language, increases as much as it can the abstractness of the concept and the arbitrariness of the sign and stretches to the limit the link between signifier and signified. The open-work structure of the concept is here maximally exploited: unlike what happens in prose, it is all the potential of the signified that the poetic sign tries to actualize, in the hope of at last reaching something like the transcendent quality of the thing, its natural (not human) meaning. Hence the essentialist ambitions of poetry, the conviction that it alone catches *the thing in itself*, inasmuch, precisely, as it wants to be an anti-language. All told, of all those who use speech, poets are the least formalist, for they are the

[10] Classical poetry, on the contrary, would be, according to such norms, a strongly mythical system, since it imposes on the meaning one extra signified, which is *regularity*. The alexandrine, for instance, has value both as meaning of a discourse and as signifier of a new whole, which is its poetic signification. Success, when it occurs, comes from the degree of apparent fusion of the two systems. It can be seen that we deal in no way with a harmony between content and form, but with an *elegant* absorption of one form into another. By *elegance* I mean the most economical use of the means employed. It is because of an age-old abuse that critics confuse *meaning* and *content*. The language is never anything but a system of forms, and the meaning is a form.

[11] We are again dealing here with the *meaning*, in Sartre's use of the term, as a natural quality of things, situated outside a semiological system (*Saint-Genet*, p. 283).

133

only ones who believe that the meaning of the words is only a form, with which they, being realists, cannot be content. This is why our modern poetry always asserts itself as a murder of language, a kind of spatial, tangible analogue of silence. Poetry occupies a position which is the reverse of that of myth: myth is a semiological system which has the pretension of transcending itself into a factual system; poetry is a semiological system which has the pretension of contracting into an essential system.

But here again, as in the case of mathematical language, the very resistance offered by poetry makes it an ideal prey for myth: the apparent lack of order of signs, which is the poetic facet of an essential order, is captured by myth, and transformed into an empty signifier, which will serve to *signify* poetry. This explains the *improbable* character of modern poetry: by fiercely refusing myth, poetry surrenders to it bound hand and foot. Conversely, the *rules* in classical poetry constituted an accepted myth, the conspicuous arbitrariness of which amounted to perfection of a kind, since the equilibrium of a semiological system comes from the arbitrariness of its signs.

A voluntary acceptance of myth can in fact define the whole of our traditional Literature. According to our norms, this Literature is an undoubted mythical system: there is a meaning, that of the discourse; there is a signifier, which is this same discourse as form or writing; there is a signified, which is the concept of literature; there is a signification, which is the literary discourse. I began to discuss this problem in *Writing Degree Zero*, which was, all told, nothing but a mythology of literary language. There I defined writing as the signifier of the literary myth, that is, as a form which is already filled with meaning and which receives from the concept of Literature a new signification.[12] I suggested

---

[12] *Style*, at least as I defined it then, is not a form, it does not belong to the province of a semiological analysis of Literature. In fact, style is a substance constantly threatened with formalization. To start with, it can perfectly well become degraded into a mode of writing: there is a 'Malraux-type' writing, and even in Malraux himself. Then, style can also become a particular language, that used by the writer *for himself and for himself alone*. Style then becomes a sort of solipsistic myth, the language which the writer speaks *to himself*. It is easy to understand that at such a degree of solidification, style calls for a deciphering. The works of J. P. Richard are an example of this necessary critique of styles.

134

that history, in modifying the writer's consciousness, had provoked, a hundred years or so ago, a moral crisis of literary
language: writing was revealed as signifier, Literature as signification; rejecting the false nature of traditional literary language,
the writer violently shifted his position in the direction of an
anti-nature of language. The subversion of writing was the
radical act by which a number of writers have attempted to
reject Literature as a mythical system. Every revolt of this kind
has been a murder of Literature as signification: all have postulated the reduction of literary discourse to a simple semiological
system, or even, in the case of poetry, to a pre-semiological system.
This is an immense task, which required radical types of behaviour: it is well known that some went as far as the pure and
simple scuttling of the discourse, silence — whether real or
transposed — appearing as the only possible weapon against the
major power of myth: its recurrence.

It thus appears that it is extremely difficult to vanquish myth
from the inside: for the very effort one makes in order to escape
its stranglehold becomes in its turn the prey of myth: myth can
always, as a last resort, signify the resistance which is brought
to bear against it. Truth to tell, the best weapon against myth is
perhaps to mythify it in its turn, and to produce an *artificial
myth*: and this reconstituted myth will in fact be a mythology.
Since myth robs language of something, why not rob myth? All
that is needed is to use it as the departure point for a third
semiological chain, to take its signification as the first term of a
second myth. Literature offers some great examples of such
artificial mythologies. I shall only evoke here Flaubert's *Bouvard
and Pécuchet*. It is what could be called an experimental myth,
a second-order myth. Bouvard and his friend Pécuchet represent
a certain kind of bourgeoisie (which is incidentally in conflict
with other bourgeois strata): their discourse *already* constitutes
a mythical type of speech; its language does have a meaning, but
this meaning is the empty form of a conceptual signified, which
here is a kind of technological unsatedness. The meeting of
meaning and concept forms, in this first mythical system, a
signification which is the rhetoric of Bouvard and Pécuchet. It

135

is at this point (I am breaking the process into its components for the sake of analysis) that Flaubert intervenes: to this first mythical system, which already is a second semiological system, he superimposes a third chain, in which the first link is the signification, or final term, of the first myth. The rhetoric of Bouvard and Pécuchet becomes the form of the new system; the concept here is due to Flaubert himself, to Flaubert's gaze on the myth which Bouvard and Pécuchet had built for themselves: it consists of their natively ineffectual inclinations, their inability to feel satisfied, the panic succession of their apprenticeships, in short what I would very much like to call (but I see storm-clouds on the horizon): bouvard-and-pécuchet-ity. As for the final signification, it is the book, it is *Bouvard and Pécuchet* for us. The power of the second myth is that it gives the first its basis as a naivety which is looked at. Flaubert has undertaken a real archaeological restoration of a given mythical speech: he is the Viollet-le-Duc of a certain bourgeois ideology. But less naive than Viollet-le-Duc, he has strewn his reconstitution with supplementary ornaments which demystify it. These ornaments (which are the form of the second myth) are subjunctive in kind: there is a semiological equivalence between the subjunctive restitution of the discourse of Bouvard and Pécuchet and their ineffectualness.[13]

Flaubert's great merit (and that of all artificial mythologies: there are remarkable ones in Sartre's work), is that he gave to the problem of realism a frankly semiological solution. True, it is a somewhat incomplete merit, for Flaubert's ideology, since the bourgeois was for him only an aesthetic eyesore, was not at all realistic. But at least he avoided the major sin in literary matters, which is to confuse ideological with semiological reality. As ideology, literary realism does not depend at all on the language spoken by the writer. Language is a form, it cannot possibly be either realistic or unrealistic. All it can do is either to be mythical or not, or perhaps, as in *Bouvard and Pécuchet*, counter-mythical. Now, unfortunately, there is no antipathy between realism and

[13] A subjunctive form because it is in the subjunctive mode that Latin expressed 'indirect style or discourse', which is an admirable instrument for demystification.

myth. It is well known how often our 'realistic' literature is mythical (if only as a crude myth of realism) and how our 'literature of the unreal' has at least the merit of being only slightly so. The wise thing would of course be to define the writer's realism as an essentially ideological problem. This certainly does not mean that there is no responsibility of form towards reality. But this responsibility can be measured only in semiological terms. A form can be judged (since forms are on trial) only as signification, not as expression. The writer's language is not expected to *represent* reality, but to signify it. This should impose on critics the duty of using two rigorously distinct methods: one must deal with the writer's realism either as an ideological substance (Marxist themes in Brecht's work, for instance) or as a semiological value (the props, the actors, the music, the colours in Brechtian dramaturgy). The ideal of course would be to combine these two types of criticism; the mistake which is constantly made is to confuse them: ideology has its methods, and so has semiology.

137

Mary Douglas

The Meaning of Myth

With special reference to 'La Geste d'Asdiwal'

Social anthropology, as we know it, was born of a professedly empirical approach. And it was first developed in Britain. These two marks, of being British and empirical, are not accidentally linked. This is the home of philosophical scepticism, an attitude of thought which has insulated us more effectively than the North Sea and the Channel from Continental movements of ideas. Our intellectual climate is plodding and anti-metaphysical. Yet, in spite of these traditions, we cannot read much of Lévi-Strauss without feeling some excitement. To social studies he holds out a promise of the sudden lift that new methods of science could give. He has developed his vision so elaborately and documented it so massively from so many fields of our subject that he commands our attention.

He has developed most explicitly in connection with myth his ideas of the place of sociology within a single grand discipline of Communication. This part of his teaching draws very broadly on the structural analysis of linguistics, and on cybernetics and communication theory in general, and to some extent on the related theory of games. Briefly, its starting-point is that it is the nature of the mind to work through form. Any experience is received in a structured form, and these forms or structures, which are a condition of knowing, are generally unconscious (as, for example, unconscious categories of language). Furthermore, they vary little in modern or in ancient times. They always consist in the creation of pairs of opposites, which are balanced against one another and built up in various (algebraically representable) ways. All the different kinds of patterned activity can be analysed according to the different structures they produce. For example, social life is a matter of interaction between persons. There are three different types of social communication. First, there is kinship, the structure underlying

49

31

the rules for transferring women; second, there is the economy, that is the structure underlying transfer of goods and services; third, there is the underlying structure of language. The promise is that if we can get at these structures, display and compare them, the way is open for a true science of society, so far a will-o'-the-wisp for sociologists.

So far myth has not been mentioned. Lévi-Strauss recognizes that its structures belong to a different level of mental activity from those of language, and the technique of analysis must be correspondingly different. The technique is described in his 'Structural Study of Myth' (1955) and is also made very clear in Edmund Leach's two articles (1961, 1962) in which he applies the technique to the Book of Genesis. It assumes that the analysis of myth should proceed like the analysis of language. In both language and myth the separate units have no meaning by themselves, they acquire it only because of the way in which they are combined. The best comparison is with musical notation: there is no musical meaning in a single isolated note. Describing the new science of mythologics which is to parallel linguistics, Lévi-Strauss unguardedly says that the units of mythological structure are sentences. If he took this statement seriously it would be an absurd limitation on analysis. But in fact, quite rightly, he abandons it at once, making great play with the structure underlying the meaning of a set of names. What are sentences, anyway? Linguists would be at a loss to identify these units of language structure which Lévi-Strauss claims to be able to put on punched cards and into a computing machine as surely and simply as if they were phonemes and morphemes. For me and for most of us, computer talk is a mysterious language very apt for prestidigitation. Does he really mean that he can chop a myth into semantic units, put them through a machine, and get out at the other end an underlying pattern which is not precisely the one he used for selecting his units? The quickness of the hand deceives the eye. Does he further believe that this underlying structure is the real meaning or sense of the myth? He says that it is the deepest kind of sense, more important than the uninitiated reader would suspect. However, I do not think it is fair to such an ebullient writer to take him literally. In other contexts it is plain that

50

Lévi-Strauss realizes that any myth has multiple meanings and that no one of them can be labelled the deepest or the truest. More of this later.

From the point of view of anthropology, one of his novel departures is to treat all versions of a myth as equally authentic or relevant. This is right, of course. Linguistic analysis can be applied to any literary unit, and the longer the better, so long as there is real unity underlying the stretches of language that are analysed together. Why stop short at one of Shakespeare's historical plays? Why not include the whole of Shakespeare? Or the whole of Elizabethan drama? Here Lévi-Strauss gives one of his disturbing twists of thought that make the plodding reader uneasily suspect that he is being duped. For by 'version' we find that Lévi-Strauss means both version and interpretation. He insists that Freud's treatment of the Oedipus myth must be put through the machine together with other earlier versions. This challenging idea is not merely for the fun of shocking the bourgeois mythologist out of his search for original versions. Freud used the Oedipus myth to stand for his own discovery that humans are each individually concerned with precisely the problem of 'birth from one' or 'birth from two' parents. On Lévi-Strauss's analysis of its structure, this problem is revealed as underlying the Oedipus cycle. So there is no inconsistency between Freud and Sophocles. But the reference to Freud interestingly vindicates Lévi-Strauss on a separate charge. Some must feel that the themes which his technique reveals are too trivial and childish either to have been worth the excavation, or to have been worth the erecting of an elaborate myth series in the first place. But after Freud no one can be sure that an individual's speculation about his own genesis is a trivial puzzle without emotional force.

I admit that the use of all interpretations of a great myth might not always so triumphantly vindicate this method. Meyer Fortes (1959) treated Oedipus rather differently in *Oedipus and Job in West Africa*. Compare St Augustine, Simone Weil (1950), and Edmund Leach (1962) on the Biblical story of Noah drunk in the vineyard: for one the drunken, naked Noah is Christ humiliated; for the other he is the dionysian mysteries too austerely rejected by the Jewish priesthood, and for the

51

last the tale is a trite lesson about Hebrew sexual morality. I will say more below of how these 'versions' would look coming out of the mythologic computer. At this stage of the discussion we should treat the computer as a red herring and forget for the moment the quest for the real meaning. We can then begin seriously to evaluate Lévi-Strauss's approach to mythology.

First, we should recognize his debt to the dialectical method of Hegelian-Marxist philosophy. The dialectic was Hegel's speculation about the nature of reality and about the logical technique by which it could be grasped. When Lévi-Strauss says that mythic thought follows a strict logic of its own, he means a Hegelian logic of thesis, antithesis, and synthesis, moving in ever more complex cycles to comprehend all the oppositions and limitations inherent in thought. According to Lévi-Strauss, the structure of myth is a dialectic structure in which opposed logical positions are stated, the oppositions mediated by a restatement, which again, when its internal structure becomes clear, gives rise to another kind of opposition, which in its turn is mediated or resolved, and so on.

On the assumption that it is the nature of myth to mediate contradictions, the method of analysis must proceed by distinguishing the oppositions and the mediating elements. And it follows, too, that the function of myth is to portray the contradictions in the basic premises of the culture. The same goes for the relation of myth to social reality. The myth is a contemplation of the unsatisfactory compromises which, after all, compose social life. In the devious statements of the myth, people can recognize· indirectly what it would be difficult to admit openly and yet what is patently clear to all and sundry, that the ideal is not attainable.

Lévi-Strauss does not stick his neck out so far as to say that people are reconciled better or worse to their makeshift arrangements and contradictory formulae – but merely that myth makes explicit their experience of the contradictoriness of reality.

A summary of 'La Geste d'Asdiwal'[1] best demonstrates how this is to be understood. It is a cycle of myths told by the Tsimshian tribes. These are a sparse population of migratory hunters and fishers who live on the Pacific coast, south of Alaska. They are culturally in the same group with Haida and

52

Tlingit, northernmost representatives of Northwest Coast culture. Topographically their territory is dominated by the two parallel rivers, Nass and Skeena, which flow southwest to the sea. In the summer they live on vegetable products collected by women, and in winter on marine and land animals and fish killed by the men. The movements of fish and game dictate their seasonal movements between sea and mountains, and the northern and southern rivers. The Tsimshian were organized in dispersed matrilineal clans and lived in typical Northwest Coast composite dwellings which housed several families. They tended to live with their close maternal kin, generally practising avunculocal residence at marriage and the ideal was to marry a mother's brother's daughter.

The myth begins during the winter famine in the Skeena valley. A mother and daughter, separated hitherto by their marriages but now both widowed by the famine, set out from East and West, one from upstream and one from downstream of the frozen Skeena, to meet each other half-way. The daughter becomes the wife of a mysterious bird who feeds them both and when she gives birth to a miraculous child, Asdiwal, its bird father gives him a magic bow and arrow, lance, snow-shoes, cloak, and hat which make him invisible at will, invincible, and able to produce an inexhaustible supply of food. The old mother dies and the bird father disappears. Asdiwal and his mother walk West to her natal village. From there he follows a white bear into the sky where it is revealed as Evening-Star, the daughter of the Sun. When Asdiwal has succeeded, thanks to his magic equipment, in a series of impossible tasks, the Sun allows him to marry Evening-Star, and, because he is homesick, to take his wife back to the earth generously supplied with magic food. On earth, because Asdiwal is unfaithful to her, his sky wife leaves him. He follows her half-way to the sky, where she kills him with a thunderbolt. His father-in-law, the Sun, brings him to life and they live together in the sky until Asdiwal feels homesick again. Once home, Asdiwal finds his mother is dead and, since nothing keeps him in her village, he continues walking to the West. This time he makes a

53

Tsimshian marriage, which starts off well, Asdiwal using his magic hunting-weapons to good effect. In the spring he, his wife, and her four brothers move along the coast northwards, towards the River Nass, but Asdiwal challenges his brothers-in-law to prove that their sea-hunting is better than his land-hunting. Asdiwal wins the contest by bringing home four dead bears from his mountain hunt, one for each of the four brothers, who return empty handed from their sea expedition. Furious at their defeat, they carry off their sister and abandon Asdiwal, who then joins some strangers also going North towards the Nass for the candlefish season. Once again, there are four brothers, and a sister whom Asdiwal marries. After a good fishing season, Asdiwal returns with his in-laws and wife to their village, where his wife bears them a son. One day, however, he boasts that he is better than his brothers-in-law at walrus-hunting. Put to the test, he succeeds brilliantly, again infuriating his wife's brothers, who abandon him without food or fire to die on a rocky reef. His bird father preserves him through a raging storm. Finally, he is taken by a mouse to the underground home of the walruses whom he has wounded. Asdiwal cures them and asks in exchange a safe return. The King of the Walruses lends Asdiwal his stomach as a boat, on which he sails home. There he finds his faithful wife, who helps him to kill her own brothers. But again Asdiwal, assailed by homesickness, leaves his wife and returns to the Skeena valley, where his son joins him. When winter comes, Asdiwal goes hunting in the mountains, but forgetting his snow-shoes, can go neither up nor down and is changed into stone.

This is the end of the story. In the analysis which follows, Lévi-Strauss draws out the remarkably complex symmetry of different levels of structure. Asdiwal's journeys take him from East to West, then North to the Nass, then Southwest to the sea fishing of walrus, and finally Southeast back to the Skeena River. So the points of the compass and the salient points of order of Tsimshian migration are laid out. This is the geographical sequence. There is another sequence concerned with residence at marriage, as follows.

54

The two women who open the tale have been separated by the daughter's virilocal residence at marriage. Living together, they set up what Lévi-Strauss calls a 'matrilocal residence of the simplest kind, mother and daughter'. Lévi-Strauss counts the first marriage of the bird father of Asdiwal as matrilocal. Then the sky marriage of Asdiwal himself with Evening-Star is counted as matrilocal, and matrilocal again the two human marriages of Asdiwal, until after he has come back from the walrus kingdom, when his wife betrays her brothers. So, Lévi-Strauss remarks that all the marriages of Asdiwal are matrilocal until the end. Then the regular pattern is inverted and 'patrilocalism triumphs' because Asdiwal abandons his wife and goes home, accompanied by his son. The story starts with the reunion of a mother and daughter, liberated from their spouses (and paternal kin in the case of the daughter), and ends with the reunion of a father and son, liberated from their spouses (and maternal kin in the case of the son). To the English anthropologist some of this symmetry and inversion seems rather far-fetched. The evidence for counting the bird marriage as matrilocal is dubious and the sky marriage is plain groom service. The rejection of the third wife is hardly 'patrilocalism'. But more about inversion below. I want to go into details of another sociological sequence which produces two more pairs of oppositions which are also inverted at the end.

The same symmetry is traced in the cosmological sequence. First, the hero sojourns in the sky where he is wounded and cured by the sky people; then he makes an underground sojourn where he finds underground people whom *he* has wounded, and whom *he* cures. There is a similar elaboration of recurring themes of famine and plenty. They correspond faithfully enough to the economic reality of Tsimshian life. Using his knowledge of another myth of the region, Lévi-Strauss explains their implication. The Northwest Coast Indians attribute the present condition of the world to the disturbances made by a great Crow, whose voracious appetite initiated all the processes of creation. So hunger is the condition of movement, glut is a static condition. The first phase of the Asdiwal tale opposes Sky and Earth, the Sun and the earthly human. These oppositions the hero overcomes, thanks to his bird father. But Asdiwal breaks

55

the harmony established between these elements: first he feels homesick, then, once at home, he betrays his sky wife for a terrestrial girl, and then, in the sky, he feels homesick again. Thus the whole sky episode ends on a negative position. In the second phase, when Asdiwal makes his first human marriage, a new set of oppositions are released: mountain-hunting and sea-hunting; land and sea.

Asdiwal wins the contest as a land-hunter, and in consequence is abandoned by his wife's brothers. Next time Asdiwal's marriage allies him with island-dwellers, and the same conflict between land and sea takes place, this time on the sea in a boat, which Asdiwal has to leave in the final stage of the hunt in order to climb onto the reef of rock. Taken together, these two phases can be broken down into a series of unsuccessful mediations between opposites arranged on an ever-diminishing scale: above and below, water and earth, maritime hunting and mountain-hunting. In the sea hunt the gap is almost closed between sea- and mountain-hunting, since Asdiwal succeeds where his brothers-in-law fail because he clambers onto the rock. The technique by which the oppositions are reduced is by paradox and reversal: the great mountain-hunter nearly dies on a little half-submerged rock; the great killer of bears is rescued by a little mouse; the slayer of animals now cures them; and, most paradoxical of all, the great provider of food himself has provender become – since he goes home in the stomach of a walrus. In the final dénouement, Asdiwal, once more a hunter in the mountains, is immobilized when he is neither up nor down, and is changed to stone, the most extreme possible expression of his earthly nature.

Some may have doubted that myths can have an elaborate symmetrical structure. If so, they should be convinced of their error.

Lévi-Strauss's analysis slowly and intricately reveals the internal structure of this myth. Although I have suggested that the symmetry has here and there been pushed too hard, the structure is indisputably there, in the material and not merely in the eye of the beholder. I am not sure who would have argued to the contrary, but myths must henceforth be conceded to have a structure as recognizable as that of a poem or a tune.

56

But Lévi-Strauss is not content with revealing structure for its own sake. Structural analysis has long been a respectable tool of literary criticism and Lévi-Strauss is not interested in a mere literary exercise.

He wants to use myth to demonstrate that structural analysis has sociological value. So instead of going on to analyse and compare formal myth structures, he asks what is the relation of myth to life. His answer in a word is 'dialectical'. Not only is the nature of reality dialectical, and the structure of myth dialectical, but the relation of the first to the second is dialectical too.

This could mean that there is a feedback between the worlds of mythical and social discourse – a statement in the myth sets off a response which modifies the social universe, which itself then touches off a new response in the realm of myth, and so on. Elsewhere, Lévi-Strauss (1962b, pp. 283-284) has shown that this complex interaction is indeed how he sees the relation between symbolic thought and social reality. And he even attempts to demonstrate with a single example how this inter-action takes place (1963b; cf. 1962b, Ch. IV). But in his analysis of myth itself he leaves out this meaning of dialectic. This is a pity, but perhaps inevitable because there is so little historical information about the tribes in question, and still less about the dating of different versions of the myth.

Rather, he develops the idea that myth expresses a social dialectic. It states the salient social contradictions, restates them in more and more .modified fashion, until in the final statement the contradictions are resolved, or so modified and masked as to be minimized. According to Lévi-Strauss, the real burden of the whole Ásdiwal myth and the one burning issue to which all the antinomies of sky and earth, land and sea, etc., are assimilated, is the contradiction implicit in patrilocal, matrilateral cross-cousin marriage. This comes as a surprise, since there has never been any mention whatever of matrilateral cross-cousin marriage in the myth of Asdiwal. But the Asdiwal story has a sequel. His son, Waux, grows up with his maternal kin, and his mother arranges for him to marry a cousin. He inherits his father's magic weapons and becomes, like him, a great hunter. One day he goes out hunting, having forgotten his

57

magic spear which enables him to split rocks and open paths through the mountains. There is an earthquake. Waux sees his wife in the valley and shouts to her to make a sacrifice of fat to appease the supernatural powers. But his wife gets it wrong and thinks he is telling her to eat the fat, on which she proceeds to stuff herself until, gorged, she bursts and turns into a rock. Waux, now without either his father's spear or his wife's help, also turns into stone. With this story the Asdiwal cycle is completed. Waux's wife dies of glut, thus reversing the opening gambit in which Asdiwal's mother is started on her journey by a famine. So the movement set going by famine ends in the immobility of fullness. Asdiwal's marriages were all with strangers. Waux makes the approved Tsimshian marriage with his maternal cousin, but she ends by ruining him; the myth makes thus the comment that matrilateral cross-cousin marriage is nothing but a feeble palliative for the social ills it seeks to cure.

Lévi-Strauss points out that the Tsimshian, along with other Northwest Coast cultures, do not benefit from the equilibrium which cross-cousin marriage could produce for them in the form of a fixed hierarchy of wife-givers and wife-receivers. They have chosen instead to be free to revise their whole system of ranking at each marriage and potlatch. So they are committed to deep-seated disequilibrium. Following Rodney Needham (1962), one suspects that this far-fetched reference to Lévi-Strauss's theory of elementary structures of kinship is misplaced. There is no reason to suppose that matrilateral cross-cousin marriage among the Tsimshian is prescribed. However, in reaching these basic antagonisms of social structure, Lévi-Strauss feels he has got to the rock bottom of the myth's meaning.·

'All the paradoxes . . . geographic, economic, sociological, and even cosmological, are, when all is said and done, assimilated to that less obvious yet so real paradox which marriage with the matrilateral cousin attempts but fails to resolve . . . ' (*supra*, pp. 27, 28).

A great deal of this myth certainly centres on marriage,

58

though very little on the cross-cousin marriage which is preferred. Lévi-Strauss says that the whole myth's burden is a negative comment on social reality. By examining all the possibilities in marriage and showing every extreme position to be untenable, it has as its core message to reconcile the Tsimshian to their usual compromises by showing that any other solution they attempt is equally beset with difficulty. But as I have said, we cannot allow Lévi-Strauss to claim the real meaning of such a complex and rich myth. His analysis is far from exhaustive. Furthermore, there are other themes which are positive, not negative, as regards social reality.

In the first place, this area of Northwest Coast culture combines a very elaborate and strict division of labour between the sexes with a strong expression of male dominance. The myth could well be interpreted as playing on the paradox of male dominance and male dependence on female help. The first hero, Asdiwal, shows his independence of womankind by betraying his first wife. He is betrayed by his second wife, abandons his third wife, but in the sequel his son, Waux, dies because of his wife's stupidity and greed – so the general effect is that women are necessary but inferior beings, and men are superior. Surely this is a positive comment?

In the second place, the potlatch too is built on a paradox that the receiver of gifts is an enemy. One-up-manship, in potlatch terms, brings success, rank, and followers, but two-up-manship inflicts defeat on the opponent and creates hostility. Asdiwal went too far when he brought four huge bears down from the mountain to confront his empty-handed brothers-in-law. Here again, the myth is positive and true to life, so no wonder they abandoned him. The ambivalent attitude in Northwest Coast culture to the successful shaman is a third theme that can plausibly be detected in the myth. Great shamans are always victims of jealousy. Asdiwal, the great shaman, is abandoned. So the myth is plain and simply true to life.

I feel that we are being asked to suspend our critical faculties if we are to believe that this myth mirrors the reverse of reality. I shall return again to give a closer look at the social realities of Tsimshian life.

59

The ideas of reversal and of inversion figure prominently in Lévi-Strauss's argument. First, he suggests that the myth is the reverse of reality in the country of its origin. Then he has formulated a curious law according to which a myth turns upside down (in relation to its normal position) at a certain distance from its place of origin. These are both developed in the Asdiwal analysis. Third, a myth which appears to have no counterpart in the ritual of the tribe in which it is told is found to be an inversion of the rites of another tribe (cf. Lévi-Strauss, 1956). On this subject the stolid English suspicion of cleverness begins to crystallize.

If ever one could suspect a scholar of trailing his coat with his tongue in his cheek, one would suspect this law of myth-inversion. The metaphor is borrowed from optics, without any explanation of why the same process should be observed in the unrelated science of mythics:

> 'When a mythical schema is transmitted from one population to another, and there exist differences of language, social organization or way of life which make the myth difficult to communicate, it begins to become impoverished or confused. But one can find a limiting situation in which, instead of being finally obliterated by losing all its outlines, the myth is inverted and regains part of its precision' (*supra*, p. 42).

So we must expect that exported myths will give a negative or upside-down picture of what the original myth portrayed. Is the scholar being ingenuous, or disingenuous? He must recognize that opposition is a pliable concept in the interpreter's hands. The whole notion of dialectic rests on the assumption that opposition can be unequivocally recognized. But this is an unwarranted assumption, as appears from a critical reading of his treatment of a Pawnee myth (Lévi-Strauss, 1956).

To demonstrate the relation of myth to rite he takes the Pawnee myth of the pregnant boy. An ignorant young boy suddenly finds he has magical powers of healing and the makings of a great shaman. An old-established shaman, always accompanied by his wife, tries to winkle his secret from him. He fails, since there is no secret learning to transmit, and then ensorcells the boy. As a result of the sorcery the boy becomes

60

pregnant, and goes in shame and confusion to die among wild beasts. But the beasts cure him and he returns with even greater power, and kills his enemy. The analysis distinguishes at least three sets of oppositions.

Shamanistic powers through initiation : without initiation
child : old man
confusion of sex : distinction of sex

Lévi-Strauss then invites us to consider what rite this Pawnee myth corresponds to. His problem, which seems very artificial, is that there is at first sight no correlated rite. The myth underlines the opposition of the generations, and yet the Pawnee do not oppose their generations: they do not base their cult associations on age-classes, and entry to their cult societies is not by ordeals or by fee; a teacher trains his pupil to succeed him on his death. But, as he puts it, all the elements of the myth fall into place confronted with the symmetrical and opposite ritual of the neighbouring Plains Indian tribes. Here the shamanistic societies are the inverse of those of the Pawnee, since entry is by payment and organization is by age. The sponsor and his sponsored candidate for entry are treated as if in a father-son relation, the candidate is accompanied by his wife, whom he offers for ritual intercourse to his sponsor. 'Here we find again all the oppositions which have been analysed on the plane of the myth, with inversion of all the values attributed to each couple.' The initiated and uninitiated are as father to son, instead of as enemies; the uninitiated knows less than the initiated, whereas in the myth he is the better shaman; in the ritual of the Plains Societies it is the youth who is accompanied by his wife, while in the myth it is the old man. 'The semantic values are the same but changed in relation to the symbols which sustain them. The Pawnee myth exposes a ritual system which is the inverse, not of that prevailing in this tribe, but of a system which does not apply here, and which belongs to related tribes whose ritual organization is the exact opposite.'

Mere difference is made to qualify as opposition. Some of the oppositions which Lévi-Strauss detects in myth are undeniably part of the artistic structure. But opposition can be imposed on any material by the interpreter. Here we have an unguarded

61

example of the latter process. To me it seems highly implausible that we can affirm any opposition worthy of the name between cult organization with age-grading and entrance fees, and cult organization by apprenticeship without age-grading. Old male with wife versus young man without wife, and with confusion of sex, these seem equally contrived as oppositions. If the alleged oppositions are not above challenge, the whole demonstration of inversion falls to the ground.

Here we should turn to the relation of myth to literature in general. Lévi-Strauss recognizes that a myth is 'a work of art arousing deep aesthetic emotion' (Jakobson & Lévi-Strauss, 1962, p. 5). But he strenuously rejects the idea that myth is a kind of primitive poetry (Lévi-Strauss, 1963a, p. 210). 'Myth,' he says, 'should be placed in the gamut of linguistic expressions at the end opposite to that of poetry. . . . Poetry is a kind of speech which cannot be translated except at the cost of serious distortions; whereas the mythical value of the myth is preserved even through the worst translation.' He goes on in terms more emotional than scientific to declare that anyone can recognize the mythic quality of myth. Why does he want so vigorously to detach myth criticism from literary criticism? It is on the literary plane that we have his best contribution to the subject of mythology. He himself wrote a splendid vindication of his own technique of literary analysis by working it out with Jakobson on a sonnet of Baudelaire (Jakobson & Lévi-Strauss, 1962). This essay is an exercise in what T. S. Eliot calls 'the lemon-squeezer school of criticism, in which the critics take a poem to pieces, stanza by stanza, line by line, and extract, squeeze, tease, press every drop of meaning out of it' (Eliot, 1957, p. 112). After reading the analysis, we perceive the poem's unity, economy, and completeness, and its tremendous range of implication.

When the lemon-squeezer technique is applied to poetry it has a high rate of extraction and the meaning flows out in rich cupfuls. Furthermore, what is extracted is not a surprise – we can see that it was there all the time. Unfortunately, something goes wrong when the technique is applied to myth: the machine seems to spring a leak. Instead of more and richer depths of understanding, we get a surprise, a totally new theme, and often a paltry one at that. All the majestic themes which we had previously thought the Oedipus myth was about – destiny, duty, and self-knowledge, have been strained off, and we are left with a worry about how the species began. When Edmund Leach applies the same technique to the Book of Genesis, the rich metaphysical themes of salvation and cosmic oneness are replaced by practical rules for the regulation of sex. When Lévi-Strauss has finished with the Tsimshian myth it is reduced to anxieties about problems of matrilateral cross-cousin marriage (which anyway only apply to the heirs of chiefs and headmen). It seems that whenever anthropologists apply structural analysis to myth they extract not only a different but a lesser meaning. The reasons for this reductionism are important. First, there is the computer analogy, for the sake of which Lévi-Strauss commits himself to treating the structural units of myth as if they were unambiguous. This takes us back to the basic difference between words and phonemes. The best words are ambiguous, and the more richly ambiguous the more suitable for the poet's or the myth-maker's job. Hence there is no end to the number of meanings which can be read into a good myth. When dealing with poetry, Lévi-Strauss gives full value to the rich ambiguity of the words. When dealing with myth he suggests that their meaning is clear cut, lending itself to being chopped into objectively recognizable, precisely defined units. It is partly in this process of semantic chopping that so much of the meaning of myth gets lost.

But there is another reason, more central to the whole programme. There are two possible objectives in analysing a piece of discourse.[2] One is to analyse the particular discourse itself, to analyse what has been said. The other is to analyse the language, seen as the instrument of what is said. No reason has so far been given to suppose that the structure of discourse is necessarily similar to that of language. But there is reason to point out that if the language analogy is adopted, research will look for a similar structure, a logic of correlations, opposi-tions, and differences (Ricoeur, 1963). We can say that the first kind of analysis, of what has been said in a discourse, aims at discovering a particular structure. This is what the literary critics do and what Jakobson and Lévi-Strauss did in 'Les

63

Chats', and what Lévi-Strauss in practice does most of the time. This kind of analysis is not intended to yield a compressed statement of the theme. It is not reductionist in any sense. The other kind of analysis discovers a formal or general structure which is not particular to any given stretch of language. For instance, the alexandrine or the sonnet form is not particular to a given poem, and to know that a particular poem has been written in sonnet form tells you nothing about what that poem is about. In the same way, a grammatical structure is formal. A book of grammar gives the conditions under which communication of a certain kind can take place. It does not give a communication.

Lévi-Strauss claims to be revealing the formal structures of myths. But he can never put aside his interest in what the myth discourse is about. He seems to think that if he had the formal structure it would look not so much like a grammar book as like a summary of the themes which analysing the particular structure of a myth cycle has produced. Hence the reductionist tendency is built in to his type of myth analysis. He falls into the trap of claiming to discover the real underlying meanings of myths because he never separates the particular artistic structure of a particular set of myths from their general or purely formal structure. Just as knowing that the rhyme structure is a, b, b, a, does not tell us anything about the content of a sonnet, so the formal structure of a myth would not help very much in interpreting it. Lévi-Strauss comes very near this when he says (Lévi-Strauss, 1957) that the structural analysis of a Pawnee myth consists of a dialectical balancing of the themes of life and death. It might have been better to have said that it was a balanced structure of pluses and minuses, or of positives and negatives. If he had actually used algebra to present the pattern he discerned, then Edmund Leach might have been less tempted to speculate on the similarity of mythic themes all over the world. He himself had found a structure of pluses and minuses in the Garden of Eden myth (1961) and remarked that the recurrence of these themes of death versus life, procreation versus vegetable reproduction, have the greatest psychological and sociological significance. But I think that their significance is that of verb/noun relations in language.

64

Their presence signifies the possibility of finding in them formal structures. But they are not the formal myth structures that we have been promised. These can hardly be knowable in ordinary language. If they are to be discovered special terms will have to be invented for recording them, comparable to the highly specialized terminology of grammar. To say simply that myth structures are built of oppositions and mediations is not to say what the structures are. It is simply to say that there are structures.

I will return later to the question of whether these formal myth structures are likely to be important for sociology. At this stage of publication (though three new volumes are in the press), Lévi-Strauss has not succeeded in revealing them. I should therefore do better to concentrate on the particular artistic structures he has revealed.

The meaning of a myth is partly the sense that the author intended it to convey, and the sense intended by each of its recounters. But every listener can find in it references to his own experience, so the myth can be enlightening, consoling, depressing, irrespective of the intentions of the tellers. Part of the anthropologist's task is to understand enough of the background of the myth to be able to construct its range of reference for its native hearers. To this Lévi-Strauss applies himself energetically, as for example when he finds that the myth of the creative Great Crow illuminates the themes of hunger and plenty in Tsimshian life.

From a study of any work of art we can infer to some extent the conditions under which it was made. The maidservant who said of St Peter, 'His speech betrays him as a Galilean' was inferring from his dialect; similarly the critic who used computer analysis to show that the same author did not write all the epistles attributed to St Paul. This kind of information is like that to be obtained from analysing the track of an animal or the finger-prints of a thief. The anthropologist studying tribal myths can do a job of criticism very like that of art critics who decide what 'attribution' to give to a painting or to figures in a painting. Lévi-Strauss, after minute analysis of the Asdiwal myth, could come forward and, like a good antiquarian, affirm that it is a real, genuine Tsimshian article. He can guarantee

65

that it is an authentic piece of Northwest Coast mythology. His analysis of the structure of the myth can show that it draws fully on the premises of Tsimshian culture.

Inferences, of course, can also be made within the culture; the native listener can infer a moral, and indeed myths are one of the ways in which cultural values are transmitted. Structural analysis can reveal unsuspected depths of reference and inference meaning for any particular series of myths. In order to squeeze this significance out, the anthropologist must apply his prior knowledge of the culture to his analysis. He uses inference the other way round, from the known culture to the interpretation of the obscure myth. This is how he discerns the elements of structure. All would agree that this is a worth-while task. But in order to analyse particular structures, he has to know his culture well first.

At this stage we should like to be able to judge how well Lévi-Strauss knows the social reality of the Tsimshian. Alas, very little is known about this tribe. He has to make do with very poor ethnographic materials. There are several minor doubts one can entertain about his interpretation of the facts, but the information here is altogether very thin. A critic of Lévi-Strauss (Ricoeur) has been struck by the fact that all his examples of mythic thought have been taken from the geo-graphical areas of totemism and never from Semitic, pre-Hellenic, or Indo-European areas, whence our own culture arose. Lévi-Strauss would have it that his examples are typical of a certain kind of thought, a type in which the arrangement of items of culture is more important and more stable than the content. Ricoeur asks whether the totemic cultures are not so much typical as selected, extreme types? This is a very central question which every anthropologist has to face. Is *La Pensée sauvage* as revealed by myth and rite analysis typical, or peculiar, or is it an illusion produced by the method? Here we are bound to mention Lévi-Strauss's idea of mythic thinking as *bricolage*. The *bricoleur*, for whom we have no word, is a crafts-man who works with material that has not been produced for the task he has in hand. I am tempted to see him as an Emmett engineer whose products always look alike whether they are bridges, stoves, or trains, because they are always composed of

66

odd pieces of drainpipe and string, with the bells and chains and bits of Gothic railing arranged in a similar crazy way. In practice this would be a wrong illustration of *bricolage*. Lévi-Strauss himself is the real Emmett engineer because he changes his rules as he goes along. For mythic thought a card-player could be a better analogy, because Emmett can use his bits how he likes, whereas the *bricolage* type of culture is limited by pattern-restricting rules. Its units are like a pack of cards continually shuffled for the same game. The rules of the game would correspond to the general structure underlying the myths. If all that the myths and rites do is to arrange and rearrange the elements of the culture, then structural analysis would be exhaustive, and for that reason very important.

At the outset of any scientific enterprise, a worker must know the limitations of his method. Linguistics and any analysis modelled on linguistics can only be synchronic sciences. They analyse systems. In so far as they can be diachronic it is in analysing the before-and-after evolution of systems. Their techniques can be applied to any behaviour that is systematic. But if the behaviour is not very systematic, they will extract whatever amount of regularity there is, and leave a residue. Edmund Leach has shown that the techniques of Lévi-Strauss can be applied to early Greek myths, to Buddhist, and to Israelite myths. But I suppose he would never claim that the analysis is exhaustive. In the case of his analysis of Genesis, I have already mentioned above that the residue is the greater part.

Lévi-Strauss in his publications so far seems blithely unconscious that his instrument can produce only one kind of tune. More aware of the limitations of his analysis, he would have to restrict what he says about the attitude of mythic thought to time, past and future. Structural analysis cannot but reveal myths as timeless, as synchronic structures outside time. From this bias built into the method there are two consequences. First, we cannot deduce anything whatever from it about the attitudes to time prevailing in the cultures in question. Our method reduces all to synchrony. Everything which Lévi-Strauss writes in *La Pensée sauvage* about time in certain cultures or at a certain level of thinking, should be rephrased to apply only to the method he uses. Second, if

67

49

myths have got an irreversible order and if this is significant, this part of their meaning will escape the analysis. This, as Ricoeur points out, is why the culture of the Old Testament does not fit into the *bricolage* category.

We know a lot about the Israelites and about the Jews and Christians who tell and retell these stories.[3] We know little about the Australian aborigines and about the no longer surviving American Indian tribes. Would this be the anthropologist's frankest answer to Ricoeur? We cannot say whether the *bricolage* level of thought is an extreme type or what it is typical of, for lack of sufficient supporting data about the examples. But we must say that the *bricolage* effect is produced by the method of analysis. For a final judgement, then, we can only wait for a perfect experiment. For this, richly abundant mythical material should be analysed against a known background of equally rich ethnographic records. We can then see how exhaustive the structural analysis can be and also how relevant its formulas are to the understanding of the culture.

NOTES

1. See pp. 1-47 of this book. The next few pages constitute Dr Douglas's summary of Lévi-Strauss's text (see Introduction) [E.R.L.].
2. In what follows I am indebted to the Rev. Dr Cyril Barett, S.J. for criticism.
3. Lévi-Strauss's own justification for *not* applying his method to Biblical materials seems to rest on the proposition that we do not know enough about the ancient Israelites! (See *Esprit*, November 1963, p. 632) but cf. Leach (1966) *passim* [E.R.L.].

REFERENCES

ELIOT, T. S. 1957. *On Poetry and Poets*. London: Faber & Faber.

FORTES, M. 1959. *Oedipus and Job in West African Religion*. Cambridge: Cambridge University Press.

JAKOBSON, R. & LÉVI-STRAUSS, C. 1962. 'Les Chats' de Charles Baudelaire. *L'Homme* 2: 5-21.

LEACH, E. R. 1961. Lévi-Strauss in the Garden of Eden: An Examination of some Recent Developments in the Analysis of Myth. *Transactions of the New York Academy of Sciences*. Series 2: 386-396.

—— 1962. Genesis as Myth. *Discovery*, May: 30-35.

—— 1966. The Legitimacy of Solomon: Some Structural Aspects of

68

Old Testament History. *European Journal of Sociology* 7: 58-101.

LÉVI-STRAUSS, C. 1955. The Structural Study of Myth. *Journal of American Folklore* 28: 428-444. Reprinted with modifications in C. Lévi-Strauss, 1963a.

—— 1956. Structure et dialectique. In *For Roman Jakobson on the Occasion of his Sixtieth Birthday*. The Hague: Mouton. Reprinted in C. Lévi-Strauss, 1963a.

—— 1957. Le symbolisme cosmique dans la structure sociale et l'organisation cérémonielle des tribus américaines. *Serie Orientale Roma*, XIV. Institut pour l'Étude de l'Orient et de l'Extrême-Orient, Rome, pp. 47-56.

—— 1958. La Geste d'Asdiwal. *École Pratique des Hautes Études, Section des Sciences Religieuses*. Extr. Annuaire 1958-1959: 3-43. Reprinted in *Les Temps modernes*, March 1961 [see pp. 1-47 of this book].

—— 1958a. *Anthropologie structurale*. Paris: Plon. (English translation, 1963a. *Structural Anthropology*. New York: Basic Books.)

—— 1962b. *La Pensée sauvage*. Paris: Plon.

—— 1963b. The Bear and the Barber. *Journal of the Royal Anthropological Institute* 93, Part I: 1-11.

NEEDHAM, R. 1962. *Structure and Sentiment*. Chicago: University of Chicago Press.

RICOEUR, P. 1963. Structure et hermeneutique. *Esprit*, November: 598-625.

WEIL, SIMONE. 1950. *Attente de Dieu*. Paris: La Colombe.

69

1

THE ARCHAIC TRIAD:
THE DOCUMENTS

In the preceding pages several references have been made to one of the oldest structures to be found in Roman religion: the association, in certain circumstances, of Jupiter, Mars, and Quirinus. In historical times this triad no longer has much vitality, and evidences of it are found only in a few obviously archaic ceremonies, rituals, and priesthoods. It is nevertheless the oldest vestige of the first stage of theology available to us, and as such it requires that we investigate it first. Moreover, as individuals Mars and Jupiter have always been the most important figures of the pantheon; as for Quirinus, he poses a complex problem, the solution of which involves many others; according to the side one chooses, the interpretation not merely of the triad but of numerous other divinities is differently oriented.

It is to G. Wissowa's credit that he drew attention, in the very beginning of his book, to the existence of the pre-Capitoline triad, even though he did not make use of it as fully as he might have. Here is his presentation, from the second edition (p. 23):

The three *flamines maiores* assure the service of Jupiter, Mars, and Quirinus, and this triad [*dieser Dreiverein*] of gods is also the one which appears as dominant in the most diverse sacred formulas dating from the earliest times. The order of precedence of the highest priests is based on the same conception, which was still flourishing at the end of the Republic, and which placed the *Rex sacrorum* above all the others, followed successively by the *flamines Dialis, Martialis,* and *Quirinalis,* with the *Pontifex Maximus* forming the last term (Fest. p. 185).[1] The less this corresponds to the real proportions of power and importance of these various priests in later periods, the greater is

1. = pp. 299–300 L².

the probability that this listing reflects a hierarchy, in force in the earliest times, of the divinities represented by these various priests.

And a note enumerates as follows the formulary uses mentioned at the end of the first sentence:

In the ritual of the Salii, Serv. *Aen.* 8.663; after the conclusion of a treaty by the ferials, Pol. 3.25.6; in the formula of *deuotio*, Liv. 8.9.6; after the consecration of the *spolia opima*, Fest. p. 189,[2] Plut. *Marc.* 8; Serv. *Aen.* 6.860 (when, in the last formula, Festus says "Janus Quirinus" instead of "Quirinus," the other evidences prove that this is an inadvertence). An analogous triad seems to have been placed at the head of the theological structure of the Umbrians, for in the Iguvine Tables Jupiter, Mars, and Vofionus share the distinctive surname of Grabovius.

This balance sheet, completed (Wiss., pp. 133–34) by a circumstance related to the cult of Fides, is rather summary and must be corrected at some points, but it stands. One cannot fail to be astonished that the man who drew it up and who wrote, with regard to the Iguvine triad, the important word *Göttersystem* "theological structure," should later have studied the three Roman gods separately, without troubling himself over their interrelationships or over the meaning of the *System* which he had glimpsed, at Rome and Iguvium. Since 1912 the exegetes of Roman religion have not paid it much attention. Only in recent times has it given rise to two radically opposed conceptions. One of these is expressed in the series to which I have given the common title *Jupiter Mars Quirinus* (1941–48); the other, coming as a reaction by various authors, is most notably set forth in Kurt Latte's *Römische Religionsgeschichte* (1960), which has recently replaced Wissowa's book in the *Handbuch der Altertumswissenschaft*. In short, while it seems necessary to me to use this triad as a point of departure for the understanding of the oldest Roman religion, Latte fails to see in it anything but a late and accidental and, moreover, badly documented grouping. One seeks in vain in his manual for a discussion of the question. The Umbrian parallel is nowhere mentioned. The other elements of the dossier occur in scattered notes, each fact being examined as if the others did not exist, in connection with some other subject, and without reference to the triad. Each of these investigations, with only one isolated and therefore unimportant exception,

2. = p. 302 L².

has as its end result the depreciation or elimination of the evidence. Thus, before we reflect on the meaning of the triad, we must put to the philological proof the documents which establish its existence and which the latest criticism tries to deny.

Two of these documents have already been thoroughly examined in my "Preliminary Remarks," for the sake of the problems of method which they raise.

1. Concerning the *ordo sacerdotum*, which Latte discusses on pages 37 and 195 of his book, I have demonstrated[3] that it is not possible to set the date of its establishment as late as the second half of the fourth century, or to explain the "selection" of the three flamens called *maiores* as one of the historical accidents of this period. I shall confine myself to quoting the text of Festus in which the *ordo* is set forth (pp. 299–300 L[2]):

It is the *rex* who is regarded as the greatest (of these priests), then comes the *flamen Dialis*, after him the *Martialis*, in fourth place the *Quirinalis*, and in fifth the *pontifex maximus*. Consequently, at a feast the *rex* sits above all the priests; the *Dialis* above the *Martialis* and the *Quirinalis*; the *Martialis* above the latter, and both above the *pontifex*: the *rex* because he is the most powerful; the *Dialis* because he is the priest of the universe which is called *dium*; the *Martialis* because Mars is the father of the founder of Rome; the *Quirinalis* because Quirinus was summoned from Cures to be associated with the Roman empire; and the *pontifex maximus* because he is the judge and arbiter of the affairs of gods and men.

We are concerned here only with the fact of the hierarchy, not with the reasons by which Festus justifies it. Note that the explanations of the *Martialis* and the *Quirinalis* are based on the commonly accepted version of the "history" of the origins. Let us merely add that Latte, in order to reduce the importance of the evidence, stresses that the precedences of the five priests are indicated only on the occasion of banquets. Is it not unlikely, however, that the order of precedence at banquets should have been different from that observed at other gatherings? In addition, as concerns the three flamens, it is less the order of the priests than that of their gods which is given, and this order is constant in all the other testimonies.

2. The formula of *deuotio* (Liv. 8.9.8), in which, after Janus, the gods of the major flamens are invoked, has been quoted in full

3. Above, pp. 102–3.

55

above.[4] It has been shown that the two reasons offered by Latte (p. 5, n. 1) for regarding this formula as a forgery do not prove his thesis: *fero*, in the phrase *ueniam peto feroque*, does not have the meaning he assigns to it; and the order of enumeration, with the *diui Nouensiles* in first place and the *dii Indigetes* in second, which seems to contradict the meaning then ascribed to the two words, actually confirms that the historian correctly copied an authentic formula.

3. One of the two competing traditions concerning the *spolia opima*, the one which is generally agreed to be the most ancient, lists as their recipients, respectively, Jupiter (of the *prima*), Mars (of the *secunda*), and Quirinus (of the *tertia*): thus Varro (in Fest. p. 302 L²) and Servius (*Aen.* 6.859). This piece of information is the only one accepted by the latest critic. Thus it is enough merely to mention it here. Later it will provide useful facts for the interpretation of the triad.[5]

4. Once a year, "the flamens" went to sacrifice at the chapel of Fides, under very special conditions.[6] Livy attributes the establishment of the rites to Numa, who was, according to general opinion, the founder of all the *sacra*. He describes them as follows: "He also established an annual worship of Faith, to whose chapel he ordered that the flamens should proceed in a two-horse hooded carriage, and that they should offer the sacrifice with their right hands wrapped up as far as the fingers."

Until recent years, making allowance for the context, flamens had been understood here to designate the three *flamines maiores*, those of Jupiter, Mars, and Quirinus. In fact, Livy's account occurs in his enumeration of the religious ceremonies instituted by the legendary King Numa (1.20–21). First he speaks of the creation of the priests, the first of whom are correctly and conjointly the three *flamines maiores* (20.1–2), followed by the Vestals, then the Salii, and finally the pontiffs (20.3–7). After reflections concerning the happy effect on the Romans of these institutions (21.1–2), and a mention of his supposed counsellor,

4. Above, p. 103.

5. Below, pp. 172–73.

6. See now the articles of P. Boyancé: "Fides et le serment," *Coll. Lat.* 58 (*Hommages à A. Grenier*) (1962): 329–41; "Fides Romana et la vie internationale," *Institut de France, Séance publique des cinq Académies 25 October 1962*, pp. 1–16; "Les Romains, peuple de la fides," *LH* 23 (1964): 419–35. See also L. Lombardi, *Dalla "fides" alla "bona fides"* (1961); and V. Bellini, "Deditio in fidem," *Revue historique du droit français et étranger* 42 (1964): 448–57, especially as a means of creating a connection of the *cliens/patronus* type. Detailed bibliography in Catalano, *SSR*, p. 81, n. 31, and in J. P. Boucher, *Etudes sur Properce* (1965), pp. 485–87.

the nymph Egeria (21.3), the historian proceeds to the sacrifices and ceremonies invented by Numa (21.4–5), and the sacrifice to Fides heads the list. It is thus natural to think that in this text, where everything is precise and technical, the *flamines* who appear in 21.4 are the ones—the only ones—who have been involved up to that point, and that they are the ones who are named in 20.1–2, the three *maiores*. Such is the general opinion, shared, for example, by Otto in his article "Fides" in the *RE* (6 [1909], col. 2292, lines 5–14): "From the cult of Fides an ancient and very remarkable ritual has been handed down to us.... The three great flamens drove to her sanctuary in a covered vehicle drawn by two horses"; such also is Wissowa's opinion (1902, p. 123; 1912, pp. 133–34): "In fact, the cult itself is certainly more ancient than the establishment of the temple [of Fides, around 250, on the Capitol], since we know that the three flamens proceeded once a year to the sanctuary of Fides (the one which had preceded the Capitoline temple) in a covered vehicle, and offered her a sacrifice...."

In note 4 on page 237 of his book, without mentioning the current opinion, Latte offers as self-evident another interpretation of the word *flamines*, intended to destroy the evidence: "Livy uses *flamines*, in accordance with the linguistic usage of his time, without technical force, to mean *sacerdotes*; from this it does not follow that Fides has a special flaminate." If the final remark is certainly true (but who ever intimated that there was a flamen of Fides?), the suggestion which precedes it is doubly improbable. We have just seen that the style and intention of the historian's chapters 20–21 dissuade us from supposing an "untechnisch" use of *flamen* (a use which does not seem to occur in Livy),[7] and that the coherent plan of these same chapters suggests, on the contrary, that we clarify 21.4 by means of 20.1–2. On the other hand, if we understand the word as Latte proposes, the plural *flamines* at 21.4 is not justified. Livy had no reason to evoke in this sentence a succession through the ages of single, individual titularies of a particular priesthood of Fides,[8] the only use of the plural which would agree with usage,[9] and accordingly *flamines* here must

7. A few chapters further on, while discussing Ancus, Livy writes (1.33.1): *Ancus, demandata cura sacrorum flaminibus sacerdotibusque aliis* . . .

8. However, this is just what Latte does (p. 237, n. 4), when he boldly translates *flamines* by a singular: "Wir erfahren, dass ihr der Priester einmal im Jahr . . . ein Opfer brachte."

9. This is how the plural is justified in texts like Gaius 1.112 (*flamines maiores, id est Diales Martiales Quirinales, item reges sacrorum* . . .): Gaius is considering these priests throughout history; similarly *Dialibus* in Tac. *Ann.* 3.71.4; etc.

refer to a group of priests, all of whom are present and active at the same time. Are we then to suppose that Fides was served by a sodality which has left no other traces?

5. Servius (*Aen.* 8.663) says that the Salii, the priests who used in their ceremonies the *ancilia*, the buckler which fell from heaven and its eleven indistinguishable copies, are *in tutela Jouis Martis Quirini*.

This statement does not depend on the text of Virgil with which it is associated, and is not suggested by it. Servius has thus given us here an independent note, and one which contains no surprises, since each of the three gods does in fact have a personal connection with the Salii. If, according to the legend of the foundation, it was Jupiter who caused the *ancile* to fall from heaven, it is Mars and Quirinus who respectively patronize the two teams of priests throughout history. The form in which we know the legend of the foundation is apparently recent and shows Greek influence, but the *ancilia* themselves are ancient, probably not having in the first centuries of Rome the connotation of *pignora imperii*, but rather that of talismans of annual security. What god other than the sovereign Jupiter was qualified to give such talismans to the community? And what other god was more able to make an object fall from the sky? As for the attribution of one of the colleges of Salii to Mars and of the other to Quirinus, whatever its meaning may be, it is definite. Nobody rejects the former, and the latter is no less well attested, despite what Latte writes (p. 113, n. 3): "The attestation is weak: a discourse in Livy, 5.52.7, and a somewhat distorted reference by Statius, *Silv.* 5.2.129." Not to mention the poet's text, which is not negligible,[10] it is hard to see how the fact that the historian's text occurs in a "discourse" and not in the body of the

---

10. R. Schilling, "Janus, le dieu introducteur, le dieu des passages," *MEFR*, 1960, p. 123, n. 4, writes: "Let us note that the meaning of this opposition [Quirinus-peace, Mars-war, see below, pp. 259–61] was never lost. When Statius (*S.* 5.128 ff.) composes a poem in honor of Crispinus, who is a 'Salian of the Hill,' he distributes the roles vested in Mars and Quirinus in conformity with tradition: to Mars (and Athena) the art of battle, to Quirinus the defensive arms:

> Monstrabunt acies Mauors Actaeaque uirgo
> ... umeris quatere arma Quirinus
> qui tibi tam tenero permisit plaudere collo
> nubigenas clipeos intactaque caedibus arma.

The last line designates the *ancilia* and the javelins used to strike them: observe the stress of *intacta caedibus arma*." It is possible that this last expression alludes solely to the fact that the arms of the Salii were used only in rites, not in war. In any case, this text proves definitely that the *Salii Collini* belonged to Quirinus.

narrative diminishes its credibility. Whether *contio* or *narratio*, everything that appears in Livy is by Livy, and is equally based on the information available to Livy. Moreover, it is not true that we have no other evidence. When Dionysius of Halicarnassus, who says in another place that the *Salii Palatini* belong only to Mars (fragment 14.2.2: καλίας τις Ἄρεος, designating the *sacrarium Saliorum* on the Palatine; cf. Val. Max. 1.8.11), undertakes (2.70.2) to present conjointly the *Salii Palatini* and the *Salii Agonenses* or *Collini*, he defines them as "dancers and singers of the armed gods [τῶν ἐνοπλίων θεῶν]." These armed gods, in the plural, are obviously not Mars alone, but Mars and Quirinus, the two gods whom the same historian, through an inadequate interpretation of Quirinus but one normal at this period, combines elsewhere (2.48.2) under the common epithet "warrior divinities [δαιμόνων πολεμιστῶν]."

Apart from any interpretation, and considering only the Roman data, the verdict rendered by Latte in the last words of note 3 on page 113 is arbitrary: "Serv. *Aen.* 8.663, *Salios qui sunt in tutela Iouis Martis Quirini* is surely false [*ist sicher falsch*]." However we are to understand the concept of *tutela*, the rites and the instruments of the Salii still involve the three gods.[11]

The Jupiter-Mars-Quirinus triad is thus not illusory, and the documents which attest it are valid.[12] How are we to interpret it?

11. Latte also refuses to admit that the Salii are priests (pp. 115, 120); let us define them, if he prefers, as men who specialized in certain religious functions.

12. It will have been noted that none of the testimonies implies that Quirinus is identified with Romulus, which is contrary to Latte's thesis discussed above, pp. 106–7.

2

INTERPRETATION:
THE THREE FUNCTIONS

For as long as people have been willing to discuss it, the pre-Capitoline triad has been generally regarded as the result of Rome's precocious history.

Giving a liberal interpretation to the classic legends about the origins of the city, holding especially to the idea of synoecism, of the fusion of two ethnically different populations, Latin and Sabine, certain scholars have admitted, in agreement with one of the two variants, that Quirinus was the god of the Sabine component, a kind of Sabine Mars, who was juxtaposed with the Latin Mars, and that Jupiter, who was shared by the two nations, was diplomatically placed at the head of this compromise. In the course of my "Preliminary Remarks," the weakness of this Sabine thesis is emphasized.[1] It is sufficient to add here that the variant which assigns Quirinus to the Sabines is obviously based on an etymological approximation, a connection with the name of the Sabine city of Cures, which the linguists have been unable to confirm.

Abandoning the Sabine component and ethnic considerations in general, others support the idea of original dualism by basing it on topographical considerations. The population of the *collis Quirinalis*, whatever it was and wherever it came from, had Quirinus as its principal god, as the populations of the Palatine had Mars, and it was the joining of these originally independent settlers in a unified city which brought about the juxtaposition of the local gods, Quirinus and Mars, in the pantheon. But as we saw in the "Preliminary Remarks," if the name *collis Quirinalis* actually means "the hill of Quirinus," there is no proof that this denomination antedates the synoecism—or, to be

1. Above, pp. 60–78.

more prudent, let us say the absorption of the *collis* into the *urbs*—and it is possible as well that a "Palatine" god named Quirinus may have seen his cult transferred to this northern outpost, just as the "Palatine" Jupiter was put in possession of the Capitol. In reality, there is no free choice between these theoretically possible theses. The interpretation of Quirinus as a primitive local god collides with a massive fact which condemns any attempt to explain the triad in terms borrowed from the history or the location of Rome, and which, consequently, the authors of these attempts refrain from mentioning. This fact is the existence among the Umbrians of Iguvium, whose pantheon is partially known to us through the famous *Tabulae*, of a completely similar triad.[2] Three gods also appear there, whose grouping in an organic structure proceeds both from their common and exclusive epithet, *Grabouio-*,[3] and from the three parallel rituals in which they figure. These gods, in order, are *Jou-*, *Mart-*, and *Vofiono-*, and their succession, to judge from one important detail, is truly a hierarchy: if each of these gods receives as a sacrifice, with the same ceremonial, three cattle (with the offering to the third specified as *buf trif calersu* "tres boues callidos," that is, with white forehead or face and the rest of the body of another color), in contrast the minor gods who are attached to them receive unequal victims: respecively, three pregnant sows, three suckling pigs, and three lambs. At Rome, in the theory of the consecration of the *spolia opima*, it is notable that the only liturgical circumstance in which we hear of different victims being offered to Jupiter, Mars, and Quirinus, that of Quirinus is an *agnus mas* (as opposed to a *bos* for Jupiter and the *solitaurilia* = *suouetaurilia* for Mars).[4] Finally, the comparison of the three names at Iguvium with those at Rome brings out a remarkable fact: while

2. See my "Remarques sur les dieux Grabovio- d'Iguvium," *RPh* 28 (1954): 225–34, reprinted, with many changes, as *IR*, part II, chap. 2; "Notes sur le début du rituel d'Iguvium (E. Vetter, *Handbuch* . . . 1, 1953, pp. 171–79)," *RHR* 147 (1955): 265–67. See especially I. Rosenzweig, *Ritual and Cults of Pre-Roman Iguvium* (1937); cf. R. Bloch, "Parenté entre religion de Rome et religion d'Ombrie, thèmes de recherches," *REL* 41 (1963): 115–22. Bibliography of the Tables (notably editions and translations of G. Devoto, E. Vetter, V. Pisani, G. Bottiglioni, J. W. Poultney), most recently in A. Ernout, *Le dialecte ombrien* (1961), pp. 5–6 (pp. 14–47, text and Latin translation of the Tables); cf. A. J. Pfiffig, *Religio Iguvina* (1964), pp. 11–31, text and German translation, followed by a most astonishing commentary: the author is one of those who understand Etruscan.

3. On *Grabouio*, see G. Garbini, *Studi linguistici in onore di V. Pisani* (1969), pp. 391–400 ("Grabovius").

4. Below, p. 240.

Jou- and *Mart-*, shared by the two lists, are substantives, the third god is designated in both places by an adjective, a derivative in *-no* of a nominal stem.[5] These facts are enough to establish that the two lists are not separable. And this statement has an important consequence.

Neither form of the divine grouping can be the outcome of chance, a historical accident.[6] It is unlikely, for example, that a fusion of inhabitants into a unified whole under different circumstances and with necessarily very different components, should twice have produced, independently, the same religious compromise, expressed in two divine hierarchies which resemble each other so closely. Thus it is certainly a question of a grouping of gods antedating the foundation both of Iguvium and of Rome, imported and maintained by the two groups of founders and inherited from their common past.

If the explanation of the grouping is neither local nor historical, it can only be of another kind. The grouping is meaningful; it outlines by the association of three different and hierarchized divine types a religious conception in three stages. In short, it constitutes a theological structure, and is indeed, as Wissowa said, a *Göttersystem* and not merely a *Götterversammlung*. It is this structure which we must try to understand.

Finally, since we are concerned with a pre-Roman and pre-Umbrian structure, and hence one which was inherited from a stage nearer to the Indo-European unity than is Rome, there will be occasion to compare it with what is known of the oldest theological structures of the other Indo-European peoples. To reject this help, as several specialists do, cannot be justified by any reason of fact or of principle: the "Preliminary Remarks" of the present volume illustrate its possibility and its usefulness. Naturally, however, it is on the basis of the Roman data that the interpretation must be formed, with the comparison providing aid and control on delicate points and giving to the whole its true dimensions.

5. V. Pisani, "Mytho-Etymologica," *Rev. des études indo-européennes* (Bucharest) 1 (1938): 230–33, and, independently, E. Benveniste, "Symbolisme social dans les cultes gréco-italiques," *RHR* 129 (1945): 7–9, propose a very probable etymology for *Vofiono-*, which makes it the exact equivalent of **Couirio-no-:*Leudhyo-no-*. The phonetic correspondences (*l, eu, dh > u, o, f*) are entirely regular; for **leudhyo-*, cf. German *Leute*, etc. Other etymologies of *Vofiono-* are not very likely: see my "Remarques ..." (above, n. 2), p. 226, n. 1.

6. And borrowing is evidently excluded. A detailed discussion appears in my article, "A propos de Quirinus," *REL* 33 (1955): 105–8.

Which Roman data are we to use in this investigation? We shall gradually have to bring in the entire theology of the three gods, as well as their history. For they do have a history. If Mars shows scarcely any development, the Capitoline Jupiter, whose cult was established during the articulation of the *regnum* and the *libertas*, is in certain respects a new type. As for Quirinus, his identification with Romulus in the account of the origins has certainly altered and complicated his definition. To be sure, we must not exaggerate these changes, and we shall see that the Capitoline god preserved a great deal, and, as the identification of Quirinus with Romulus cannot have been entirely arbitrary, the very changes which it produced are apt to reveal the ancient traits of the figures involved. But, for the specific problem in which we are engaged, we must be exacting and must limit ourselves at first to what is taught by the behavior of the three flamens of these gods. On the one hand, as I have said more than once, these *maiores* priests are in fact true fossils, stubbornly resisting change; in the historical period, not one of them was ever charged with new duties; their number never varied, and their archaic nature is obvious (the rules of the *Dialis*; the *Martialis* and the sacrifice of the October Horse). On the other hand, they themselves form, in the *ordo* and in the cult of Fides, a human triad in which the differential characteristics must not be divorced from those which distinguish the divine triad. At the most, certain social or political facts of the regal period can be connected with this first piece of evidence.

The status of the *flamen Dialis* and of his wife, the *flaminica*, is the best known of the three: containing a great number of strange items, it has interested the antiquaries and the annalists.[7] A certain number of these items are intended solely to assure the continued presence of the priest in Rome and his physical communication with Roman soil (he may not leave Rome; the feet of his bed are coated with a thin layer of mud, and he may not go three days without lying on it), but others clarify the nature of his god.

Certain items refer to the sky, attesting that Jupiter is in the heavens. For example, the *flamen Dialis* may remove his under tunic only in covered places, in order that he may not appear naked under the

7. Unless otherwise indicated, the data given here occur in Gell. 10.15, *de flaminis Dialis deque flaminicae caerimoniis.*

sky *tanquam sub oculis Jouis.* Again, he is not allowed to remove *sub diuo* the most distinctive part of his costume, the *apex* of his cap. Moreover, it must be admitted that at all times the sky god was the hurler of thunderbolts; if there is nothing in what we know of the behavior of the *Dialis* which corresponds to this trait, that of his wife fills the gap: when she sees a thunderbolt, the *flaminica* is *feriata* "until she shall have appeased the gods" (Macr. 1.16.8).

But this naturalistic aspect is not the only one. The connections of the *flamen Dialis* and the *rex*, which have already been mentioned, are definite, and must date from earlier than republican times. Livy explains their principle, evidently based on the pontifical doctrine, in his chapter on the alleged foundations by Numa, where he sums up so well the essential features of each priest (1.20. 1–2):

> He [Numa] then turned his attention to the appointment of priests, al-
> though he performed very many priestly duties himself, especially those which
> now belong to the Flamen Dialis. But inasmuch as he thought that in a war-
> like nation there would be more kings like Romulus than like Numa, and that
> they would take the field in person, he did not wish the sacrificial duties of the
> kingly office to be neglected. and so appointed a flamen for Jupiter, as his
> perpetual priest, and provided him with a conspicuous dress and the royal
> curule chair. To him he added two other flamens, one for Mars, the other for
> Quirinus.

The curule chair was not the unique sign of a mystical link with power: the only one of the priests with the Vestals, the *flamen Dialis* was preceded by one lictor (Plut. *Q.R.* 113), and he alone had the privilege of sitting in the Senate (Liv. 27.8.8).[8] Through these definitions and symbols we catch sight of a characteristic of the earliest Jupiter: he himself was *rex*, and he protected the human *rex*. Even in republican times, when this title had become suspect and hateful, it remained *fas* to give it to Jupiter, and to him alone (Cic. *Rep.* 1.50; Liv 3.39.4).

Other rules governing the *flamen Dialis* (principally Gell. 10.15), the most likely interpretation of which is that they extend to the priest the traits of his god, reveal a Jupiter who is above the oath, above the law, completely free. Alone of the Romans, the *flamen Dialis* is

---

8. The *flaminica* and the *regina* are the only ones to wear the headdress called (*in*)*arculum,* Serv. *Aen.* 4.137; cf. Paul. p. 237 L².

exempt from the oath, *iurare Dialem fas nunquam est*. By virtue of his position he suspends the execution of punishments: if a chained man enters his house, he must be set free, and the chains must be carried up to the roof and thrown down from there into the street; if a man who is being led away to be scourged casts himself in supplication at the feet of the *Dialis*, it is a sacrilege to beat him on that day. A personal symbolism confirms this freedom, this absence of ties: the *Dialis* has no knot on his cap or on his girdle or elsewhere; he may not even wear a ring which is not open and hollow.

Differentially, other rules separate him clearly from the warlike area of human activity. He may not see the army, *classem procinctam*, arrayed outside the *pomerium*. The horse is particularly repugnant to him: he must not mount it.

Finally, another group of rules makes the *Dialis* the pure and sacred being par excellence, the incarnation of the sacred. He is *quotidie feriatus*, which means that for him no day is secular. Day and night he keeps on his person some item of costume which expresses his function. No fire but the sacred fire may be carried out of his house. He must always have near his bedposts a casket containing sacred cakes, *strues* and *ferctum*. The most sacred of the marriage forms, the *confarreatio*, besides being demanded of him and his parents, also requires his presence. He avoids contact with everything which may defile, and especially with that which is dead or suggests death: corpses, funeral pyres, and uncooked meat.[9]

Thus, the already complex figure of a personal god emerges at the head of the triad: celestial and fulgurant, but also kingly; active in the areas of power and the law, but not of battle, which, like the horse, is Mars's concern; the most sacred among sacred beings and the source of sacredness. It would be artificial to try to assign a chronological order to the elements of this coherent representation; particularly artificial to claim that in the beginnings this god was merely a Jupiter of the peasants, the master of good and bad weather and the sender of rain, and to assert that the rest of his qualities were later additions. The *regnum*, as we have seen, is also very old, older than Rome, and the functional pair *rex–flamen Dialis* has its counterparts in Ireland as well as in India.[10] Frazer too drastically reduced the Latin

9. On the role of the *flamen Dialis* at the August Vinalia, see below, pp. 184–85.
10. Above, pp. 16–17.

rex to magico-agricultural duties, and to the role of guarantor of fertility; he was the leader in all things, primarily in the political area, and in earlier times, without doubt, in the religious area: these are the parts of the royal function which Jupiter controlled in the visible world and discharged himself in the invisible world.

We know little about the *flamen Martialis*; he was not involved in a maze of interdictions and obligations, like the *Dialis*, and this was probably an essential part of his nature rather than the result of a slackening of rules. He would not have fulfilled his true function if he had been subjected to rules which had meaning only in the theology of Jupiter.[11] We have no direct knowledge of any of his sacred duties. Nevertheless it is very probable that he was active in a ceremony which goes back to the earliest times and which definitely characterizes the earliest Mars: the sacrifice of a horse to this god, performed on 15 October, on the Field of Mars. If the summary information which we have concerning the *Equus October* does not actually specify the officiating priest, a macabre imitation of it, which was performed in Caesar's time, in which two mutinous soldiers took the place of the horse, was carried out, according to Dio Cassius (43.24.4) "by the pontiffs and the priest of Mars." Later we shall have to examine this ceremony in detail, or at least what incomplete sources tell us about it,[12] but here the only important thing is the character of the ritual act in which the *flamen Martialis* participated. This character is clearly warlike. The victim is a "war horse," ἵππος πολεμιστής, and moreover has just been the "winner"

11. Serv. *Aen*. 8. 552: *more enim uetere sacrorum neque Martialis neque Quirinalis omnibus caerimoniis tenebantur quibus flamen Dialis.* If the *flamen Martialis* may mount a horse (ibid.), it is not because of a relaxation of his statute, but because the horse belongs to the domain of Mars (below, p. 216). That the position proper to the *Martialis* was rather strict appears, for example, in Val. Max. 1.1.2, where we see a grand pontiff preventing a consul who is at the same time a flamen of Mars from going to war in Africa, *ne a sacris discederet*; but the *caerimoniae Martiae* which required his presence are not known.

12. Below, pp. 215–28, and "*QII* 17 (Le 'sacrifice humain' de 46 av. J. C.)," *REL* 41 (1963): 87–89. There is no doubt that the manner of execution was taken from the October Horse (it too was performed on the Field of Mars, and the heads were also carried to the Regia); moreover, Dio Cassius specifies that the execution was performed in the manner of a religious ritual ἐν τρόπῳ τινὶ ἱερουργίας. It is certainly to the *Equus October*, the only sacrifice of a horse at Rome, that Pliny refers, *N.H.* 28.146: horse's gall, he says, is regarded as a poison; *ideo flamini sacrorum equum tangere non licet, cum Romae publicis sacris equus etiam immolatur*; the flamen here must be the *Martialis*, and the method of killing (by thrusts of a javelin) allowed him to sacrifice the animal without touching it.

in a race, ὁ νικήσας δεξίος, and it is not immolated with a knife but with the thrust of a javelin κατάκοντίζειν (Pol. 12.4b).[13]

The role attributed to Mars in the royal legends allows us to glimpse what his place in the ideology then was, his point of entry into the social order. Even though he may be the father of the founding twins he does not at any point act in association with the monarchy. It is not to Mars but to Jupiter that his son Romulus trusts the protection of his work. If it is said of Numa that he created the flamen of Mars and his group of Salii, this is not an indication of affinity but merely the result of the bias which attributes to this king the establishment of all the great priesthoods. During the monarchy he does not play a significant role, but at the end, with the expulsion of the Tarquins and the establishment of the Republic, he is abruptly thrust into the place of honor. The oath normally belongs in Jupiter's province; however, in the annalistic tradition when Brutus, *tribunus Celerum*, that is, the leader of the army, swears to avenge the rape of Lucretia by expelling the kings, it is Mars whom he invokes; and the fallen king's land lying along the Tiber is consecrated to Mars, receiving the name of *campus Martius*. One has the impression, in this insurrection of the Latin military aristocracy against the Etruscan kings and in general against the *regnum*, that Mars is ideologically opposed to the traditional Jupiter, whom the Capitoline dedication has not yet reconciled, on approval, with the *libertas*.

With regard to the first two gods of the triad, we see that the collection of the oldest facts already sets the general tone for what they will continue to be throughout all of Roman history, despite inevitable adaptations to changing circumstances. Even when he assumes military tasks on the Capitol, the celestial and fulgurant Jupiter will be for the consuls and for the state the ruler and the resource which he was for the king, and, with the features of Zeus,

---

13. In his inaugural lecture at the Collège de France, 4 December, 1945, p. 12 (*Philologica* I, [1946]: 10), A. Ernout ingeniously attributed another, nonwarlike duty to the *flamen Martialis*: ". . . Such was this distich which the *flamen Martialis* pronounced on the day of the Meditrinalia, a feast in honor of Meditrina 'the healing ⟨goddess⟩,' in order to dispel illness: *Nouum uetus uinum bibo | nouo ueteri morbo medeor* (Varro L.L. 6.21)." I do not believe that this can be deduced from the text: *Octobri mense Meditrinalia dies dictus a medendo, quod Flaccus flamen Martialis dicebat, hoc die solitum uinum nouum et uetus libari et degustari medicamenti causa ; quod facere solent etiam nunc multi quum dicant : nouum uetus uinum bibo*, etc. Flaccus, the flamen of Mars, is thus only the *source* of the information. Ernout maintains this interpretation in his edition of Pliny, *N.H.* 28 (1962), p. 125, n. 4.

he will still remain the most august of the divinities. Mars will always patronize physical force and the spiritual violence whose principal application is war and whose outcome is victory. The career of Quirinus has been less straightforward. What do we learn from the observation of his priest?

We know three circumstances, and only three, in which the *flamen Quirinalis* participated ritually: at the time of the summer Consualia (21 August), at the time of the Robigalia (25 April), and probably at the time of the Larentalia (23 December). Until quite recent times, they had scarcely been doubted. G. Wissowa, who usually had better inspiration, had been the only one to think that they were secondary (p. 155): the meaning and the function of the god having been forgotten, he says, his priest had become idle, and in order to provide employment for this priest he had been given new duties, unconnected with those which he formerly performed and which had also been forgotten. This thesis is definitely untenable. The Romans never treated the traditional priests in this way, particularly not the other major flamens. When the meaning of a priesthood became blurred, along with the theology which supported it, they allowed it to fade away, preserving its honors, and created new priests in order to fill new needs. Moreover, several of the divinities served by the *flamen Quirinalis* are among the most archaic. The name of Consus, among others, bears the mark of great antiquity. Finally, considering the realities of Rome, it is hard to imagine the shift of these few old cults without priests to an old priest without a cult, which Wissowa conjectures. At least Wissowa does not question the facts of the problem. On the contrary, this is exactly what Latte does. Let us consider them in succession, saving the case of the Larentalia for another occasion, since it involves a particular difficulty; however, if it is to be retained, as probably it should be, it can only confirm the other facts.[14]

The calendar contains two feasts of Consus, the god of stored grains (*condere*), on 21 August and 15 December; each is followed, after a similar interval (25 August and 19 December), by a feast of the goddess Ops, the personification of abundance and, in the earliest times especially, of agricultural abundance. This arrangement proves a con-

14. See below, pp. 268–69.

nection between the two divinities, which is not at all surprising and which confirms the epithet of Ops in the August cult: *Consiua*.[15] As so often happens, we have scanty information concerning the details of the rites. In the case of the Opeconsivia of 25 August, it can be thought that the grand pontiff and the Vestals officiated, but this is only an inference: all that is said in the only text (Varr. *L.L.* 6.21) which speaks of Ops Consiva is that she had a sanctuary in the Regia of the Forum, so sacred that the only ones allowed to enter it were the Vestals and the grand pontiff, who is designated as usual by the phrase *sacerdos publicus*. As for the Consualia of 21 August, an equally unique text (Tert. *Spect.* 5) says plainly that on this day the *flamen Quirinalis* and the Vestal virgins sacrificed at the underground altar which Consus had in the Circus. The two operations are different, and, if the Vestals take part in both—as they definitely do in the Consualia and as they probably do in the feast of Ops Consiva—it is because the two divinities are strictly interdependent and because the affinity of the priestesses for one also involves an affinity for the other. Latte, however, shows no hesitation in setting aside Tertullian's testimony, on the pretext of an alleged "confusion" committed by Tertullian with regard to Consus—a confusion of which in fact he is not guilty.[16] The Christian doctor is then supposed to have made mistake after mistake, and, not being aware of anything but the *opeconsiua dies* of 25 August, to have replaced 25 August by 21 August, the Forum and the Regia by the Circus, Ops by Consus, and finally—one wonders how and why, since the *pontifex* was surely the *mentio facilior*—the grand pontiff by the flamen of Quirinus. The rite of 21 August, expressly affirmed in this text, is thus evaporated to the advantage of the rite of 25 August, which is itself only a reconstruction. If one is not determined in advance to destroy the dossier of the *flamen Quirinalis* item by item, is it not wiser to accept that which is not suspicious, and to continue to think that 21 August, the feast of Consus, had its

15. The connection established by the ferial between Consus and the agricultural Abundance is confirmed by the fact that Consus is one of the old divinities (Seia, Segeta, etc.) of the valley of the Circus, all of them agrarian. The best etymology of his name is still the one which connects it with *condere*. The form *Consualia* may be analogical (*Februalia*, etc.), or it may be based on a verbal substantive in -*u*; there is nothing in it to suggest an Etruscan origin. Contrary opinion in A. Ernout, *Philologica* 2, (1957): 174. See below, pp. 267–68.

16. "Religion romaine et critique philologique, 2, le *flamen Quirinalis* aux *Consualia*," *REL* 39 (1961): 91–93.

rites at the altar of Consus, that 25 August, the feast of Ops, had its rites in the sanctuary of Ops, and that it was the *flamen Quirinalis* who celebrated the former?

The Robigalia involve the sacrifice of a dog and a sheep to Robigus, the personification of wheat rust. This is one of the rare malevolent powers to receive a cult. According to the calendar of Praeneste (*CIL*, I², 316–17), the feast takes place near the fifth milestone on the Via Claudia. Ovid, who uses poetic license when he names the divinity "Robigo" as the blight itself, is the only one to speak of a *lucus* consecrated to this spirit, and he says that he met the celebrants of the feast when he was returning from Nomentum. This scarcely agrees with the localization given by the calendar, since the traveler coming from Nomentum returns to Rome by the *via Nomentana* and not by the *via Claudia*. From Mommsen (who cites Ov. *Pont.* 1.8.43–44) to Bömer (*Fast.* 2: 287), various plausible ways of reconciling these two statements have been proposed, and of course it is possible, after all, that Ovid was guilty of an oversight on this point. But it is scarcely thinkable that he was mistaken about the salient features in the ceremony: on the one hand, the nature of the victims, of which one, the dog, is unusual, and on the other hand, the sacrificing priest. This priest is the *flamen Quirinalis*, into whose mouth the poet puts a long prayer consistent with a conception of Quirinus which was particularly cultivated by Augustan propaganda, and which we shall examine later: that of a peaceable Quirinus. Latte's judgment here seems to hesitate. On page 67 he does not contest the presence of the priest: "At the fifth milestone of the Via Claudia the *flamen Quirinalis* sacrifices a sheep and a dog"; but on page 114, note 1, he decides on the other hand that Ovid's uncertainty regarding the name (*Robigo* instead of *Robigus*) and the difficulties of itinerary caused by the mention of Nomentum completely invalidate his testimony concerning the priest. This is to mix up the incidental detail, in which the poet has taken one or perhaps two small liberties, and the essential fact, in which he could not commit an error without destroying the interest and the usefulness of the whole passage.

Even though the presence of his flamen there is not affirmed, we must cite here the festival of Quirinus himself, the Quirinalia of 17 February, which belong to the most ancient known cycle of annual ceremonies. The only ritual which is indicated for this day is the one

which bears the name of *stultorum feriae*, the last part of the Fornacalia (Ov. *F.* 2.513–32).[17] The Fornacalia, the feast of the roasting of
grains, were celebrated separately by each of the thirty curiae, but
not on a fixed date, which explains the absence of the name in the
calendars. Each year the *Curio maximus* decided the days and posted
them in the Forum. But there were laggards—the *stulti*—who through
carelessness or ignorance allowed the day assigned to their curia
to pass. On 17 February they had a "day of catching-up" on which,
as a group, they were supposed to set themselves aright. What is
the connection between the "feast of fools" and the Quirinalia?
Is it a simple coincidence of two independent rituals on the same day?
Or were they even identical? This latter view is represented by
Festus, p. 412 (cf. p. 361) L², and by the eighty-ninth *Roman Question*
of Plutarch, and two reasons recommend it. First, there is the fact
that if the Quirinalia are not the feast of fools, no Roman writer and
no antiquary has given the slightest indication regarding their content; but rituals just do not disappear so completely; on the contrary,
at Rome they often survive the loss of their theological justification.
Second—but this will not take on interest until after our next considerations of the very meaning of the name of Quirinus—there is
the fact that the feast of fools concludes operations which fully involve the structure of the *curiae*, under the authority of the *Curio
maximus*. I do not think, therefore, that Latte is correct when he writes
(p. 113): "The feast of the Quirinalia, on 17 February, was later so
completely forgotten that the final ceremony of the Fornacalia, the
stultorum feriae, could be set on this day." This is to attribute to the
Romans responsible for theology and especially for the cult more
freedom than they acknowledged to themselves; moreover, how
are we to undertand the word "later"? Do not the Fornacalia and their
conclusion furnish, in their subject matter and in their curiate organization, the guarantee of their antiquity?

17. On the Fornacalia, see L. Delatte, *Recherches sur quelques fêtes mobiles du calendrier
romain* (1937), pp. 13–22. The character of "god of the dead" which some have tried to
draw from the date of the Quirinalia (H. Wagenvoort, *Studies in Roman Literature, Culture,
and Religion* [1956], p. 182) is not supported by the facts. Only the calendar of Polemius
Silvius places the death of Romulus on 17 February (Quirinalia, quo die Romulus occisus a
suis); all the other sources associate this legend with 7 July (Nonae Caprotinae). Ovid, F. 2.481–
512, speaks of the transformation of Romulus into Quirinus at the beginning of his
treatment of the Quirinalia, but leaves it associated with *Capreae Palus*, thus with the *Nonae
Caprotinae* of July.

A sensible consideration is enough to render improbable the disqualifications, in the dossier of Quirinus, of the offices of his flamen and the content of his festival: if the duties of the *flamen Quirinalis* at the Consualia and at the Robigalia are, respectively, a mistake by Tertullian and an invention by Ovid, if the coincidence of the Quirinalia and of the last act of the Fornacalia is accidental and without meaning, then by what miracle did these three accidents have as their convergent result the concern of Quirinus with the same thing, namely, with grain, at three important moments in its life as a foodstuff: first, when rust threatens it; then when it is stored in the granaries; and finally when the Romans, organized in the *curiae*, prolong its preservation by roasting it? If we do not have any preconceived ideas, two lessons emerge from this convergence: it must be part of the definition of Quirinus, in contrast with Jupiter and Mars, that he collaborates closely with other divinities, to the extent of lending them his flamen; and this collaboration concerns grain, insofar as it is harvested and processed by the Romans, to their advantage.[18]

As for the social sector in which the god is interested, the evidence of the Quirinalia confirms what is suggested by the most likely etymology of his name.[19] Since the time of Kretschmer, *Quirīnus* has generally been recognized as a derivative in -*no*- (of the type *dominus*, from *domo*-), formed on an ancient **co-uirio*-, which would have designated the community of the *uiri*, or might even have been the proper name of their habitat ("*Quirium*"). We must probably simplify this etymology by abandoning the imaginary neuter **couirio*- and the equally imaginary hill called **Quirium*, and being satisfied with the feminine **couiria*-, which survives in the form *cūria*, designating the smallest division of each of the primitive tribes.[20] Quirinus may be, not the god of each *cūria* and of its *curiales*, but the god of the whole

18. The interpretation of G. Rohde, *Die Kultsatzungen der römischen Pontifices*, RVV 25 (1936): 121–24, is vitiated by the theory which makes Quirinus a god "adopted" when synoecism took place.

19. Among the other ancient explanations of the name of Quirinus, the association with the city of Cures is no longer defended. The etymology based on a Sabine *curis, quiris* "spear" (the authenticity of which is guaranteed by a related Celtic word) is rather unlikely: (1) Sabine *qu* causes difficulty; (2) the spear belongs to Mars rather than to Quirinus; (3) the *Quirites*, as opposed to the *milites*, can scarcely have been defined by the spear or by any other weapon; (4) on the basis of the "spear," how are we to explain *curia*?

20. R. Adrados, *El sistema gentilicio decimal de los Indo-europeos occidentales y las origines de Roma* (1948), pp. 35–59, thinks that the *curia* was not originally a division of the *tribus*, but a direct (military) "mustering"; for him, in primitive times, *curia* = *decuria*.

curiate organization, of the people as a whole, regarded not as an indistinct *moles*, but in its fundamental divisions. Another word, inseparable from these, has had a great career: *Quirites*, from **co-uirites*, the specific name of the Romans viewed from the standpoint of their civil and political organization. It is certainly not an accident if one of the feminine abstractions which pontifical science gave to Quirinus as an associate was the plural *Virites* (cf. *uiritim*), which might be translated as "the individualities": in other words, the materials of the synthesis (*co-uirites*) over which the masculine Quirinus presides.

Thus, below the celestial, royal, and highly sacred Jupiter, and below the warlike Mars, the older god Quirinus seems to have been the patron of the Roman people, and, whether by himself or by the action of his flamen in the service of specialized divinities, to have watched particularly over the Romans' supply of grain.

The conceptual religious structure which is manifested in these three hierarchized terms is now familiar to Indo-Europeanists. It can be observed, with the special peculiarities of each of the societies, among the Indians and Iranians as well as among the ancient Scandinavians and, with more pronounced alterations, among the Celts. To judge from some survivals which are to be found despite the early reorganization of the traditions, it was also known to several waves of Greek invaders, the Achaeans and the Ionians. I have proposed, for the sake of brevity, to call this structure "the ideology of the three functions." The principal elements and the machinery of the world and of society are here divided into three harmoniously adjusted domains. These are, in descending order of dignity, sovereignty with its magical and juridical aspects and a kind of maximal expression of the sacred; physical power and bravery, the most obvious manifestation of which is victory in war; fertility and prosperity with all kinds of conditions and consequences, which are almost always meticulously analyzed and represented by a great number of related but different divinities, among whom now one, now the other, typifies the whole in formulary enumerations of gods. The "Jupiter-Mars-Quirinus" grouping, with the nuances appropriate to Rome, corresponds to the lists which occur in Scandinavia and in Vedic and pre-Vedic India: Óðinn, Þórr, Freyr; Mitra-Varuṇa, Indra, Nāsatya.

73

For about thirty years, numerous studies of the whole and of details have been published on this subject by me or by scholars better qualified than I to explore the material in various areas: in the German collection for which this *Roman Religion* was originally written, the books which G. Widengren, J. de Vries, and W. Betz devote to the Iranian, Celtic, and Germanic religions are or will be based on the examination of this structure. For Vedic India,[21] I can only refer the reader to the most recent scrutiny of the subject, "Les trois fonctions dans le *Rg Veda* et les dieux indiens de Mitani," published in the *Bulletin de l'Académie royale de Belgique, Classe des lettres et des sciences morales et politiques* 47 (1961): 265–98, and to the basic works by Stig Wikander. A provisional critical analysis of what had been proposed up to 1956 has been published under the title *L'idéologie tripartie des Indo-Européens*, Collection Latomus, vol. 24 (1956).[22] The study continues to make progress, to undergo completion and correction, and the constantly renewed discussions which must be carried on contribute to this improvement. In a parallel development, a slower investigation is attempting to determine which societies throughout the world, outside of the Indo-Europeans, have succeeded in formulating and placing at the center of their thought these three needs which are in fact basic everywhere, but which the majority of human groups have been content merely to satisfy, without theorizing about them: sacred power and knowledge, attack and defense, and the nourishment and well-being of all.

In all the ancient Indo-European societies in which this ideological framework exists, it is a problem to know whether, and up to what point, the structure of the three functions is also expressed in the actual structure of society. For there is a difference between making an explicit survey of these three needs and causing a division of social behavior to correspond to them in practice, as men being then more or less exhaustively divided into functional "classes," into *Stände—Lehrstand, Wehrstand, Nährstand*, as it has sometimes been expressed in a phrase which is assonant but inadequate, especially in

21. This is not the place to criticize the volume written by J. Gonda for the same collection, *Die Religionen Indiens*, vol. 1: *Veda und älterer Hinduismus* (1960), in which the author speaks several times of my work. I have also examined his method of discussion several times and I shall probably return to it elsewhere.

22. Cf. also *Les dieux des Germains, essai sur la formation de la religion scandinave* (1959).

its first term. It seems certain, in all areas, that the rapid successes of the columns of Indo-European conquerors were due to the existence of specialists in war, notably in chariotry, such as the Indo-Iranian *márya*, of whom the Egyptian and Babylonian chronicles have preserved the terrified memory. The astonishing resemblances which have been pointed out between the druids and the brahmans and between the Irish *rí* and the Vedic *rájan* seem likewise to indicate that in at least one part of the Indo-European world the ancient types of the administrator of sacred matters and the trustee of politico-religious power survived long migrations. Thus the two higher functions must have been guaranteed by the differentiated groups of the general population, which was often enlarged by the addition of conquered natives, and on which the third function devolved. But it is also certain that at the end of these great travels, after they had settled down, the greater part of the Indo-European-speaking groups sooner or later, often very soon, abandoned this framework in actual practice. It thus remained only ideological and formed a means of analyzing and understanding the world, but with regard to social organization it offered at best only an ideal cherished by the philosophers and a legendary view of the beginnings. The light of history overtakes Greece at the moment when this change was accomplished almost everywhere, at the point where the functional meaning of the Ionian tribes was no more than a mythical fact. Among the Indo-Iranians themselves, India is the only region in which this archaic division was hardened, through an inverse evolution, in its system of the three arya *varṇa*—*brāhmaṇa, kṣatriya, vaiśya*—which dominate the non-arya fourth, the *śūdra*. If the Avesta and the Mazdean books which depend on it speak at length about the three estates (or about the four, the fourth being, as in Ionia, that of the artisans), we nevertheless know that human society was not actually divided in this way, at least not in an exhaustive or stable way, either in the Achaemenid empire or in the other Iranian societies of the Near East.

The problem must thus arise at Rome as well. But it arises under almost desperate conditions, since too many centuries elapsed between the origins and the account which the annalists gave of them for us to be able to expect authentic information concerning the earliest social organization. If in the eighth century there was any

survival of a division of society into three classes, respectively oper-
ating the three functions, its last traces quickly disappeared, at any
rate before the end of the regal period. It was probably one of the
accomplishments of the Etruscan domination to achieve its destruction. In my "Preliminary Remarks,"[23] I insist upon the fact
that the legend about the war between the Latins of Romulus and
the Sabines of Titus Tatius and their subsequent fusion was consistent
in its development and in the significance of its episodes with the
type of story that, in other Indo-European areas, forms the basis of
legends concerning the formation of the complete divine society,
starting with the original separation and hostility of its future components. This kind of story occurs among the Scandinavians (war,
then fusion of the Æsir and Vanir) and among the Indians (conflict,
then close association of the higher gods and the Nāsatya): on the one
hand are the gods representing the first and second functions, magical
power and warlike power, on the other hand the gods of fertility,
health, riches, etc.; similarly Romulus, the son of a god and the
beneficiary of Jupiter's promises, sometimes joined by his Etruscan
ally Lucumon, the expert in war, is originally opposed to Titus
Tatius, the leader of the wealthy Sabines and the father of the Sabine
women, and then forms with him a complete and viable society.
Now, this legend, in which each of the three leaders, with his respective following, is thoroughly characterized in terms of one of the
functions—reread in particular lines 9–32 of the first *Roman Elegy*
of Propertius—is intended to justify the oldest known division, the
three tribes of which these leaders are the eponyms, the companions
of Romulus becoming the *Ramnes*, those of Lucumon the *Luceres*,
and those of Titus Tatius the *Titienses*. May we assume from this that
the three primitive tribes (whose names, be it said in passing, have
an Etruscan ring, and thus were either changed or at least retouched
under the last kings) had in effect a functional definition, with the
Ramnes controlling political government and the cult (like the
companions of "Remus" in Propertius 4.1.9–26), the Luceres being
specialists in war (like Lucumon in the same text of Propertius,
26–29), and the Titienses being defined by their wealth of sheep (like
the Tatius of Propertius, 30)? The question remains open. I have
offered a number of reasons for an affirmative answer, but none is

23. Above, pp. 60–78.

compelling.[24] In the fourth and third centuries the fabricators of Roman history had only a very vague idea of the pre-Servian tribes, and it is possible that the Ramnes, the Luceres, and the Titienses had received their functional coloration only from the "legend of the origins," which was inherited from the Indo-European tradition and, as such, was faithfully trifunctional. But for the present study, an analysis of tenacious ideas and not a pursuit of inaccessible facts, this uncertainty is not very serious. It is more important for us to recognize the implicit philosophy, the theory of the world and of society which supports the legends of the origins, than to try to isolate from it the part which belongs to history.

The interpretation of the divine triad allows a better understanding of the reasons which account for its being invoked in several of the formulas and rituals cited above.[25] Generally speaking, wherever the three gods appear together, society as a whole and as a structure is concerned, using simultaneously for its advantage all the great principles of divine and human action.

Fides, Good Faith, is the patroness of all relations between persons and groups of persons; without her nothing is possible, on any level; on her depend the reciprocal concord and trust of the Romans, the harmonious adjustment of the rights and duties of all, regardless of where they were born or brought up, not to mention the stable peace or the just war with the foreigner, or the equitable arrangements between men and gods. One may thus conceive that the three major flamens take part in her cult, and that all three, crossing the city in the same vehicle and sacrificing together, demonstrate the total agreement of the powers they represent.

The danger from which the *deuotio* must deliver the army, the *populus Romanus Quiritium*, as the formula puts it, is no less total. It is thus natural that the suppliant, before his collective and indistinct references to *Diui Nouensiles*, *dii Indigetes*, and then to *Diui quorum est potestas nostrorum hostiumque*, should address himself, between the god of beginnings and the specialists of the battle and of the piece

24. This is the matter of chap. 2 of *NR*, pp. 86–127 ("Properce et les tribus," study of the variants with two and three races), and of the second part of *JMQ* 4 (1948): 113–71: "Les trois tribus primitives de Rome," summed up in *Idéol.*, pp. 12–15. See now *ME* 1: 15–16, 290–302, 428–36, and *IR*, pt. II, chap. 5 ("Les trois tribus primitives").

25. Above, pp. 141–47.

of ground where it takes place, to the divine triad which has power over the three constituent elements of social life.

The *ancile*, the bilobate buckler which fell from the sky, and the eleven indistinguishable copies which were made from it and which share in its sacredness, are one of the principal groups of talismans at Rome. Their number doubtless alludes to the full annual cycle considered in terms of its divisions, but, throughout this cycle, their power protects another totality, that of the Roman people. When we study Mars and Quirinus more fully and differentially, we shall try to understand the meaning of the juxaposition of their two groups of Salii in the rites of spring and autumn. But for now we can mention that several other Indo-European peoples possessed talismans which had fallen from the sky: for example, the golden objects which the Scythians honored every year (Herod. 4.5); or the three stones honored at Orchomenos under the name of Charites (Paus. 9.38.1). These talismans refer explicitly to the three functions: in the case of the Charites this is apparent from the invocation of the fourteenth *Olympic* (3–7), which is well interpreted by the scholiast (wisdom, beauty, valor);[26] as for the Scythian talismans, it appears in their very enumeration (cultic cup, warrior's axe, and the plow with its yoke).[27] In the case of the Salii, the *tutela Jouis Martis Quirini* expresses in a different way the same trifunctional and thus total meaning of the talismans which are in their charge.[28]

We can also usefully take up here the old theory of the *spolia opima*, the only item of ritual evidence which Latte has spared. This theory is known in two variants. One, defining *opima* as only those

26. See F. Vian, "La triade des rois d'Orchomène," *Coll. Lat.* 45 (*Hommages à G. Dumézil*) (1960): 216–24, esp. pp. 218–19.

27. "La préhistoire indo-iranienne des castes," *JA* 216 (1930): 109–30; "Les trois trésors des ancêtres dans l'épopée Narte," *RHR* 157 (1960): 141–54; "La société scythique avait-elle des classes fonctionelles?" *IIJ* 5 (1962): 187–202; *ME* 1: 446–52, 485–503. My interpretation (1930) of the Scythian objects which fell from the sky would improve that of A. Christensen, and has itself been improved (with respect to the connection of the yoke and the plow on the analogy of an Avestan expression) by E. Benveniste, "Traditions indo-iraniennes sur les classes sociales," *JA* 230 (1939): 532–33.

28. For other groups of mythical talismans with trifunctional meaning—which did not fall from the sky—see *Idéol.* p. 25 (§19), with the corresponding references, 97–98: the jewels of the Irish Tuatha dé Danann; the objects fabricated for the gods by the Vedic Ṛbhu and by the Eddic Black Elves. In contrast with the Scythian, Irish, and Vedic objects, if not the Charites-stones of Orchomenos, the *ancilia* are uniform: on this subject see L. Gerschel, "Sur un schème trifonctionnel dans une famille de légendes germaniques," *RHR* 150 (1956): 55–92, esp. 56–59, 68–69.

spolia quae dux populi Romani duci hostium detraxit, says that they are offered uniformly to Jupiter Feretrius, and confines itself to noting the rarity of such an exploit. In fact, only three leaders are supposed to have succeeded in accomplishing it: Romulus himself, the conqueror of Acron king of Caenina, and the reputed founder of the cult; Cossus, the conqueror of Tolumnius, the king of Veii (428); and lastly Marcellus, the conqueror of Viridomarus, the chief of Insubres (222). The other variant is more highly nuanced. It can be read in the greatest detail in Festus (p. 302 L²), who bases his account on the Books of the Pontiffs as reported by Varro, and who also cites, from the same source, a "law of Numa Pompilius"; the text contains some corrupted words and some lacunae which can be reconstructed or filled out with assurance, but it also presents a certain basic confusion from which one can escape only by interpretation, by assuming a more coherent doctrine. The *spolia opima* exist every time the conquered party is the *dux hostium*, even if the conqueror is not the Roman *dux* in person. As in the preceding variant, there are three kinds; this number, however, is no longer the result of accidental historical circumstances but forms part of the definition: the first *spolia* must be offered to Jupiter Feretrius, the second to Mars, and the third to "Janus Quirinus." On the occasion of the first, an ox is sacrificed in the name of the state; for the second, the *solitaurilia* (which probably means the *suouetaurilia*, a boar, a ram, and a bull); for the third, a lamb. Moreover, the man who has won these spoils at the expense of the enemy leader receives in the first case three hundred pieces of money, probably two hundred in the second, and in the third only one hundred.[29]

In this variant as in the other, the adjectives *prima, secunda, tertia* have generally been understood in terms of time,[30] and Servius (*Aen.* 6.859) does not hesitate to write, confusing the two variants, that Romulus (in conformity with the law of his successor, Numa!) offered the *prima spolia opima* to Jupiter Feretrius, Cossus the *secunda* to Mars, and Marcellus the *tertia* to Quirinus. To be sure, this interpretation is not impossible, since we are dealing with legend, and legend will support anything, but it is strange. It attributes to Numa not merely a prescription but a prophecy announcing that in all

---

29. On the meaning of this *lex regia*, see G. C. Picard, cited below, p. 237, n. 49 (end.)
30. Which I myself have done up to now.

Roman history there would be only three occasions for celebrating the ritual and indicating the successive varieties of this ritual. Consequently Latte (pp. 204–5), by completing and harmonizing the text of Festus, prefers another, more satisfactory interpretation; but he sees in it, for what reason I do not know, a mark of "the influence of the pontiffs on the systematization of Roman religion"; after all, casuistry is as old as the world. "Thus," he says, "the consecration to Jupiter of the arms of an enemy leader was bound to the condition that the Roman who had killed him should exercise a command, with his own auspices. In the same sense, there were *secunda* or *tertia spolia*, according to whether the exploit had been accomplished by the commander of a Roman force without independent auspices, or by a common soldier. In these last two cases they had to be consecrated not to Jupiter Feretrius, but to Mars and to Janus Quirinus." Thus, *prima*, *secunda*, and *tertia* are here understood as indications not of time, but of value or degree. If this interpretation is correct, the distribution of the three kinds of *spolia opima* among the gods is remarkably consistent with the trifunctional explanation of the triad. Jupiter receives the *spolia* from the hand of the *rex*, or of the republican leader substituted for the *rex*, to whom he has given signs during the taking of the auspices; Mars receives the *spolia* acquired by the officer functioning strictly as a military technician, without the personal auspices which would have given him religious meaning,[31] as in the first case; finally, Quirinus receives the *spolia* conquered by a mass soldier, who is in no way distinguished from the organized mass implied in the name *Co-uirīnus*.[32] Do we not find here the trifunctional distinction of the three gods, but aligned with the circumstance, which is warlike and which obliges the three gods to characterize their "men" by their relation to a single warlike act, leaving for the last, Quirinus, only a feeble, but still authentic part of his definition?

We have been reminded recently, in passing, that among other Indo-European peoples, the "third function" was parceled out among a whole troop of divine patrons, in contrast to the small number of patrons of sovereignty and the single patron of warlike power.

31. The discussions of the ancients about the exact title and command of Cossus are not important here.

32. Compare the use of the singular *Quiris* in the meaning of "any Roman of the lower class": Juv. 8.47 (*ima plebe Quiritem*), Ov. *Am.* 1.7.29 (*minimum de plebe Quiritem*), 3.14.9 (*ignoto meretrix corpus iunctura Quiriti*).

The explanation is easy: save perhaps in our societies of the atomic era, commanding, praying, and fighting are relatively simple modes of conduct as compared with the innumerable particular patterns of behavior which are demanded by the exploitation of different soils, the raising of various kinds of animals, and the administration of increasingly differentiated riches, as well as the supervision of health and fertility, and the enjoyment of the pleasures of the senses. Vedic India, for example, groups on this level, near the Aśvin, who exert a multiform benevolence, goddesses like Sarasvatī, the personification of the river; the Waters; the goddesses specializing in generation; Pūṣan, the master of herds; Draviṇodā, the giver of riches; and many others.

As we have seen, a similar situation has been revealed at Rome by the remarkable schedule of activities of the *flamen Quirinalis*. While the *Dialis*, and probably the *Martialis*, are strictly bound to the cult of their respective gods, the *Quirinalis* officiates in the service of the agricultural Consus as the masculine counterpart of Ops, performs a propitiatory sacrifice to Robigus, the god of wheat rust, and probably takes part in the *parentatio* of the mysterious Larentia, the fabulously wealthy and generous benefactress of the Roman people.

This diversity, which caused Wissowa to believe that the priest of Quirinus had been dispossessed of his old, properly Quirinal functions, and subsequently reemployed in various new duties, is on the contrary consistent with the nature of the god, if one understands it as we have done. But the legend of the origins of Rome provides a striking statement and development of this theologem.

When Romulus and Titus Tatius—personages who incarnate and illustrate the first and third functions in this epic scene[33]—bring their war to an end and found the complete Roman society, each of them fulfills his religious duty and institutes cults in accordance with his respective function. Thus while Romulus institutes only one, that of Jupiter, Titus Tatius is said to introduce to Rome a whole series of cults, which Varro lists (*L.L.* 5.74): *uouit Opi, Florae, Vedioui Saturnoque, Soli, Lunae, Volcano et Summano, itemque Larundae, Termino, Quirino, Vortumno, Laribus, Dianae Lucinaeque*.[34] To be sure, this list

33. Above, pp. 66–73.
34. Varro here does not yield to his "Sabinism": he claims to get his information from the "annals": *nam ut annales dicunt, uouit Opi*, etc. Several names in this list occur in Dion. 2.50.3, but the author gives up the attempt to render the others in Greek; Aug. *Ciu. D.*

is a composite one and in part anachronistic, containing such divinities as Diana, Sol, and Luna who do not belong to the oldest Roman stock; and like the Jupiter Stator attributed to Romulus, it bears the mark of the century in which the first annalists worked. Nevertheless, with respect to the meaning and the level of the gods, it is remarkably homogeneous and consistent with the "Sabine component," as it was understood by these annalists. Of the fourteen divinities who thus accompanied Quirinus, seven are concerned in diverse ways with agriculture and the rustic life (Ops—the associate in the calendar of the god of the Consualia; Flora, Saturnus, Terminus, Vortumnus; Volcanus, to whom a sacrifice was made on 23 August, at the same time as to Ops and Quirinus, very probably as a precaution against the burning of the crops; and the Lares, the patrons of soil allotments and of crossroads); two favor births (Diana and Lucina); two (Sol and Luna) are stars which Roman religion retains only in their roles as regulators of the seasons and the months; and one, or perhaps two (Vedius and Larunda—probably a variant of the name of the beneficiary of the Larentalia) have or were accepted as having a connection with the underworld. In short—and the almost unknown Summanus does not contradict this—these gods share among themselves the portions, the dependencies, and the appendages of the domain of prosperity and fertility, and Quirinus is only one member of this great family.

One result of the parceling out of the third function, at Rome and elsewhere, is that none of the gods who patronize it partially can represent it completely in the schematic lists which sum up the tripartite structure. Even the god whom dominant usage installs in this rank in the "canonical list" is not and cannot be a perfect representative. The reason for choosing him in preference over others is

---

4.23.1, gives the same shortened list, but instead of attributing to Romulus only a single foundation (Jupiter), he has him establish, symmetrically with Tatius, an entire list of cults (*Janum Jouem Martem*, etc., and even *Herculem*! through a displacement of what appears in Liv. 1.7.15). The Christian doctor thus spoils the clear opposition between unity (on the first level) and multiplicity, apportionment (on the third); cf. a Germanic fact with the same significance, in *La saga de Hadingus* (1953), pp. 109–10. During the course of this book I shall often use the expression "the gods of Titus Tatius" as a brief designation of this grouping of gods. I trust that my critics will do me the favor of believing that I do not attribute their foundation to someone named Titus Tatius, or to anyone else; in my eyes, the expression has only a theological meaning, not a historical one.

often clear. Among the Vedic Indians, for example, the listing Mitra-Varuṇa, Indra, and Nāsatya, which I have mentioned above, has been confirmed among the para-Indians of the Euphrates by the discovery of a Mitannian-Hittite treatise dating from the fourteenth century B.C. In the third term, the twin Nāsatya, or Aśvin, are saviors in every respect, famed for their powers of healing, like the Greek Dioscuri; moreover a specific fact suggests that originally one of them patronized the raising of horses and the other the raising of cattle, that is, the two kinds of animals of interest to the archaic Indo-Iranian societies;[35] finally their character as twins places them in a symbolic relationship with fertility in general. This does not prevent them from yielding their authority over the third function, in other versions of the list, to the aquatic goddesses, in others to Pūṣan, a more precise specialist than themselves in cattle-breeding, and in still others to the collective notion of "*Viśve Devāḥ*," which then probably takes on the meaning of "organized mass of the gods," the gods regarded as a unit, in their triple division, without regard to their singularities.[36] This last divine specification recalls the earthly *vaiśya*, the third of the social classes: these are the members of the *viśaḥ*, the "clans," which are thus defined by their social frameworks, while the first two classes receive names (*brāhmaṇá*, *kṣatríya*) derived from those of their principles (*bráhman*, sacred principle, whatever its precise meaning may be; *kṣatrá* "power").

At Rome it is precisely this notion of an organized mass,[37] exemplified in the name *Quirinus*, which was retained in the canonical list, but Quirinus by himself represents in so small a way the whole of the "third function" that he seems to have been set in this place of honor solely to put his flamen at the disposition of more material aspects on the same level: the care of grain, and the underworld. Even his feast is ambiguous, associating a treatment of grain with a view of the people distributed in *curiae*, under the control of the *Curio maximus*.

---

35. S. Wikander, "Pāṇḍavasagan och Mahābhāratas mytiska förutsättningar," *Religion och Bibel* 6 (1947): 27–39, translation and commentary in my *JMQ* 4: 37–85 (pp. 48–50 on the twins; cf. p. 59); "Nakula et Sahadeva," *Orientalia Suecana* 6 (1957): 65–95 (pp. 79–84 on the differentiations of the twins with regard to horses and cattle); see now *ME* 1: 73–89.

36. *JMQ* 4: 156–61.

37. Perhaps this may explain an indication by Plin. *N.H.* 15. 120–21: two myrtles once stood in front of the temple of Quirinus; one was called the patrician myrtle, the other the plebeian myrtle; the former died, and the other grew and flourished along with the progress of the plebs.

From this we may imagine that in particular circumstances the canonical Jupiter-Mars-Quirinus list had been felt to be inadequate, or even improper, and that the third term had been replaced by another divinity of the third function, one of what we might call "the gods of Titus Tatius," to use once more the terms of the legend. One of these circumstances, which again involves the *rex*, must be mentioned.[38]

In the republican era, the Regia of the Forum, the "house of the king," is the center of religious affairs. It is within its walls that the deliberations of the pontiffs take place and that the great pontiff himself resides. If it is not properly a temple, it at least contains sacred objects and serves as a setting for cultic ceremonies. The objects and the ceremonies, both evidently archaic, have been preserved, like the *rex* himself, and sheltered from further ideological developments. Though it was burned and rebuilt several times, excavations have revealed the very simple plan which corresponds closely to what we know of its usages from other sources. And it is likely that the *reges* had a Regia of this kind before they descended into the valley, at the very time when their domain was confined to the Palatine.[39] In the Forum's Regia, of reduced dimensions, the principal structure is trapezoid, almost rectangular, and is divided into three consecutive sections, one greater than the other two, which are roughly equal in size. Beyond the pontiffs' administration, the religious activities indicated there are of three quite different types, concerning two of which the texts say expressly that they take place in two particular *sacraria*, two chapels. It is natural to identify these chapels with the two smaller sections, and to attribute the principal section, the accessory buildings, and the court to the other uses.

1. Certain acts are guaranteed by the sacred personages of the highest rank, the *rex*, the *regina*, and the *flaminica Dialis*: on all *nundinae* the *flaminica* sacrifices a ram to Jupiter (Macr. 1.16.30); on 9 January, at the Agonalia, the first feast of the year, the *rex*

38. I sum up here "Les cultes de la Regia, les trois fonctions et la triade Jupiter Mars Quirinus," *Lat.* 13 (1954): 129–39. See Lugli, *RA*, pp. 212–15 (*Regia pontificis*).

39. For the problem treated here, the age of the Regia whose ruins still survive is unimportant, Frank Brown, "The Regia," *MAAR* 12 (1935): 67–88, and plates IV–VIII. Recent excavations have brought to light constructions from the seventh and sixth centuries, F. Brown, "New Soundings in the Regia: The Evidence for the Early Republic," in *Les origines de la République romaine, Entretiens sur l'Antiquité classique de la Fondation Hardt* 13 (1957): 47–64, and three plans.

offers a ram to Janus, the god of "January" and of all beginnings (Ov. *F.* 1.318; Varr. *L.L.* 3.12); on all calends the *regina sacrorum* immolates either a sow or a ewe to Juno. If Janus and Juno, whom the royal couple serve, are here considered regulators of time in the most general sense (the beginning of each year, the beginning of each month), the Jupiter of the *nundinae*, who is served by the *flaminica Dialis*, seems to have a political meaning. In fact the legend attributes the institution of this monthly occasion to Servius Tullius, "so that the people might come in a crowd from the country to the city, to arrange the affairs of the city and the country" (Cassius, in Macr. 1.16.33); "so that people might come in from the country to Rome to do their marketing and to receive the laws; so that the acts of the leaders and of the Senate might be proclaimed to a more numerous audience and, after having been proposed on three consecutive *nundinae*, that they might be readily known to one and all" (Rutilius, ibid. 34).[40] To sum up, all these cults resorted to the first function, to the administration of the life of the world as well as that of the state.

2. A *sacrarium Martis*, in the Regia, shelters the warlike talismans of Rome examined at length in my "Preliminary Remarks."[41] Here are kept the *hastae Martis* whose shaking is a menacing omen; here, when war is declared, the designated general comes first to make the shields move (*commouebat*), and then the "spear of the statue," while saying: *Mars uigila!* (Serv. *Aen.* 8.3; 7.603). It is probably also in this *sacrarium* that the sacrifice mentioned by Cincius (in Fest. p. 419 L²) takes place, which was offered in the Regia by the *Saliae uirgines*, dressed in the costume of the Salii, *cum apicibus paludatae*.

3. Finally a second *sacrarium*, to which another discussion has introduced us,[42] belongs to Ops Consiva, the Abundance who is related to Consus. It is known from an indication by Varro (*L.L.* 6.21) and from a mention by Festus (p. 354 L²). The former says that this chapel was so holy (*adeo sanctum*, a likely correction for the unintelligible *ita actum*) that only the Vestal virgins and the *sacerdos publicus*, that is, the grand pontiff, could enter it; the latter speaks of a vessel of a

---

40. See A. K. Michels, *The Calendar of the Roman Republic* (1967), pp. 84–89 ("Nundinal letters and *Nundinae*") and 191–206 (app. 3: "*Nundinae* and the *trinum nundinum*").

41. Above, pp. 23–26.

42. Above, pp. 156–58.

particular type (*praefericulum*), *quo ad sacrificia utebantur in sacrario Opis Consiuae.*

Thus the "house of the king" joins, or rather juxtaposes in three places, the cults which clearly involve sacred sovereignty, war, and abundance. What is more natural than that the king of the whole society, despite his special affinity for the first function, should be active in the other two? But the principal interest of the grouping lies in the fact that Ops, another divinity of the "group of Titus Tatius," should be given the representative role which the canonical list, that of the major flamens, assigns to Quirinus. It is not under the aspect of the people as consumers, but directly under that of the food to be consumed, that the Regia harbors the third function.[43]

This first examination of the triad, as we have seen, has not been fruitless. Voluntarily confined to what the personal statute or the activities of the three *flamines maiores* tell us, and to certain allied facts, it surely does not exhaust all of Jupiter, all of Mars, or all of Quirinus in the era of the monarchy, but it provides a solid and specific balance sheet, and certain fixed and coordinate points, starting from which, little by little, the complete dossiers of the three gods can be explored. It is to this extension of the investigation that we shall first proceed, with the double intention of enriching the original picture which we have formed of each god and of following him throughout his history.

But we must recall a rule of procedure which is often forgotten, at the risk of great confusion. In describing a divinity, the definition of his mode of action is more characteristic than the list of places where he is active or of the occasions for his services. An important divinity is inevitably solicited by everybody and for everything, sometimes in unexpected places, far removed from his principal province. Nevertheless he acts there, and if we confine ourselves to registering these unusual locations of this activity, we are in danger of joining it with-

43. Information in Gell. 4.6, corroborates this interpretation. According to *antiquae memoriae*, one day when the *hastae Martis* had shaken in the Regia, a senatus consultum ordered one of the consuls to sacrifice to Jupiter and to Mars *hostiis maioribus*, and to appease those of the other gods who he thought should be appeased, specifying, however, that if *succidaneae* victims are requested (to replace the victims which would not have been accepted by the experts: *si primis hostiis litatum non erat*), the consul would also sacrifice to Robigus. It will be recalled that the Robigalia are one of the occasions at which the *flamen Quirinalis* officiates; see above, p. 158.

out any appraisal of relative importances to the other, principal locations, and saying that the divinity cannot be given a limited description, that he is "omnivalent" or "indeterminate." On the contrary, if we do not concern ourselves with *where*, but with *how* he acts, we may almost always state that he preserves a constant behavior and constant methods, even in his most aberrant activities. The object of the study is to determine this behavior and these methods. A peasant will invoke a warlike god for the protection of his field: the god will remain no less warlike in this activity, and will not be "agrarian" in the ordinary sense of the word, in the sense in which Ceres is. A general will expect and solicit from a sovereign god the happy outcome of his war: the god, even in this circumstance, will still remain sovereign, and not warlike. Jupiter and Mars provide good illustrations of this rule.

LÉVI-STRAUSS IN THE GARDEN OF EDEN: AN EXAMINATION OF SOME RECENT DEVELOPMENTS IN THE ANALYSIS OF MYTH*

Edmund Leach

Center for Advanced Study in the Behavioral Sciences, Stanford, Calif.

The study of myth has always had a central place in anthropological studies, but the views of anthropologists have varied greatly both on matters of definition and of interpretation. In this respect the celebrities of the past 80 years fall into 2 classes. First, there is a group of writers whom we may call *symbolists* — among whom I would class James G. Frazer, Sigmund Freud, and Ernst Cassirer in his earlier phase — who assume that the elements of myth are to be understood as symbols that are pieced together into a nonrational story much as in a fairy tale or dream. These writers hold that the "purpose" or "meaning" of myth is one of two kinds: (1) myth "explains the inexplicable," for example, the origin of the world, the origin of death; (2) myth is a kind of word magic that purports to alter the harsh facts of reality by manipulating symbolic representations of these facts.

Common to all the symbolist writers is the view that a myth can be understood as "a thing in itself" without any direct reference to the social context in which it is told; the meaning can be discovered from a consideration of the words alone.

The second group of writers are the functionalists — among whom I would class Emile Durkheim and his associates, Jane Harrison, B. Malinowski, and Cassirer in his later phase. The key theme here is the assumption of an intimate and direct association between myth and social action; the myth and its associated rite are held to be two aspects of the the same unitary whole.

The most explicit formulation of this doctrine was provided by Malinowski in his well known essay *Myth in Primitive Psychology* (Malinowski, 1926). Myth provides a "charter" or justification for facts in the present day social situation. For example, in the Trobriand myth of emergence, it

*This paper was presented at a joint meeting of the Division and the American Ethnological Society on January 23, 1961.

The Division of Biochemistry held a meeting on January 24, 1961, at which Maynard E. Pullman of the Public Health Research Institute, New York, N. Y., presented a paper entitled "Components of the Energy-Coupling Mechanism of Oxidative Phosphorylation." This paper will not be published by the Academy.

The Division of Microbiology held a meeting on January 27, 1961, at which Karl Maramorosch of the Boyce-Thompson Research Institute, Yonkers, N. Y., presented a paper entitled "The Mystery of Cadang-Cadang." This paper will be published as an Annal of the Academy.

is recorded that the brother and sister founder ancestors of each matrilineal subclan emerged from holes in the ground, the position of which is
precisely recorded by tradition. Each ancestral hole is located in territory that is today regarded as the hereditary property of the subclan descendants of the original founder ancestors. Thus a tale that considered
in isolation, has all the appearance of fantasy is seen to "make sense"
when related to its social context. Within the framework of Trobriand
ideas this myth has the force of a legal precedent in a court of law.

As C. Lévi-Strauss puts it: "This theory assumes that myth and rite
are homologous ... the myth and the rite reproduce each other, the one at
the level of action the other at the level of ideas." (Lévi-Strauss, 1956
p. 289).

It is a necessary corollary of this functionalist thesis that myth can be
studied *only* within its social context. A myth divorced from its associated rite can have no meaning. Myth is never "a thing in itself."

British social anthropologists of my generation were brought up to
believe that, on this issue, Malinowski was right. Detailed modifications
of his original theory might be possible but the essentials of the argument
were unassailable.

One consequence of this acceptance of the functionalist thesis has
been that the collections of "literary myths" that exist in ethnographic
libraries and in the sacred writings of the more sophisticated religions
have come to be neglected by the professional anthropologist. Such myths,
in the form in which we now have them, are clearly "divorced from their
ritual context," hence, according to the functionalist dogma, they cease
to be of interest.

The same line of reasoning eliminates from the field of serious academic discussion the whole of the works of Frazer and other exponents
of the Frazerian "comparative method." Many of the comparisons to which
Frazer draws our attention are very striking but, since Frazer consistently ignored the context of his evidence, it is a matter of functionalist
dogma that we *must* ignore the apparent implications.

In a number of essays published over the last four years Lévi-Strauss
has quite explicitly repudiated the functionalist thesis (the key document
is Lévi-Strauss, 1955) in favor of a revised form of "symbolist" analysis
that he calls structural. Lévi-Strauss denies the existence of any causal
link by which myth overtly justifies the patterning of social action or
vice versa. He concedes that myths and rites that occur in the same cultural environment may very well share a common structure. Hence if the
elements of a myth or the elements of an associated rite are treated as
the elements in a logical statement, the myth and the rite may appear to
"say the same thing." Nevertheless, myth and rite are independent and
each can be studied in isolation.

According to Lévi-Strauss the best method of ascertaining the "meaning" of a myth is to assemble together all the variant forms in which it has been recorded regardless of their date or source. What we are looking for is the fundamental essence, and this essence, according to Lévi-Strauss, is a matter of logical structure that will persist throughout all the diversities of form by which the myth story has been perpetuated. A comparison of the different versions of a single myth complex will reveal this common structural nexus, and it is this common structure that really gives "meaning" and importance to those who recount the myth.

If we accept this view, then it follows that, despite anything that Malinowski may appear to have demonstrated, the social anthropologist is fully entitled to study myth as "a thing in itself" without regard to detailed consideration of social or ritual context. I do not ask anyone to suspend his critical judgement. Lévi-Strauss' thesis has many weaknesses and some of them seem a good deal more damaging than the alleged weaknesses of functionalism. Nevertheless, he has made out a case. At the very least he has demonstrated that the functionalist thesis, in its more orthodox form, is unnecessarily inhibiting. He has reopened what had begun to look like a closed argument. We need not accept Lévi-Strauss' views in every particular, but it is quite clear that the proper understanding of myth is once again a very open question.

As Lévi-Strauss himself recognizes, his new theory is exceedingly difficult to put to the test. In effect he postulates that the symbolic elements in a myth are analogous to neutral pebbles of diverse colors. One cannot discover what the elements "mean" by any straight forward technique of intuition or verbal interpretation; all that one can do is observe how the pebbles are grouped together into patterns. In principle, this patterning (or structure) of the symbols in relation to each other is a matter of statistics. Lévi-Strauss maintains that a really thorough application of the method would entail the use of punched cards and the services of an electronic computer (Lévi-Strauss, 1955). Since most of us operate under the delusion that some myths appear meaningful in a fairly straight forward way this kind of intellectual sophistication may arouse suspicion; nevertheless I suggest that the matter be given serious consideration.

If we accept Lévi-Strauss' view, the heart of the matter is that myth furnishes a "logical" model by means of which the human mind can evade unwelcome contradictions, such as that human beings cannot enjoy life without suffering death or that rules of incest (which specify that legitimate sex relations can only be between members of opposed kin groups) conflict with a doctrine of unilineal descent. The function of myth is to "mediate" such contradictions, to make them appear less final than they really are and thus more acceptable. This end is not served by isolated myths but by clusters of myths that are similar in some ways but different in others so that, in accumulation, they tend to blur the edges of real (but unwelcome) category distinctions.

90

Among the examples that Lévi-Strauss has used to illustrate his thesis are the following:

(1) He claims that an analysis of certain Pueblo Indian myths shows that the central problem that the myth cluster seeks to resolve is the opposition between life and death. In the myths we find a threefold category distinction: agriculture, hunting, and war. Agriculture is a means to life for man but entails the death of animals. It is thus a mediating middle category.

In another version of the same myth cluster a further threefold category distinction emerges: grass-eating animals, ravens, and predatory animals. Grass-eating animals are vegetarians; they need not kill in order to live. Ravens and predators are meat eaters; but ravens need not kill in order to eat. In accumulation, therefore, argues Lévi-Strauss, this succession of symbol patterns creates a logical model that asserts (or seems to assert) that, after all, life and death are *not* just the back and front of the same penny, that death is *not* the necessary consequence of life (Lévi-Strauss, 1955).

(2) Lévi-Strauss furnishes other examples. For instance, he claims, rather surprisingly, that the central problem with which the myth of Oeiipus is concerned is that of autochthonous creation. In the beginning man was created; but who precisely was created? A man plus a woman of the same kind? If so, then the perpetuation of mankind must have depended upon incest and we are all born in sin. Or was there a double creation — a man plus a woman of a different kind? In that case what are these two original kinds, and how can we justify a claim to descent from one line of ancestors rather than another?

Perhaps you wonder what all this has to do with the Oedipus myth as you know it, and I do not pretend that the Lévi-Straus example is easy to follow. FIGURE 1 may help. Lévi-Strauss assumes that the myth has a logical form corresponding to the equation: $a:b :: c:d$ (*op. cit.*, pp. 55-56). The theme of incest (the overemphasis of kinship solidarity) is balanced against the themes of patricide and fratricide (the underemphasis of kinship solidarity) and this corresponds to a similar balance between the highly ambivalent sphinx and Oedipus, who, in isolation, is incomplete and crippled. The sphinx is a kind of merging of the two parent figures Jocasta and Laios. Oedipus' legitimate task is to eliminate the sphinx. He accomplishes this end by sinning doubly — incest with Jocasta and patricide against Laios. Oedipus does not actually kill the sphinx. The sphinx, which is primarily female, commits suicide, as does Jocasta. The cause of the suicide is that Oedipus answers the riddle — the answer being, in effect: "the son grows into the father and replaces him" (Lévi-Strauss, 1958 p. 238). On this analysis the myth centers around a problem of patrilineal descent: the requirement that fathers shall be perpetuated in their sons without the intervention of women, which in simple fact is

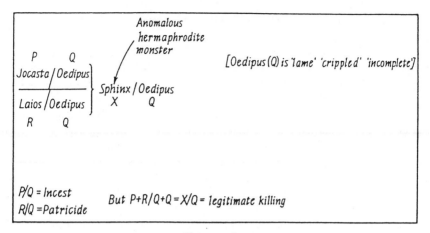

FIGURE 1.

plainly impossible. However, the impossibility is "resolved" in the myth
by mediating the antithesis between male and female parents into the ambivalent person of the sphinx. Lévi-Strauss is somewhat free with his
editing of the mythology, and I have been decidedly free with my editing
of Lévi-Strauss. For further enlightenment I must ask you to read him in
the original.

For my part I find the whole analysis extremely interesting. I feel that
Lévi-Strauss has a case. We ought to investigate the hypothesis with all
the means at our disposal: with or without resort to mathematical com-
puters.

With all this in mind I decided to take another look at the story of the
creation as recorded in Genesis. How well do the various theories about
myth that I have mentioned stand up when put to the test against this
basic myth of our own society?

The first point that struck me was that the different types of theories
that I have mentioned throw the emphasis on different aspects of the
story, or rather stories for, as is well known, there are two distinct creation stories in Genesis.

The symbolists favor the story concerning the Garden of Eden. Frazer
and Freud and most medieval artists are in agreement that the core of the
story is the matter of Eve and the serpent and the forbidden fruit. From
this point of view the myth seems to provide a rather elementary example
of the use of phallic symbolism. Frazer, however, made the further penetrating observation that the Tree of the Knowledge of Good and Evil,
from which Eve's apple comes, is unambiguously stated to be the Tree of
Death that stands opposed to another special tree, the Tree of Life.
Moreover, while Adam and Eve were forbidden to eat of the Tree of Death
they were not, in the first instance, forbidden to eat of the Tree of Life.
(Genesis 2, v. 17).

A functionalist approach would be quite different. The story of the seven-day creation provides a mythical charter for the seven-day week. Also, in a more round about way, the creation story provides a charter for the Jewish rules of taboo as recorded in Leviticus, chapter 11.

The creation story specifies all living things as belonging to a very limited number of precisely defined categories: fowls of the air, fish, cattle, beasts, and creeping things. Similarly the plants are categorized as grass, herb-yielding seed (cereals), and fruit trees. It is further specified that the animals are intended to eat the grass while the cereals and the fruit and the meat of the animals themselves are intended for man's exclusive benefit (Genesis 1 vv. 29 and 30). As Mary Douglas has pointed out (Douglas, 1959), the creatures classified as "abominations" in Leviticus 11 are those that break out of these tidy categories: water creatures with no fins, flying creatures with 4 legs, animals and birds that eat meat or fish, and certain animals that are indiscriminate in their eating habits such as dogs and pigs.*

This functionalist treatment of the material leads to an orthodox thesis about the close association of ideas concerning taboo, sacredness, and abnormality (Radcliffe-Brown, 1952, chapter VII).

Having said all this one notices that it is only the first part of the creation story that seems to serve as a "charter" in Malinowski's sense. The second part — the Garden of Eden story that appeals so strongly to the symbolists — has no obvious implications for the functionalist. Thus neither the symbolist nor the functionalist approaches can be considered adequate. Each tells us something but neither offers an answer to the total question: What is Genesis 1 to 4 all about?

However, if we now apply a Lévi-Strauss style of analysis everything takes on a completely new shape; moreover it is a shape that recurs in both parts of the story and is repeated again in a third form in the Cain and Abel story that follows. The complex diagram (FIGURE 2) has been designed to display this structure. At every step we find the assertion of of a category opposition followed by the introduction of a "mediating" category. The seven-day creation story (upper section of the diagram) may be analysed as follows:

Genesis 1, vv. 1 to 5 (not on diagram). Light divided from darkness. Initial introduction of concept of category opposition, heaven versus earth.

Genesis 1, vv. 6 to 8 (column 1 of diagram). Fresh water above (fer-

---

*The thesis that tabooed animals are always "anomalous" in respect to the categories of the creation story holds good in nearly every case but not all. Thus it is not obvious to me why a camel should be an anomaly. The treatment of "creeping things" in Leviticus 11, vv. 29 to 43, is particularly illuminating in the light of the argument given below. The text starts out by attempting to distinguish as abominable certain special "anomalous creeping things," namely the weasel, the mouse, the tortoise, the ferret, the chameleon, the lizard, the snail, and the mole, but this leads logically to the conclusion that creeping things are anomalous *ab initio*, so that at v. 41 we are told that *all* creeping things without exception are abominations.

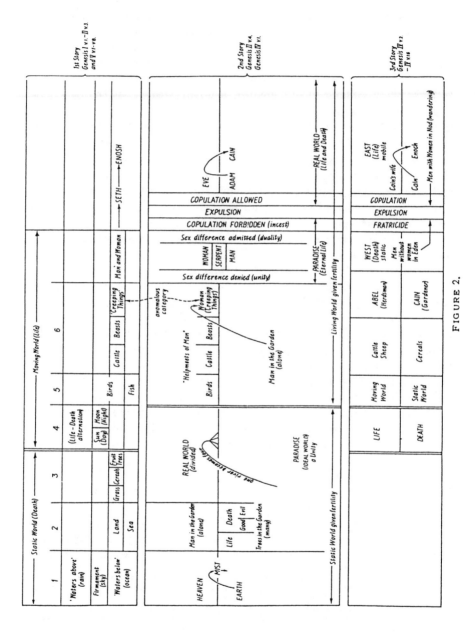

FIGURE 2.

tile rain) opposed to (salt) water below (sea). Mediated by firmament (sky).

Genesis 1, vv. 9 and 10 (column 2 of diagram). Sea opposed to dry land.

Genesis 1, vv. 11 and 12 (column 3 of diagram). Mediated by grass, herb-yielding seed, and fruit trees. These grow on dry land but need water. Very significantly, they are classed as things "whose seed is in itself" (thereby contrasted with such creatures as animals and birds, which are divided into males and females).

The creation of the world as a static (that is, dead) entity is now complete, and this whole phase of creation is opposed to the creation of moving (that is, living) things.

Genesis 1, vv. 13 to 18 (column 4 of diagram). The mobile sun and moon are placed in the firmament of column 1. Light and darkness, opposed at the beginning of the story, are now presented as alternations. By implication the life-death opposition is also an alternation.

Genesis 1, vv. 20 to 23 (column 5 of diagram). Fish and birds are living things corresponding to the category opposition of column 2 but they also mediate the oppositions between sky and land and between salt water and fresh water.

Genesis 1, vv. 24 and 25 (column 6 of diagram, left half). Cattle, beasts, and creeping things (that is, domestic animals, wild animals, and anomalous animals) correspond to the static triad of column 3 but are not allocated accordingly. Only grass is allocated to the animals, the rest is reserved for man (vv. 29 and 30).

Genesis 1, vv. 26 and 27 (Column 6 of diagram, right half). The final act of creation is the simultaneous creation of man and woman: "Male and female created he them."

The whole system of living creatures is instructed to "be fruitful and multiply," but the problems of life versus death and incest versus procreation are not faced.

The Garden of Eden story that now follows attacks from the start these very problems that have been evaded in the first version. We start again with a category opposition of heaven versus earth, but this is mediated by a fertilizing mist that is drawn up out of the dry infertile earth (Genesis 2, vv. 4 to 6). The same theme recurs throughout the story. Living Adam is formed from "the dust of the ground " (v. 7); so are the living animals (v. 19). The dry lands of the real world are fertilized by a river that comes out of the ground of Eden. In Eden (Paradise) it is a unitary river; in the real world it is divided (vv. 10 to 14). Finally fertile Eve is formed from the rib of infertile Adam (vv. 22 and 23).

The opposition of Heaven and Earth (Column 1) is followed by the opposition of Man and the Garden and, in the Garden, are trees that include a Tree of Life and a Tree of Death (column 2: Genesis 2, vv. 8 and 9). Notice that the Tree of Death is called the "Tree of Knowledge of Good and Evil" which might also be called the "knowledge of sexual difference," or the "knowledge of logical categories." The theme is repeated: isolated unitary categories such as man alone, life alone, one river, occur only in ideal Paradise; in the real world things are multiple and divided; man needs a partner, woman; life has a partner, death.

The other living things are now created because of the loneliness of Man in Eden. The categories are cattle (domestic animals), birds, and beasts (wild animals). These are unsatisfactory as helpmeets of Man, so Eve is drawn from Adam's rib: "they are of one flesh." (columns 5 and 6: Genesis 2, vv. 18 to 24). Comparison of the two stories at this stage shows that Eve in Eden is, from a structural point of view, the same category as "the creeping things" of the first story. Creeping things were anomalous in the category opposition "cattle versus beasts;" Eve is anomalous in the category opposition "man versus animal;" and finally "the serpent" (a creeping thing) is anomalous in the category opposition "man versus woman." The parallels here with the Oedipus–Sphinx story are here extremely close, as may be seen from FIGURES 1 and 3. The

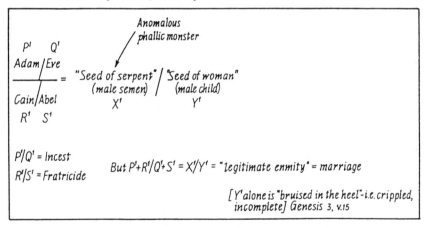

FIGURE 3.

Bible does not specify the serpent's sex. Mediaeval artists made it female, Freud might have argued for a male; the structural argument suggests hermaphrodite qualities.

Adam and Eve eat the apple and become aware of sexual difference, and death becomes inevitable (Genesis 3, vv. 3 to 8) — also of course pregnancy and life becomes possible. Significantly, Eve does not become pregnant until after they have been expelled from Paradise (Genesis 4, v. 1). The curse that is imposed on the serpent deserves especial note (Genesis 3, vv. 14 and 15). There is to be enmity between the serpent and the woman and between "the seed of the serpent" and the "seed of the woman" — the latter being specified as male; "*he* shall bruise thy head; and thou shalt bruise *his* heel."

One is inevitably reminded of Levi-Strauss' point that autochthonous heroes are very commonly lame (Levi-Strauss, 1955). Indeed the whole formula parallels that of Oedipus. If "the seed of the serpent" be here read as "the semen of the father," while "the seed of the woman" be read as the son of the father by his impregnated wife, the curse refers to the opposition between man and woman and the hostility between father and son. It might even be taken as a "charter" for circumcision.

Finally, although very briefly, let us notice that the Cain and Abel story repeats the same story over again. The opposition between Cain the gardener and Abel the herdsman is the same opposition as that between the first three days of the creation and the last three days, the static world versus the living. Cain must eliminate his brother and substitute a wife in order that a sterile homosexual world shall become a fertile heterosexual world (Genesis 4, v. 17). Some extra elements come in here. The dead world of Eden-paradise is said to lie to the west, the living world (significantly called Nod "wandering") lies to the east (Genesis 4, v. 16); moreover, although Cain is cursed for the sin of fratricide in terms nearly identical to those imposed on Adam for the sin of incest (compare Genesis 3, vv. 17 to 19 with Genesis 4, v. 11 and 12) he is also declared a sacred person whose life is protected* (v. 15). Cain is the ancestor of "wanderers" in general — pastoralists, traveling musicians, traveling metal-workers (Genesis 4, vv. 19 to 24) — groups with special skills but not servile outcastes.

I do not claim that this kind of "structural" analysis is the one and only legitimate procedure for the interpretation of myth. It seems to me that whether any particular individual finds this kind of thing interesting or stimulating must depend on personal temperament; some may think it is too like a conjuring trick. For my part, I do find it interesting. All I have done here is to show that the component elements in some very familiar stories are in fact ordered in a pattern of which many have not been previously aware. However, the pattern *is* there; I did not invent it, I have merely demonstrated that it exists. No one will ever again be able to read the early chapters of Genesis without taking this pattern into account. Whether the analysis has any "value" for anthropologists or for anyone else I am not sure, but at least it surely throws new light on the mysterious workings of what Durkheim used to call the "collective conscience."

* Cain's peculiar status as a divinely protected person has been examined from a functionalist point of view by Schapera (1955). Here I am concerned only with the strict structural parallelism between the expulsion of Adam from Paradise followed by the pregnancy of Eve (Genesis 4, v. 1) and the expulsion of Cain from paradise followed by the pregnancy of Cain's wife (Genesis 4, vv. 16 and 17).

References

DOUGLAS, M. 1959. Leviticus XL Lecture delivered at University College. London, England. Unpublished.

LÉVI-STRAUSS, C. 1955. The structural study of myth. *In* Myth: A symposium. T. A. Sebeok, Ed. Bibliographical and Special Series of the American Folklore Society. 5. Indiana Univ. Press. Bloomington, Ind.

LÉVI-STRAUSS, C. 1956. Structure et dialectique. *In* For Roman Jakobson: Essays on the Occasion of his Sixtieth Birthday. : 289-294. Mouton. The Hague, Netherlands.

LÉVI-STRAUSS, C. 1958. Anthropologie Structurale. Libraire Plon. Paris, France.

MALINOWSKI, B. 1926. Myth in Primitive Psychology. Kegan Paul. London, England.

RADCLIFFE-BROWN, A. R. 1952. Structure and Function in Primitive Society. Chap. VII. Cohen and West. London, England.

SCHAPERA, L 1955. The Sin of Cain. J. Roy. Anthropol. Inst. 85.

ISIDOR LEVIN

Vladimir Propp: An Evaluation on His Seventieth Birthday

"Fame is ultimately nothing but the sum of all the misunderstandings that collect around a new name," Rilke once wrote in reference to Rodin.

Professor Vladimir Propp's name is, of course, not a new one; he celebrated his seventieth birthday on April 29, 1965. Likewise, some of the misunderstandings are now out of date. Nevertheless, they ought to be cleared up in the interest of the history of scholarship, for these misunderstandings do not affect his name as such, since Propp is world famous in his field, but rather his work[1] and perhaps even the reputation of Soviet folkloristics.

Vladimir Propp was born in Petersburg, the son of a family whose ancestors had been German colonists. A close inner affinity with the Russian character, which left a lasting impress on the mentality of this group of people, was further deepened by the presence of St. Anne's German-Russian school. In 1913 Propp matriculated at the local university, registering for course work in Germanics and Slavics as a student of the philological faculty. He left the university in 1918 with a diploma in Russian philology, and was soon vigorously engaged in the teaching of German and Russian in several secondary schools. He continued to serve in this capacity until 1926, during what was the most difficult period for the secondary school in Russia. Then came teaching appointments in several technological institutes, where he enjoyed a position of authority in the program in German. During this period Professor Propp did a great deal to encourage and extend the study of the German language in Leningrad (01-04).[2]

[1] For a bibliography of his most important publications, see the appendix.
[2] All subsequent numbers in parentheses refer to items in the appended bibliography.

In 1932 he was called to a position at the university which, in the meantime, had been split up into several separate schools, and is still an active member of its faculty. Since about 1938 this accomplished language teacher has functioned chiefly as a professor of folklore. After the death of Mark Azadovskij, as long as folklore was able to maintain an independent professorial chair, Propp was its occupant. After this time, folklore was incorporated, both theoretically and organizationally, into the department of Russian literature. Professor Propp's successful activities have prospered within this framework down to the present day, and his work has also occasionally been expanded to include the Institute for Russian Literature of the Academy (*IRLi.*, Folklore Division). This proven and highly regarded teacher has introduced numerous students to the discipline of folklore. Today there are scholars holding appointments in Leningrad, as well as in several remote research centers in the Soviet Union and even abroad, who praise him as their master.

Here in Russia, the very vigorous septuagenarian (in the twenty years I have had the pleasure of his acquaintance, he has hardly changed — and may he thus remain with us for a long time to come) is at once both the most prominent folklorist and the senior member of a controversial and controversy-filled cohort of scholars.

Perhaps Propp would have become a botanist, had he not felt more strongly the calling to botanize in the not less flowery fields of folk literature.

Already in his early works on the "morphology" of the folktale (which are perhaps the fruit of a hobby he pursued during those always insufficient leisure hours), Propp established himself as a hard-working researcher and penetrating systematizer in the tradition of Linné. Nevertheless, he would have been destined to remain an outsider to folklore, if his structural studies were not *today* in harmony with general literary scholarship and Marxist theory, both of which have exerted a lasting influence on folklore research.

Both structural analysis and the analysis of content (or as Propp puts it, the "history of the magic tale as a genre") are feasible only if the scope and content of the material to be investigated have already been established.

In order to gain control over the increasing number of folktale variants, and to render them meaningfully and easily accessible to "morphological" literary research, Propp advanced a number of principles for the construction of an index which would, in his opinion, eventually come to

replace the Type Index (2). In an attempt to avoid the notorious frag-
mentation and suspected atomization of their organically artistic content,
Propp sought, even at the stage of cataloguing, to group the items of
content in a broad-meshed network, and thus to arrange them in clearly
patterned forms. Propp began with the idea that a certain degree of
abstraction is also necessary when constructing a lexicon, and consequently
he offered a system of generic concepts, such as form, movement, attributes, etc., which, in his opinion, encompassed quite concrete arrangements of motifs. According to Propp, this leads to essential, non-acciden-
tal motif arrangements (he calls them "elements"), which would then
need to be subjected to further investigation. Propp was not convinced
about the reality of the Aarne-Thompson tale types, and for that reason
he considered them useless as a basis for comparative research.

Of course, the practical usefulness of this index would ultimately
depend on the consistency employed by both the compiler and the user
in classifying the material. For this purpose Propp offers an *a priori*
questionnaire (2) by means of which each variant should be tested. To
my knowledge, this questionnaire was never actually put to use.

Although this work represented only a preliminary first step in that direction, its basic concern was with the thematic history of the magic tale as a
distinct genre. Nevertheless, Propp attempted to create some kind of order
out of the already then enormous amount of material on the basis of its
form and structure. Here Propp set out at an early date on a path of inquiry which many only now have begun to regard as practicable. His investigation of the morphology of the folktale was to point the way (3).

In the preliminary announcement about the work (1) — and I have
translated the passage literally in order to provide the reader with a
sample of Propp's scholarly style — it is stated:

The investigation proceeds from the observation that the most dissimilar *dramatis personae* in diverse folktales behave in a similar manner. The *Baba Yaga*
(witch), as well as the *Lešij* (forest spirit), or the bear, yes, even a little old man
approaching from the opposite direction, etc., can all put the hero to a test and
reward him. The attributes of the actors change, and the manner in which
the function (=action) is carried out may also differ (i.e., the means of testing
may change), but the functions, as such, are constantly repeated. The same
functions confront us in various narrative materials (*sujets*). This observation
compels us to examine the folktales according to the functions of the *dramatis
personae*. The established repeatability of the functions suggests that the number of these functions found in magic tales must really be quite limited. To

test this assumption, one must first and foremost identify the functions. On the basis of an analysis of one hundred folktales from Afanas'ev's collection (Nos. 51 to 151 inclusive) (19), it has become apparent that only about thirty can be found. These findings are confirmed by the material in other folktale collections. (1, p. 48)

Even the sequence of the functions — today we might prefer the term *Handlungsführung* (plot-guide) in German — supposedly remains the same. And, aside from insignificant, mechanically distorted variants, there is, in his opinion, only *one* system, only *one* sequence of events. This system forms the basis of that structure which is peculiar to a definite class of folktales. In other words, Propp believes that it is possible to discover an all-embracing plot-guide in the contents of the genre of the magic tale, a genre which he considers to be a "folktale class."

Although he could not possibly have foreseen this result, Propp's suggested plot-guide, the narration or story peculiar to a given genre, corresponds precisely to the interpretation of the folktale as a characteristic activity of the human psyche which was later put forth by psychoanalytically-oriented research.

Thus, in Propp's view, the magic tale recognizes a mere thirty-one functions (i.e., actions) in its genre-specific plot-guide, no matter how different the bearers of the action may appear to be. All *dramatis personae*, according to their action, may be classified into six categories: (1) villains, (2) mediators, (3) heroes, (4) gift-givers, (5) helpers, and (6) objects of a quest.

The thirty-one actions and six actors (*dramatis personae*) provide a system of morphological and structural coordinates that yields about 150 elements of composition, and permits any magic tale (for according to Propp there is only *one* folktale type) to be outlined and catalogued, in a manner analogous to the Linnaean system of plants or Mendeleev's classification of the chemical elements. A "transformation" of the thematic contents evolves within the genre-bound framework of these structural possibilities (4, p. 71).

But how, then, did the iridescent profusion of traditional Aarne-Thompson types come about? Are the thematic materials* of folktales associated with each other genetically?

Stimulated by a far-reaching analogy between the organic world and that of the folktale, Propp attempts to understand the manifold contents

* Translator's Note: The crucial term, *Stoff*, has been rendered interchangeably in this translation as "thematic materials," "theme," "narrative plot," or "content."

of folktales as the result of a *transformation* (4, p. 70). To this Darwinian-minded philologist, not only the variants of *one* tale type in Aarne's sense (and again I emphasize that Propp has often contested the reality of these tale types), but rather all the various A-T types themselves appear as a diversely caused transformation of *one* original subject matter. According to Propp, this transformation of narrative plot is realized as:

1. Reduction (shortening, loss of detail)
2. Amplification (expansion)
3. Distortion
4. Metamorphosis (female figures appearing as men, etc.)
5. Intensification
6. Weakening
7. Folktale-internal Replacement
8. Habitual Substitution
9. Religiously Motivated Substitution
10. Superstitious Substitution
11. Archaizing Substitution
12. Literary Innovation
13. Modification
14. Replacement from Unknown Sources
15. Folktale-internal Assimilation
16. Habitual Assimilation
17. Religious Assimilation
18. Superstitious Assimilation
19. Literary Assimilation
20. Archaic Assimilation

Propp, moreover, states that, if necessary, he is quite ready to accept further kinds of transformation should they be demonstrated (4, pp. 78-86).

Based on these considerations, the author also proposes formal criteria for judging the relative originality of the thematic materials of magic tales and for their chronological classification (4, pp. 77ff.). These are: (1) that imagination precedes rationality; (2) that the heroic element is primary, and that humor or parody in the treatment of the same material is secondary; (3) that the primary element is always logical, the secondary frequently illogical; and (4) that international forms are always older than national forms.

To be sure, Propp recognizes that to investigate even one of his 150 elements on the basis of the total international evidence would prove to be an impossible task for a single scholar. For this reason he feels obliged to confine his phenomenological descriptions to repertories which are nationally or regionally limited in scope.

Instead of laboring over tale type monographs in an attempt to learn something about the history of one narrative *plot*, Propp argues for local analyses of the above-mentioned 150 motif combinations, and finds it extremely suggestive that, by doing this, motifs in the Finnish sense, from everywhere in the world and from disparate kinds of tale types, would be subjected to a sort of comparison which Aarne had earlier cautioned scholars against. Propp hoped in this way to obtain new insights into the "ultimate causes" of those analogies and correspondences which appear in folklore materials. As it turns out, this approach was, albeit devoid of any theoretical intents, unfortunately also a practice among certain Russian scholars during those baroque days.

Just *what* Propp understood by motif research is illustrated in his early studies (5; see also 7 and 9). Using the relevant critical literature of earlier scholarship, Propp addresses himself to the problem of examining the motif of the miraculous birth in folktales (9) with respect to the so-called facts of historical reality, in order, thereby, to uncover the source of the motif (9, p. 94). After attempting a phenomenology of this motif on the basis of African, Australian, Russian, and other evidence, the author refers to myths and beliefs in which he thinks he sees the *ad hoc* source for this particular item of folktale content. This procedure is later employed as a general method (6; 8; 11; 12).

Exactly *how* Propp conceives of the relationship between fantastic folktale or legend materials and "historical reality" is explained in his contribution on the history of the Oedipus theme (11, p. 138). Here, in his view, an obsolete version of reality leaves residual traces in art, and in folktales in particular. Later an amalgamation with more recent, often habitual features takes place, and this results then in forms such as winged horses and the like, which could never actually have existed in "reality." This process, manifesting itself in folk literature, can also be demonstrated, in terms of the ideas of N. Ja. Marr, to be operative in linguistic materials (9, p. 139). Using the Oedipus theme, Propp tried to trace the steps of the changes and to illuminate the reasons for their general significance, a problem which, even given the state of contemporary research, might not prove so simple to resolve.

The basis for the changes in content, the "transformation," may often lie outside of the tale itself, as, for example, in religious mentality (4, p. 75; 12, p. 10; 12, pp. 15 ff.; 13, p. 146). Propp believes that it was just these obsolete religious concepts which served as a basis for various art forms, and among them the folktale. According to Propp, the cultic and religious element as such is fundamental to the genre of the magic tale. By this he probably does not intend to mean the higher religions, since their inclusion would result in a confusion of the folktale, legend, and myth, genres whose distinct structural and temporal separation Propp is careful to maintain. It is important to keep in mind that the religious (Propp occasionally calls it "magical") mentality is regarded here by a Marxist as a determinant of the genre. Now this presupposes a competence in religious history and psychology seldom found among Soviet readers, and hence also proved to be a point very easy for the public to misunderstand.

The legitimacy of Propp's morphological-structuralistic attempts to formulate a historical-materialistic poetics of folk literature within the framework of Marxist philology was seriously doubted by several academic functionaries at that time. The scholar was dubbed with the dubious epithet "formalist," although the historical relationships which he had excluded from the study for technical reasons had already partially been explored by the same author. Nevertheless, he did not despair. More to rehabilitate himself in the face of suspicions of being a formalist, rather than to habilitate as a university lecturer, Propp submitted a very strong doctoral dissertation on "The Historical Roots of the Magic Tale" in 1939 (12).

In this study he set himself the task of discovering the "historical cause that gave rise to the magic tale" — a very presumptuous undertaking for a professional folktale scholar belonging to the guild of the Finnish school, but one quite appropriate for a student of literature (or poetologist) like himself (12, p. 5). Propp considers the folktale generally to be a superstructure erected on a pre-capitalistic base (12, p. 9), containing traces of extinct forms of social life. These traces, in his opinion, are still discernible today, and he points out that one might well discover the sources of many folktale motifs in such residues (12, pp. 11 ff.,), without, however, going into the history of the problem in detail. But the folktale, he continues, also reinterprets defunct customs. The fact that this rationalization and reinterpretation became a possibility and indeed a necessity is evidence for Propp that the conditions of life have changed. Thus, the content (*sujet*) of the folktale did not arise simply as a reflection of actual reality as such, but rather stems from its denial (12, p. 14).

The narrative plot of folktales corresponds to the very antithesis of reality. Of course, by no means does Propp attempt to trace back each and every instance of "primitive stupidity" (as Engels might say) *mutatis mutandis* to reality, in order thereby to substantiate his purely philosophical statements. Whatever is not representable as "related to reality" is traced back, à la Marr, to the laws of "thought" (12, p. 19; 13, p. 146). But the path leading to semantic studies remains open and unutilized, since the "intermediate stage of myth," which appears in the course of the changes undergone by the thematic materials, was excluded from discussion in this study (12), probably for reasons relating to the theory of the genre.

As a literary scholar, Propp makes no effort to prove the relationships between folktale motifs and social reality via primitive religion and cult, but chooses only to point out their existence. He illustrates this by means of a limited phenomenology in which the records from so-called "primitive" peoples are used as genuine, unfalsified documents of the European cultural past.

A glance at the table of contents is sufficient to reveal to the specialist what kind of forms will be investigated (12, p. 338). The chapters are devoted to certain folktale features, and are correspondingly entitled: "The Secret Forest," "Magic Gifts," "The Bride," etc. Only the most common motifs were selected for the later revised publication of the doctoral dissertation (12). His method of proof and general theory emerges with sufficient clarity from each section here, as well as from his earlier works (5; 7; 8; 9; 11). According to Propp, no tale type can be studied in isolation, nor can any motif be examined without reference to the whole, that is, without being related to or contrasted with other elements (12, pp. 8; 4, p. 72).

Space does not permit us here to explore this thesis critically or in greater detail. Professional narrative research, which Propp often rightly subjects to criticism (4, p. 72; 12, p. 6), has overlooked the work. Perhaps only the Italian translation of the book (12) will stimulate narrative scholars to a debate of the author's entire theory, and perhaps my synopsis here may serve as a modest contribution in this direction.

But the habilitation thesis soon found itself in need of a re-habilitation of its own, since the seemingly unique Russian materials presumably had not been adequately evaluated in the study. To vindicate himself Propp chose the more indigenous genre of the *bylina* (17), which he regards as a form of sung heroic epic poetry. He *a priori* excludes anything humorous or ballad-like in nature, eliminating likewise the "historical narrative song" from his discussion. Thus, this study even omits *bylina* materials which are found decomposed in prose form. This is indeed a striking feature of a conception of folk literature national in its orientation and framed in terms of the history of genres, a view which contemporary scholarship has yet to accept. Given these presuppositions, he was, none the less, able to present the *bylina* as a national phenomenon, quite to the satisfaction of every Russian patriot. Propp rejects on principle the reconstruction of spatially and temporally bound "prototypes," based on the total recorded corpus of a *bylina* theme, as a valid method of research (17, pp. 19 ff.). He derives support for this view from the work of the late A. Nikiforov, who is supposed to have finally succeeded in methodically "unmasking" the so-called "Finnish School" in a brief 1934 paper[3] — the Finns, of course, never noticing a thing.

No less resolute, Propp also comes to critical terms with his native Russian predecessors in the field of *bylina* scholarship, and in doing so harks back to the esthetic views of V. Belinskij (1811-1848) (14).

Since Propp is concerned with the esthetics, and not the thematic history of the *byliny*, he unfortunately does not choose to treat numerous significant details in the monographic sections of the work, although the text is still valuable today as a result of its excellect bibliographical appendix (17, pp. 521-547).

Propp does, however, direct his attention to the *ideological content of* the *byliny* as a genre (15; 22; 27). The *byliny* are thus divided into periods solely on the basis of the current prevailing ideology (probably in the sense of Julius Wiegand[4]), and are linked together with the heterogeneous, fixed evolution of the Russian *state*.

Propp presented a detailed treatment of his conception of the development of Russian heroic poetry at the Fourth International Congress of

[3]   See "Finskaja škola pered krizisom" [The Finnish School Faces a Crisis], *Sovetskaja ètnografija*, 1934, No. 4, 141-144.
[4]   See his *Geschichte der deutschen Dichtung in strenger Systematik nach Gedanken, Stoffen und Form* (Cologne, 1922).

Slavicists in Moscow (27). I presume his arguments are familiar to those in the field.

In his capacity as a literary scholar, Propp has also given serious thought to the problem of the "Essence of Folklore" (13), ideas which I feel are rather meant for the field of folklore studies per se. The German folklorist will be suprised by the thesis of this Soviet scholar that the investigation of the ideational and material culture of the peasant within the framework of a *single* and unified discipline, such as German *Volkskunde* conceives itself to be (and in my opinion actually is), necessarily implies a patronizing attitude toward the peasant, as long as the so-called upper-class counterparts such as architecture, the history of technology, literature, and music are treated as *separate* disciplines (13, p. 139). In so thinking, Propp disassociates himself from the *Volkskunde-Völkerkunde* controversy, and seeks wherever possible to make folkloristics an international discipline.

In addition, Propp, whose entire approach has been to drive the dilettantes out of folktale research by maintaining its connections with ethnography, makes a plea for a methodological union with literary scholarship (13, pp. 14f.). He feels that without any ethnography at all, the materialistic and historical study of folklore would be quite unthinkable, since folkloristics must try to account for the *history* of a phenomenon (13, pp. 145ff.). But its beginnings lie far in the past, and it is ethnography that is concerned with just this chronological period. Consequently, it would be amiss to divorce folklore studies completely from ethnological research. Propp holds the view that folklore is an ideological science, and thus that the most suitable methodological approaches are those which have, in each case, been pre-formed in our thinking by contemporary ideology.

One of the tasks of folkloristics is the exhaustive study of genres. The genre must be painstakingly researched with regard to style and language, i.e., with regard to structure. It is imperative that we clarify the specific poetics of folklore phenomena. It is characteristic that Propp has not infrequently preferred to link the study of folklore sooner with that of language than with the study of literature (13, p. 142). Like language, which is, in actual fact, not an invention of the individual, folklore is also subject to the same regular changes, whenever the necessary conditions are ripe for it.

The comparison between language and folklore (which Propp makes

precisely along the lines of Günter Müller, but which Propp derives from
N. Marr) represented the attempt, as I now understand it, to free
the study of folklore from its all too rigid dependence on literature.
But both the comparison and the attempt proved unsuccessful.

Propp's discussions of legends and folk drama, written for teaching
purposes, are also worth noting (16, pp. 378-407).

Propp enjoys the reputation of being a master editor, and expressed
some basic thoughts on the subject in one of his reviews (R5). The new
edition of Afanas'ev's folktales (19) which Propp supervised, can always
be held up to Soviet publishers as a model in the field. Propp's activities
in editing and textual criticism have been fairly comprehensive (18; 22;
29; R6).

Propp's contributions to the history of Russian folkloristics are quite
valuable (14; 20; 21). These writings, as well as his other occasional
articles, often contain the quite topical and highly polemical confessions
of Propp the *theoretician*, the man who consciously continues in the
footsteps of the great revolutionary Russian democrats (25; 26; 30; 31;
34; 3; R1-15).

Two of Propp's works on Russian popular calendar festivals are likewise of importance to the folklorist (28; 32). In these studies he proposes
a historicizing explanation of peasant customs. This subject has been lying fallow here in this country for several decades, and it is encouraging
for the history of scholarship that no less a scholar has tackled the problem.
The evidence cited and the secondary literature are confined to Russian
materials and are all taken from the last century, but neither of these
works is lacking in contemporary social significance. Circumstances per-
mitting, they should be well suited to serve the needs of a more elevated
type of atheistic propaganda (28, p. 272; 32, p. 3). Here again, an old
but very new field of research is made accessible to the academic layman.

Propp's work is characterized by a cathechetical clarity in the formulation of complicated problems and a pedagogically dogmatic manner
in presenting them. As a result, he has earned the lasting praise of all
those who need and value an effective teacher. This probably accounts
for the fact that Propp, as an educator *par excellence*, has largely excluded the remote, inaccessible literature, especially that of foreign colleagues, from his works. But the specialist notes that he nevertheless
has mastered most of the relevant information. It would be regrettable
if this point were misunderstood.

At present the grand old man is at work on the Russian folksong. Here it turns out that the venerable philologist seems not only to be familiar with the latest questions *about* the folksong, but that he still knows how to enjoy them spontaneously — a gift that must always be admired in a folklorist, not to mention a sensitive connoisseur of Goethe and Rilke such as Propp is.

I was assured by several people that Propp was looking forward with great anticipation to his announced role as director of the symposium on the "Classification of Folk Literature" at the 1964 Ethnological Congress in Moscow. Had he not been forced to cancel his participation because he was temporarily indisposed, as the expression goes, I would most certainly have been spared the difficult job of serving as the interpreter at the symposium, since Vladimir Propp is sufficiently knowledgeable about the outside world, is well-known owing to his collaboration on the *International Folklore Bibliography* and *Demos*, and is even familiar to the readers of this journal through Archer Taylor's essay.[5] He corresponds with many noted scholars abroad and is absolutely proficient in each of their languages.

What we might have enjoyed hearing him say at the Congress, can hopefully be gleaned in part from his paper on the principles of the classification of folklore genres (34).

The subject of Propp's studies, first and last, has always been the poetics of the creative process. Furthermore, this entails a historical poetology such as was already envisioned here in this country by Aleksander Veselovskij (1838-1906) (6). According to this view, the literary scholar as poetologist must of necessity refer back to the presumably early genres contained in *folk* literature. For this reason, Propp is pre-eminently a folklorist.

The fact that a certain set of thematic materials belongs to a definite original genre, and that both these materials and the genre are already manifest at the level of *structure*, is, at the present time, the principal law of any poetics. Thus Propp, probably in every one of his folkloristic writings, has shown himself to be a pioneering literary scholar without equal.

Both the seemingly pure study of form to which his early works were devoted, as well as the concern for the supposed history of themes (which for Propp was strictly a question of the history of genres) that is expressed

[5] "The Biographical Pattern in Traditional Narrative," *Journal of the Folklore Institute*, Vol. I, No. 1/2 (1964), 114-129.

in his later works, were to be used by the author, his older, and even his younger followers, for the highest literary-historical purposes, in point of fact for the development of a philosophical theory of poetics. For this reason Propp was unfortunately never basically concerned with the substantive richness of the materials he drew on, but strove merely for an *ad hoc* valid, intuitively grounded *verstehende Phänomenologie*, in terms of which thematic content ceases to be a material entity and becomes rather the expression of a higher set of laws which must then be fathomed.

Propp, who initially was to deny the reality of the customary folktale types (a fact which did not, by the way, prevent him, at a much later date, from producing one of the most reliable supplements to the Aarne-Andreev catalogue [19]), nevertheless has no doubts about the actual existence of the magic tale, the legend, and the *bylina*, as such. Propp proceeds from the view that any "ultimate relationships" and valid laws which may evolve are, in every case, limited to *one* genre alone. Hence, Propp always chose to restrict his studies to one definite genre at a time, not only when he was working along structural-analytical lines, but also when he focused on the history of themes, even when the contents were by no means firmly linked with just one particular genre pattern. That is to say, Propp assumes that there had to be, and must now still be, a certain affinity between content, genre, and historical period, or rather, mode of production. According to this view, this affinity would correspond to a definite structure of the configuration of motifs. Since the number of nuclear motifs is, of necessity, limited, it must therefore be possible to comprehend these motifs in terms of a system, to enumerate them, and finally to interpret the motifs with ease within the framework of whatever ideological conception is valid at the moment. Propp's train of thought here sounds like a Marxist version of Helmut de Boor's hypotheses,[6] and speaks for the ubiquity of similar scientific ideas under diverse social and political conditions.

Propp attempted to understand the emergence and disappearance of distinct thematic materials *within* the confines of a genre (for him this is called a "transformation" and is closely linked with morphology) not only in chronological terms, but rather even more as a part of the history of ideas.

Just as Julius Wiegand[7] in his time believed it possible to construct

[6] See "Märchenforschung," *Zeitschrift für Deutschkunde*, XLII (1928), 561-581.
[7] Wiegand, op. cit., n. 4.

a literary history in which one could define the essential themes and motifs for each age and generation, Propp also tried to suggest certain folktale motifs for the primitive "epochs" of Morgan and Engels, and also epic ideas for the later "historical" periods. In doing so, Propp declared himself an adherent of Marxism-Leninism, the dominant ideology of his homeland, embracing this ideology however at a much higher level than what was customary in this country among folklorists at that time, and in a mode which even today is not accessible to all.

But Propp most probably arrived at an early stage in his work at the final assumption that the thematic materials were interpretable, and that from structure we might learn something valuable about the history of the creative processes of the human intellect, in fact, about the very history of folk-culture itself. Even Professor Propp feels that this is a premise which can only be pointed out, but never conclusively proved.

Just because this affinity between content and genre, and between both of these in turn, and the historical period, i.e., mode of production, serves as a premise for a point of departure, it can hardly be substantiated on the basis of already available results of research. Indeed, many may regard Propp's accomplishments as a welcome demonstration that *no* such affinity actually exists, and they will then be sincerely grateful to Propp for having convinced them that the method of studying folklore by means of the genres is too impracticable to be attempted, at least given the present state of our knowledge.

Seen in terms of the history of the field, Propp must be ranked among those scholars who, already back in the 1920's, were trying to fathom the mystery of the literary genre and its formal structure. We need only mention such figures as Julius Petersen,[8] Karl Viëtor,[9] Günter Müller,[10] their immediate offspring André Jolles,[11] Robert Petsch,[12] Walter Berendsohn,[13] and, more recently, the work of Max Lüthi, Wolfgang Kayser,[14] Claude Lévi-Strauss[15] and Alan Dundes.[16]

[8]   "Zur Lehre von den Dichtungsgattungen," in *Festschrift für August Sauer* (Stuttgart, 1925), pp. 72ff.
[9]   "Probleme der literarischen Gattungsgeschichte," in Viëtor, *Geist und Form* (Bern, 1952), pp. 292-309.
[10]   "Bemerkungen zur Gattungspoetik," *Philosophischer Anzeiger*, Vol. III (1929), 129-147.
[11]   *Einfache Formen* (Leipzig, 1929).
[12]   *Wesen und Formen der Erzählkunst* (Halle/Saale, 1934).
[13]   "Einfache Formen," in Lutz Mackensen (ed.), *Handwörterbuch des deutschen Märchens* (Berlin, 1930-33), I, pp.484-498.

In the Soviet Union this brand of literary criticism was for a long time properly represented only by Vladimir Propp. Much later Lüthi also arrived at an independent so-called "folktale biology,"[17] i.e., at the discovery that there is a regularity of some sort in the structure of a unit of content. This statement could also be applied to the work of other structuralists. Nowadays such kinds of regularities — and I hope I will not be misunderstood here — just seem to be dangling there, suspended in the air wherever one goes.

But since Propp himself generally pays little attention to the secondary literature in his writings (I perceive in this a habit of the philosophers: the Jolles volume, *Einfache Formen*, for example, contains no references to works consulted and no footnotes whatsoever), I feel it is hardly proper for me to pursue the problem of historical relationships any further here. I will save that for the next anniversary celebration.

Propp's works are, however, especially valuable to our discipline for precisely the simple reason that, often enough, he independently thought through to the same conclusions reached by writers whose works, fortunately or unfortunately, as the case may be, were not accessible to him at the right time. In a sense, his conclusions can thus be evaluated as corroborating evidence for controversial hypotheses, particularly in those cases in which the material is not conducive to empirical proof. It should therefore not surprise us that the latest generation of American folklorists — let me mention Dundes as a representative example — have recently discovered "Propp" for themselves.[18] "The stone which the builders rejected has become the chief cornerstone,"[19] namely, the cornerstone of a most promising theoretical system. And perhaps his works also contain the smaller portion of those insights for which someday Soviet folklorists too may be grateful to him!

Leningrad, U.S.S.R.

Translated from the German by William Templer and Allen Hershberger

[14] *Das sprachliche Kunstwerk*, 9th ed. (Bern, 1963).
[15] "L'Analyse morphologique de contes russes," *International Journal of Slavic Linguistics and Poetics*, III (1960), 122-149.
[16] *The Morphology of North American Indian Folktales* (= *FF Communications*, 195) (Helsinki, 1964).
[17] *Das europäische Volksmärchen* (Bern, 1947; 2nd ed. 1960); *Es war einmal...* (Göttingen, 1962).
[18] See Matthew 13:57: "... A prophet is not without honor except in his own country and in his own house."
[19] Psalms 118:22.

Selected Bibliography

Teaching of German:

(01) V. Ja. Propp and I. F. Vejert, *Rabočaja kniga po nemeckomu jazyku dlja studentov-èkonomistov* [German Workbook for Economics Students] (Leningrad, 1929; 2nd ed., 1930).
(02) ——, *Nemeckaja xrestomatija dlja studentov-èkonomistov* [Readings in German for Economics Students] (Leningrad, 1929).
(03) *Povtoritel'nyj kurs nemeckoj grammatiki* [German Review Grammar] (Leningrad, 1929).
(04) "Problema artiklja v sovremennom nemeckom jazyke" [Problem of the Article in Contemporary German], *Sbornik pamjati akad. L. V. Ščerby* (Leningrad, 1951), pp. 213-226.

Folklore Studies:

(1) "Morfologija russkoj volšebnoj skazki" [Morphology of the Russian Magic Tale], *Skazočnaja komissija v 1926 g. VGO* (Leningrad, 1927), pp. 48-50.
(2) "O sostavlenii alfavitnyx ukazatelej k sobranijam skazok" [On Compiling Alphabetical Indexes for Collections of Folktales], *Skazočnaja komissija v 1927 g. VGO* (Leningrad, 1928), pp. 64-79.
(3) *Morfologija skazki* (Moscow-Leningrad, 1928). 152 pp. Reviewed by Dmitrij Zelenin, *Slavische Rundschau*, I (1929), 286-287. English translation, *Morphology of the Folktale*, in *International Journal of American Linguistics*, XXIV, 4 (Oct., 1958). Reviewed by Melville Jacobs, *Journal of American Folklore*, LXXII (1959), 195-196; and Claude Lévi-Strauss, *International Journal of Slavic Linguistics and Poetics*, III (1960), 122-158.
(4) "Transformacii volšebnyx skazok" [Transformations of Magic Tales], *Poètika*, IV (1928), 64ff.
(5) "Volšebnoe derevo na mogile" [Magic Tree on the Grave], *Sovetskaja ètnografija* 1934, No. 1/2, 128-152.
(6) "Sravnitel'naja mifologija i eë metod" [Comparative Mythology and Its Method], in A. N. Veselovskij, *Sobranie sočinenij*, XVI (Leningrad, 1938), 295-304.
(7) "Mužskoj dom v russkoj skazke" [Male House in the Russian Folktale], *Učenye zapiski LGU*, No. 20, *Serija filolog. nauk*, I (1939), 174-199.
(8) "Ritual'nyj smex v fol'klore" [Ritual Laughter in Folklore], *Učenye zapiski LGU*, No. 46, *Serija filolog. nauk*, III (1939), 151-176.
(9) "Motif čudesnogo roždenija" [Motif of the Miraculous Birth], *Učenye zapiski LGU*, No. 81, *Serija filolog. nauk*, XII (1941), 67-98.
(10) "Čukotskij mif i giljackij èpos" [Chukot Myth and Gilyak Epic], *Naučnyj bjulleten' LGU*, No. 4 (1945), 138-176.
(11) "Èdip v svete fol'klora" [Oedipus in the Light of Folklore], *Učenye zapiski LGU*, No. 72, *Serija filolog. nauk*, IX (1946), 138-176.
(12) *Istoričeskie korni volšebnoj skazki* [Historical Roots of the Magic Tale] (Leningrad, 1946), 340 pp. Essay review, based on the unpublished dissertation, by Dmitrij Zelenin — *Ethos*, V (1940), 54-58. Italian translation, *Le radici storiche dei racconti di fate*. Trans. by C. Coisson, with a preface by G. Cocchiara (Turin, 1949). Essay review by Paolo Toschi, *Lares*, XV (1949), 137-149; reprinted in Toschi, *"Rappresaglia" di studi di letteratura popolare* (Florence, 1956), pp. 45-63.

(13) "Specifika fol'klora" [Essence of Folklore], *Trudy jubilejnoj naučnoj sessii LGU, Sekcija filolog. nauk* (Leningrad, 1946), pp. 138-152.

(14) "Belinskij o narodnoj poèzii" [Belinskij on Folk Poetry], *Vestnik LGU*, No. 12 (1953), 95-120.

(15) "Jazyk bylin kak sredstvo xudožestvennoj izobrazitel'nosti" [Language of the Byliny as a Means of Artistic Depiction], *Učenye zapiski LGU*, No. 173, *Serija filolog. nauk*, XX (1954), 375-403.

(16) "Legenda" [Legend], *Russkoe narodnoe poètičeskoe tvorčestvo*, vol. I, book 2 (Moskow-Leningrad, AN SSSR, 1955), pp. 386-407.

(17) *Russkij geroičeskij èpos* [Russian Heroic Epic] (Leningrad, 1956, 2nd ed., 1958). 550 pp.

(18) "Tekstologičeskoe redaktirovanie zapisej fol'klora" [Textual Editing of Folklore Records], *Russkij fol'klor*, I (1956), 196-206.

(19) A. N. Afanas'ev. *Narodnye russkie skazki* [Russian Folktales] (Preparation of texts, introductory essay and notes by V. Ja. Propp.), 3 vols. (Moscow, 1957; 2nd ed., 1958).

(20) "Molodoj Dobroljubov ob izučenii narodnoj pesni" [The Young Dobroljubov on the Study of Folksongs], *Učenye zapiski LGU*, No. 229, *Serija filolog. nauk*, XXX (1957), 145-159.

(21) "Vladimir Ivanovič Čičerov zum Gedächtnis," *Deutsches Jahrbuch für Volkskunde*, III (1957), 481-482.

(22) *Byliny* (Preparation of texts, introductory essay and notes by V. Ja. Propp and B. N. Putilov.), 2 vols. (Moscow, 1958).

(23) "Pesnja o gneve Groznogo na syna" (Song on the Wrath of Ivan the Terrible against His Son], *Vestnik LGU*, No. 14, *Serija istorii, jazyka i literatury*, III (1958), 75-103.

(24) "Motivy lubočnyx povestej v stixotvorenii Puškina 'Son' 1816 g." [Motifs from Broadside Stories in Pushkin's Poem "Sleep" 1816], *Trudy Otdela drevnerusskoj literatury IRLI, AN SSSR*, XIV (1958), 535-538.

(25) V. Ja. Propp, et al., "Problemy izučenija narodno-poètičeskogo tvorčestva" [Problems in the Study of Russian Folk Poetic Creation], *Izvestija OLJa AN SSSR*, XVIII, No. 6 (1959), 473-489.

(26) V. Ja. Propp, et al., *Voprosy sovetskoj nauki. Izučenie narodno-poètičeskogo tvorčestva* [Questions of Soviet Science. The Study of Folk Poetic Creation] (Moscow, 1960).

(27) "Osnovnye ètapy razvitija russkogo geroičeskogo èposa" [Basic Stages in the Development of the Russian Epic], *Issledovanija po slavjanskomu literaturovedeniju i fol'kloristike. Doklady sovetskix učenyx na IV Meždunarodnom s'ezde slavistov* (Moscow, AN SSSR, 1960), pp. 284-312.

(28) "Istoričeskaja osnova nekotoryx zemledel'českix obrjadov" [Historical Basis of Some Agricultural Ceremonies], *Ežegodnik Muzeja istorii, religii i ateizma*, V (Leningrad, 1961), 272-297.

(29) *Narodnye liričeskie pesni* [Lyric Folk Songs] (Preparation of texts, introductory essay and notes by V. Ja. Propp.) (Leningrad, 1961). 610 pp.

(30) "Ob istorizme russkogo èposa" [On the Historicism of the Russian Epic], *Russkaja literatura*, No. 2 (1962), 87-92.

(31) "Fol'klor i dejstvitel'nost'" [Folklore and Reality], *Russkaja literatura*, No. 3 (1963), 62-84.

(32) *Russkie agrarnye prazdniki. Opyt istoriko-ètnografičeskogo issledovanija* [Russian Agrarian Holidays. An Experiment in Historical Ethnographical Research]

(Leningrad, 1963). 143 pp. Review by G. Nosova, *Deutsches Jahrbuch für Volkskunde*, X (1964), 196-199.

(33) "Märchen der Brüder Grimm im russischen Norden," *Deutsches Jahrbuch für Volkskunde*, IX (1963), 104-112.

(34) "Principy klassifikacii fol'klornyx žanrov" [Principles of the Classification of Folklore Genres], *Sovetskaja ètnografija*, 1964, No. 4, 147-154.

(35) "Žanrovyj sostav russkogo fol'klora" [Genre-structure of Russian Folklore], *Russkaja literatura*, No. 4 (1964), 58-76.

Reviews:

(R1) Will-Erich Peuckert, *Volkskunde des Proletariats* (Frankfurt am Main, 1931) — *Sovetskij fol'klor*, No. 2-3 (1936), 427-428.

(R2) Gustav Jungbauer, *Geschichte der deutschen Volkskunde* (Prague, 1931) — *Sovetskij fol'klor*, No. 2-3 (1936), 428-430.

(R3) V. I. Malyšev, *Povest' o Suxane* [Story about Suxan] — *Russkij fol'klor*, II (1957), 348-350.

(R4) Carl Stief, *Studies in the Russian Historical Song* (Copenhagen, 1953) — *Russkij fol'klor*, II (1957), 350-352.

(R5) *Narty. Èpos osetinskogo naroda* [Narty, Epic of the Ossetic People] (Moscow, 1957) — *Russkij fol'klor*, III (1958), 395-399.

(R6) P. G. Bogatyrev (ed.), *Russkoe narodnoe poètičeskoe tvorčestvo* [Russian Folk Poetic Creation] (Moscow, 1956) — *Russkaja literatura*, No. 2 (1958), 230-233.

(R7) V. I. Čičerov, *Zimnij period russkogo narodnogo zemledel'českogo kalendarja XVI-XIX vv.* [Winter Period in the Russian Folk Agricultural Calendar, Sixteenth to Nineteenth Centuries] (Moscow, 1957) — *Deutsches Jahrbuch für Volkskunde*, IV (1958), 570-572.

(R8) *Deutsches Jahrbuch für Volkskunde*, I-III (1955-1957) — *Russkij fol'klor*, IV (1959), 447-454.

(R9) *Russkie narodnye pesni Povolž'ja* [Russian Folksongs from the Volga Region, Vol. I. Songs Recorded in the Kujbyšev Area], I (Moscow-Leningrad, 1959) — *Deutsches Jahrbuch für Volkskunde*, V (1959), 479-481.

(R10) P. Rubcov, *Narodnye pesni Leningradskoj oblasti* [Folksongs of the Leningrad Region] (Moscow, 1958) — *Deutsches Jahrbuch für Volkskunde*, VI (1960), 492.

(R11) B. N. Putilov and B. M. Dobrovol'skij, *Istoričeskie pesni XIII-XVI vekov* [Historical Songs of the Thirteenth to Sixteenth Centuries] (Moscow-Leningrad, 1960) — *Voprosy literatury*, No. 2 (1962), 207-209; also in *Deutsches Jahrbuch für Volkskunde*, IX (1963), 412-414.

(R12) M. J. Mel'c, *Russkij fol'klor. Bibliografičeskij ukazatel' 1945-1959* [Russian Folklore. Bibliography 1945-1959] (Moscow-Leningrad, 1961) — *Sovetskaja ètnografija*, 1962, No. 2, 156-158.

(R13) Giuseppe Cocchiara, *Istorija fol'kloristiki v Evrope* [History of Folklore Studies in Europe]. Trans. from Italian (Moscow, 1960) — *Sovetskaja ètnografija*, 1962, No. 4, 210-212.

(R14) B. N. Putilov, *Russkij istoriko-pesennyj fol'klor XIII-XVI vekov* [Russian Hisrical Song Folklore of the Thirteenth to Sixteenth Centuries] (Moscow-Leningrad, 1960) — *Deutsches Jahrbuch für Volkskunde*, IX (1963), 414-415.

(R15) Hermann Strobach, *Bauernklagen* (Berlin, 1964) — *Sovetskaja ètnografija*, 1964, No. 5, 162-165.

For a more complete bibliography of Propp's publications on folklore, see *Russkij fol'klor*, X (1966), 337-343.

THE STRUCTURAL STUDY OF MYTH

By Claude Lévi-Strauss

"It would seem that mythological worlds have been built up only to be shattered again, and that new worlds were built from the fragments."

Franz Boas, in Introduction to James Teit, *Traditions of the Thompson River Indians of British Columbia*, Memoirs of the American Folklore Society, VI (1898), 18.

1.0. Despite some recent attempts to renew them, it would seem that during the past twenty years anthropology has more and more turned away from studies in the field of religion. At the same time, and precisely because professional anthropologists' interest has withdrawn from primitive religion, all kinds of amateurs who claim to belong to other disciplines have seized this opportunity to move in, thereby turning into their private playground what we had left as a wasteland. Thus, the prospects for the scientific study of religion have been undermined in two ways.

1.1. The explanation for that situation lies to some extent in the fact that the anthropological study of religion was started by men like Tylor, Frazer, and Durkheim who were psychologically oriented, although not in a position to keep up with the progress of psychological research and theory. Therefore, their interpretations soon became vitiated by the outmoded psychological approach which they used as their backing. Although they were undoubtedly right in giving their attention to intellectual processes, the way they handled them remained so coarse as to discredit them altogether. This is much to be regretted since, as Hocart so profoundly noticed in his introduction to a posthumous book recently published,[1] psychological interpretations were withdrawn from the intellectual field only to be introduced again in the field of affectivity, thus adding to "the inherent defects of the psychological school . . . the mistake of deriving clear-cut ideas . . . from vague emotions." Instead of trying to enlarge the framework of our logic to include processes which, whatever their apparent differences, belong to the same kind of intellectual operations, a naive attempt was made to reduce them to inarticulate emotional drives which resulted only in withering our studies.

1.2. Of all the chapters of religious anthropology probably none has tarried to the same extent as studies in the field of mythology. From a theoretical point of view the situation remains very much the same as it was fifty years ago, namely, a picture of chaos. Myths are still widely interpreted in conflicting ways: collective dreams, the outcome of a kind of esthetic play, the foundation of ritual. . . . Mythological figures are considered as personified abstractions, divinized heroes or decayed gods. Whatever the hypothesis, the choice amounts to reducing mythology either to an idle play or to a coarse kind of speculation.

1.3. In order to understand what a myth really is, are we compelled to choose between platitude and sophism? Some claim that human societies merely express,

[1] A. M. Hocart, *Social Origins* (London, 1954), p. 7.

through their mythology, fundamental feelings common to the whole of mankind, such as love, hate, revenge; or that they try to provide some kind of explanations for phenomena which they cannot understand otherwise: astronomical, meteorological, and the like. But why should these societies do it in such elaborate and devious ways, since all of them are also acquainted with positive explanations? On the other hand, psychoanalysts and many anthropologists have shifted the problems to be explained away from the natural or cosmological towards the sociological and psychological fields. But then the interpretation becomes too easy: if a given mythology confers prominence to a certain character, let us say an evil grandmother, it will be claimed that in such a society grandmothers are actually evil and that mythology reflects the social structure and the social relations; but should the actual data be conflicting, it would be readily claimed that the purpose of mythology is to provide an outlet for repressed feelings. Whatever the situation may be, a clever dialectic will always find a way to pretend that a meaning has been unravelled.

2.0. Mythology confronts the student with a situation which at first sight could be looked upon as contradictory. On the one hand, it would seem that in the course of a myth anything is likely to happen. There is no logic, no continuity. Any characteristic can be attributed to any subject; every conceivable relation can be met. With myth, everything becomes possible. But on the other hand, this apparent arbitrariness is belied by the astounding similarity between myths collected in widely different regions. Therefore the problem: if the content of a myth is contingent, how are we going to explain that throughout the world myths do resemble one another so much?

2.1. It is precisely this awareness of a basic antinomy pertaining to the nature of myth that may lead us towards its solution. For the contradiction which we face is very similar to that which in earlier times brought considerable worry to the first philosophers concerned with linguistic problems; linguistics could only begin to evolve as a science after this contradiction had been overcome. Ancient philosophers were reasoning about language the way we are about mythology. On the one hand, they did notice that in a given language certain sequences of sounds were associated with definite meanings, and they earnestly aimed at discovering a reason for the linkage between those sounds and that meaning. Their attempt, however, was thwarted from the very beginning by the fact that the same sounds were equally present in other languages though the meaning they conveyed was entirely different. The contradiction was surmounted only by the discovery that it is the combination of sounds, not the sounds in themselves, which provides the significant data.

2.2. Now, it is easy to see that some of the more recent interpretations of mythological thought originated from the same kind of misconception under which those early linguists were laboring. Let us consider, for instance, Jung's idea that a given mythological pattern—the so-called archetype—possesses a certain signification. This is comparable to the long supported error that a sound may possess a certain affinity with a meaning: for instance, the "liquid" semi-vowels with water, the open vowels with things that are big, large, loud, or heavy, etc., a kind of theory which still has its supporters.[2] Whatever emendations the original formulation may now call for, everybody will agree that the Saussurean principle of the arbitrary character of the linguistic signs was a prerequisite for the acceding of linguistics to the scientific level.

[2] See, for instance, Sir R. A. Paget, "The Origin of Language...," *Journal of World History*, I, No. 2 (UNESCO, 1953).

2.3. To invite the mythologist to compare his precarious situation with that of the linguist in the prescientific stage is not enough. As a matter of fact we may thus be led only from one difficulty to another. There is a very good reason why myth cannot simply be treated as language if its specific problems are to be solved; myth *is* language: to be known, myth has to be told; it is a part of human speech. In order to preserve its specificity we should thus put ourselves in a position to show that it is both the same thing as language, and also something different from it. Here, too, the past experience of linguists may help us. For language itself can be analyzed into things which are at the same time similar and different. This is precisely what is expressed in Saussure's distinction between *langue* and *parole,* one being the structural side of language, the other the statistical aspect of it, *langue* belonging to a revertible time, whereas *parole* is non-revertible. If those two levels already exist in language, then a third one can conceivably be isolated.

2.4. We have just distinguished *langue* and *parole* by the different time referents which they use. Keeping this in mind, we may notice that myth uses a third referent which combines the properties of the first two. On the one hand, a myth always refers to events alleged to have taken place in time: before the world was created, or during its first stages—anyway, long ago. But what gives the myth an operative value is that the specific pattern described is everlasting; it explains the present and the past as well as the future. This can be made clear through a comparison between myth and what appears to have largely replaced it in modern societies, namely, politics. When the historian refers to the French Revolution it is always as a sequence of past happenings, a non-revertible series of events the remote consequences of which may still be felt at present. But to the French politician, as well as to his followers, the French Revolution is both a sequence belonging to the past—as to the historian—and an everlasting pattern which can be detected in the present French social structure and which provides a clue for its interpretation, a lead from which to infer the future developments. See, for instance, Michelet who was a politically-minded historian. He describes the French Revolution thus: "This day . . . everything was possible. . . . Future became present . . . that is, no more time, a glimpse of eternity." It is that double structure, altogether historical and anhistorical, which explains that myth, while pertaining to the realm of the *parole* and calling for an explanation as such, as well as to that of the *langue* in which it is expressed, can also be an absolute object on a third level which, though it remains linguistic by nature, is nevertheless distinct from the other two.

2.5. A remark can be introduced at this point which will help to show the singularity of myth among other linguistic phenomena. Myth is the part of language where the formula *traduttore, traditore* reaches its lowest truth-value. From that point of view it should be put in the whole gamut of linguistic expressions at the end opposite to that of poetry, in spite of all the claims which have been made to prove the contrary. Poetry is a kind of speech which cannot be translated except at the cost of serious distortions; whereas the mythical value of the myth remains preserved, even through the worst translation. Whatever our ignorance of the language and the culture of the people where it originated, a myth is still felt as a myth by any reader throughout the world. Its substance does not lie in its style, its original music, or its syntax, but in the *story* which it tells. It is language, functioning on an especially high level where meaning succeeds practically at "taking off" from the linguistic ground on which it keeps on rolling.

2.6. To sum up the discussion at this point, we have so far made the following claims: 1. If there is a meaning to be found in mythology, this cannot reside in the isolated elements which enter into the composition of a myth, but only in the way those elements are combined. 2. Although myth belongs to the same category as language, being, as a matter of fact, only part of it, language in myth unveils specific properties. 3. Those properties are only to be found *above* the ordinary linguistic level; that is, they exhibit more complex features beside those which are to be found in any kind of linguistic expression.

3.0. If the above three points are granted, at least as a working hypothesis, two consequences will follow: 1. Myth, like the rest of language, is made up of constituent units. 2. These constituent units presuppose the constituent units present in language when analyzed on other levels, namely, phonemes, morphemes, and semantemes, but they, nevertheless, differ from the latter in the same way as they themselves differ from morphemes, and these from phonemes; they belong to a higher order, a more complex one. For this reason, we will call them *gross constituent units*.

3.1. How shall we proceed in order to identify and isolate these gross constituent units? We know that they cannot be found among phonemes, morphemes, or semantemes, but only on a higher level; otherwise myth would become confused with any other kind of speech. Therefore, we should look for them on the sentence level. The only method we can suggest at this stage is to proceed tentatively, by trial and error, using as a check the principles which serve as a basis for any kind of structural analysis: economy of explanation; unity of solution; and ability to reconstruct the whole from a fragment, as well as further stages from previous ones.

3.2. The technique which has been applied so far by this writer consists in analyzing each myth individually, breaking down its story into the shortest possible sentences, and writing each such sentence on an index card bearing a number corresponding to the unfolding of the story.

3.3. Practically each card will thus show that a certain function is, at a given time, predicated to a given subject. Or, to put it otherwise, each gross constituent unit will consist in a relation.

3.4. However, the above definition remains highly unsatisfactory for two different reasons. In the first place, it is well known to structural linguists that constituent units on all levels are made up of relations and the true difference between our gross units and the others stays unexplained; moreover, we still find ourselves in the realm of a non-revertible time since the numbers of the cards correspond to the unfolding of the informant's speech. Thus, the specific character of mythological time, which as we have seen is both revertible and non-revertible, synchronic and diachronic, remains unaccounted for. Therefrom comes a new hypothesis which constitutes the very core of our argument: the true constituent units of a myth are not the isolated relations but *bundles of such relations* and it is only as bundles that these relations can be put to use and combined so as to produce a meaning. Relations pertaining to the same bundle may appear diachronically at remote intervals, but when we have succeeded in grouping them together, we have reorganized our myth according to a time referent of a new nature corresponding to the prerequisite of the initial hypothesis, namely, a two-dimensional time referent which is simultaneously diachronic and synchronic and which accordingly integrates the characteristics of the *langue* on one hand, and those of the *parole* on the other. To put it in even more linguistic terms, it is as though a phoneme were always made up of all its variants.

4.0. Two comparisons may help to explain what we have in mind.

4.1. Let us first suppose that archaeologists of the future coming from another planet would one day, when all human life had disappeared from the earth, excavate one of our libraries. Even if they were at first ignorant of our writing, they might succeed in deciphering it—an undertaking which would require, at some early stage, the discovery that the alphabet, as we are in the habit of printing it, should be read from left to right and from top to bottom. However, they would soon find out that a whole category of books did not fit the usual pattern: these would be the orchestra scores on the shelves of the music division. But after trying, without success, to decipher staffs one after the other, from the upper down to the lower, they would probably notice that the same patterns of notes recurred at intervals, either in full or in part, or that some patterns were strongly reminiscent of earlier ones. Hence the hypothesis: what if patterns showing affinity, instead of being considered in succession, were to be treated as one complex pattern and read globally? By getting at what we call *harmony*, they would then find out that an orchestra score, in order to become meaningful, has to be read diachronically along one axis—that is, page after page, and from left to right—and also synchronically along the other axis, all the notes which are written vertically making up one gross constituent unit, i.e. one bundle of relations.

4.2. The other comparison is somewhat different. Let us take an observer ignorant of our playing cards, sitting for a long time with a fortune-teller. He would know something of the visitors: sex, age, look, social situation, etc. in the same way as we know something of the different cultures whose myths we try to study. He would also listen to the séances and keep them recorded so as to be able to go over them and make comparisons—as we do when we listen to myth telling and record it. Mathematicians to whom I have put the problem agree that if the man is bright and if the material available to him is sufficient, he may be able to reconstruct the nature of the deck of cards being used, that is: fifty-two or thirty-two cards according to case, made up of four homologous series consisting of the same units (the individual cards) with only one varying feature, the suit.

4.3. The time has come to give a concrete example of the method we propose. We will use the Oedipus myth which has the advantage of being well-known to everybody and for which no preliminary explanation is therefore needed. By doing so, I am well aware that the Oedipus myth has only reached us under late forms and through literary transfigurations concerned more with esthetic and moral preoccupations than with religious or ritual ones, whatever these may have been. But as will be shown later, this apparently unsatisfactory situation will strengthen our demonstration rather than weaken it.

4.4. The myth will be treated as would be an orchestra score perversely presented as a unilinear series and where our task is to re-establish the correct disposition. As if, for instance, we were confronted with a sequence of the type: 1,2,4,7,8,2,3,4,6,8,1,4,5,7, 8,1,2,5,7,3,4,5,6,8 . . . , the assignment being to put all the 1's together, all the 2's, the 3's, etc.; the result is a chart:

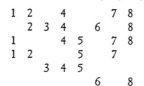

4.5. We will attempt to perform the same kind of operation on the Oedipus myth, trying out several dispositions until we find one which is in harmony with the principles enumerated under 3.1. Let us suppose, for the sake of argument, that the best arrangement is the following (although it might certainly be improved by the help of a specialist in Greek mythology):

Kadmos seeks his sister Europa ravished by Zeus			
		Kadmos kills the dragon	
	The Spartoi kill each other		
			Labdacos (Laios' father) = *lame* (?)
	Oedipus kills his father Laios		
			Laios (Oedipus' father) = *left-sided* (?)
		Oedipus kills the Sphinx	
Oedipus marries his mother Jocasta			
	Eteocles kills his brother Polynices		Oedipus = *swollen-foot* (?)
Antigone buries her brother Polynices despite prohibition			

4.6. Thus, we find ourselves confronted with four vertical columns each of which include several relations belonging to the same bundle. Were we to *tell* the myth, we would disregard the columns and read the rows from left to right and from top to bottom. But if we want to *understand* the myth, then we will have to disregard one half of the diachronic dimension (top to bottom) and read from left to right, column after column, each one being considered as a unit.

4.7. All the relations belonging to the same column exhibit one common feature which it is our task to unravel. For instance, all the events grouped in the first column on the left have something to do with blood relations which are over-emphasized, i.e. are subject to a more intimate treatment than they should be. Let us say, then, that the first column has as its common feature the *overrating of blood relations*. It is obvious that the second column expresses the same thing, but inverted: *underrating of blood relations*. The third column refers to monsters being slain. As to the fourth, a word of clarification is needed. The remarkable connotation of the surnames in Oedipus' father-line has often been noticed. However, linguists usually disregard it, since to them the only way to define the meaning of a term is to investigate all the contexts in which it appears, and personal names, precisely because they are used as such, are not accompanied by any context. With the method we propose to follow the objection disappears since the myth itself provides its own context. The meaningful fact is no longer to be looked for in the eventual sense of each name, but in the fact that all the names have a common feature: i.e. that they may eventually mean something and that all these hypothetical meanings (which may well remain hypothetical) exhibit a common feature, namely they refer to *difficulties to walk and to behave straight.*

4.8. What is then the relationship between the two columns on the right? Column three refers to monsters. The dragon is a chthonian being which has to be killed in order that mankind be born from the earth; the Sphinx is a monster unwilling to permit men to live. The last unit reproduces the first one which has to do with the *autochthonous origin* of mankind. Since the monsters are overcome by men, we may thus say that the common feature of the third column is *the denial of the autochthonous origin of man.*

4.9. This immediately helps us to understand the meaning of the fourth column. In mythology it is a universal character of men born from the earth that at the moment they emerge from the depth, they either cannot walk or do it clumsily. This is the case of the chthonian beings in the mythology of the Pueblo: Masauwu, who leads the emergence, and the chthonian Shumaikoli are lame ("bleeding-foot," "sore-foot"). The same happens to the Koskimo of the Kwakiutl after they have been swallowed by the chthonian monster, Tsiakish: when they returned to the surface of the earth "they limped forward or tripped sideways." Then the common feature of the fourth column is: *the persistence of the autochthonous origin of man.* It follows that column four is to column three as column one is to column two. The inability to connect two kinds of relationships is overcome (or rather replaced) by the positive statement that contradictory relationships are identical inasmuch as they are both self-contradictory in a similar way. Although this is still a provisional formulation of the structure of mythical thought, it is sufficient at this stage.

4.10. Turning back to the Oedipus myth, we may now see what it means. The myth has to do with the inability, for a culture which holds the belief that mankind is autochthonous (see, for instance, Pausanias, VIII, xxix, 4: vegetals provide a *model* for humans), to find a satisfactory transition between this theory and the knowledge that human beings are actually born from the union of man and woman. Although the problem obviously cannot be solved, the Oedipus myth provides a kind of logical tool which, to phrase it coarsely, replaces the original problem: born from one or born from two? born from different or born from same? By a correlation of this type, the overrating of blood relations is to the underrating of blood relations as the attempt to escape autochthony is to the impossibility to succeed in it. Although experience contradicts theory, social life verifies the cosmology by its similarity of structure. Hence cosmology is true.

4.11.0. Two remarks should be made at this stage.

4.11.1. In order to interpret the myth, we were able to leave aside a point which has until now worried the specialists, namely, that in the earlier (Homeric) versions of the Oedipus myth, some basic elements are lacking, such as Jocasta killing herself and Oedipus piercing his own eyes. These events do not alter the substance of the myth although they can easily be integrated, the first one as a new case of auto-destruction (column three) while the second is another case of crippledness (column four). At the same time there is something significant in these additions since the shift from foot to head is to be correlated with the shift from: autochthonous origin negated to: self-destruction.

4.11.2. Thus, our method eliminates a problem which has been so far one of the main obstacles to the progress of mythological studies, namely, the quest for the *true* version, or the *earlier* one. On the contrary, we define the myth as consisting of all its versions; to put it otherwise: a myth remains the same as long as it is felt as such. A striking example is offered by the fact that our interpretation may take into account, and is certainly applicable to, the Freudian use of the Oedipus myth. Although the Freudian problem has ceased to be that of autochthony *versus* bisexual reproduction, it is still the problem of understanding how *one* can be born from *two:* how is it that we do not have only one procreator, but a mother plus a father? Therefore, not only Sophocles, but Freud himself, should be included among the recorded versions of the Oedipus myth on a par with earlier or seemingly more "authentic" versions.

5.0. An important consequence follows. If a myth is made up of all its variants, structural analysis should take all of them into account. Thus, after analyzing all the known variants of the Theban version, we should treat the others in the same way: first, the tales about Labdacos' collateral line including Agavé, Pentheus, and Jocasta herself; the Theban variant about Lycos with Amphion and Zetos as the city founders; more remote variants concerning Dionysos (Oedipus' matrilateral cousin), and Athenian legends where Cecrops takes the place of Kadmos, etc. For each of them a similar chart should be drawn, and then compared and reorganized according to the findings: Cecrops killing the serpent with the parallel episode of Kadmos; abandonment of Dionysos with abandonment of Oedipus; "Swollen Foot" with Dionysos *loxias,* i.e. walking obliquely; Europa's quest with Antiope's; the foundation of Thebes by the Spartoi or by the brothers Amphion and Zetos; Zeus kidnapping Europa and Antiope and the same with Semele; the Theban Oedipus and the Argian Perseus, etc. We will then have several two-dimensional charts, each dealing with a variant, to be organized in a three-dimensional order

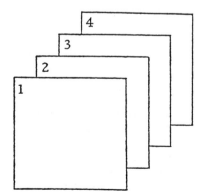

Fig. 1.

so that three different readings become possible: left to right, top to bottom, front to back. All of these charts cannot be expected to be identical; but experience shows that any difference to be observed may be correlated with other differences, so that a logical treatment of the whole will allow simplifications, the final outcome being the structural law of the myth.

5.1. One may object at this point that the task is impossible to perform since we can only work with known versions. Is it not possible that a new version might alter the picture? This is true enough if only one or two versions are available, but the objection becomes theoretical as soon as a reasonably large number has been recorded (a number which experience will progressively tell, at least as an approximation). Let us make this point clear by a comparison. If the furniture of a room and the way it is arranged in the room were known to us only through its reflection in two mirrors placed on opposite walls, we would theoretically dispose of an almost infinite number of mirror-images which would provide us with a complete knowledge. However, should the two mirrors be obliquely set, the number of mirror-images would become very small; nevertheless, four or five such images would very likely give us, if not complete information, at least a sufficient coverage so that we would feel sure that no large piece of furniture is missing in our description.

5.2. On the other hand, it cannot be too strongly emphasized that all available variants should be taken into account. If Freudian comments on the Oedipus complex are a part of the Oedipus myth, then questions such as whether Cushing's version of the Zuni origin myth should be retained or discarded become irrelevant. There is no one true version of which all the others are but copies or distortions. Every version belongs to the myth.

5.3. Finally it can be understood why works on general mythology have given discouraging results. This comes from two reasons. First, comparative mythologists have picked up preferred versions instead of using them all. Second, we have seen that the structural analysis of *one* variant of *one* myth belonging to *one* tribe (in some cases, even *one* village) already requires two dimensions. When we use several variants of the same myth for the same tribe or village, the frame of reference becomes three-dimensional and as soon as we try to enlarge the comparison, the number of dimensions required increases to such an extent that it appears quite impossible to handle them intuitively. The confusions and platitudes which are the outcome of comparative mythology can be explained by the fact that multi-dimensional frames of reference cannot be ignored, or naively replaced by two- or three-dimensional ones. Indeed, progress in comparative mythology depends largely on the cooperation of mathematicians who would undertake to express in symbols multi-dimensional relations which cannot be handled otherwise.

6.0. In order to check this theory,[3] an attempt was made in 1953-54 towards an exhaustive analysis of all the known versions of the Zuni origin and emergence myth: Cushing, 1883 and 1896; Stevenson, 1904; Parsons, 1923; Bunzel, 1932; Benedict, 1934. Furthermore, a preliminary attempt was made at a comparison of the results with similar myths in other Pueblo tribes, Western and Eastern. Finally, a test was undertaken with Plains mythology. In all cases, it was found that the theory was sound, and light was thrown, not only on North American mythology, but also on a previously unnoticed kind of logical operation, or one known only so far in a wholly

[3] Thanks are due to an unsolicited, but deeply appreciated, grant from the Ford Foundation.

different context. The bulk of material which needs to be handled almost at the beginning of the work makes it impossible to enter into details, and we will have to limit ourselves here to a few illustrations.

6.1. An over-simplified chart of the Zuni emergence myth would read as follows:

INCREASE			DEATH
mechanical growth of vegetals (used as ladders)	emergence led by Beloved Twins	sibling incest	gods kill children
food value of wild plants	migration led by the two Newekwe		magical contest with people of the dew (collecting wild food *versus* cultivation)
		sibling sacrificed (to gain victory)	
food value of cultivated plants		sibling adopted (in exchange for corn)	
periodical character of agricultural work			
hunting	war led by two war-gods		war against Kyanakwe (gardeners *versus* hunters)
warfare			salvation of the tribe (center of the world found)
		sibling sacrificed (to avoid flood)	

DEATH	PERMANENCY

6.2. As may be seen from a global inspection of the chart, the basic problem consists in discovering a mediation between life and death. For the Pueblo, the problem is especially difficult since they understand the origin of human life on the model of vegetal life (emergence from the earth). They share that belief with the ancient Greeks, and it is not without reason that we chose the Oedipus myth as our first example. But in the American case, the highest form of vegetal life is to be found in agriculture which is periodical in nature, i.e. which consists in an alternation between life and death. If this is disregarded, the contradiction surges at another place: agriculture provides food, therefore life; but hunting provides food and is similar to warfare which means death. Hence there are three different ways of handling the problem. In the Cushing version, the difficulty revolves around an opposition between activities yielding an immediate result (collecting wild food) and activities yielding a delayed result—death has to become integrated so that agriculture can exist. Parsons' version goes from hunting to agriculture, while Stevenson's version operates the other way around. It can be shown that all the differences between these versions can be rigorously correlated with these basic structures. For instance:

	CUSHING	PARSONS	STEVENSON
Gods ⎱ Kyanakwe ⎰	allied, use fiber strings on their bows (gardeners)	Kyanakwe alone, use fiber string	Gods ⎱ Men ⎰ allied, use fiber string

	VICTORIOUS OVER	VICTORIOUS OVER	VICTORIOUS OVER
Men	alone, use sinew (hunters) (until men shift to fiber)	Gods ⎱ Men ⎰ allied, use sinew string	Kyanakwe alone, use sinew string

Since fiber strings (vegetal) are always superior to sinew strings (animal) and since (to a lesser extent) the gods' alliance is preferable to their antagonism, it follows that in Cushing's version, men begin to be doubly underprivileged (hostile gods, sinew string); in Stevenson, doubly privileged (friendly gods, fiber string); while Parsons' version confronts us with an intermediary situation (friendly gods, but sinew strings since men begin by being hunters). Hence:

	CUSHING	PARSONS	STEVENSON
gods/men	−	+	+
fiber/sinew	−	−	+

6.3. Bunzel's version is from a structural point of view of the same type as Cushing's. However, it differs from both Cushing's and Stevenson's inasmuch as the latter two explain the emergence as a result of man's need to evade his pitiful condition, while Bunzel's version makes it the consequence of a call from the higher powers —hence the inverted sequences of the means resorted to for the emergence: in both Cushing and Stevenson, they go from plants to animals; in Bunzel, from mammals to insects and from insects to plants.

6.4. Among the Western Pueblo the logical approach always remains the same; the starting point and the point of arrival are the simplest ones and ambiguity is met with halfway:

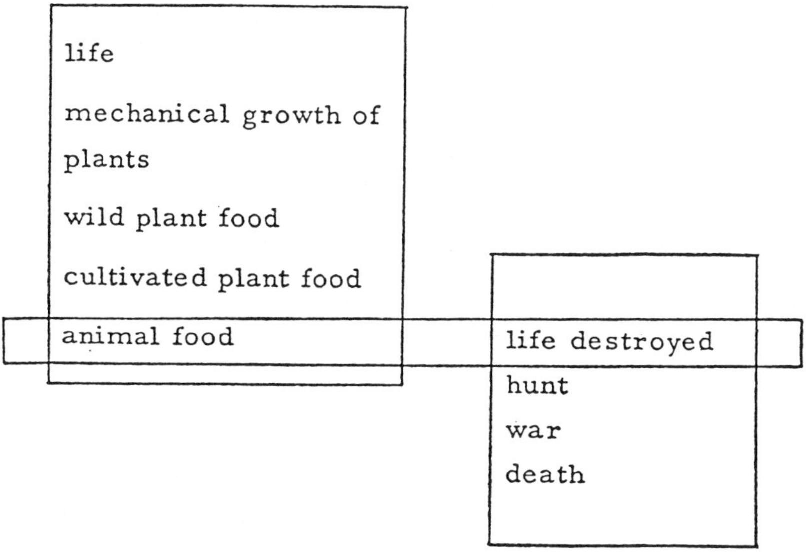

Fig. 2.

The fact that contradiction appears in the middle of the dialectical process has as its result the production of a double series of dioscuric pairs the purpose of which is to operate a mediation between conflicting terms:

1. 3 divine messengers 2 ceremonial clowns   2 war-gods

2. homogeneous pair: siblings (brother   couple (hus-   heterogeneous pair:
   dioscurs (2 brothers) and sister)   band and wife) grandmother/grandchild

which consists in combinatory variants of the same function; (hence the war attribute of the clowns which has given rise to so many queries).

6.5. Some Central and Eastern Pueblos proceed the other way around. They begin by stating the identity of hunting and cultivation (first corn obtained by Game-Father sowing deer-dewclaws), and they try to derive both life and death from that central notion. Then, instead of extreme terms being simple and intermediary ones duplicated as among the Western groups, the extreme terms become duplicated (i.e., the two sisters of the Eastern Pueblo) while a simple mediating term comes to the foreground (for instance, the Poshaiyanne of the Zia), but endowed with equivocal attributes. Hence the attributes of this "messiah" can be deduced from the place it occupies in the time sequence: good when at the beginning (Zuni, Cushing), equivocal in the middle (Central Pueblo), bad at the end (Zia), except in Bunzel where the sequence is reversed as has been shown.

6.6. By using systematically this kind of structural analysis it becomes possible to organize all the known variants of a myth as a series forming a kind of permutation group, the two variants placed at the far-ends being in a symmetrical, though inverted, relationship to each other.

7.0. Our method not only has the advantage of bringing some kind of order to what was previously chaos; it also enables us to perceive some basic logical processes which are at the root of mythical thought. Three main processes should be distinguished.

7.1.0. The trickster of American mythology has remained so far a problematic figure. Why is it that throughout North America his part is assigned practically everywhere to either coyote or raven? If we keep in mind that mythical thought always works from the awareness of oppositions towards their progressive mediation, the reason for those choices becomes clearer. We need only to assume that two opposite terms with no intermediary always tend to be replaced by two equivalent terms which allow a third one as a mediator; then one of the polar terms and the mediator becomes replaced by a new triad and so on. Thus we have:

INITIAL PAIR	FIRST TRIAD	SECOND TRIAD
Life		
	Agriculture	
		Herbivorous animals
		Carrion-eating animals (raven; coyote)
	Hunt	
		Prey animals
	War	
Death		

With the unformulated argument: carrion-eating animals are like prey animals (they eat animal food), but they are also like food-plant producers (they do not kill what they eat). Or, to put it otherwise, Pueblo style: ravens are to gardens as prey animals are to herbivorous ones. But it is also clear that herbivorous animals may be called first to act as mediators on the assumption that they are like collectors and gatherers (vegetal-food eaters) while they can be used as animal food though not themselves hunters. Thus we may have mediators of the first order, of the second order, and so on, where each term gives birth to the next by a double process of opposition and correlation.

7.1.1. This kind of process can be followed in the mythology of the Plains where we may order the data according to the sequence:

Unsuccessful mediator between earth and sky
(Star husband's wife)

Heterogeneous pair of mediators
(grandmother/grandchild)

Semi-homogeneous pair of mediators
(Lodge-Boy and Thrown-away)

While among the Pueblo we have:

> Successful mediator between earth and sky
> (Poshaiyanki)
>
> Semi-homogeneous pair of mediators
> (Uyuyewi and Matsailema)
>
> Homogeneous pair of mediators
> (the Ahaiyuta)

7.1.2. On the other hand, correlations may appear on a transversal axis; (this is true even on the linguistic level; see the manifold connotation of the root *pose* in Tewa according to Parsons: coyote, mist, scalp, etc.). Coyote is intermediary between herbivorous and carnivorous in the same way as mist between sky and earth; scalp between war and hunt (scalp is war-crop); corn smut between wild plants and cultivated plants; garments between "nature" and "culture"; refuse between village and outside; ashes between roof and hearth (chimney). This string of mediators, if one may call them so, not only throws light on whole pieces of North American mythology—why the Dew-God may be at the same time the Game-Master and the giver of raiments and be personified as an "Ash-Boy"; or why the scalps are mist producing; or why the Game-Mother is associated with corn smut; etc.—but it also probably corresponds to a universal way of organizing daily experience. See, for instance, the French for vegetal smut; *nielle,* from Latin *nebula;* the luck-bringing power attributed to refuse (old shoe) and ashes (kissing chimney-sweepers); and compare the American Ash-Boy cycle with the Indo-European Cinderella: both phallic figures (mediator between male and female); master of the dew and of the game; owners of fine raiments; and social bridges (low class marrying into high class); though impossible to interpret through recent diffusion as has been sometimes contended since Ash-Boy and Cinderella are symmetrical but inverted in every detail (while the borrowed Cinderella tale in America—Zuni Turkey-Girl—is parallel to the prototype):

	EUROPE	AMERICA
Sex	female	male
Family Status	double family	no family
Appearance	pretty girl	ugly boy
Sentimental status	nobody likes her	in hopeless love with girl
Transformation	luxuriously clothed with supernatural help	stripped of ugliness with supernatural help

etc.

7.2.0. Thus, the mediating function of the trickster explains that since its position is halfway between two polar terms he must retain something of that duality, namely an ambiguous and equivocal character. But the trickster figure is not the only conceivable form of mediation; some myths seem to devote themselves to the task of exhausting all the possible solutions to the problem of bridging the gap between *two* and *one*. For instance, a comparison between all the variants of the Zuni emergence myth provides us with a series of mediating devices, each of which creates the next one by a process of opposition and correlation:

$$\text{messiah} > \text{dioscurs} > \text{trickster} > \frac{\text{bisexual}}{\text{being}} > \frac{\text{sibling}}{\text{pair}} > \frac{\text{married}}{\text{couple}} > \frac{\text{grandmother-}}{\text{grandchild}} > \frac{\text{4 terms}}{\text{group}} > \text{triad}$$

In Cushing's version, this dialectic is accompanied by a change from the space dimension (mediating between sky and earth) to the time dimension (mediating between summer and winter, i.e., between birth and death). But while the shift is being made from space to time, the final solution (triad) re-introduces space, since a triad consists in a dioscur pair *plus* a messiah simultaneously present; and while the point of departure was ostensibly formulated in terms of a space referent (sky and earth) this was nevertheless implicitly conceived in terms of a time referent (first the messiah calls; *then* the dioscurs descend). Therefore the logic of myth confronts us with a double, reciprocal exchange of functions to which we shall return shortly (7.3.).

7.2.1. Not only can we account for the ambiguous character of the trickster, but we may also understand another property of mythical figures the world over, namely, that the same god may be endowed with contradictory attributes; for instance, he may be *good* and *bad* at the same time. If we compare the variants of the Hopi myth of the origin of Shalako, we may order them so that the following structure becomes apparent:

$$(\text{Masauwu}: x) \simeq (\text{Muyingwu}: \text{Masauwu}) \simeq (\text{Shalako}: \text{Muyingwu}) \simeq (y: \text{Masauwu})$$

where x and y represent arbitrary values corresponding to the fact that in the two "extreme" variants the god Masauwu, while appearing alone instead of associated with another god, as in variant two, or being absent, as in three, still retains intrinsically a relative value. In variant one, Masauwu (alone) is depicted as helpful to mankind (though not as helpful as he could be), and in version four, harmful to mankind (though not as harmful as he could be); whereas in two, Muyingwu is relatively more helpful than Masauwu, and in three, Shalako more helpful than Muyingwu. We find an identical series when ordering the Keresan variants:

$$(\text{Poshaiyanki}: x) \simeq (\text{Lea}: \text{Poshaiyanki}) \simeq (\text{Poshaiyanki}: \text{Tiamoni}) \simeq (y: \text{Poshaiyanki})$$

7.2.2. This logical framework is particularly interesting since sociologists are already acquainted with it on two other levels: first, with the problem of the pecking order among hens; and second, it also corresponds to what this writer has called *general exchange* in the field of kinship. By recognizing it also on the level of mythical thought, we may find ourselves in a better position to appraise its basic importance in sociological studies and to give it a more inclusive theoretical interpretation.

7.3.0. Finally, when we have succeeded in organizing a whole series of variants in a kind of permutation group, we are in a position to formulate the law of that group. Although it is not possible at the present stage to come closer than an approximate formulation which will certainly need to be made more accurate in the future, it seems that every myth (considered as the collection of all its variants) corresponds to a formula of the following type:

$$f_x(a) : f_y(b) \simeq f_x(b) : f_{a-1}(y)$$

where, two terms being given as well as two functions of these terms, it is stated that a relation of equivalence still exists between two situations when terms and relations are inverted, under two conditions: 1. that one term be replaced by its contrary; 2. that an inversion be made between the *function* and the *term* value of two elements.

7.3.1. This formula becomes highly significant when we recall that Freud considered that *two traumas* (and not one as it is so commonly said) are necessary in order to give birth to this individual myth in which a neurosis consists. By trying to apply the formula to the analysis of those traumatisms (and assuming that they correspond to conditions 1. and 2. respectively) we should not only be able to improve it, but would find ourselves in the much desired position of developing side by side the sociological and the psychological aspects of the theory; we may also take it to the laboratory and subject it to experimental verification.

8.0. At this point it seems unfortunate that, with the limited means at the disposal of French anthropological research, no further advance can be made. It should be emphasized that the task of analyzing mythological literature, which is extremely bulky, and of breaking it down into its constituent units, requires team work and secretarial help. A variant of average length needs several hundred cards to be properly analyzed. To discover a suitable pattern of rows and columns for those cards, special devices are needed, consisting of vertical boards about two meters long and one and one-half meters high, where cards can be pigeon-holed and moved at will; in order to build up three-dimensional models enabling one to compare the variants, several such boards are necessary, and this in turn requires a spacious workshop, a kind of commodity particularly unavailable in Western Europe nowadays. Furthermore, as soon as the frame of reference becomes multi-dimensional (which occurs at an early stage, as has been shown in 5.3.) the board-system has to be replaced by perforated cards which in turn require I.B.M. equipment, etc. Since there is little hope that such facilities will become available in France in the near future, it is much desired that some American group, better equipped than we are here in Paris, will be induced by this paper to start a project of its own in structural mythology.

8.1.0. Three final remarks may serve as conclusion.

8.1.1. First, the question has often been raised why myths, and more generally oral literature, are so much addicted to duplication, triplication or quadruplication of the same sequence. If our hypotheses are accepted, the answer is obvious: repetition has as its function to make the structure of the myth apparent. For we have seen that the synchro-diachronical structure of the myth permits us to organize it into diachronical sequences (the rows in our tables) which should be read synchronically (the columns). Thus, a myth exhibits a "slated" structure which seeps to the surface, if one may say so, through the repetition process.

8.1.2. However, the slates are not absolutely identical to each other. And since the purpose of myth is to provide a logical model capable of overcoming a contradiction (an impossible achievement if, as it happens, the contradiction is real), a theoretically infinite number of slates will be generated, each one slightly different from the others. Thus, myth grows spiral-wise until the intellectual impulse which has originated it is exhausted. Its growth is a continuous process whereas its structure remains discontinuous. If this is the case we should consider that it closely corresponds, in the realm of the spoken word, to the kind of being a crystal is in the realm of physical matter.

This analogy may help us understand better the relationship of myth on one hand to both *langue* and *parole* on the other.

8.1.3. Prevalent attempts to explain alleged differences between the so-called "primitive" mind and scientific thought have resorted to qualitative differences between the working processes of the mind in both cases while assuming that the objects to which they were applying themselves remained very much the same. If our interpretation is correct, we are led toward a completely different view, namely, that the kind of logic which is used by mythical thought is as rigorous as that of modern science, and that the difference lies not in the quality of the intellectual process, but in the nature of the things to which it is applied. This is well in agreement with the situation known to prevail in the field of technology: what makes a steel ax superior to a stone one is not that the first one is better made than the second. They are equally well made, but steel is a different thing than stone. In the same way we may be able to show that the same logical processes are put to use in myth as in science, and that man has always been thinking equally well; the improvement lies, not in an alleged progress of man's conscience, but in the discovery of new things to which it may apply its unchangeable abilities.

École Pratique des Hautes Études, Sorbonne
Paris, France

Claude Lévi-Strauss

The Story of Asdiwal

Since 1963 Lévi-Strauss and his associates have published a variety of 'structural analyses' of myth, but prior to the appearance of Le Cru et le cuit *in the autumn of 1964 'La Geste d'Asdiwal' was, by general consent, the most successful of all these pieces. 'Asdiwal' has twice appeared in French, but this is the first English translation. The Editor is deeply indebted to Professor Lévi-Strauss for granting permission to publish the translation and to Mr Nicholas Mann for making it.*

I

This study of a native myth from the Pacific coast of Canada has two aims. First, to isolate and compare the *various levels* on which the myth evolves: geographic, economic, sociological, and cosmological – each one of these levels, together with the symbolism proper to it, being seen as a transformation of an underlying logical structure common to all of them. And, second, to compare the *different versions* of the myth and to look for the meaning of the discrepancies between them, or between some of them; for, since they all come from the same people (but are recorded in different parts of their territory), these variations cannot be explained in terms of dissimilar beliefs, languages, or institutions.

The story of Asdiwal, which comes from the Tsimshian Indians, is known to us in four versions, collected some sixty years ago by Franz Boas (1895; 1902; 1912; 1916).

We shall begin by calling attention to certain facts which must be known if the myth is to be understood.

The Tsimshian Indians, with the Tlingit and the Haida, belong to the northern group of cultures on the Northwest Pacific coast. They live in British Columbia, immediately south of Alaska, in a region which embraces the basins of the Nass and Skeena Rivers, the coastal region stretching between their

1

135

estuaries, and, further inland, the land drained by the two rivers and their tributaries. The Nass in the North and the Skeena in the south both flow in a northeast-southwesterly direction, and are approximately parallel. The Nass, however, is slightly nearer North-South in orientation, a detail which, as we shall see, is not entirely devoid of importance.

This territory was divided between three local groups, distinguished by their different dialects: in the upper reaches of the Skeena, the Gitskan; in the lower reaches and the coastal region, the Tsimshian themselves; and in the valleys of the Nass and its tributaries, the Nisqa. Three of the versions of the myth of Asdiwal were recorded on the coast and in Tsimshian dialect (Boas, 1895, pp. 285-288; 1912, pp. 71-146; 1916, pp. 243-245 and the comparative analysis, pp. 792-824), the fourth at the mouth of the Nass, in Nisqa dialect (Boas, 1902, pp. 225-228). It is this last which, when compared with the other three, reveals the most marked differences.

Like all the peoples on the Northwest Pacific Coast, the Tsimshian had no agriculture. During the summer, the women's work was to collect fruit, berries, plants, and wild roots, while the men hunted bears and goats in the mountains and seals and sea-lions on the coastal reefs. They also practised deep-sea fishery, catching mainly cod and halibut, but also herring nearer the shore. It was, however, the complex rhythm of river-fishing that made the deepest impression upon the life of the tribe. Whereas the Nisqa were relatively settled, the Tsimshian moved, according to the seasons, between their winter villages, which were situated in the coastal region, and their fishing-places, either on the Nass or the Skeena.

At the end of the winter, when stores of smoked fish, dried meat, fat, and preserved fruits were running low, or were even completely exhausted, the natives would undergo periods of severe famine, an echo of which is found in the myth. At such times they anxiously awaited the arrival of the candlefish[1] which would go up the Nass (which was still frozen to start with) for a period of about six weeks in order to spawn (Goddard, 1934, p. 68). This would begin about 1 March, and the entire Skeena population would travel along the coast in boats as far as the Nass in order to take up position on the fishing-grounds,

2

which were family properties. The period from 15 February to 15 March was called, not without reason, the 'Month when Candlefish is Eaten' and that which followed, from 15 March to 15 April, the 'Month when Candlefish is Cooked' (to extract its oil). This operation was strictly taboo to men, whereas the women were obliged to use their naked breasts to press the fish; the oil-cake residue had to be left to become rotten from maggots and putrefaction and, despite the pestilential stench, it had to be left in the immediate vicinity of the dwelling-houses until the work was finished (Boas, 1916, pp. 398-399 and 44-45).

Then everyone would return by the same route to the Skeena for the second major event, which was the arrival of the salmon fished in June and July (the 'Salmon Months'). Once the fish was smoked and stored away for the year, the families would go up to the mountains, where the men would hunt while the women laid up stocks of fruit and berries. With the coming of the frost in the ritual 'Month of the Spinning Tops' (which were spun on the ice), people settled down in permanent villages for the winter. During this period the men used sometimes to go off hunting again for a few days or a few weeks. Finally, towards 15 November, came the 'Taboo Month', which marked the inauguration of the great winter ceremonies, in preparation for which the men were subjected to various restrictions.

Let us remember, too, that the Tsimshian were divided into four non-localized matrilineal clans, which were strictly exogamous and divided into lineages, descent lines, and households: the Eagles, the Ravens, the Wolves, and the Bears, also, that the permanent villages were the seat of chiefdoms (generally called 'tribes' by native informants); and finally that Tsimshian society was divided into (three) hereditary castes with bilateral inheritance of caste status (each individual was supposed to marry according to his rank): the 'Real People' or reigning familes, the 'Nobles', and the 'People', which last comprised all those who (failing a purchase of rank by generous potlatches) were unable to assert an equal degree of nobility in both lines of their descent (Boas 1916, pp. 478-514; Garfield, 1939, pp. 173-174 and 177-178; Garfield, Wingert & Barbeau, 1951, pp. 1-34).

3

II

Now follows a summary of the story of Asdiwal taken from Boas (1912) which will serve as a point of reference. This version was recorded on the coast at Port Simpson in Tsimshian dialect. Boas published the native text together with an English translation.

Famine reigns in the Skeena valley; the river is frozen and it is winter. A mother and her daughter, both of whose husbands have died of hunger, both remember independently the happy times when they lived together and there was no dearth of food. Released by the death of their husbands, they simultaneously decide to meet and set off at the same moment. Since the mother lives down-river and the daughter up-river, the former goes eastwards and the latter westwards. They both travel on the frozen bed of the Skeena and meet half-way.

Weeping with hunger and sorrow, the two women pitch camp on the bank at the foot of a tree, not far from which they find, poor pittance that it is, a rotten berry, which they sadly share.

During the night, a stranger visits the young widow. It is soon learned that his name is Hatsenas,[2] a term which means, in Tsimshian, a bird of good omen. Thanks to him, the women start to find food regularly, and the younger of the two becomes the wife of their mysterious protector and soon gives birth to a son, Asdiwal (Asiwa, Boas, 1895; Asi-hwil, Boas, 1902).[3] His father speeds up his growth by supernatural means and gives him various magic objects: a bow and arrows which never miss for hunting, a quiver, a lance, a basket, snow-shoes, a bark raincoat, and a hat, all of which will enable the hero to overcome all obstacles, make himself invisible, and procure an inexhaustible supply of food. Hatsenas then disappears and the elder of the two women dies.

Asdiwal and his mother pursue their course westwards and settle down in her native village, Gitsalasert, in the Skeena Canyon (Boas, 1912, p. 83). One day a white she-bear comes down the valley.

Hunted by Asdiwal, who almost catches it thanks to his

4

magic objects, the bear starts to climb up a vertical ladder. Asdiwal follows it up to the heavens, which he sees as a vast prairie, covered with grass and all kinds of flowers. The bear lures him into the home of its father, the sun, and reveals itself to be a beautiful girl, Evening-Star. The marriage takes place, though not before the Sun has submitted Asdiwal to a series of trials, to which all previous suitors had succumbed (hunting wild goat in mountains which are rent by earthquakes; drawing water from a spring in a cave whose walls close in on each other; collecting wood from a tree which crushes those who try to cut it down; a period in a fiery furnace). But Asdiwal overcomes them all thanks to his magic objects and the timely intervention of his father. Won over by his son-in-law's talents, the Sun finally approves of him.

Asdiwal, however, pines for his mother. The Sun agrees to allow him to go down to earth again with his wife, and gives them, as provisions for the journey, four baskets filled with inexhaustible supplies of food, which earn the couple a grateful welcome from the villagers, who are in the midst of their winter famine.

In spite of repeated warnings from his wife, Asdiwal deceives her with a woman from his village. Evening-Star, offended, departs, followed by her tearful husband. Half-way up to heaven, Asdiwal is struck down by a look from his wife, who disappears. He dies, but is at once regretted and is brought back to life by his celestial father-in-law.

For a time, all goes well; then, once again, Asdiwal feels a twinge of nostalgia for earth. His wife agrees to accompany him as far as the earth, and there bids him a final farewell. Returning to his village, the hero learns of his mother's death. Nothing remains to hold him back, and he sets off again on his journey downstream.

When he reaches the Tsimshian village of Ginaxangioget, he seduces and marries the daughter of the local chief. To start with, the marriage is a happy one, and Asdiwal joins his four brothers-in-law on wild goat hunts, which, thanks to his magic objects, are crowned with success. When spring approaches, the whole family moves house, staying first at Metlakatla, and then setting off by boat for the river Nass,

5

going up along the coast. A head wind forces them to a halt and they camp for a while at Ksemaksén. There, things go wrong because of a dispute between Asdiwal and his brothers-in-law over the respective merits of mountain-hunters and sea-hunters. A competition takes place – Asdiwal returns from the mountains with four bears that he has killed, while the brothers-in-law return empty-handed from their sea expedition. Humiliated and enraged, they break camp, and, taking their sister with them, abandon Asdiwal.

He is picked up by strangers coming from Gitxatla, who are also on their way to the Nass for the candlefish season.

As in the previous case, they are a group of four brothers and a sister, whom Asdiwal wastes no time in marrying. They soon arrive together at the River Nass, where they sell large quantities of fresh meat and salmon to the Tsimshian, who have already settled there and are starving.

Since the catch that year is a good one, everyone goes home: the Tsimshian to their capital at Metlakatla and the Gitxatla to their town Laxalan, where Asdiwal, by this time rich and famous, has a son. One winter's day, he boasts that he can hunt sea-lions better than his brothers-in-law. They set out to sea together. Thanks to his magic objects, Asdiwal has a miraculously successful hunt on a reef, but is left there without food or fire by his angry brothers-in-law. A storm gets up and waves sweep over the rock. With the help of his father, who appears in time to save him, Asdiwal, transformed into a bird, succeeds in keeping himself above the waves, using his magic objects as a perch.

After two days and two nights the storm is calmed, and Asdiwal falls asleep exhausted. A mouse wakes him and leads him to the subterranean home of the sea-lions whom he has wounded, but who imagine (since Asdiwal's arrows are invisible to them) that they are victims of an epidemic. Asdiwal extracts the arrows and cures his hosts, whom he asks, in return, to guarantee his safe return. Unfortunately, the sea-lions' boats, which are made of their stomachs, are out of use, pierced by the hunter's arrows. The king of the sea-lions therefore lends Asdiwal his own stomach as a canoe and instructs him to send it back without delay. When he reaches

6

land, the hero discovers his wife, and his son alike, inconsolable. Thanks to the help of this good wife, but bad sister (for she carries out the rites which are essential to the success of the operation), Asdiwal makes killer-whales out of carved wood and brings them to life. They break open the boats with their fins and bring about the shipwreck and death of the wicked brothers-in-law.

But once again Asdiwal feels an irrepressible desire to revisit the scenes of his childhood. He leaves his wife and returns to the Skeena valley. He settles in the town of Ginadâos, where he is joined by his son, to whom he gives his magic bow and arrows, and from whom he receives a dog in return.

When winter comes, Asdiwal goes off to the mountains to hunt, but forgets his snow-shoes. Lost, and unable to go either up or down without them, he is turned to stone with his lance and his dog, and they can still be seen in that form at the peak of the great mountain by the lake of Ginadâos (Boas, 1912, pp. 71-146).

III

Let us keep provisionally to this version alone in order to attempt to define the essential points of its structure. The narrative refers to facts of various orders. First, the physical and political geography of the Tsimshian country, since the places and towns mentioned really do exist. Second, the economic life of the natives which, as we have seen, governs the great seasonal migrations between the Skeena and Nass Valleys, and during the course of which Asdiwal's adventures take place. Third, the social and family organization, for we witness several marriages, divorces, widowhoods, and other connected events. Lastly, the cosmology, for, unlike the others, two of Asdiwal's visits, one to heaven and the other below the earth, are of a mythological and not of an experiential order.

First of all, the geographical framework.

The story begins in the Skeena valley, when the two heroines leave their villages, one upstream, the other downstream, and meet half-way. In the version that Boas recorded at the Nass

7

estuary (1902) it is stated that the meeting-place, this time on the Nass, is called Hwil-lê-ne-hwada, 'Where-they-met-each-other' (Boas, 1902, p. 225).

After her mother's death, the young woman and her son settle in her native village (i.e. her father's, where her mother had lived from the time of her marriage until her husband's death): the downstream village. It is from there that the visit to heaven takes place. This village, called Gitsalasert, 'People of the (Skeena) Canyon', is situated not far from the modern town of Usk (Garfield, 1939, p. 175; Boas, 1912, pp. 71, 276). Although the Tsimshian dialect was spoken there, it was outside the 'nine towns' which strictly speaking formed the Tsimshian province (Boas, 1912, p. 225).

On his mother's death, Asdiwal continues his journey downstream, that is to say, westwards. He settles in the town of Ginaxangioget, where he marries. This is in proper Tsimshian country on the lower reaches of the Skeena. Ginaxangioget is in fact a term formed from the root of git = 'people' and $gi.k$ = 'hemlock tree' from which comes $Ginax$-$angi.k$ 'the people of the firs' (Garfield, 1939, p. 175). And Ginaxangioget was one of the nine principal towns of the Tsimshian (Boas, 1916, pp. 482-483; Swanton, 1952, p. 606, gives 'Kinagingeet, near Metlakatla').

When Asdiwal leaves with his in-laws for the Nass to fish candlefish there, they go first by the Skeena estuary, then take to the sea, and stop at the capital city of the Tsimshian, Metlakatla – a recent town of the same name, founded by natives converted to Christianity, is to be found on Annette Island in Alaska (Beynon, 1941; Garfield, Wingert & Barbeau, 1951, pp. 33-34).

Old Metlakatla is on the coast, north of Prince Rupert and half-way between the Skeena and Nass estuaries. Ksemaksén, where the first quarrel takes place, and where Asdiwal is first abandoned by his brothers-in-law, is also on the coast, a little further north.

The Tsimshian-speaking tribe called Gitxatla, which is independent of those centres around Metlakatla, is a group of islanders living on Dolphin Island, south of the Skeena Estuary. Their name comes from git 'people' and $qxatla$ 'channel' (Garfield, 1939, p. 175. Also Boas, 1916, 483. Swanton, 1952,

8

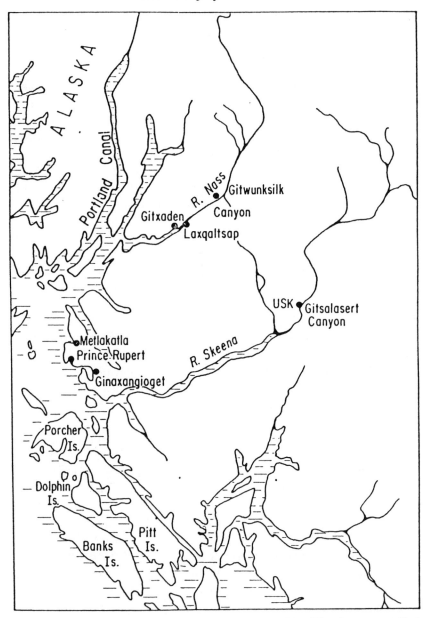

p. 607, gives 'Kitkatla, on Porcher Island'). Having travelled
from East to West, Asdiwal accompanies them to the Nass,
that is to say in a South-North direction, then in the opposite

9

143

direction, to 'their town', off-shore from which (and probably to the West, since it was a deep-sea expedition) the visit to the sea-lions takes place.

From there, Asdiwal returns to the Skeena, that is to say this time from West to East. The story ends at Ginadâos, Ginadoiks perhaps, from *git* 'people', *na* 'of', *doiks* 'rapid current'; the name of a torrent which flows into the Skeena (Garfield, 1939, p. 176; cf. also Boas, 1912, p. 223: Ginadâiks, 'one of the nine towns of the Tsimshian').

Let us now consider the economic aspect. The activities of this order which are brought to notice by the myth are no less real than the geographical places and the populations evoked in the preceding paragraphs. Everything begins with a period of winter famine such as was well known to the natives in the period between mid-December and mid-January, before the moment at which, theoretically, the spring salmon arrived, which was just before the arrival of the candlefish; the period called 'the Interval' (Boas, 1916, pp. 398-399). After his visit to the heavens, Asdiwal takes part in the spring migrations to the Nass for the candlefish season; then we are told of the return of the families to the Skeena in the salmon season.

These seasonal variations – to use Marcel Mauss's expression – are on a par with other differences none the less real which are emphasized by the myth, notably that between the land-hunter (personified by Asdiwal, born on the river and upstream, that is to say inland) and the sea-hunter, personified first by the People of the Firs who live downstream on the estuary, and then, still more clearly, by the inhabitants of Dolphin Island.

When we move on to the sociological aspects, there is a much greater freedom of interpretation. It is not a question of an accurate documentary picture of the reality of native life, but a sort of counterpoint which seems sometimes to be in harmony with this reality, and sometimes to part from it in order to rejoin it again.

The initial sequence of events evokes clearly defined sociological conditions. The mother and daughter have been separated by the latter's marriage, and since that time each has lived

10

with her own husband in his village. The elder woman's husband was also the father of the younger woman, who thus left her native village to follow her own husband upstream. We can recognize this as a society where, although there is a system of matrilineal filiation, residence is patrilocal, the wife going to live in her husband's village; and where the children, although they belong to their mother's clan, are brought up in their father's home and not in that of their maternal kin.

Such was the (real) situation among the Tsimshian. Boas emphasizes it several times: 'In olden times it was customary for a great chief to take a princess from each tribe to be his wife. Some had as many as sixteen or eighteen wives . . .' which would clearly be impossible if a man had to live in his wife's native village. More generally, says Boas: 'There is ample evidence showing that the young married people lived with the young man's parents', so that 'the children grew up in their father's home' (Boas, 1916, pp. 355, 529, 426; cf. also pp. 420, 427, 441, 499-500).

But, in the myth, this patrilocal type of residence is quickly undermined by famine, which frees the two women from their respective obligations and allows them, upon the death of their husbands, to meet (significantly enough) half-way. Their camping at the foot of the tree on the bank of the frozen river, equidistant from up-river and down-river, presents a picture of a matrilocal type of residence reduced to its simplest form, since the new household consists only of a mother and her daughter.

This reversal, which is barely hinted at, is all the more remarkable because all the subsequent marriages (in the myth) are going to be matrilocal, and thus contrary to the type found in reality.

First, Hatsenas's marriage with the younger woman. Fleeting though this union between a human being and a supernatural being may be, the husband still lives in his wife's home, and therefore in her mother's home. The matrilocal trend is even more apparent in the version recorded on the Nass. When his son Asi-hwil has grown up, Hatsenas (who here is called Hôux) says to his wife: 'Your brothers are coming to look for you. Therefore I must hide in the woods.' A short time after he had left, the brothers came, and left again the following morning,

11

laden with supplies of meat given to the women by their protector:

> 'As soon as they left, Hôux returned. The [women] told him that their brothers had asked them to return home. Then Hôux said "Let us part. You may return to your home; I will return to mine." On the following morning many people came to fetch the women and the boy. They took them to Gitxaden. The boy's uncles gave a feast and his mother told them the boy's name, Asi-hwil . . .' (Boas, 1902, p. 227).

Not only does the husband seem an intruder, regarded with suspicion by his brothers-in-law, and afraid that they might attack him, but, contrary to what (really) happens among the Tsimshian and in other societies characterized by the association of matrilineal filiation and patrilocal residence (Boas, 1916, p. 423; Malinowski, 1932), the food gifts go from the sister's husband to the wife's brothers.

Matrilocal marriage, accompanied by antagonism between the husband and his in-laws, is further illustrated by Asdiwal's marriage to Evening-Star; they live in her father's home, and the father-in-law shows so much hostility towards his son-in-law that he sets him trials which are deemed to be fatal.

Matrilocal, too, is Asdiwal's second marriage in the land of the People of the Firs, which is accompanied by hostility between the husband and his brothers-in-law because they abandon him and persuade their sister to follow them.

The same theme is expressed in the third marriage in the land of the People of the Channel, at any rate to start with. For after Asdiwal's visit to the sea-lions the situation is reversed: Asdiwal recovers his wife, who had refused to follow her brothers, and was wandering in search of her husband. What is more, she collaborates with him to produce the 'machination' – in the literal and the figurative sense – by means of which he takes revenge on his brothers-in-law. Finally, patrilocality triumphs when Asdiwal abandons his wife (whereas, in the previous marriages, it had been his wife who had abandoned him) and returns to the Skeena where he was born, and where his son comes alone to join him. Thus having begun with the

12

story of the *reunion of a mother and her daughter*, freed from their affines or *paternal kin*, the myth ends with the story of the *reunion of a father and his son*, freed from their affines or *maternal kin*.

But if the initial and final sequences in the myth constitute from a sociological point of view a pair of oppositions, the same is true, from a cosmological point of view, of the two supernatural voyages which interrupt the hero's 'real' journey. The first voyage takes him to the heavens, and into the home of the Sun, who first tries to kill him and then agrees to bring him back to life. The second takes Asdiwal to the subterranean kingdom of the sea-lions, whom he has himself killed or wounded, but whom he agrees to look after and to cure. The first voyage results in a marriage which, as we have seen, is matrilocal, and which, moreover, bears witness to a maximal exogamous separation (between an earth-born man and a woman from heaven). But this marriage will be broken up by Asdiwal's infidelity with a woman of his own village, which may be seen as a suggestion of a marriage which, if it really took place, would, so to speak, neutralize matri-locality (since husband and wife would come from the same place) and would be characterized by an endogamous proximity which would also be maximal (marriage within the village). It is true that the hero's second supernatural voyage, to the subterranean kingdom of the sea-lions, does not lead to a marriage, but in any case, as has already been shown, this visit brings about a reversal in the matrilocal tendency of Asdiwal's successive marriages, for it separates his third wife from her brothers, the hero himself from his wife, their son from his mother, and leaves only one relationship in existence: that between the father and his son.

IV

In this analysis of the myth, we have distinguished four levels: the geographic, the techno-economic, the sociological, and the cosmological. The first two are exact transcriptions of reality; the fourth has nothing to do with it, and in the third, real and imaginary institutions are interwoven. Yet in spite of these differences, the levels cannot be separated out by the native

13

mind. It is rather that everything happens as if the levels were provided with different codes, each being used according to the needs of the moment, and according to its particular capacity, to transmit the same message. It is the nature of this message that we shall now consider.

Winter famines are a recurrent event in the economic life of the Tsimshian. But the famine which starts the story off is also a cosmological theme. All along the Northwest Pacific Coast, in fact, the present state of the universe is attributed to the havoc wrought in the original order by the demiurge Giant or Raven (Txamsen, in Tsimshian) during travels which he undertook in order to satisfy his irrepressible voracity. Thus Txamsem is perpetually in a state of famine, and famine, although a negative condition, is seen as the *'primum movens'* of Creation.[4] In this sense we can say that the hunger of the two women in our myth has a cosmic significance; these heroines are not so much legendary persons as incarnations of principles which are at the origin of place-names.

One may schematize the initial situation as follows:

Mother	(is opposed to) Daughter
Elder	(,, ,, ,,) Younger
Downstream	(,, ,, ,,) Upstream
West	(,, ,, ,,) East
South	(,, ,, ,,) North

The meeting takes place at the half-way point, a situation which, as we have seen, corresponds to a neutralization of patrilocal residence and to the fulfilment of the conditions for a matrilocal residence which is as yet only hinted at. But since the mother dies on the very spot where the meeting and the birth of Asdiwal took place, the essential movement, which her daughter begins by leaving the village of her marriage 'very far upstream' (Boas, 1912, p. 71), is in the direction East-West, as far as her native village in the Skeena Canyon, where she in her turn dies, leaving the field open for the hero.

Asdiwal's first adventure presents us with an opposition: heaven/earth which the hero is able to surmount by virtue of the intervention of his father, Hatsenas, the bird of good omen. The latter is a creature of the atmospheric or middle heaven and consequently well qualified to play the role of mediator between

14

the earth-born Asdiwal and his father-in-law the Sun, ruler of the highest heaven. Even so, Asdiwal does not manage to overcome his earthly nature, to which he twice submits, first in yielding to the charms of a fellow-countrywoman and then in yielding to nostalgia for his home village. Thus there remains a series of unresolved oppositions:

Low	High
Earth	Heaven
Man	Woman
Endogamy	Exogamy

Pursuing his course westwards, Asdiwal contracts a second matrilocal marriage which generates a new series of oppositions:

Mountain-hunting	Sea-hunting
Land	Water

These oppositions too are insurmountable, and Asdiwal's earthly nature carries him away a third time, with the result that he is abandoned by his wife and his brothers-in-law.

Asdiwal contracts his last marriage not with the river-dwellers, but with islanders, and the same conflict is repeated. The opposition continues to be insurmountable, although at each stage the terms more closer together. This time it is in fact a question of a quarrel between Asdiwal and his brothers-in-law on the occasion of a hunt on a reef when the seas are running high; that is to say, on land and water at the same time. In the previous incident, Asdiwal and his brothers-in-law had gone their separate ways, one inland and on foot, the others out to sea and in boats. This time they go together in boats, and it is only when they land that Asdiwal's superiority is made manifest by the use he makes of the magic objects intended for mountain-hunting:

> 'It was a very difficult hunt on account of the waves which swept past [the reef] in the direction of the open sea. While they were speaking about this, [Asdiwal] said: "My dear fellows I have only to put on my snowshoes and I'll run up the rocks you are talking about".' He succeeds in this way, whilst his brothers-in-law, incapable of landing, stay shame-facedly in their boats (Boas, 1912, pp. 125-126).

15

Asdiwal, the earth-born master of the hunt, finds himself abandoned on a reef in high seas; he has come to the furthest point of his westward journey; so much for the geographic and economic aspects. But, from a logical point of view, his adventures can be seen in a different form – that of a series of impossible mediations between oppositions which are ordered in a descending scale: high and low, water and earth, sea-hunting and mountain-hunting, etc.

Consequently, on the spatial plane, the hero is completely led off his course, and his failure is expressed in this *maximal separation* from his starting-point. On the logical plane, he has also failed because of his immoderate attitude towards his brothers-in-law, and by his inability to play the role of a mediator, even though the last of the oppositions which had to be overcome – between the types of life led by the land- and sea-hunters – is reduced to a *minimal separation*. There would seem to be a dead end at this point; but from neutral the myth goes into reverse and its machinery starts up again.

The king of the mountains (in Nass dialect, Asdiwal is called Asi-hwil, which means 'Crosser of Mountains') is caught on a mockery of a mountain, and doubly so because, on the one hand, it is nothing more than a reef and, on the other, it is surrounded and almost submerged by the sea. The ruler of wild animals and killer of bears is to be saved by a she-mouse, a mockery of a wild animal.[5] She makes him undertake a *subterranean journey*, just as the she-bear, the supreme wild animal, had imposed on Asdiwal a *celestial journey*. In fact, the only thing that is missing is for the mouse to change into a woman and to offer the hero a marriage which would be symmetrical to the other, but opposite to it; and although this element is not to be found in any of the versions, we know at least that the mouse is a fairy: Lady Mouse-woman, as she is called in the texts, where the word *ksem*, a term of respect addressed to a woman, is prefixed to the word denoting a rodent. Following through the inversion more systematically than had been possible under the preceding hypothesis, this fairy is an old woman incapable of procreation: an 'inverse wife'.

And that is not all. The man who had killed animals in their hundreds goes this time to heal them and win their love.[6] The

16

bringer of food (who repeatedly exercises the power he received from his father in this respect for the benefit of his family) becomes food, since he is transported in the sea-lion's stomach.[7]

Finally, the visit to the subterranean world (which is also, in many respects, an 'upside-down world') sets the course of the hero's return, for from then onwards he travels from West to East, from the sea towards the mainland, from the salt water of the ocean to the fresh water of the Skeena.

This overall reversal does not affect the development of the plot, which unfolds up to the final catastrophe. When Asdiwal returns to his people and to the initial patrilocal situation, he takes up his favourite occupation again, helped by his magic objects. But he *forgets* one of them, and this mistake is fatal. After a successful hunt, he finds himself trapped half-way up the mountain-side: 'Where might he go now? He could not go up, he could not go down, he could not go to either side' (Boas, 1912, p. 145). And on the spot he is changed to stone, that is to say paralysed, reduced to his earth-born nature in the stony and unchangeable form in which he has been seen 'for generations'.

V

The above analysis leads us to draw a distinction between two aspects of the construction of a myth: the sequences and the schemata (*schèmes*).[8] The sequences form the apparent content of the myth; the chronological order in which things happen: the meeting of the two women, the intervention of the supernatural protector, the birth of Asdiwal, his childhood, his visit to heaven, his successive marriages, his hunting and fishing expeditions, his quarrels with his brothers-in-law, etc.

But these sequences are organized, on planes at different levels (of abstraction), in accordance with schemata, which exist simultaneously, superimposed one upon another; just as a melody composed for several voices is held within bounds by constraints in two dimensions, first by its own melodic line which is horizontal, and second by the contrapuntal schemata (settings) which are vertical. Let us then draw up an inventory of such schemata for this present myth.

1. *Geographic Schema.* The hero goes from East to West, then

17

151

he returns from West to East. This return journey is modulated
by another one, from the South to the North and then from the
North to the South, which corresponds to the seasonal migra-
tions of the Tsimshian (in which the hero takes part) to the
River Nass for the candlefish season in the spring, then to the
Skeena for the salmon-fishing in the summer.

NORTH

EAST————————→WEST————————→EAST

SOUTH

2. *Cosmological Schema.* Three supernatural visits establish
a relationship between terms thought of respectively as 'below'
and 'above': the visit to the young widow by Hatsenas, the
bird of good omen associated with the atmospheric heavens;
the visit by Asdiwal to the highest heavens in pursuit of
Evening-Star; his visit to the subterranean kingdom of the
sea-lions under the guidance of Lady Mouse-woman. The end
of Asdiwal, trapped in the mountain, then appears as a
neutralization of the intermediate mediation (between atmospheric heaven and earth) established at his birth but which
even so does not enable him to bring off two further extreme
mediations (the one between heaven and earth considered as
the opposition low/high and the other between the sea and the
land considered as the opposition East/West):

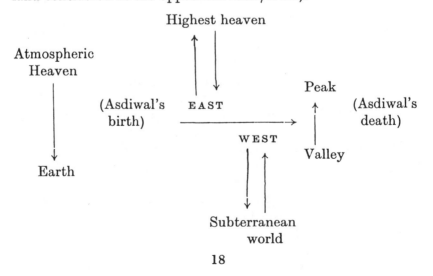

18

152

3. *Integration.* The above two schemata are integrated in a third consisting of several binary oppositions, none of which the hero can resolve, although the distance separating the opposed terms gradually dwindles. The initial and final oppositions: high/low and peak/valley are 'vertical' and thus belong to the cosmological schema. The two intermediate oppositions (water/land and sea-hunting/mountain-hunting) are 'horizontal' and belong to the geographic schema. But in fact the final opposition (peak/valley), which is also the narrowest contrast, brings into association the essential characteristics of the two preceding schemata: it is 'vertical' in form but 'geographical' in content. This double aspect, natural and supernatural, of the opposition between peak and valley is already specified in the myth, since the hero's perilous situation is the result of an earthquake brought about by the gods (see below, p. 22). Asdiwal's failure (in that, because he forgot his snow-shoes, he is trapped half-way up the mountain) thus takes on a threefold significance: geographical, cosmological, and logical:

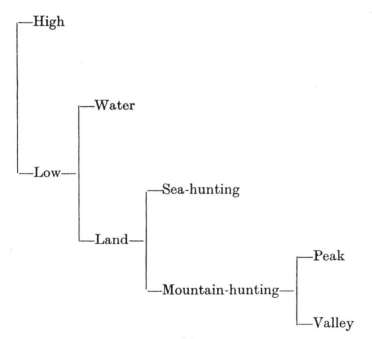

19

When the three schemata are reduced to their bare essentials in this way, retaining only the order and amplitude of the oppositions, their complementarity becomes apparent.

Schema 1 is composed of a sequence of oscillations of constant amplitude: East – North – West – South – East.

Schema 2 starts at a zero point (the meeting half-way between upstream and downstream) and is followed by an oscillation of medium amplitude (atmospheric heavens – earth), then by oscillations of maximum amplitude (earth – heaven, heaven – earth, earth – subterranean world, subterranean world – earth) which die away at the zero point (half-way up, between peak and valley).

Schema 3 begins with an oscillation of maximum amplitude (high-low) which dies away in a series of oscillations of decreasing amplitude (water – land; sea-hunting – mountain-hunting; valley – peak).

4. *Sociological Schema.* To start with, patrilocal residence prevails. It gives way progressively to matrilocal residence (Hatsenas's marriage), which becomes murderous (Asdiwal's marriage in heaven), then merely hostile (the marriage in the land of the People of the Firs), before weakening and finally reversing (marriage among the People of the Channel) to allow a return to patrilocal residence.

The sociological schema has not, however, a closed structure like the geographic schema, since, at the beginning, it involves a mother and her daughter, in the middle, a husband, his wife, and his brothers-in-law, and, at the end, a father and his son.[9]

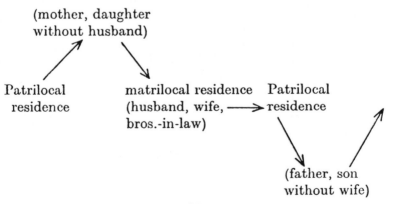

20

154

5. *Techno-economic Schema.* The myth begins by evoking a winter famine; it ends with a successful hunt. In between, the story follows the (real-life) economic cycle and the seasonal migrations of the native fishermen:

$$\text{Famine} \longrightarrow \begin{array}{c} \text{Fishing} \\ \text{for} \\ \text{Candlefish} \end{array} \longrightarrow \begin{array}{c} \text{Salmon} \\ \text{Fishing} \end{array} \longrightarrow \begin{array}{c} \text{Successful} \\ \text{Hunt} \end{array}$$

6. *Global Integration.* If the myth is finally reduced to its two extreme propositions, the initial state of affairs and the final, which together summarize its operational function, then we end up with a simplified diagram:

(Initial State)   (Final State)

$$\left.\begin{array}{l} \text{FEMALE} \\ \text{EAST-WEST} \\ \text{FAMINE} \\ \text{MOVEMENT} \end{array}\right\} \text{axis} \text{———} \left\{\begin{array}{l} \text{MALE} \\ \text{HIGH-LOW} \\ \text{REPLETION} \\ \text{IMMOBILITY} \end{array}\right. \text{axis}$$

Having separated out the codes, we have analysed the structure of the message. It now remains to decipher the meaning.

VI

In Boas (1916) there is a version of the story of Asdiwal that is remarkable in several respects. First, it brings a new character into play: Waux, the son of Asdiwal's second marriage, who seems to be a doublet of his father, although his adventures take place after those of Asdiwal. In chronological order, they form supplementary sequences of events. But these *later* sequences are organized in schemata which are at the same time *homologous* to those which have been described and more *explicit* than them. Everything seems to suggest that, as it draws to its close, the obvious narrative (the sequences) tends to approach the latent content of the myth (the schemata); a convergence which is not unlike that which the listener discovers in the final chords of a symphony.

> When Asdiwal's second wife (his first earth-born wife) bore him a son, he was called Waux. That means 'very light', for this son used to fly away like a spark.[10]
> The father and son loved each other very much and always

21

hunted together. And thus it was a cause of great sorrow to Waux when his uncles forced him to follow them after they had left his father (Asdiwal) at Ksemaksén. The mother and son had even secretly tried to find Asdiwal and had only abandoned the attempt when they were convinced that he must have been devoured by some wild animal.

Waux, following in his father's footsteps, became a great hunter. Before his mother died, she made him marry a cousin, and the young couple lived happily. Waux continued to hunt on his father's hunting-grounds, sometimes in company with his wife, who gave birth to twins.

Soon Waux's children went hunting with him, as he had formerly done with his father. One day he went with them into an unexplored region. The children slipped on the mountain and were both killed. The following year Waux returned to the same place to hunt, armed with all the magic objects he had inherited from his father, except the lance, which he forgot. Taken unawares by an earthquake, he tried in vain to make his wife (whom he saw in the valley) understand that he needed her ritual help. He shouted to her to sacrifice fat to the supernatural powers in order to appease them. But the wife could not hear and misunderstood, repeating not what her husband had said, but what she wanted to do herself, 'You want me to eat fat?' Discouraged, Waux agreed, and his wife sated herself with fat and cold water. Satisfied, she lay down on an old log. Her body broke apart and was changed into a veined flint which is still found all over that place today.

Waux, because he had forgotten the lance which enabled him to split the rock and open a way through the mountain, and having lost his last chance of placating the elements because of the misunderstanding which had arisen between his wife and himself, was turned to stone, as were also his dog and all his magic objects. They are still there to this day (Boas, 1916, pp. 243-245).

Several significant permutations will be noticed if this is compared with the version which we have taken as a point of reference.

22

Asdiwal had an only son (in fact, as we have seen, two only sons, born of consecutive marriages and confused into one single one in the story), whereas Waux has twins. We do not know much about these twins, but it is tempting to set up a parallel between them and the two magic dogs that Asi-hwil was given by his father in the River Nass version: one red, the other spotted – that is, marked by a contrast which suggests (when compared with the symbolic colour systems so common among the North American Indians) divergent functions.

Moreover, the existence of twins already provides a pointer. In the American series of mediators, twins represent the weakest term, and come at the bottom of the list, after the Messiah (who unites opponents) and the trickster (in whom they are in juxtaposition). The pair of twins brings opposites into association but at the same time leaves them individually distinct (see Lévi-Strauss, 1963a, Ch. xi, 'The Structural Study of Myth').

The change from a single mediator to a pair of twins is thus a sign of a weakening in the function of the mediator, all the clearer because only shortly after their appearance on the mystical scene the twins die in unexplored territory without having played any part.

Like Asdiwal, Waux ends by being turned to stone as a result of forgetting a magic object; the identity of this object, however, changes from one version to another. In Asdiwal, it is the snow-shoes; in Waux the lance. These magic objects are the instruments of mediation given to the hero by his supernatural father. Here, again, there is a gradation; the snow-shoes make it possible to climb up and down the steepest slopes; the lance enables its owner to go straight through walls of rock. The lance is thus a more radical means than the snow-shoes, which come to terms with the obstacle rather than doing away with it. Waux's omission seems more serious than Asdiwal's. The weaker mediator loses the stronger instrument of mediation and his powers are doubly diminished as a result.

Thus the story of Waux follows a dialectic regression; but, in another sense, it reveals a progression, since it is with this variant that a structure which had remained open in certain respects is finally closed.

Waux's wife dies of *repletion*. That is the end of a story which

23

opened by showing Asdiwal's (or Asi-hwil's) mother a victim of *starvation*. It was this famine which set her in *motion*, just as, now, abuse of food brings Waux's wife to a *halt*. And before leaving this point let us note that in fact the two characters of the initial sequence were two women who were *single, unfed*, and *on the move*, whereas those of the final sequence were a *couple* composed of a husband and his wife, one a *bringer of food* (who is not understood) and the other *overfed* (because she does not understand), and both *paralysed* in spite of this opposition (but also perhaps because of the negative complementarity that it expresses).

The most important transformation is that represented by the marriage of Waux. It has been seen that Asdiwal contracted a series of marriages, all equally unsuccessful. He cannot choose between his supernatural bride and his fellow-country-women; he is abandoned (though against her will, it is true) by his Tsimshian spouse. His Gitxatla wife remains faithful to him and even goes so far as to betray her brothers; it is he who abandons her. He ends his days, having joined forces with his son again, in a celibate state.

Waux, on the other hand, marries only once, but this marriage proves fatal for him. Here, however, it is a case of a marriage *arranged* by Waux's mother (unlike Asdiwal's *adventurous* marriages) and a marriage with a *cousin* (whereas Asdiwal marries complete *strangers*), or more precisely, with his cross-cousin, his mother's brother's daughter (which explains the intermediary role played by his mother).[11]

As Boas explains in the text quoted in the footnote above, there was a preference for marriage with the mother's brother's daughter among the Tsimshian, especially in the noble classes from which our heroes are drawn. Garfield doubts whether the practice was strictly in accordance with mythical models (Garfield, 1939, pp. 232-233), but the point is of secondary importance, since we are studying schemata with a normative function. In a society like that of the Tsimshian, there is no difficulty in seeing why this type of marriage could be thought ideal. Boys grew up in their fathers' homes, but sooner or later they had to go over to their maternal uncle when they inherited his titles, prerogatives, and hunting-grounds (Boas, 1916, p. 411,

24

where he contradicts p. 401. We shall return to this contradiction later.) Marriage with the matrilateral cousin provided a solution to this conflict.

Furthermore, as has often been found to be the case in other societies of the same type, such a marriage made it possible to overcome another conflict: that between the patrilineal and matrilineal tendencies of Tsimshian society, which, as we have seen above, is very deeply conscious of the two lines (p. 3. See also on this point E. Sapir, 1915, pp. 6 and 27, and Garfield, Wingert & Barbeau, 1951, pp. 17-25). By means of such a marriage, a man ensures the continued existence of his hereditary privileges and of such titles as he might have within the limits of a small family circle (Swanton, 1909; Wedgewood, 1928; Richards, 1914).

I have shown elsewhere that it is unlikely that this interpretation may be seen as the universal origin of cross-cousin marriage (Lévi-Strauss, 1949, pp. 158-159). But in the case of a society which has feudal tendencies, it certainly corresponds to real motives which contributed to the survival, or to the adoption, of the custom. The final explanation of this custom must, however, be sought in those characteristics which are common to all societies which practised it.

The Tsimshian myths provide, furthermore, a surprising commentary on the native theory of marriage with the matrilateral cross-cousin in the story of the princess who refuses to marry her cousin (her father's sister's son).

No less cruel than she was proud, the princess demands that her cousin prove his love by disfiguring himself. He slashes his face and then she rejects him because of his ugliness. Reduced to a state of despair, the young man seeks death and ventures into the land of Chief Pestilence, master of deformities. After the hero has undergone rigorous trials, the chief agrees to transform him into a Prince Charming.

Now his cousin is passionately attracted to him, and the young man, in his turn, demands that she sacrifice her beauty, but only in order to heap sarcasm upon her head. The now hideous princess tries to move Chief Pestilence to pity, and at once the maimed and deformed race of people who make

25

up his court set upon the unfortunate woman, break her bones and tear her apart.

Boas's informant sees in this tale the myth which lies at the origin of the rites and ceremonies celebrated at the marriages of cross-cousins.

'There was a custom among our people that the nephew of the chief had to marry the chief's daughter, because the tribe of the chief wanted the chief's nephew to be the heir of his uncle and to inherit his place after his death. This custom has gone on, generation after generation, all along until now, and the places of the head men have thus been inherited.'

But, the informant goes on, it is because of the disaster that struck the rebellious princess that it was decided that on such occasions 'no young woman should have any say about her marriage. . . . Even though the young woman does not want to marry the man, she has to consent when the agreement has been made on both sides to marry them' (that is to say after negotiations between the maternal descent groups of the young people).

'When the prince and princess have married, the tribe of the young man's uncle mobilize. Then the tribe of the young woman's uncle also mobilize and they have a fight. The two parties cast stones at each other, and the heads of many of those on each side are hit. The scars made by the stones on the heads of each chief's people are signs of the marriage pledge'.[12]

In his commentary Boas notes that this myth is not peculiar to the Tsimshian, but is found also among the Tlingit and the Haida, who are likewise matrilineal and likewise faithful to the same type of marriage. Thus it is clear that it portrays a fundamental aspect of the social organization of these peoples, which consists in a hostile equilibrium between the matrilineal lineages of the village chiefs. In a system of generalized exchange, such as results, in these feudal families, from the preferential marriage with the mother's brother's daughter, the

26

families are, so to speak, ranged around a more or less stable circle, in such a way that each family occupies, at least temporarily, the position of 'wife-giver' with respect to some other family and of 'wife-taker' with respect to a third. Depending on the society, this lopsided structure (lopsided, because there is no guarantee that in giving one will receive) can achieve a certain equilibrium – more apparent, however, than real – in several ways: democratically, by following the principle that all marriage exchanges are equivalent; or, on the contrary, by stipulating that one of the positions (wife-giver, wife-taker) is, by definition, superior to the other. But given a different social and economic context, this amounts in theory, if not in practice, to the same thing, since each family must occupy both positions (Lévi-Strauss, 1949; 1963a, pp. 311-312). The societies of the Northwest Pacific Coast could not, or would not, choose one of these points of balance, and the respective superiority or inferiority of the groups involved was openly contested on the occasion of each marriage. Each marriage, along with the potlatches which accompanied and preceded it, and the transfers of titles and property occasioned by it, provided the means by which the groups concerned might gain an advantage over each other while at the same time putting an end to former disputes. It was necessary to make peace but only on the best possible terms. French mediaeval society offers, in terms of patrilineal institutions, a symmetrical picture of a situation which had much in common with the one just described.

In such circumstances, is there anything amazing about the horrid little story in which the natives see the origin of their marriage institutions? Is there anything surprising in the fact that the ceremony of marriage between first cousins takes the form of a bloody battle? When we believe that, in bringing to light these antagonisms which are inherent in the structure of Tsimshian society, we are 'reaching rock bottom' (in the words of Marcel Mauss), we express in this geological metaphor an approach that has many points of comparison with that made by the myths of Asdiwal and Waux. All the paradoxes conceived by the native mind, on the most diverse planes: geographic, economic, sociological, and even cosmological, are, when all is

27

said and done, assimilated to that less obvious yet so real paradox which marriage with the matrilateral cousin attempts but fails to resolve. But the failure is *admitted* in our myths, and there precisely lies their function.

Let us glance at them again in this light. The winter famine which kills the husbands of the two original heroines frees them from patrilocal residence and enables them first to meet and then to return to the daughter's native village, which will correspond, for her son, to a matrilocal type of residence. Thus a shortage of food is related to the sending out of young women, who return to their own descent groups when food is scarce. This is symbolic of an event which is illustrated in a more concrete fashion each year, even if there is no famine, by the departure of the candlefish from the Nass and then of the salmon from the Skeena. These fish come from the open sea, arrive from the South and the West, and go up the rivers in an easterly direction. Like the departing fish, Asdiwal's mother continues her journey westwards and towards the sea, where Asdiwal discovers the disastrous effects of matrilocal marriage.

The first of his marriages is with Evening-Star, who is a supernatural being. The correlation of female heaven and male earth which is implicit in this event is interesting from two points of view.

First, Asdiwal is in a way fished up by the She-Bear who draws him up to heaven, and the myths often describe grizzly bears as *fishing for salmon*.[13] Like a salmon too, Asdiwal is fished up in a net by the compassionate Sun after he has crashed to earth.[14] But when Asdiwal returns from his symmetrically opposite visit to the subterranean kingdom of the sea-lions, he travels in one of their stomachs, like a food; comparable to the *candlefish* which are scooped up from the bed of the River Nass, the 'Stomach River'. Furthermore, the hero now goes in the opposite direction, no longer from East to West like the food disappearing, but from West to East like the food returning.

Second, this reversal is accompanied by another: from matrilocal to patrilocal residence; and this reversal is in itself a variable of the replacement of a celestial journey by a sub-

28

terranean one, which brings Asdiwal from the position of: earth, male, dominated, to that of: earth, male, dominant.

Patrilocal residence is no more successful for Asdiwal. He gets his son back but loses his wife and his affines. Isolated in this new relationship, and incapable of bringing together the two types of filiation and residence, he is stuck half-way at the moment when he has almost reached his goal; at the end of a successful hunt, he has reconquered food but lost his freedom of movement. Famine, which causes movement, has given way to abundance, but at the price of paralysis.

We can then now better understand how Waux's marriage with his matrilateral cousin, following that of his father, symbolizes the futile last attempts of Tsimshian thought and Tsimshian society to overcome their inherent contradictions. For this marriage fails as the result of a *misunderstanding* added to an *omission*: Waux had succeeded in staying with his maternal kin while at the same time retaining his father's hunting-grounds; he had managed to inherit in both the maternal and the paternal lines at the same time; but, although they are cousins, he and his wife remain alienated from one another, because cross-cousin marriage, in a feudal society, is a palliative and a decoy. In these societies, women are always objects of exchange, but property is also a cause of battle.

VII

The above analysis suggests an observation of a different kind: it is always rash to undertake, as Boas wanted to do in his monumental *Tsimshian Mythology*, 'a description of the life, social organization and religious ideas and practices of a people . . . as it appears from their mythology' (Boas, 1916, p. 32).

The myth is certainly related to given (empirical) facts, but not as a *re-presentation* of them. The relationship is of a dialectic kind, and the institutions described in the myths can be the very opposite of the real institutions. This will in fact always be the case when the myth is trying to express a negative truth. As has already been seen, the story of Asdiwal has landed the great American ethnologist in no little difficulty, for Waux

29

is there said to have inherited his father's hunting-grounds, while other texts, as well as eye-witness observation, reveal that a man's property, including his hunting-grounds, went to his sister's son, that is to say from man to man in the maternal line.[15]

But Waux's paternal inheritance no more reflects real conditions than do his father's matrilocal marriages. In real life, the children grew up in the patrilocal home. Then they went to finish their education at their maternal uncle's home; after marrying, they returned to live with their parents, bringing their wives with them, and they settled in their uncle's village only when they were called upon to succeed him. Such, at any rate, was the case among the nobility, whose mythology formed a real 'court literature'. The comings and goings were one of the outward signs of the tensions between lineages connected by marriage. Mythical speculation about types of residence which are exclusively patrilocal or matrilocal do not therefore have anything to do with the reality of the structure of Tsimshian society, but rather with its inherent possibilities and its latent potentialities. Such speculations, in the last analysis, do not seek to depict what is real, but to justify the shortcomings of reality, since the extreme positions are only *imagined* in order to show that they are *untenable*. This step, which is fitting for mythical thought, implies an admission (but in the veiled language of the myth) that the social facts when thus examined are marred by an insurmountable contradiction. A contradiction which, like the hero of the myth, Tsimshian society cannot understand and prefers to forget.

This conception of the relation of the myth to reality no doubt limits the use of the former as a documentary source. But it opens the way for other possibilities; for in abandoning the search for a constantly accurate picture of ethnographic reality in the myth, we gain, on occasions, a means of reaching unconscious categories.

A moment ago it was recalled that Asdiwal's two journeys – from East to West and from West to East – were correlated with types of residence, respectively matrilocal and patrilocal. But in fact the Tsimshian have patrilocal residence, and from this we can (and indeed must) draw the conclusion that one of the orientations corresponds to the direction implicit in a

30

real-life 'reading' of their institutions, the other to the opposite direction. The journey from West to East, the return journey, is accompanied by a return to patrilocality. Therefore the direction in which it is made is, for the native mind, the only real direction, the other being purely imaginary.

That is, moreover, what the myth proclaims. The move to the East assures Asdiwal's return to his element, the Earth, and to his native land. When he went westwards it was as a bringer of food putting an end to starvation; he made up for the absence of food while at the same time travelling in the same direction as that taken by food when it departed. Journeying in the opposite direction, in the sea-lion's stomach, he is symbolically identified with food, and he travels in the direction in which the food (of actual experience) returns.

The same applies to matrilocal residence; it is introduced as a negative reality, to make up for the non-existence of patrilocal residence caused by the death of the husbands.

What then is the West–East direction in native thought? It is the direction taken by the candlefish and the salmon when they arrive from the sea each year to enter the rivers and race upstream. If this orientation is also that which the Tsimshian must adopt in order to obtain an undistorted picture of their concrete social existence, is it not because they see themselves as being *sub specie piscis*; that they put themselves in the fishes' place, or rather that they put the fish in their place?

This hypothesis, arrived at by a process of deductive reasoning, is indirectly confirmed by ritual institutions and mythology.

Fishing and the preparation of the fish are the occasion for all kinds of ritual among the natives of the Northwest Coast. We have already seen that the women must use their naked breasts to press the candlefish in order to extract the oil from it, and that the remains must be left to rot near the dwellings in spite of the smell. The salmon does not rot, since it is dried in the sun or smoked. But there are further ritual conditions which must be observed: for instance, it must be cut up with a primitive knife made of a mussel shell, and any kind of stone, bone, or metal blade is forbidden. Women set about this operation sitting on the ground with their legs apart (Boas, 1916, pp. 449-450 and 919-932 (Nootka)).

31

These prohibitions and prescriptions seem to represent the same intention: to bring out the immediacy of the relationship between fish and man by treating fish as if it were a man, or at any rate by ruling out, or limiting to the extreme, the use of manufactured objects which are part of culture; or, in other words, by denying or underestimating the differences between fish and men.

The myths, for their part, tell of the visit of a prince to the kingdom of the salmon, whence he returns, having won their alliance, himself transformed into a fish. All these myths have one incident in common: the prince is welcomed by the salmon and learns that he may in no circumstances eat the same food as they, but must not hesitate to kill and eat the fish themselves, regardless of the fact that they thenceforth appear to him in human form (Boas, 1916, pp. 192-206, 770-778, 919-932).

It is at this point that the mythical identification hits upon the only real relationship between fish and men: one of food. It persists, even in the myth, as an alternative: either to eat like salmon (although one is a man) or to eat salmon (although they are like men). This latter solution is the right one, and thanks to it they are reborn from their bones, which had been carefully collected and then immersed or burned. But the first solution would be an *abuse of identification*, of man with salmon, not of salmon with man. The character in the myth who was guilty of this was transformed into a root or a rock – like Asdiwal – condemned to immobility and perpetually bound to the earth.

Starting with an initial situation characterized by irrepressible movement, and ending in a final situation characterized by perpetual immobility, the myth of Asdiwal expresses in its own way a fundamental aspect of the native philosophy. The start presents us with the absence of food; and everything which has been said above leads us to think that the role of Asdiwal, as bringer of food, consists in (bringing about) a negation of this absence, but that is quite another thing from (saying that Asdiwal's role equates with) the presence of food. In fact, when this presence is finally obtained, with Asdiwal taking on the aspect of 'food itself' (and no longer that of 'bringer of food'), the result is a state of inertia.

But starvation is no more a tolerable human condition than is

32

immobility. Therefore we must conclude that for these natives the only positive form of existence is a *negation of non-existence*. It is out of the question to develop this theory within the limits of the present work. But let us note in passing that it would shed new light on the *need for self-assertion* which, in the potlatch, the feasts, the ceremonies, and the feudal rivalries, seems to be such a particular characteristic of the societies of the Northwest Pacific Coast.

VIII

There is one last problem which remains to be solved, that which is posed by the differences between the Nass River version and those recorded on the coast, in which the action takes place on the Skeena. Up to now we have followed these latter ones, which are very similar to each other. Boas even says that the two versions are 'practically identical'.[16] Let us now look at the Nass version.

Famine reigns in the two villages of Laxqaltsap and Gitwunksilk – it is possible to place them: the first is the present Greenville on the Nass estuary,[17] and the second is on the lower Nass, but further upstream.[18] Two sisters, separated by marriage, each live in one of the villages. They decide to join forces, and meet half-way in a place which is named in memory of this event. They have a few provisions. The sister from down-river has only a few hawberries, the one from up-river, a small piece of spawn. They share this and bewail their plight.

One of the sisters – the one from up-river – has come with her daughter, who does not enter the story again. The one from down-river, the younger of the two, is still unmarried. A stranger visits her at night. He is called Hôux, which means 'Good Luck'. When he learns of the state of the women, he miraculously provides food for them, and the younger woman soon gives birth to a son, Asi-hwil, for whom his father makes a pair of snow-shoes. At first they are useless, but once perfected, they bestow magic powers on their wearer. Asi-hwil's father also gives him two magic dogs, and

33

a lance which can pass through rock. From then on, the hero reveals himself to be a better hunter than other supernatural beings against whom he is matched.

Then follows the episode of Hôux's retreat from his brothers-in-law which has been summarized above (see pp. 11-12). They carry off their sister and their nephew at Gitxaden, down-stream from Nass Canyon.[19] There, the hero is drawn towards the sky by the slave of a supernatural being, disguised as a white bear; but he does not succeed in reaching the heavenly abode and returns to earth having lost track of the bear.

He then goes to Tsimshian country, where he marries the sister of the sea-lion hunters. He humiliates them by his superiority, is abandoned by them, visits the sea-lions in their subterranean kingdom, looks after them and cures them, gets a canoe made of their intestines which brings him back to the coast, where he kills his brothers-in-law with artificial killer-whales. He finds his wife and never leaves her again (Boas, 1902, pp. 225-229).

Clearly, this version is very poor. It has very few episodes, and when compared with Boas (1912) which has been our point of reference up to now, the sequence of events seems very confused. It would, however, be quite wrong to treat the Nass version simply as a weakened echo of the Skeena ones. In the best-preserved part, the initial sequence of events, it is as if the richness of detail had been preserved, but at the cost of permutations which, without any doubt, form a system. Let us therefore begin by listing them, distinguishing the elements which are common to both versions from the elements which have been transformed.

In both cases, the story begins in a river valley: that of the Skeena, that of the Nass. It is winter, and famine reigns. Two related women, one living upstream and the other downstream, decide to join forces, and meet half-way.

Already, several differences are apparent:

Place of the Action	Nass	Skeena
State of the River	?	Frozen

34

Situation of the Two Villages	Not far apart	'Very far apart'[20]
Relationship between the Two Women	Sisters	Mother and daughter
Civil Status	{ 1 married / 1 unmarried }	2 widows

These differences, it is clear, are equivalent to a *weakening of all the oppositions* in the Nass version. This is very striking in the (contrasted) situations of the two villages and even more so in the (contrasted) relationships between the two women. In the latter there is a constant element, the relationship of elder to younger, which is manifested in the form: *mother/ daughter* in the one case, and *elder sister/younger sister* in the other, the first couple living *farther apart* from one another than the second and being brought together by a *more radical event* (the double simultaneous widowhood) than the second (of whom only one is married – it is not stated whether she has lost her husband).

One may also prove that the Nass version is a weakening of the Skeena version and that the Skeena version is not a strengthened form of the other. The proof lies in the vestigial survival of the original mother/daughter relationship in the form of the maternity of the elder sister, who is accompanied by her daughter, a detail which in every other respect has no function in the Nass version:

(a) [mother : daughter] :: [(mother + daughter) : non-mother] the constant element being given by the opposition between *retrospective fertility* and *prospective fertility*.

But these differences, which one could consider as being 'more' or 'less', and in this sense quantitative, are accompanied by others which are genuine inversions.

In the Skeena version, the elder of the two women comes from down-river, the younger from up-river. In the Nass variant, the contrary is true, since the pair (mother + daughter) comes from Gitwunksilk, upstream of the Canyon, and the unmarried sister (who will marry the supernatural protector and is therefore identical with the daughter in the Skeena version) arrives from Laxqaltsap, which is downstream.

In the Skeena version, the women are completely empty-

35

169

handed, reduced to sharing *a single rotten berry*, found at their meeting-place ('a few berries' in Boas, 1895). Once again, the Nass version shows a weakening, since the women bring provisions, though they are in fact very meagre: a handful of berries and a piece of spawn:

	Down-river	*Up-river*
Skeena version:	0———→rotten←———0	
	berry	
Nass version:	berries———→	←———spawn

It would be easy to show that on the Northwest Pacific Coast and in other regions of America, decomposition is considered as the borderline between food and excrement.[21] If, in the Skeena version, a single berry (*quantatively*, the minimal food) is the bearer of decomposition (*qualitatively*, the minimal food), then it is because berries in themselves are thought of *specifically* as a weak kind of food, in contrast with strong foods.

Without any doubt, in the Skeena version the two women are deliberately associated not with any particular food, but with the lack of any sort of food. This 'dearth of food' however, though a negative category, is not an empty category, for the development of the myth gives it, in retrospect, a content. The two women represent 'absence of food', but they are also bound respectively to the East and to the West, to the land and to the sea. The myth of Asdiwal tells of an opposition between two types of life, also bound up with the same cardinal points and the same elements: mountain-hunters on the one side, fishermen and sea-hunters on the other (Boas, 1916, p. 403: 'The sea-hunter required a training quite different from that of the mountain-hunter'). In the Skeena version the 'alimentary' opposition is therefore double: (1) between animal food (at the extreme positions) and vegetable food (in the intermediate position) and (2) between sea-animal (West) and land-animal (East), thus:

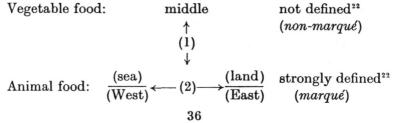

Vegetable food: middle   not defined[22]
                           ↑   (*non-marqué*)
                          (1)
                           ↓

Animal food: (sea)/(West) ←— (2) —→ (land)/(East)   strongly defined[22]
                                                        (*marqué*)

36

From this we obtain the formula:

(*b*) [land : sea] :: [(sea + land) : middle]

and the analogy of this with (*a*) [p. 35] is immediately obvious.

The alimentary system of the Nass version is based on a *simplified structure* (with two terms instead of three) and on *weakened oppositions*. From being 'not-defined', vegetable food moves to a state of being 'weakly defined'; from a borderline state between 'food' and 'absence of food', it becomes a positive food, both quantitatively (a handful of berries) and qualitatively (fresh berries). This vegetable food is now opposed not to animal food as such, a category which is strongly defined (and here distinguished by a minus sign (-1)), but to the weakest imaginable manifestation of this same animal food (to which we still assign a plus sign ($+1$)). This contrast between 'weakly defined animal food' and 'strongly defined animal food' is exhibited in three ways:

fish and not meat

fish spawn and not fish

a piece 'as big as the finger'

Thus we have a system:

sea   ⎰land
West   ⎮East
vegetable food ⎱ weakly   ⎰ animal food
(relatively   ⎰ ← defined → (relatively
abundant in   ⎱ opposition   weak in
quantity)   ⎰ quality)

From the point of view of the alimentary system, the correlation between the two variants of the myth can thus be expressed by the following formulae:

(c_1) [($-$meat) : ($-$fish)] :: [dx(meat + fish) : dx(vegetable food)]

or in simplified form (ignoring the minute quantity dx):

(c_2) [meat : fish] :: [(meat + fish) : (vegetable food)]

where the sum of (meat + fish) constitutes the category of animal food. It will be noticed, once again, that there is an analogy between the three formulae *a*, *b*, and *c*.

The two types of food in the Nass version are berries (downstream) and spawn (upstream). Spawn is an animal food from the river, berries a vegetable food from the land (earth), and,

37

of all earth-grown foods, this (in contrast to the game that is hunted in the mountains) is the one most commonly associated with the river banks (Boas, 1916, p. 404: 'Women go out jointly by canoe or walking in the woods to gather berries').

Thus the transformation which has occurred in the process of transferring the story from the one version to the other can, from this point of view, be written as follows:

(*d*) [West : East] :: [sea : land] :: [water : land (earth)]
:: [river : bank]

But the opposition between the river and its banks is not only a weakened form of the fundamental contrasts between 'East' and 'West' and between 'land (earth)' and 'water', which are most strongly defined in the opposition: sea/land. It is also a *function* of this last opposition.

In fact, the opposition river/bank is more strongly defined inland (where the element 'water' is reduced to 'river') than towards the coast. There the opposition is no longer so pertinent because, in the category 'water', the sea takes precedence over the river, and in the category 'land (earth)', the coast takes precedence over the bank. One can thus understand the logic of the reversal whereby, *up-river*, we are led to put:

(*d*) [water : land (earth)] :: [river : bank]

whereas *down-river* – when the whole of the river and its banks are assimilated into the category 'land,' this time in opposition to the category 'sea' – we are led to write:

(*e*) [water : land (earth)] :: [sea : (river + bank)]

where the combination (river + bank) has, by permutation, been moved into the position originally occupied by 'land'.

Since (*d*) and (*e*) can be recast in the form:

(*f*) [land : water] :: [(river + bank) : sea]

which is analogous to formulae (*a*), (*b*), and (*c*), this example shows how a mythological transformation can be expressed by a series of equivalences, such that the two extremes are radically inverted (cf. Lévi-Strauss, 1963a, pp. 228-229).

In fact, in the last stage of the transformation, the (down-stream, West) position is occupied by a vegetable food, that is to say by an 'earth-food', while the (upstream, East) position is occupied by an animal food, which, since it consists of fish-spawn, comes from the river and is therefore a 'water-food'.

38

The two women, reduced to their common denominator, which is the relationship older/younger, have thus, in coherent fashion, had their positions changed over with respect to the relationship upstream/downstream.[23]

Consequently, in the Skeena version, the weak opposition between river and bank is *neutralized* (this is expressed in the myth by specifying that the river is frozen and that the women walk on the ice) in favour of the strong opposition between sea and land which is, however, negatively evoked (since the women are defined by their lack of the foods which are associated with their respective (territorial) positions). In the Nass version it is the strong opposition which is neutralized, by weakening and inversion, in favour of the weak opposition between river and bank, which is positively evoked (since in this case the women are provided, albeit meagrely, with the appropriate foods).

Parallel transformations are to be found in the episode of the supernatural protector as related by the two versions. In that of the Skeena, he provides meat alone, in an ever-increasing quantity (in order: little squirrel, grouse, porcupine, beaver, goat, black bear, grizzly bear, caribou); in the Nass version, he provides meat and fish at the same time in such large quantities that in the one case the hut is 'full of meat and fish' but only 'full of dried meat' in the other. In the Skeena version this balance between the two types of life is brought about only much later and in a transitory way: during Asdiwal's third marriage with the sister of the Gitxatla people, when, accompanied by his brothers-in-law, he is abundantly provided with 'salmon and fresh meat' which he sells to the starving Tsimshian (cf. Boas, 1902, pp. 225-226, and Boas, 1912, pp. 74-77 and 120-123).

On the other hand, Asdiwal's father gives him magic objects which are immediately effective (Skeena version), whereas those given to Asi-hwil have to be gradually perfected (Nass version). In each case, the hero returns from the West like the food, transported in the insides of a sea-lion; but in the second case the change from stomach (Skeena) to intestines (Nass) suggests a food that is nearer to putrefaction, a theme that is final here and no longer initial (a rotten berry and rotten bark

39

were the women's first food in the Skeena version). Nor must it be forgotten that, from this point of view, the candlefish, the only hope of escaping from starvation (in Tsimshian, candlefish is called: *hale-mâ'tk*, which means 'saviour') must be tolerated up to the point of decomposition – otherwise the fish would be offended and would never return.

IX

How can a concrete content be given to this double mechanism of the *weakening of oppositions*, accompanied by a *reversal of correlations* the formal coherence of which we have now established? It should first be noted that the inversion is given in the respective geographical positions of the two populations: the Nisqa, people of the Nass, are found in the North; the Tsimshian (whose name means: 'inside the river Skeena' from *K-sia'n*: 'Skeena') in the South. In order to marry on (relatively speaking) foreign territory, the Nass hero goes to the land of the Tsimshian, that is to say, towards the Skeena, in the South; and the Skeena-born Asdiwal's last marriage shows him, up to the time of the break, camping with his in-laws on the Nass and thus in the North. Each population spontaneously forms symmetrical but inverse conceptions of the same country.

But the myths bear witness to the fact that the duality: Skeena valley/Nass valley, which, with the region in between, forms the Tsimshian country (in the broadest sense) is seen as an opposition, as are also the economic activities which are respectively associated with each of the two rivers:

A young man of miraculous birth decided to go up to heaven while night reigned on earth. Changed into a leaf, he impregnated the daughter of the Master of the Sun, who bore a son called Giant. The child seized the sun, made himself master of daylight and went down to earth where he found himself a companion, Logobola, who was master of mist, water, and marshes. The two boys had a competition, and after several undecided contests they decided to shoot arrows and play for the River Skeena against the River Nass. Giant won by a trick and was so overjoyed that he spoke in Tsimshian – in

40

the dialect of the lower reaches of the Skeena – to voice his feelings 'And Logobola says: "You won, Brother Giant. Now the candlefish will come to Nass River twice every summer." And Txamsem (Giant) said, "And the salmon of Skeena River shall always be fat." Thus they divided what Txamsem had won at Nass river. . . . After which the two brothers parted.' One of the versions recorded by Boas says: 'Txamsem went down to the ocean and Logobola went southward to the place he had come from' (Boas, 1916, p. 70. Cf. also Boas, 1902, p. 7ff.).

In any case, the symmetry of the geographical positions provides only the beginning of an explanation. We have seen that the reversal of correlations is itself the function of a general weakening of all the oppositions which cannot be explained merely by a substitution of South for North and North for South. In passing from the Skeena to the Nass, the myth becomes distorted in two ways, which are structurally connected: first, it is reduced and, second, it is reversed. In order to be admissible, any interpretation must take account of both of these aspects.

The Skeena people and the Nass people speak similar dialects (Boas, 1911). Their social organization is almost identical.[24] But their modes of life are profoundly different. We have described the way of life on the Skeena and on the coast, characterized by a great seasonal movement which is in fact two-phased: between the winter towns and the spring camps on one hand, and then between the spring candlefish season on the Nass and the summer salmon-fishing on the Skeena.

As for the Nass people, it does not seem that they made periodic visits to the Skeena. The most that we are told is that those who lived very far up the Nass were called 'kit'anwi'likc', 'people who left their permanent villages from time to time', because they came down towards the Nass estuary each year, but only for the candlefish season (Sapir, 1915, p. 3). The largest seasonal migrations of the Nisqa seem thus to have been limited to the Nass, while those of the Tsimshian were based on a much more complex Skeena-Nass system. The reason is that the candlefish only visit the Nass, which therefore becomes the

41

meeting-place of all the groups who anxiously await the arrival
of their 'saviour', whereas the salmon goes up both rivers
indiscriminately. Thus the Nisqa lived in one valley, and the
Tsimshian in two.

Since this is so, all the natives are able to conceptualize the
duality Nass/Skeena as an opposition which correlates with
that of candlefish/salmon. There can be no doubt about it,
since the myth which lays the foundation of this opposition was
recorded by Boas in two practically identical versions, one in
Nass dialect, the other in Skeena dialect. But an opposition
which is recognized by all need not have the same significance
for each group. The Tsimshian lived through this opposition in
the course of each year; the Nisqa were content to know about
it. Although a grammatical construction employing couplets of
antithetical terms is present in the Tsimshian tongue as a very
obvious model, and probably presents itself as such quite
consciously to the speaker,[25] its logical and philosophical
implication would not be the same in each of the two groups.
The Tsimshian use it to build up a system which is global and
coherent but which is not communicable in its entirety to
people whose concrete experiences are not stamped with the
same duality; perhaps, also, the fact that the course of the Nass
is less definitely orientated from East to West than is that of
the Skeena adds to the obscurity of the topographical schema
(among the Nisqa).

Thus we arrive at a fundamental property of mythical
thought, other examples of which might well be sought elsewhere. When a mythical schema is transmitted from one
population to another, and there exist differences of language,
social organization or way of life which make the myth difficult
to communicate, it begins to become impoverished and confused.
But one can find a limiting situation in which instead of being
finally obliterated by losing all its outlines, the myth is inverted
and regains part of its precision.

Similar inversions occur in optics. An image can be seen in
full detail when observed through any adequately large
aperture. But as the aperture is narrowed the image becomes
blurred and difficult to see. When, however, the aperture is
further reduced to a pinpoint, that is to say, when *communica-*

42

tion is about to vanish, the image is inverted and becomes clear again. This experiment is used in schools to demonstrate the propagation of light in straight lines, or in other words to prove that rays of light are not transmitted at random, but within the limits of a structured field.

This study is in its own way an experiment, since it is limited to a single case, and the elements isolated by analysis appear in several series of concomitant variations. If the experiment has helped to demonstrate that the field of mythical thought, too, is structured, then it will have achieved its object.

NOTES

1. The candlefish (*olachen*) is a small very oily fish caught in very large numbers. Valued mainly for its oil, the meat can be eaten in times of scarcity [E.R.L.].

2. Hatsenas (Boas, 1912), Hadsenas (Boas, 1895): it is a bird like the robin but not a robin (Boas, 1912, pp. 72-73). In another myth the robin announces the summer (cf. Boas, 1912, pp. 200-201). The term 'robin' is applied to a variety of birds by the English and the Americans. It would be rash to try to identify the species. According to Boas (1895), Hadsenas means 'luck', and describes a bird sent as a messenger from Heaven (p. 286).

   In this work, which has no linguistic pretentions, the transcription of native terms has been simplified to the extreme, keeping only those distinctions which are essential for avoiding ambiguities between the terms quoted.

3. The name Asdiwal certainly has several connotations. The Nass form, Asi-hwil, means 'Crosser of Mountains' (Boas, 1902, p. 226) but cf. also '*asdiwal*', 'to be in danger' (Boas, 1912, Glossary, p. 257) and Asewaelgyet: a different name for and special variety of the Thunder Bird (Barbeau, 1950, Vol. I, pp. 144-145 and Vol. II, p. 476).

4. For a summary and comparative analysis of all the texts which have been listed as referring to the greed of the Demiurge, see Boas (1916, p. 636 ff.).

5. As the smallest mammal to appear in mythology, and also because in the mythology of the Northwest Coast the mouse represents the animals of the earth at their most modest level: that of domestic life. The mouse is in fact the domestic animal of the earth. With this distinction she is entitled to the tiny offering of fat which drips from woollen ear-ornaments when they are thrown into the fire in her honour.

6. 'The love of the master of the sea-lions and of his whole tribe increased very much' (Boas, 1912, p. 133).

7. The Tsimshian of the Nisqa group 'look to the river [Nass] for their food supply, which consists principally of salmon and candlefish. Indeed it is owing to the enormous numbers of the latter fish that run in to spawn in the early spring that the name Nass, meaning "the stomach, or food depot" has been given to the river' (G. T. Emmons, 1910).

8. In Lévi-Strauss's writings the notion of a structured conceptual scheme (*schème conceptuel*), which lies at the back of explicit cultural forms and

43

consists in the main of elements linked in binary opposition, is of basic importance. See, in particular *La Pensée sauvage* (1962b, p. 173). Throughout this translation the French *schème* has been consistently rendered as English 'schema' and French *opposition* as English 'opposition' even though in places it might have been more elegant to write 'framework' or 'setting' for *schème*, and 'contrast' or 'antithesis' for *opposition* [E.R.L.].

9. As we shall see later, the apparent gap in the cycle is explained by the fact that in the story of Waux, Asdiwal's son, the closure will be the result of a matrilateral marriage which ends in a terminal situation: husband and wife without children.

10. Asdiwal himself had inherited from his father the lightness and speed of a bird, qualities which are ideally suited to a hunter who, according to native thought, should be as light-footed as a bird on the wing (Boas, 1916, p. 403). Boas's informant considers Waux as Asdiwal's only child (Boas, 1916, p. 243). This is a mistake, for Asdiwal also had a son by his third marriage (Boas, 1912, pp. 123, 133, 135). But this point is unimportant since the third marriage was simply a doublet of the second.

11. Boas's informant seems to have made a mistake which Boas has only partially corrected. In Boas (1916) the text is as follows 'Before his mother died she wanted her son to marry one of her own cousins, and he did what his mother wanted him to do' (p. 244). Thus it would be a cousin of the mother and not of the son. The corresponding native text is to be found in Durlach (1928, p. 124) of which herewith a transcription (in simplified signs): na gauga(?) dem dzake na'ot da hasa'x a dem naksde lguolget a k!âlda lgu-txaât. . . .

The kinship term *txaâ* denotes the father's sister's or the mother's brother's children – that is to say, all cross-cousins. *Lgu-* is a diminutive. The suffix -*t* is a third person possessive. In his summary of the story of Waux, Boas repeats the suspect phrase: 'He marries one of his mother's cousins' (Boas, 1916, p. 825). But in the commentary he corrects his interpretation by placing this example quite rightly with all those he quotes of marriages with a matrilateral cross-cousin. 'The normal type of marriage, as described in the traditions, is that between a young man and his mother's brother's daughter. Thus . . . a mother requests her daughter to marry her cousin (244)' (Boas, 1916, p. 440). Since p. 244 only mentions Waux's marriage, it is clear that this time Boas rectifies the kinship relations, but confuses the sex of the husband and wife. From this there arises a new contradiction, for this cousin would be the father's sister's daughter. The real meaning seems to be: before dying, his mother wanted him to marry one of his own cousins.

12. Boas (1916, pp. 185-191): Describing the marriage ceremonies of the Nisqa as reported by another informant, Boas explains that the fight between the two groups can become so violent that one of the slaves in the suitor's guard is killed: 'This foretells that the couple will never part' (Boas, 1916, p. 531).

13. Boas (1916, p. 403). Asdiwal's double visit to heaven (which contrasts with his single journey below the earth) seems to be intended to make even clearer the analogy with salmon-fishing. In fact, his return to heaven takes place exactly as if it were a 'catch', in a net which is let down through an opening in the heavens: just like the ritual fishing for the first salmon of spring, which is carried out with a net, through a hole made in the ice which still covers the river.

14. Boas (1912, pp. 112-113). If our interpretation is correct, it must be

admitted that the explicit opposition: sky/earth is here realized in an implicit form: sky/water, which is the strongest opposition inherent in the system of the three elements as used by the myth.

This system can in fact be represented by the following formula (read the sign : to mean 'is to', the sign :: to mean 'as', the sign > to mean 'is above', and the sign / to mean 'is opposed to')

1. sky : earth :: earth : water

which can also be written

2. sky > earth > water

Then the hypothesis put forward above about the 'fishing up' of Asdiwal can be verified by the following permutation:

3. sky : water :: earth : earth

which may be said to correspond to Asdiwal's second supernatural voyage, where the opposition to water (earth) is expressed by a subterranean voyage. We are therefore perfectly entitled to put

4. sky/earth :: sky/water (where 'water' stands for 'beneath the sky')

5. earth/water :: earth/earth (where '/earth' stands for 'below the ground')

But this duplication of the 'earth' pole is only made necessary by the assimilation (in veiled terms) of the major opposition between sky and earth to the minor opposition, still implicit, between earth and water: Asdiwal is fished up like a fish off an earth which is confused with the liquid element, from the heights of a sky pictured in terrestial terms as a 'green and fertile prairie'.

From the very beginning the myth seems governed by one particular opposition which is more vital than the others, even if not immediately perceptible: that between earth and water, which is also the one most closely linked with methods of production and the objective relationships between men and the world. Formal though it be, analysis of a society's myths verifies the primacy of the infrastructures.

15. See Boas's hesitations in Boas (1916, pp. 401, 411, 412). Even Garfield, who gave the problems much attention, cannot bring herself to admit to the existence of succession in the paternal line. See Garfield, Wingert & Barbeau (1951, p. 17).

16. Boas (1916, p. 793). None the less, there are a few minor differences which suggest that Boas (1895) is a weak variant of Boas (1912).

17. J. R. Swanton (1952). 'Lakkulzap or Greenville' (p. 586); 'Gitwinksilk . . . near the mouth of Nass River' (*idem*). In any case, Barbeau's map (1950) places Gitwinksilk (Gitwinksihlt) upstream of the Canyon.

18. E. Sapir (1915): 'Greenville (laxqaltsa'p) . . .' (p. 2). According to Sapir, the Gitwankcitlku, 'people of the place where lizards live', from the third Nisqa group, starting from downstream.

19. Sapir (1915): 'Gitxate'n, people of the fish traps' (p. 3). Barbeau (1950, map) Gitrhatin, at the mouth of the estuary and downstream from the canyon.

20. That is, at any rate, what the myth emphatically affirms – but the village of the younger woman is not named.

21. Many myths treat of the loss of salmon by mankind, thanks to men's refusing a piece of mouldy fish, or to their disgust on discovering that the Mother of Salmon gives birth by her excretory canal.

22. Lévi-Strauss's distinction *marqué/non-mraqué* is here rendered 'defined'/ 'not defined', but note also the distinction 'marked'/'unmarked' as it occurs in general linguistics. In the latter context the words *man* and *author* are 'unmarked' in comparison with the words *woman* and *authoress* which are

45

179

Claude Lévi-Strauss

'marked'. Here the 'unmarked' term will be presumed to include the 'marked' category unless the latter is explicitly distinguished. For a full discussion, see Greenberg (1966).

23. The younger woman, representing prospective fertility, shows a markedly feminine character; in the elder this is not so marked. The younger must always be in the (earth) position: in the Skeena version, because she is to bear Asdiwal, master of mountains and earth-born hunter; in the Nass version for the same reason, and also because of the strictly feminine character of the gatherer of berries, which stand for earth-food. Cf. Boas (1916): 'while the men procure all the animal food except shellfish, the women gather berries and dig roots and shellfish' (p. 52, also p. 404).

24. E. Sapir (1915, pp. 3-7), where it is clear that Goddard (1934) was wrong in attributing only two exogamic divisions to the Nisqa instead of four. This mistake can probably be explained by the fact that the Nisqa, immediate neighbours of the Tlingit, find it necessary more often than the Tsimshian to apply the rule of the lowest common multiple to their social organization, so that the laws of exogamy may be respected in marriages with foreigners.

25. Boas quotes 31 pairs of 'local particles' in oppositions of the following type: up along the ground–down along the ground; up through the air–down through the air; into–out of; backwards–forwards, etc. (Boas, 1911, pp. 300-312).

REFERENCES

BARBEAU, M. 1950. Totem Poles. *National Museum of Canada Bulletin*, No. 119, Anthropological Series No. 30.

BEYNON, W. 1941. The Tsimshians of Metlakatla. *American Anthropologist* 43: 83-88.

BOAS, FRANZ. 1895. *Indianische Sagen von der Nord-Pacifischen Küste Amerikas*. Berlin.

— 1902. Tsimshian Texts. *Bulletin of Smithsonian Institution*, No. 27. Bureau of American Ethnology, Washington.

— 1911. 'Tsimshian' in *Handbook of American Indian Languages*, Part I. Smithsonian Institution, Bureau of American Ethnology, Bulletin 40, Part I.

— 1912. *Tsimshian Texts (New Series)*. Publication of American Ethnological Society, Vol. III. Leyden.

— 1916. *Tsimshian Mythology*. Annual Report Smithsonian Institution, No. 31 (1909-1910). Washington: Bureau of American Ethnology.

DURLACH, T. M. 1928. *The Relationship Systems of the Tlingit, Haida and Tsimshian*. Publications of American Ethnological Society, Vol. XI. New York.

EMMONS, G. T. 1910. 'Niska' in *Handbook of American Indians North of Mexico*. Smithsonian Institution, Bureau of American Ethnology, Bulletin 30, Part II.

GARFIELD, V. E. 1939. *Tsimshian Clan and Society*. University of Washington Publications in Anthropology, Vol. 7, No. 3.

46

GARFIELD, V. E., WINGERT, P. S. & BARBEAU, M. 1951. *The Tsimshian: Their Arts and Music*. Publications of American Ethnological Society, Vol. XVIII. New York.

GODDARD, P. E. 1934. *Indians of the Northwest Coast*. American Museum of Natural History, Handbook Series No. 10. New York.

GREENBERG, J. H. 1966. Language Universals. In T. A. Sebeok (ed.), *Current Trends in Linguistics*, Volume 3: *Theoretical Foundations*. The Hague: Mouton, pp. 62ff.

LÉVI-STRAUSS, C. 1949. *Les Structures élémentaires de la parenté*. Paris: Presses Universitaires de France.

—— 1958a. *Anthropologie structurale*. Paris: Plon (English translation, 1963a. *Structural Anthropology*. New York: Basic Books).

—— 1962b. *La Pensée sauvage*. Paris: Plon.

MALINOWSKI, B. 1932. *The Sexual Life of Savages in North-Western Melanesia*, 3rd edn. London: Routledge.

RICHARDS, J. F. 1914. Cross Cousin Marriage in South India. *Man* 14.

SAPIR, E. 1915. A Sketch of the Social Organisation of the Nass River Indians. *Museum Bulletin of the Canadian Dept. of Mines, Geological Survey*, No. XIX. Ottawa.

SWANTON, J. R. 1909. *Contributions to the Ethnology of the Haida*. Memoirs of American Museum of Natural History, Vol. VIII.

—— 1952. *The Indian Tribes of North America*. Smithsonian Institution, Bureau of American Ethnology, Bulletin 145.

WEDGEWOOD, C. H. 1928. Cousin Marriage in *Encyclopaedia Britannica*, 14th edn.

47

C. SCOTT LITTLETON

The Comparative Indo-European Mythology of Georges Dumézil

I

The purpose of this paper[1] is to discuss one of the most remarkable figures to appear in the field of comparative Indo-European mythology since the turn of the century: Professor Georges Dumézil, presently occupant of the chair of Indo-European Civilization in the Collège de France. For Dumézil, trained under the great Indo-Europeanist Antoine Meillet, and exposed to the sociology of Durkheim, Marcel Mauss, and others who in the early years of the present century were shaping a functional approach to the study of primitive religion, has added a new sociological and anthropological dimension to the traditional comparative study of Indo-European myth, epic, ritual, folklore, and society. As a result a wholly new conception of the nature of these phenomena and their relationship to one another has emerged.

In applying the fundamental Durkheimian principle[2] that the persons,

[1] The bulk of the research upon which this paper is based was done in 1961-62 under the auspices of the Center for the Study of Comparative Folklore and Mythology, University of California, Los Angeles; the writing was done in 1963 and greatly facilitated by an Occidental College Faculty Fellowship, generously provided by the John Randolph and Dora Haynes Foundation of Los Angeles. To all those concerned, the author would like to express his sincere thanks. Special thanks are due to Professors William A. Lessa, of the Department of Anthropology, and Jaan Puhvel, of the Department of Classics, University of California, Los Angeles, for their most welcome advice, assistance, and encouragement during the course of this research; the extent of this debt cannot be overestimated.

[2] Cf. Émile Durkheim, *The Elementary Forms of the Religious Life*, translated from the French by Joseph Ward Swain (New York, 1961), pp. 22-23. See also Durkheim and Marcel Mauss, "De quelques formes primitives de classification; Contributions à l'étude des représentations collectives," *L'Année Sociologique*, VI (1903), 1-72; Mauss, it should be noted, was a mentor and for many years close associate of Dumézil in the École des Hautes Études, Section des Sciences Religieuses.

183

places, events, and situations which receive expression in myths are inevitably representations of important social and cultural realities to his analysis of I-E³ materials, Dumézil has sought to demonstrate that the earliest I-E speaking societies of India, Europe, and elsewhere shared a common set of such "collective representations." Most if not all of these early I-E societies, he asserts, were characterized, at least in their earliest known periods, by a hierarchically ordered, tripartite social organization, each stratum of which was collectively represented in myth and epic by an appropriate set of gods and heroes. These three social strata, which included, in order of precedence, a priestly stratum, a warrior stratum, and a herder-cultivator stratum, together with their mythical counterparts, each made a specific contribution to the maintenance of the whole social and/or supernatural system and for this reason, apparently, Dumézil uses the term *fonction*, or "function," as a label here. Thus, the first or most important "function" (i.e., the priestly stratum and its mythical representations) was concerned with the maintenance of magico-religious and juridical order; the second "function" (i.e., the warrior stratum and its representations) was concerned with physical prowess; and the third or least important "function" as far as the Indo-Europeans were concerned (i.e., the herder-cultivator stratum and its representations) was charged with the provision of sustenance, the maintenance of physical well-being, plant and animal fertility, and other related activities. Underlying this functionally interrelated, tripartite social and supernatural system was a tripartite ideology; a tendency to conceive of phenomena in general as divided into three interrelated categories, defined in terms of the three above mentioned "functions."

In short, on the basis of his comparative analysis of the varied social and mythological forms presented by the ancient I-E speaking world, Dumézil has concluded (1) that the parent or proto-I-E society, before it broke up, was characterized by a tripartite ideology, (2) that elements of this ideology were carried by the inheritors of this society across the length and breadth of what was to become the historic I-E domain, and (3) that these elements can be discovered in most (but by no means all) of the early I-E mythical and epical literature – from the *Vedas* of ancient India to the *Eddas* of pre-Christian Iceland, from the *Mahābhārata* to the *Heimskringla*. Moreover, this tripartite ideology, whether

³ Wherever possible, and in accordance with long established linguistic usage, the abbreviation "I-E" will be substituted for "Indo-European".

expressed in myth, epic, or social organization, is asserted to be uniquely I-E, having no parallels among the ancient civilizations of the Near East, Nile Valley, China, or any other region of the Old World prior to the I-E migrations in the second millennium B.C.

These conclusions as to the nature of I-E myth and society were not reached overnight. They are indeed the result of extensive research, the direction of which has more than once altered its course. Yet as early as 1924, in his rather Frazerian doctoral dissertation, *Le festin d'immortalité*, Dumézil set forth a statement of faith, so to speak, which, though modified through the years, still guides his research.

Bref, [he observed] il s'agit de restituer, dans la préhistoire des légendes et des mythes, à côté de leur interprétation sociale, une part à l'étude de leur évolution.[4]

II

Perhaps the best way to introduce Professor Dumézil's system is to consider it in context. Let us begin, as he often begins, with the ancient I-E speaking communities of northern India.

As is well known, classical Indian social organization was composed of four main castes: The *Brahmans*, or priests, the *Kṣatriyas* (*Rajputs*), or warriors, the *Vaiśyas*, or cultivators, and the *Śūdras*, or those whose obligation it was to serve all the rest. Of these castes, only the first three were defined as *Arya*, a description which, like the word "Navaho," seems originally to have meant simply 'people' or 'human beings';[5] the *Śūdras*, thus, were "out-castes" in the best sense of the term and in

---

[4] Georges Dumézil, *Le festin d'immortalité, étude de mythologie comparée indo-européenne* (= *Annales du Musée Guimet, Bibliotheque d'études*, tome xxxiv) (Paris, 1924), p. iv.

[5] Dumézil and Paul Thieme have engaged in a long running debate over the meaning of the Skt. root *ari-*. The latter has suggested that it means 'foreigner' or 'stranger', while the former has maintained that it is simply an ethnic self-identification term, like Navaho, etc. Cf. Paul Thieme, *Der Fremdling im Rigveda* (Berlin, 1938); *Mitra and Aryaman* (= *Transactions of the Connecticut Academy of Arts and Sciences*, XLI) (New Haven, 1957), 1-96; Dumézil, "Le nom des 'Arya'," *Revue de l'Histoire des Religions*, CXXI (1941), 36-59; "Aryaman et Paul Thieme," in *L'idéologie tripartie des Indo-Européens* (= *Collection Latomus*, XXXI) (Brussels, 1958), 108-118. See also E. Laroche, "Hittite *arawa*- 'libre'," in *Hommages à Georges Dumézil* (Brussels, 1960), 124-128.

theory, at least, included the conquered, indigenous population. In its broad outlines, this system still obtains, despite the proliferation of sub-castes within each major group and the fact that today the line between *Vaiśya* and *Śūdra* is by no means clearly defined in many regions, especially in South India.

If one analyzes the ancient Sanskrit religious literature, Dumézil claims, one can see that the earliest Indian pantheon reflected this stratified social organization, especially the three *Arya* castes. Even in the oldest of all Indian texts, the *Rig Veda*,[6] there can be found three hierarchically ranked, functionally differentiated strata of gods – a pattern which appears over and over again in the later *Vedas* and *Brāhmaṇas*, and indeed persists, in a somewhat altered form, in the great Indian epic, the *Mahābhārata*.

At the highest of these three divine levels appear the sovereign gods Mitra and Varuṇa. The characteristics of these two deities are such that in Dumézil's opinion they are projections – or collective representations – of the *Brahman* caste which, of course, in the mortal scheme of things, is at the apex of the social system. Moreover, Dumézil has concluded that there exists between the two gods in question a definite division of supernatural labor as regards the management of the universe. On the one hand, Mitra is concerned with the rational and legal aspects of sovereignty; indeed, Meillet, as early as 1907, had suggested that Mitra might be the personification of the idea of 'Contract.' Varuṇa, on the other hand, represents the awesome and sometimes terrible magico-religious aspects of sovereignty. Thus, respectively, Mitra and Varuṇa reflect the two basic functions of the *Brahman*: (1) to serve as an arbiter of legal and contractual disputes, and (2) to serve as a magical and religious practitioner, conducting sacrifices, divining, performing marriages, etc. Here, then, is an example of what Dumézil has labeled the "first function": the relationship or correspondence between Mitra and Varuṇa, together with their celestial "assistants," so to speak (a set of lesser deities who share certain aspects of the sovereignty; e.g., Bhaga, Aryaman) and the priestly caste or class (as it appears to have been in the

---

[6] The hymns of the *Rig Veda* do not present a fully developed picture of the classical Indian castes or *varna*, although the roots of the words later used as caste designations (e.g., *Brahman*, from *brah-*) are indeed present; see Dumézil, *Jupiter, Mars, Quirinus* (Paris, 1941), pp. 20-30; *Mitra-Varuṇa, essai sur deux représentations indo-européennes de la souveraineté*, 2nd ed. (Paris, 1948).

earliest period). In summarizing the nature of the "first function," Dumézil[7] claims that it is concerned with "...l'administration à la fois mysterieuse et régulière du monde."

At the second supernatural level one finds a set of young, virile, warlike gods (i.e., the *Maruts*), dominated by the imposing figure of Indra, who is the personification of the warrior ideal. It is Indra who fights monsters (e.g., *Vritra*), leads armies, and, unlike Mitra and Varuṇa, generally gains his ends through the exercise of physical strength. Indra, thus, is a collective representation of the *Kṣatriya* caste, whose prime function is to protect the society against the threat or actuality of armed invasion. This relationship, then, between the warrior caste or class and its personifications constitutes the "second function" and is defined as "...le jeu de la vigueur physique, de la force, principalement mais non uniquement guerrière."[8]

Finally, at the lowest level, there appear a number of deities whose principal function is to maintain and promote plant and animal fertility, to assure bountiful harvests, and generally to preside over matters of human physical well-being and comfort. Chief among these are the *Aśvins*, or 'Divine Twins.' Also included here (and elsewhere, as we shall see) is a female figure, the goddess Sarasvatī. This lowest divine stratum, the occupants of which are seen as collectively representing the food-producing class, constitutes the "third function," which is defined as "...la fécondité, avec beaucoup de consequences et de resonances, telles que la santé, la longue vie, la tranquillité, la volupté, le 'nombre'."[9]

Thus, in brief, is the picture Dumézil draws of ancient Indian myth and society: three functionally integrated strata of men and gods, dominated by the conception of a joint or dual sovereignty shared by a pair of gods representing, respectively, juridical and magico-religious processes. Together, these strata, or "functions," form an integrated social and supernatural whole.

If the foregoing system were limited to Vedic India, it would be difficult to generalize it as I-E. But as noted earlier, Dumézil has attempted to demonstrate the presence of these same three functions, as well as the concept of joint sovereignty, in the myths and social structures of most of the ancient I-E speaking communities. Outside of India, his

[7] Dumézil, *Les dieux des Indo-Européens* (Paris, 1952), p. 7.
[8] *Ibid.*
[9] *Ibid.*

best evidence so far comes from the rest of the Indo-Iranian speaking region, as well as from those regions historically associated with Italic, Germanic, and Celtic speaking peoples.

By far the oldest datable example of tripartition among the Indo-Iranians – or any other group of I-E speakers, for that matter – can be found in the famous 14th century B.C. treaty, preserved in the archives at Boghazköy, between the Mitannian king Matiwaza and his Hittite conquerors. Matiwaza, who belonged to an Indo-Iranian (or perhaps already Indic[10]) military aristocracy which had imposed itself several centuries earlier upon the predominantly Hurrian population of this north Syrian state, invoked his gods as witnesses to the treaty and among them appear, unmistakably, and in the following order, the names Mitra-Varuna, Indara (i.e. Indra), and that of the Nāsatyas (i.e. the Aśvins). That these gods represented the same social and supernatural functions and conception of sovereignty as their later Vedic counterparts seems certain, Dumézil feels, pointing out[11] that, although relatively little is known about the social organization of 14th century B.C. Mitanni, the fact that its I-E speaking ruling class is referred to as the marya or maru (cf. Indra and his Maruts) would seem to indicate the presence at least of the I-E warrior stratum; that the other two strata were also present seems quite probable, he asserts, given the series of gods listed in the treaty.

Another, albeit much later, Indo-Iranian example can be found in Herodotus's account (4.5-6) of the Scythian origin myth, wherein three objects of burning gold, a cup, an ax, and a yoke, fall from the sky and are recovered by the youngest son of Targitaos, the primeval being. In the foregoing, our subject recognizes a clear expression of social and mythological tripartition. The three objects symbolize, respectively, the first, second, and third functions, and from their recoverer, Kolaxaïs, springs the dominant Scythian class or tribe. From Kolaxaïs's two elder brothers, who successively failed in their attempts to recover the burning implements, issue the Scythian warrior and food-producing classes. Thus, among the westernmost group of Indo-Iranians, the three I-E functions are collectively represented by three brothers, the youngest of whom is

[10]   See Thieme, "The 'Aryan' Gods of the Mitanni Treaties," *Journal of the American Oriental Society*, LXXX (1960), 301-317.
[11]   Dumézil, *Naissance d'archanges, essai sur la formation de la théologie zoroastrienne* (Paris, 1945), pp. 8-11, 15-55.

sovereign. Although the joint or dual aspects of the first function are lacking here, Dumézil feels that the rest of the evidence is clear enough to support his thesis, especially the symbolic associations of the celestial objects. The cup, for example, associated as it is with the preparation and consumption by priests of sacred beverages – an I-E pattern which has long been recognized;[12] e.g., *meade, madhu, soma, haoma* – serves as a symbolic expression of the first function in a number of ancient I-E traditions, as well as in modern European folklore.[13]

As far as Iran itself is concerned, it is in the theological reforms of Zoroaster (7th-6th centuries B.C.) that Dumézil sees the clearest expression of the I-E system. In attempting to substitute an ethical and metaphysical dualism for the ancient Iranian polytheism – a polytheism which appears to have been broadly similar to that of Vedic India – Zoroaster conceived of a series of more or less abstract beings as part of the retinue, so to speak, of the Good Principle (Ahura Mazda). These beings, labeled *Ameša Spentas* ("Immortal Benificences"), remarkably parallel the Indic gods previously discussed: *Aša* ('Order') and *Vohu Manah* ("Good Thought"), respectively, correspond to Varuṇa and Mitra and can thus be viewed as representatives of the first function; *Xšathra* ("Dominion") parallels Indra and represents the second function; the pair *Haurvatāt* ("Health") and *Ameretāt* ("Immortality") parallel the *Aśvins* and relate to the third function, as does the female figure *Ārmaiti* ("Pious Thought"), a Zoroastrian version of the archaic Iranian goddess Anāhitā and a counterpart of the previously mentioned Sarasvatī.

Before leaving the Indo-Iranian area, it should be pointed out that not all of the evidence is as clear-cut as the few examples given above would seem perhaps to indicate. For example, the ancient Iranian god Mithra, whose cult survived the Zoroastrian reforms and flourished in Iran and elsewhere until the spread of Islam and Christianity put an end to it, presents some rather difficult problems when viewed from a Dumézilian perspective. Despite the obvious onomastic similarities to Mitra, and despite the prominence of the Mithraic cult, the god exhibits both first and second function characteristics. Indeed, in the later *Avesta* (cf. especially *Yt.* 9, the so-called "Mithra *Yašt*") and in graphic art, Mithra

[12]   Dumézil, *Le festin d'immortalité.*
[13]   See Lucien Gerschel, "Sur un schème trifonctionnel dans une famille de légendes germaniques," *Revue de l'Histoire des Religions,* CL (1956), 55-92.

is usually represented as a young and virile warrior, a trait rarely if ever associated with Mitra.

Turning our attention to the West, Dumézil claims to have uncovered some excellent examples of social and supernatural tripartition in early Rome. And here, in my opinion, he has made a most important contribution to scholarship, whatever may prove to be the fate of his over-all system.

At first glance, Rome appears to have possessed a culture characterized by an abundance of ritual and a paucity of myth. There is Virgil; there is Ovid; there are numerous identifications between Roman and Greek divinities; but on the surface, at least, there seems to be little in the way of native Roman myth. However, after an exhaustive examination of the admittedly legendary early history of the city, as found in the first books of Livy and elsewhere, Dumézil has concluded that Rome's myths had indeed become euhemerized. In a brilliant series of works devoted to the subject (1941-48), he finds in the persons of Romulus, Numa, and the warlike Tullus Hostilius, the three earliest kings of Rome, the characteristic gods of the joint sovereignty (Romulus equaling Varuṇa and Numa Mitra), as well as that of the second function (Tullus Hostilius equaling Indra). The third function is less clearly evident, although Dumézil feels it was represented by the Sabines, who were traditionally viewed as devotees of luxury, "la tranquillité," and "la volupté." In the legendary Sabine War Dumézil sees an expression of an I-E mythic theme not yet mentioned: a struggle between representatives of the first two functions and those of the third, wherein the latter are defeated and thus brought into the social system. Granting his interpretation here, the foregoing would serve to explain the lowly position of the cultivator in I-E society; he was the last to be admitted to it, as far as myth is concerned. We shall have more to say about this assumed "war between the functions" when we encounter it again shortly in ancient Scandinavian myth.

On another level, that of the Roman pantheon, Dumézil also sees an expression of the tripartite system. In the so-called "pre-Capitoline" or archaic triad, consisting of Jupiter, Mars, and Quirinus, he finds, respectively, the magico-religious half of the first function, the second function, and part of the third function. The picture is completed by several obscure and little known early Roman gods: Dius Fidius, who is often coupled with Jupiter, represents the Mitra-half of the sovereignty, and Ops (related to the root of the English word 'opulent'), who is often paired with Quirinus.

Among the Germanic speaking peoples, especially the Scandinavians, the subject of our study once again claims to have uncovered some examples of mythological and social tripartition. In his *Les dieux des Germains* (1959) and elsewhere, Dumézil attempts to demonstrate that the Norse gods Othinn and Tyr respectively represent the magico-religious and juridical aspects of the sovereignty, and that Thor, the warrior, corresponds to Mars and Indra and is a second function figure. The twin gods Freyr and Njördr are seen to be third function figures, corresponding to Quirinus and Ops as well as to the *Aśvins*. In addition, Dumézil has indicated the presence of a third function female figure here, the goddess Freyja, whom he links with Sarasvatī and Anāhitā. Finally, the previously mentioned theme of a war between representatives of the first two functions and those of the third is expressed, he asserts, in the mythical conflict between the *Aesir*, the dominant group of gods, to which Othinn, Tyr, and Thor belong, and the *Vanir*, to which Freyr, Njördr, and Freyja belong. As is the case with the Sabines, the Vanir, representing the third function, are defeated and thus brought into the system.

Once again we encounter an explanation of the lowly position of the I-E cultivator, this time in Scandinavia: his gods, here the *Vanir*, who are essentially terrestrial in character and thus especially important to those who till the earth, were the last to be included in the pantheon. That this theme, expressed clearly and independently in Roman and Norse myth, reflects some historic event or events, such as a war or a series of wars between an agricultural and a non-agricultural people, wherein the latter were victorious, is, of course, highly conjectural. Yet such a victory on the part of a warlike, nomadic (or semi-nomadic), hunting and gathering people over one possessed of a more sedentary, neolithic type of economy could easily have resulted in the formation of a new and larger society, as well as a new speech community – perhaps that of the proto-Indo-Europeans.[14]

We should add immediately that Dumézil himself does not offer this

---

[14]   Cf. the theories of Trubetzkoy, who has abandoned altogether the idea of a single I-E proto-language in favor of the notion that from the beginning I-E has been a group of related languages which, in the third millennium B.C., served as a bridge between the Caucasic and Semitic speech communities to the south and the Finno-Ugric and Altaic communities to the north and east; see N. S. Trubetzkoy, "Gedanken über das Indogermanenproblem," *Acta Linguistica*, I (1939), 81-89.

conjecture; it is our own, based upon the evidence he presents. Admittedly, it may be somewhat overly euhemeristic, although it should be borne in mind that in other areas and in other times comparable events have indeed formed the basis of myths and their memory has thereby been preserved long after they ceased to be "history" in the usual sense of the term.[15]

Among the Celts, although Dumézil and his students have uncovered a number of tripartitions which do seem to relate to the three assumed I-E functions – for example, the traditions surrounding the three *Machas* of Ulster, one of whom was a prophetess, the wife of Nemed the Sacred, the second a female warrior who fought her way to the throne, and the third the beautiful wife of a farmer, to whom she brought additional riches and presented twins[16] – no over-all division of either the Irish, Brythonic, or Gallic pantheons has yet been made with any degree of certainty. This, of course, is in large part due to our imperfect knowledge of these pantheons, especially that of ancient Gaul. As far as the latter is concerned, more often than not we are forced to rely upon the *interpretatio romana*, which, it would appear, was in many cases quite arbitrary and based upon political expediency.[17] For reasons too detailed to enumerate here, Dumézil claims that the three Gallic techniques of human sacrifice, as reported by Lucan and others, represent a tripartite formula and that each technique can be seen as ensuring the social and supernatural effectiveness of one of the three I-E functions. Thus, burning in a wicker basket related to the first function, hanging from a tree related to the second, and drowning in a keg ensured the effectiveness of the third.

Elsewhere among the early I-E speaking communities the evidence is at best much less abundant and in all cases less certain. Among the Greeks, for example, despite the fact that their mythology is perhaps the best known of all the world's mythologies, only a few hints of the tripartite

[15] See William Bascom, "The Myth-Ritual Theory," *Journal of American Folklore*, LXX (1957), 103-114.
[16] Dumézil, "Le trio des Macha," *Revue de l'Histoire des Religions*, CXLVI (1954), 5-17.
[17] See Jan de Vries, "Die Interpretatio Romana der gallischen Götter," *Indogermanica: Festschrift für Wolfgang Krause* (Heidelberg, 1960), 204-213; see also Françoise Le Roux, *Les Druides* (Paris, 1961); "Études sur le Festiaire Celtique," *Ogam*, XIV (1962), 174-184.

system have as yet been detected.[18] As far as the pantheon is concerned, the Dioscuri, or 'Heavenly Twins,' do indeed seem to correspond to the *Aśvins* – an observation made long before Dumézil's time[19] – and can, in Dumézil's eyes, be reckoned as representing the third function. The other two levels, however, are not clearly defined; e.g., Zeus, like Mithra, exhibits traits characteristic of both the first and second functions. The chief of the Olympians achieves his ends through a combination of magical spells (cf. Varuṇa) and physical force (cf. Indra), and at the same time upholds universal order and the sanctity of oaths and contracts (cf. Mitra).

Perhaps the best single Greek example of mythological tripartition so far uncovered concerns the well-known "judgment of Paris," wherein the Trojan prince must choose between the regal Hera, the warlike Athena, and the voluptuous Aphrodite. So as to influence him in his choice, each goddess, here seen as a representative of one of the three functions, offers Paris a gift: Hera offers world sovereignty (first function), Athena promises military prowess (second function), and Aphrodite tenders the gift of earthly pleasure (third function). Paris chooses the latter goddess and thus, by alienating Hera and Athena (i.e., the first two functions), ensures Troy's ultimate downfall.[20]

In addition to the gods of the three functions, Dumézil asserts that in most of the I-E pantheons there are certain deities who must be viewed as essentially outside any one level of the tripartite structure; gods (and goddesses) whose function is to support or integrate this structure by summing together in their persons traits characteristic of all three levels.

---

[18]   The difficulty here, it seems, results in large part from the fact that the Greeks, like the Hittites – Dumézil has so far avoided any interpretation of Hittite religion – were so profoundly influenced by the non-I-E civilizations of the eastern Mediterranean and that this is reflected throughout their myths and epics; see Dumézil, *L'idéologie tripartie des Indo-Européens*, p. 91. Palmer, working independently, has attempted to demonstrate the presence of a tripartite, feudal social structure in the newly translated Mycenaean texts and has asserted that this same pattern was characteristic of the earlier stages of the Hittite Empire as revealed by the texts found at Boghazköy. The correctness of this demonstration remains to be confirmed. See L. R. Palmer, *Achaeans and Indo-Europeans, an Inaugural Lecture* (Oxford, 1955), 1-21; Dumézil, *L'idéologie tripartie des Indo-Européens*, p. 94, where he notes that "L. R. Palmer a brillamment propose de reconnaître la tripartition sociale indoeuropéenne dans des textes mycéniens."

[19]   Cf., for example, Sir George W. Cox, *The Mythology of the Aryan Nations* (London, 1887), p. 207.

[20]   Dumézil, "Les trois fonctions dans quelques traditions grecques," in *Hommages à Lucien Febvre,* II (Paris, 1953), 25-32.

Included here are a number of gods who, like the Roman Janus and
Vesta and the Vedic Vāyu and Agni, are primarily associated with
beginnings and endings. In ancient India, for example, Dumézil points
out that Vāyu was usually invoked at the beginning of a ritual, prior to
the invocation of Mitra and Varuṇa, and that Agni was invoked subsequent to the invocation of the *Aśvins* (or *Nāsatya*). These, then, are
what he terms "dieux premiers" and "dieux derniers"; beings who
proceed and are subsequent to the gods of the three functions.[21] Anāhitā,
Sarasvatī, Freyja, and other I-E female figures are usually classed both
as "déesses derniers" and as third function figures; some, like the Greek
Athena, seem to relate to all three functions.[22] Perhaps the clearest
example of a female figure who cuts across the system is furnished by the
trio of Irish *Machas* discussed earlier, who appear to be but aspects of a
single goddess. In any case, Dumézil sees these multi-functional gods
and goddesses, wherever they occur, as logically and functionally linked
to the over-all tripartite structure of the pantheon. They form, as he
puts it, "l'épine du système."[23]

Although it has been subjected to surprisingly little criticism from his
adversaries – who are usually more than willing to disassemble any
theory which Dumézil has constructed – this notion of an "épine"
supporting the tripartite structure is, in our opinion, one of the weaker
links in our subject's chain of ideas; and the extent to which gods such
as Janus and Vāyu belong merely to a residual category of deities not
otherwise categorizable in terms of the three assumed functions must not
be overlooked in any assessment of this idea.

Turning to matters of social organization, Dumézil hastens to point
out that, save for India, mythological tripartition far outlasted the
social tripartition upon which it originally seems to have been based.
Only in India did the archaic I-E social system "harden," so to speak.
Nevertheless, fragments of it can be found, he feels, in most if not all of
the early I-E speaking communities just discussed. We have already
mentioned the *marya* or *maru* of Mitanni as indicative of the presence of
the warrior stratum and have noted the situation presented by the Scyths,

[21] Dumézil, *Tarpeia, cinq essais de philologie comparative indo-européenne* (Paris,
1947), pp. 33-113; *Les dieux des Indo-Européens*, pp. 79-103.
[22] See F. Vian, *La guerre des géants, le mythe avant l'époque hellènistique* (Paris, 1952),
pp. 257-258.
[23] Dumézil, "La tripartition indo-européenne," *Psyche*, II (1947), 1352.

wherein three hierarchically ranked strata (or tribes) were conceived to have been founded by the sons of Targitaos. Among the ancient Iranians and Celts, Dumézil points to the presence of a clearly defined, *Brahman*-like priest class, respectively, the *Magi* (or *Magavans*) and the Druids; and in the *Avesta* he finds evidence of three other archaic Iranian social groups, composed of warriors, cultivators, and artisans – although the extent to which the latter group either represented the indigenous, pre-I-E population of Iran (cf. the *Śūdras*) or was merely an aspect of the third function is unclear.

At Rome, Dumézil cites the persistence of a priestly group (if not class), the *Flamens*; indeed, in an early work (1935)[24] he attempted to relate philologically the words *Flamen* and *Brahman*. This has not been generally accepted, but the cultural comparisons which he makes between these two sacral groups, especially as regards common sets of taboos and patterns of ritual cleanliness, are certainly suggestive;[25] e.g., neither the *Flamen dialis* nor a *Brahman* could undress completely, look at a horse, or engage in physical combat. Also, he points out that the three original Roman "tribes" – the *Ramnes* (reputedly founded by Romulus), *Luceres*, and *Titienses* – perhaps represent a division, respectively, into priests, warriors, and cultivators.

The Germanic speaking communities generally present a negative picture when it comes to social tripartition. Even the priestly segment seems to be absent.[26] Yet the presence of a *Männerbund*, or *Marut*-like

[24] Dumézil, *Flamen-Brahman* (= *Annales du Musée Guimet, Bibliothèque de vulgarisation*, tome li) (Paris, 1935).
[25] Initially, Dumézil conceived of the *Bhlag^h(s)-men*, I-E prototype of the Indic *Brahman*, the Iranian *Baresman*, and the Roman *flamen* (*Flamen-Brahman*, p. 56), as functioning primarily (or primevally, perhaps) as a substitute sacrificial victim for the *reg-* (Lat. *rex*, Skt. *rājan-*, Irish *rig-*, etc.) or 'king' rather than as a priest, and assumed that his exalted status derived from the fact that in order to be acceptable to the gods such a substitute must be equal to or greater than the actual ruler in prestige (cf. "L'histoire de Çunahçepa," *Flamen-Brahman*, pp. 21-23). Here, of course, the influence of Frazer is clearly evident; and, while continuing to hold that *Brahman*, *flamen*, etc. derive from a common I-E sacerdotal class or category, he has long since abandoned the idea of the I-E priest as a "dying god" in favor of a more sociological explanation; see Dumézil, *L'idéologie tripartie des Indo-Européens*, pp. 48-49.
[26] There are, however, some faint indications that this segment did exist in the earliest phase of Germanic society and that its place was usurped by the second or warrior function, the chief or king gradually assuming the duties of the former priests – though the inherited I-E distinction between the two functions persisted in myth (i.e., the distinction between Othinn and Thor); see Dumézil, *Mythes et dieux des Germains*, 2nd ed. (Paris, 1959).

group of young warriors surrounding the king or chief is significant; indeed, such a group also seems to have been present among the Celts, if the tales concerning Finn and the *fianna* are any indication of early Irish (and by extension, Celtic) social life. Moreover, both the Germans and the Celts seem to have been characterized by a cultivator class set apart from that of the warriors, though the distinction here, especially among the Germanic speakers, is by no means as clear as that between the *Kṣatriyas* and the *Vaiśyas*.

An interesting (though in our opinion by no means certain) example of the persistence of the I-E tripartite social heritage in Greek thought can be found in Plato's *Republic*, Dumézil suggests.[27] Plato's conception of the ideal state is indeed a tripartite one:

Elle [the ideal state] est constituée par l'agencement harmonieux de trois fonctions ... les philosophes qui gouvernent, les guerriers qui combattent, le tiers-état, laboureurs et artisans réunis, qui crée la richesse.[28]

The model upon which this Platonic conception may have been based, he asserts, is the fourfold set of early Ionian "tribes" or *bioi* ("types of life") as described by Plutarch, Strabo, and others. Although neither their names nor their functions are clear, these *bioi* seem to have included (1) priests and magistrates, (2) warriors or "guardians," (3) laborers, and (4) artisans. Lumping the last two categories together, Dumézil arrives at a class structure not unlike that of Vedic India, and asks:

Si les plus vielles des Ioniens gardaient le souvenir d'une division fonctionelle quadripartie de la société (prêtres, guerriers, agriculteurs, artisans), la cité idéale de Platon ne serait-elle pas, au sens le plus strict, une réminiscence indo-européenne?[29]

If the French mythologist is correct in seeing in Plato's tripartite conception of the ideal state a reflection of the I-E social heritage, it would seem to us to mean one of two things: (1) that despite the absence of tripartite themes in all but a few fragments of Greek myth and epic, to say nothing of her pre-Platonic philosophical literature, this heritage – discernible perhaps in the early social organization of Ionia – somehow

[27] Dumézil, *Jupiter, Mars, Quirinus*, pp. 257-260.
[28] *Ibid.*, p. 257.
[29] *Ibid.*

managed to linger on silently at least until the fourth century B.C., or (2) that Plato borrowed this conception from some other (i.e., non-Greek) I-E source, possibly Iran. There is, of course, a third possibility not compatible with Dumézil's theory here: that the Greek philosopher in question arrived at this particular conception of social tripartition wholly independently; but given the rarity of wholly new ideas, even in Plato, we are inclined toward the second alternative suggested above. Indeed, it is one that was suggested some years ago by Dumézil's eminent Iranianist colleague Duchesne-Guillemin in his most interesting and challenging book *The Western Response to Zoroaster* (1958).

Finally, as was mentioned earlier, Dumézil claims that this characteristic and uniquely I-E tendency to view phenomena as divided into three hierarchically ranked strata became a deeply ingrained habit of thought; it became, in short, an ideology. As a result, replications of tripartite formulas, including tripartitions within tripartitions, are frequently encountered by Dumézil and his colleagues. For example, it is noted that three-fold divisions of the universe, wherein the upper atmosphere is assigned to the first function, the lower atmosphere to the second, and the earth itself to the third, can be found throughout the later Indic literature; and that exhortations, like that found in the famous inscription of Darius at Behistun, to preserve the sanctity of contracts, to defend the society against foreign invasion, and to guard against famine and plague, as well as tripartite divisions of catastrophes into those affecting, respectively, the sovereignty, the military, and the food supply, are found repeatedly – from the Irish *Lebor Gabala* (or 'Book of Conquests') to the *Śatapatha Brāhmaṇa*.

Some years ago the eminent Swedish mythologist Stig Wikander, perhaps Dumézil's most brilliant disciple, discovered that a tripartite division of heroes and semi-divine beings can often be found in I-E epic and saga as well as myth.[30] For example, in the great Indian epic, the *Mahābhārata*, he has demonstrated that the five central figures, the *Pāṇḍavas*, all derive from one or another of the earlier Vedic gods: e.g., Yudiṣṭhira, the leader of the five, derives from Varuṇa and is thus a first

[30] Stig Wikander, "Pāṇḍava-sagen och Mahābhāratas mytiska förutsättingar," *Religion och Bibel*, VI (1947), 27-39. The above article was in large part translated into French by Dumézil in *Jupiter, Mars, Quirinus*, IV, *explications de textes* (Paris, 1948); see also Wikander, "Sur le fonds commun indo-iranien des épopées de la Perse et de l'Inde," *La Nouvelle Clio*, VII (1950), 310-329; "Nakula et Sahadeva," *Orientalia Suecana*, VI (1957), 66-96.

function figure; Arjuna, the great epic warrior, derives from Indra and is a second function figure.

Wikander, among others, has also pointed out that the later Norse literature, notably Snorri's *Edda*, the *Heimskringla*, and the "histories" of Saxo Grammaticus, reflect a euhemerized version of the Norse pantheon previously outlined.[31] This literature, of course, belongs to a post-Christian era, and Othinn was viewed merely as a culture hero who, escaping from the ruins of Troy, led a band of Trojan refugees (i.e., the rest of the *Aesir*) across Europe and ultimately into Scandinavia. The parallels to the *Aeneid* are obvious and suggest that the newly Christian Norse, like the Romans before them, were eager to establish ties with the ancient and prestigeful civilizations of the eastern Mediterranean. Yet even here, despite the presence of Christian symbolism and euhemerization, the tripartite ideology persisted.

More recently, Lucien Gerschel,[32] another of Dumézil's students, has demonstrated that the Romans indeed applied this inherited I-E habit of thought to an interpretation of their defeat of Carthage, an event which, of course, can be documented historically. The Carthagenians were assigned to the third function; thus Rome's final triumph was viewed (after the fact) as never having been in doubt. For it was Rome's destiny, so the *augurs* argued, to occupy a sovereign position *vis à vis* all its rivals. Gerschel has also attempted to demonstrate the persistence of this tripartite ideology in European folklore.[33]

III

As of this writing, Professor Dumézil and his contributions to an understanding of the relationship between I-E myth and society – and by extension, the relationship between myth and society in general – have received little if any attention from British and American anthropologists, even from those concerned primarily with the analysis of myth and

[31]   This euhemerized Norse myth can indeed be compared to the Indian epics; see Wikander, "Germanische und indo-iranische Eschatologie," *Kairos* (1960), 83-88. See also Dumézil, *La saga de Hadingus, du mythe au roman* (Paris, 1953).
[32]   Gerschel, "Structures augurales et tripartition fonctionnelle dans la pensée de l'ancienne Rome," *Journal de Psychologie normale et pathologique*, CL (1956), 55-92.
[33]   Gerschel, "Sur un schème trifonctionnel dans une famille de légendes germaniques," pp. 55-92.

folklore. This is unfortunate, perhaps, but understandable in light of the history of comparative I-E mythology.[34] In the earlier phases of this history, before 1900, the efforts of scholars such as Adalbert Kuhn and Max Müller usually command the attention, if not always the respect, of anthropologists, sociologists, social philosophers, etc. Yet from 1900 on, largely as a result of the rise of a more rigorous anthropology, comparative mythology rapidly lost ground. Save for Frazer and a few others whose outlook remained essentially that of the 19th century, anthropological attention as far as mythology was concerned came to be focused almost exclusively upon the myths and folktales of living primitive peoples. Among those scholars concerned with the various I-E mythologies, comparativism, associated as it was with the discarded naturism[35] of Kuhn, Müller, et al., became something to be avoided at all costs.

The last several decades, however, have seen a resurgence of comparative I-E studies, a phenomenon largely if not wholly stimulated by the efforts of Dumézil and his school. For this school, with its insistence upon a sociological interpretation of mythical data, has aroused both the respect and the ire of a generation of European linguists, classicists, folklorists, and mythologists – if not anthropologists. Since the advent of this new comparative mythology, many regional specialists, in crit-

[34] Another major reason for this must certainly lie in the fact that as yet none of Dumézil's publications have been translated into English. Moreover, the relatively few summaries, reviews, and discussions of his work are either incomplete, narrowly focused, or so critically biased as to give a thoroughly distorted impression of Dumézil's theories. Among the latter can be classed Thieme's *Mitra and Aryaman* and John Brough's "The Tripartite Ideology of the Indo-Europeans: An Experiment in Method," *Bulletin of the School of Oriental and African Studies*, XXII (London, 1959), 68-86. More favorably disposed though still inadequate English accounts of Dumézilian mythology can be found in: J. C. Tavadia, "From Aryan Mythology to Zoroastrian Theology: A Review of Dumézil's Researches," *Zeitschrift der Deutschen Morgenländischen Gesellschaft*, CIII (1953), 344-353; Gerschel, "Georges Dumézil's Comparative Studies in Tales and Traditions" (translated by Archer Taylor), *Midwest Folklore*, VII (1957), 141-147; J. Duchesne-Guillemin, *The Western Response to Zoroaster* (Oxford, 1958), pp. 38-51; Alwyn and Brinley Rees, *Celtic Heritage: Ancient Tradition in Ireland and Wales* (London, 1961), pp. 112-117.

[35] The widely held 19th century view, promulgated by Max Müller, Adalbert Kuhn, George Cox, etc., that all mythical personages (gods, heroes, etc.) are in the last analysis symbolic representations of natural phenomena of one sort or another (such as the sun, moon, fire, storms). For an excellent analysis of the "solar" school of naturism espoused by Müller, see Richard M. Dorson, "The Eclipse of Solar Mythology," in *Myth: A Symposium*, Thomas A. Sebeok, ed., (= *Bibliographical and Special Series of the American Folklore Society*, V) (Philadelphia, 1955), 15-38.

icizing what sometimes appear to be gross oversimplifications or mis-interpretations on the part of Dumézil and his students, have had to come to terms once more with the idea that particular problems in the mythologies of particular I-E speaking regions can perhaps be solved by viewing them against a broad, comparative background. What is more, such specialists have been forced to consider the proposition that this background includes a common set of myths functionally interrelated with a common set of social institutions, with a common ideology, whether in ancient Italy, Scandinavia, Iran, or even Greece. For example, Jan de Vries, a leading contemporary specialist in Germanic and Celtic mythology, has on more than one occasion[36] adopted a Dumézilian position. To a lesser degree, the same thing can be said for Celticists Alwyn and Brinley Rees[37] and Françoise Le Roux[38] and Iranianists J. Duchesne-Guillemin[39] and Kaj Barr.[40]

There are, of course, those who, like the eminent British classicist H. J. Rose and others of the so-called "primitivist" school,[41] strongly question the efficacy of this new comparativism, despite the fact that it is no longer associated in any degree with naturism. Others, while not necessarily hostile to comparativism itself, seem to resent the avowedly

---

[36] E.g., de Vries, "Der heutige Stand der germanischen Religionsforschung," *Germanisch-romanische Monatsschrift*, II (new series, 1951), 1-11; "La valeur religieuse du mot germanique *Irmin*," *Cahiers du Sud*, XXXVI (1952), 18-27; *Kelten und Germanen* (= *Bibliotheca Germanica*, IX) (Bern, 1960).

[37] Rees & Rees, *Celtic Heritage*, pp. 112-117.

[38] Le Roux, *Les Druides*, p. 8.

[39] Duchesne-Guillemin, *The Western Response to Zoroaster*, pp. 38-51; "De la dicéphalie dans l'iconographie mazdéenne," in *Festgabe für Herman Lommel* (Wiesbaden, 1960), 32-37.

[40] Kaj Barr, "Irans profet som τέλειος ἄγθρωπος," *Festskrift til L. L. Hammerich* (Copenhagen, 1952), 26-36.

[41] The "primitivists," Rose, H. Wagenvoort, J. Gonda, et al., have sought to explain Roman, Vedic, and other ancient I-E religions in terms of a dynamism not unlike the *mana* concept found among Melanesians and other contemporary primitive peoples. See, for example, H. J. Rose, Review of Georges Dumézil, *Jupiter, Mars, Quirinus* (1941) and *Servius et la Fortune* (1943) – *Journal of Roman Studies*, XXXVII (1947), 183; *Ancient Roman Religion* (London, 1950); Review of Georges Dumézil, *Rituels indo-européens à Rome* (1954) – *The Classical Review*, V (new series, 1955), 307-308; H. Wagenvoort, *Roman Dynamism: Studies in Ancient Roman Thought, Language, and Custom* (London, 1947); J. Gonda, "Some Observations on Dumézil's Views of Indo-European Mythology," *Mnemosyne*, IV (1960), 1-15. See also Dumézil, *Les dieux des Indo-Européens*, pp. 142-143; *Déesses latines et mythes védiques* (= *Collection Latomus*, XXV) (Brussels, 1956), pp. 118-123, where Rose's criticisms of *Rituels indo-européens à Rome*, etc. are answered.

sociological and social anthropological assumptions which underlie most of Dumézil's interpretations.

To date, Dumézil's severest critics have perhaps been Paul Thieme[42] and John Brough.[43] The former has quarreled with Dumézil about many technical points relating to Indo-Iranian texts and has frequently accused him of being highly selective in the data used to support the system. Brough, an Indic philologist, has attempted to uncover tripartite formulas in the Old Testament – successfully, as far as he is concerned. If, indeed, such a system were to have been present among the ancient Hebrews, then Dumézil's claim that it is uniquely I-E would certainly be less secure. However, Dumézil has pointed out that most events recorded in the Old Testament occurred long after the arrival of I-E speakers in the Near East (ca. 1700 B.C.), and that *if* Brough is correct (which he strongly doubts)[44] it could easily have been the result of diffusion.

It might be added here that there are a number of criticisms which can be levied against this school strictly from the point of view of social anthropology. For example, despite his exposure to sociological theory, Dumézil's use of the term "function" tends to be ambiguous. As has been seen, he often uses it to refer not only to what most anthropologists would consider the social functions served by the three I-E social and supernatural strata – the ways in which they contribute to the maintenance of the social and supernatural system – but also to refer to the strata themselves. This involves a conception of function which deviates rather sharply from long accepted British, American, and, indeed, French anthropological usage.[45]

Whether or not the criticisms mentioned above are justified, and there is reason to believe that some of them are, Dumézil's approach to the study of I-E mythology, combining as it does the sociological and comparativist traditions, remains in our opinion the most fruitful one

[42]   E.g., Thieme, *Mitra and Aryaman*, especially pp. 12-16. For a rejoinder, see Dumézil, *L'idéologie tripartie des Indo-Européens*, pp. 114-118.
[43]   Brough, "The Tripartite Ideology of the Indo-Europeans," especially pp. 85-86. See also Dumézil's rejoinder, "L'idéologie tripartie des Indo-Européens et la Bible," *Kratylos*, IV (1959), 97-118.
[44]   Dumézil, "L'idéologie tripartie des Indo-Européens et la Bible," pp. 116-118.
[45]   Cf. A. R. Radcliffe-Brown, "Introduction," in *African Systems of Kinship and Marriage*, Radcliffe-Brown and C. Daryll Forde, eds. (London, 1950), 1-85, especially p. 56; Robert Redfield, "Introduction," in *Social Anthropology of North American Tribes*, Fred Eggan, ed. (Chicago, 1937), pp. vii-xii; Claude Lévi-Strauss, "Social Structure," in *Anthropology Today*, A. L. Kroeber, ed. (Chicago, 1953), 524-573.

yet to be devised. In characterizing this approach, the French myth-ologist emphasizes that it

...ne se réclame d'aucun système préconcu d'explication, mais utilise les enseignements de la sociologie et de l'ethnographie comme elle a recours à l'ana-lyse linguistique des concepts. Elle n'a que deux postulats: elle admit que tout système théologique et mythologique signifie quelque chose, aide la société qui le pratique à se comprendre, à s'accepter, à être fière de son passé, confiante dans son présent et dans son avenir; elle admit aussi que la communauté de langue, chez les Indo-Européens, impliquait une mesure substantielle d'idéo-logie commune à laquelle il doit être possible d'accéder par une variété adéquate de méthode comparative.[46]

If there are errors, these errors may well prove to be the result of over-enthusiasm on the part of the researchers and not necessarily an indica-tion that the system itself is totally incorrect. Indeed, if in the main Dumézil and his students *are* correct, it occurs to us that the idea of a tripartite social system may have persisted longer in the West than it would appear at first glance. Is it possible that in the division of Medieval society into three estates, the clergy, the nobility, and the peasantry, one can, in part at least, see the persistence of an archaic, inherited I-E pattern, a pattern which came to light once more as the Germanic, Celtic, and Italic speaking peoples reorganized themselves after the decline of Greco-Roman civilization?

So far, Dumézil and his colleagues have wisely limited themselves to the earlier stages in the history of these three speech communities. Yet given their evidence for the existence of an archaic tripartite I-E ideology, the foregoing suggestion is not altogether out of the question.

Occidental College
Los Angeles, California

[46] Dumézil, *L'idéologie tripartie des Indo-Européens*, p. 91.

1

Myths

A work entitled *Mythologies* by someone known as a literary critic might be expected to deal with many things, but probably not all-in wrestling, photographs of actors, a film of *Julius Caesar*, and the image of writers on holiday. These are the first four topics of Barthes's book of that name. At first sight, they seem, moreover, to have little in common. They are, however, linked not by subject-matter, but by a common status as messages circulating within 'mass culture' (a label that I shall query but which is convenient for the moment). Barthes's task is therefore twofold: to decode the messages, and to evaluate their links with mass culture. Analysis and judgement are thus coupled. In the concluding essay of *Mythologies*, 'Le mythe, aujourd'hui', Barthes assembles a set of tools for the analysis. But this is a retrospective systematization and rationalization of what is initially a more intuitive set of procedures, and I propose to leave 'Le mythe, aujourd'hui' for later consideration.

Mythologies is a compilation of a series of articles most of which were published in the magazine *Les Lettres nouvelles* between 1954 and 1956. Their concern is with the values and attitudes implicit in the variety of messages with which our culture bombards us: advertisements, newspaper and magazine reports, photographs, and even material objects like cars and children's toys. (When high culture (Racine or Fauré) comes into question, it is because of the stock responses that govern its consumption.) Barthes calls these messages myths, partly in virtue of the etymology of 'myth' (the Greek *muthos*, speech, therefore 'message'), and partly because many of these messages are myths in another sense, mystifications. The importance of *Mythologies* lies less in subject-matter (though many of the topics are still uncomfortably relevant), than in the procedures by which it is analysed, judged, and not least transformed by and into writing. Procedures of rhetoric are indeed inseparable from the process of argument and evaluation, and this gives the text a certain exemplary status, as a persuasive discourse on forms of persuasion.

To start with, the mere fact of treating some of the topics of *Mythologies* as messages is itself a paradoxical manoeuvre, giving rise to paradoxical utterances ('paradoxical' is to be understood in its etymological sense: that which is against *doxa*, common opinion). Common sense would say that wrestling is a sport: Barthes asserts it is not a sport, but a spectacle (*MY*, 13/ 15); again, strip-tease is not about sexuality, but about de-sexualizing women (*MY*, 147/91). Both these activities, then, emit a message that belies their apparent nature. In a sense, there are thus two messages. There is a manifest message, which can be rendered by a tautological or apparently self-evident statement ('wrestling is a sport', 'strip-tease is sexy'). This message is, in short, that there is no message: common sense is impervious to signs. This primary message thus functions so as to conceal the secondary message, and so to facilitate its delivery.[1]

The common-sense view of the world largely consists in asking what the use of something is. But to bracket out an object's utilitarian function can enable one to 'hear' previously unsuspected messages. Wrestling, again: if one tries to understand it, commonsensewise, as a sport, it is unintelligible: in a real contest, a wrestler caught in a hold would struggle to conceal his agony, which could only encourage his opponent; in fact, he displays it. Or why is the foul play so blatant? Because the wrestler is not so much trying to win as fulfilling a role expected of him by the spectators: to suffer, visibly, is part of that role; and an invisible foul is useless because the function of a foul is to build up the perpetrator's character as a 'dirty bastard', to be spectacularly chastised by the 'good guy'. Physique is likewise dictated not by considerations of strength or fitness but by this need to establish a recognizable character, in the theatrical sense. The whole exercise is a play, or even a ritual confrontation between Good and Evil (*MY*, 13–24/15–26).

In other words, there is in wrestling a discrepancy between the primary common-sense message 'This is a sport (not a message)' and the secondary message 'This is a spectacle'. This discrepancy, however, is ludic and aesthetic in function. Nobody is being fooled by a wrestling match: on the contrary, the duplicity of the event is part of the spectator's pleasure. There is the pleasure of the spectacle itself, the conflict of hero and villain, Good and Evil, and the further pleasure in the fact of the spectacle's masquerading as a sporting contest. But with other messages, the duplicity is not aesthetic but ideological.

It is as if Barthes sees wrestling as a genuine manifestation of popular culture, resting on a set of values shared by performers and audience, as one might suppose Greek or Elizabethan drama to have been. The common-sense view (wrestling is a sport, but a bad one because not honestly competitive) is thus not the popular one: it would be glossed by Barthes as more of a (petty-) bourgeois reaction. Yet there are other messages that relate differently to society. Take the case of wine, which has an obvious symbolic status, as a sign of Frenchness and of virility. Here the vehicle of the myth, or message, the wine, is valued as a 'good and fine substance'. But the myth has to be questioned because spontaneously to participate in it is also to endorse what the myth conceals: the fact that wine is a commodity like any other, produced under a capitalist regime, which has turned into vineyards parts of North Africa that could have been used to produce food, and set the native Muslim population working there, when their religion holds wine in abhorrence (*MY*, 77/68).[2] The myth of wine is thus doubly alienating: it palliates the exclusion of the North African population from its own environment and culture and debars the intellectual from a whole-hearted uncomplicated relationship with what is after all a 'belle et bonne substance'.

This example shows the two-stage logic of much of *Mythologies*: a message is read into some substance, custom, attitude that seemed to carry its own justification in terms purely of practical use; and the message thus revealed turns out to be concealing the operation of socio-economic structures that require to be denounced – both because they are concealing their identity and because that identity is inherently exploitative. Thus soap-powder advertising produces powerful symbolic contrasts between two brands, so that the choice between them takes on a quasi-poetic seriousness: which tends to obscure the fact that they are produced by the same multinational company (*MY*, 38–40/40–2). This is the mystifying function of which I spoke above.

'What is "natural" must have the force of what is startling', said Brecht of the aims of his epic theatre.[3] The whole project of *Mythologies* is in line with this: it aims to make the natural, the taken-for-granted, appear strange and remote, to establish unsuspected connections, to subvert cultural hierarchies – wrestling is compared to Greek tragedy, boxing to Jansenist theology, the riders in the Tour de France to characters from Homer. Such 'defamiliariza-tion' was held by the Russian Formalists to be essential to the aesthetic effect, and there is no doubt that in *Mythologies* it serves an aesthetic effect for which the Bakhtinian term 'carnivalesque' seems appropriate.[4] But as in Brecht, its ideological function is crucial: to change the world it is necessary to convince people that its ways are not self-evident: to show that what is presented to them as 'natural' is in fact what conforms to a particular ideological world-view, serving particular social interests. To drink wine and take an interest in the Tour de France seems simply part of being French, but the forms in which both of these things are presented in daily life reflect the structures and priorities of capitalist production. The myths of wine and the epic representation of the Tour de France are thus elements of capitalist ideology. Further ideological targets are racism (*MY*, 64–7), colonialism (*MY*, 137–44), gender stereotyping (*MY*, 56–8/56–8), the judicial system (*MY*, 50–3/48–52), and Cold War propaganda (*MY*, 130–3).[5] This is, then, committed analysis, from a broadly left-wing position. Indeed one of Barthes's points is that neutrality is never anything other than taking sides by appearing not to (*MY*, 144–6/88–90). As I have hinted, the content of the analysis is not as dated as some might think, and others wish. One example among many (and their relevance is not confined to France): *Mythologies* bitterly attacks the politics of the right-wing populist Poujade, mentioning by name one of his followers, Le Pen, now the leader of the racist Front National (*MY*, 85–7, 182–90).

The critical study of myth is not just the denunciation of particular ideological positions, but the analysis of how their messages are constituted, how they come to persuade. Form is essential to myth; and the Front National gives a powerful illustration of this. Its slogan 'Two million immigrants = two million unemployed' exemplifies the arithmetical logic that Barthes shows as governing a whole class of mythical utterances. 'Two million = two million' is a tautology, a self-evident proposition, which lends a false credibility to the equation of unemployment and immigration, an equation that contrives to obscure the complexities of the national and global economic structures in which the two are by no means complementary (since jobs would be being lost in traditional industries whether or not there were immigration, and under pressures quite distinct from the specific legacy of colonialism and underdevelopment that impels North Africans to leave their homes for France). Tautological discourse is thus the language of social myopia. But obviously some more general theory of the role of form in producing mythical discourse is required. This Barthes attempts to provide in 'Le mythe, aujourd'hui'.

A myth, says Barthes, is 'a system of communication . . . a message' (*MY*, 193/117). This is superficially contradictory, but in practice perfectly clear: a myth is not just any message, but a message produced by a certain signifying mechanism. It is this formal aspect that characterizes myth, not its content – there are myths of soap powder and myths of human nature – or a particular medium – there are photographic myths, as well as verbal ones, and, as we have seen, even material objects, cars, or toys, can have the status of myths. Two media can of course be combined, as in television advertisements.

Barthes's discussion of the relationships between signs that constitute a myth is indebted to the Swiss linguist Saussure. Saussure postulated a science, of which he saw linguistics as eventually forming a part, that would study 'the life of signs within society', and he baptized it 'semiology' (from the Greek *semeion*, sign).[6] Semiology is not concerned with content as such but with the forms that enable sounds, images, gestures, etc. to function as signs. Although the content of a myth is ideological (for reasons we shall see) and therefore determined by history, the myth is something more than its content, and this something more requires formal, semiological, analysis: moreover, there is a history of forms as well as of contents.

I shall deal with Saussurean theory more fully in connection with Barthes's 'Eléments de sémiologie'. Barthes's reading of Saussure (in 1956) post-dates the composition of most of *Mythologies*, and he did not systematically attempt to reconcile his embryonic semiological practice with the fully-fledged theory (*PRB*, 409).[7]

A *sign* for Saussure is the union of a *signified*, a concept, and a *signifier*, through which that concept is manifested. A bunch of roses is a sign when the flowers stand as signifiers of the signified 'passion'. A linguistic sign – say, the word 'tree' – unites a sound, or, more precisely, a sound-image /tree/ and the concept ⟨⟨tree⟩⟩.[8] Now the mythical sign is a sign to the second power: it is constituted by the superimposition of a second tripartite schema on the one just analysed. In this, the original sign becomes the signifier of a new sign by being attached to a new concept, or signified (*MY*, 197–200/ 121–4). Take the now famous example Barthes gives, of a magazine photograph. The photograph is an assemblage of lines and colours on a sheet of paper. But (since in our culture we are familiar with photographs) we can see these lines and colours as forming the image of a man, and indeed further as representing a Black soldier in the French army saluting – which we know only because we are already familiar with codes of costume (uniform) and gesture. So the picture conveys a message, and is thus a sign on this very literal level; but that is clearly not the be-all and the end-all of the image: it is clearly intended to show (given that it comes from *Paris-Match*) that, whatever malicious and unpatriotic people may claim, France is a great empire faithfully served by black and white alike (and not an oppressive colonial regime). So the photographic sign has become the signifier of a new signified, and we have to distinguish between the first-order system of meaning, the literal one, and the second-order system within which the myth comes into being (*MY*, 201/125–6).[9]

The first-order messages belong to a self-sufficient but contingent order – the particular Black man in the photograph must have joined the French army as a result of some particular concatenation of circumstances. In that sense, the image relates to a history. Or, to take Barthes's other example, the Latin sentence *quia ego nominor leo* (because my name is Lion), is initially part of a fable, in which it serves as one of the spurious arguments by which the lion seeks to defraud his partners from their share in the collective prey.

But these messages are transformed into myths by abstraction from their particular context; the Black soldier's personal history would interfere with his serving as a living manifestation and vindication of the French Empire; when you meet *quia ego nominor leo* used as a grammatical example, you are not supposed to ask why someone might say that, simply to learn the rule it illustrates. Yet the abstraction from history must not be total: the Black soldier in the photograph is not just a conventional coded symbol of Empire (as a statue might be); it is as if his individual history is just enough present to suggest that 'French imperiality' is more than an idea – a destiny, naturally unfolding in the individual life; as if the fact that a lion did once say *quia ego nominor leo* proves the grammatical rule of the agreement of the attribute. Paradoxically, the history drained away from the signifier flows into the signified: for the concepts of 'French imperiality' or 'grammatical exemplarity' receive their content from a historical situation: which confronts people in France with the threat of their country's loss of its colonial possessions; which sets some children (and not others) learning Latin (and not computer science).[10] The concepts are reactions to the history, rather than accurate reflections of it; ironically, one of the effects of history is to conceal its own workings. 'French imperiality' is asserted as a timeless value at the very moment when its historical crisis is most cryingly obvious (*MY*, 202–4/ 126–9).

In the mythical message, then, a certain concept, social and historical in origin, seizes on a certain sign for its own ends, while sheltering behind the initial literal significance of the sign. The image of the Black soldier saluting the flag communicates its factual nature to the non-factual concept of 'French imperiality'. Thus the French Empire, as an idea or value, comes to impose itself with the straightforwardness of an empirical fact; and thus the message is enabled to conceal its identity as such. It is this appropriation of a sign as an alibi for another message that Barthes finds ethically objectionable: myth is a 'theft of language' (*MY*, 217–18/142–3). And it is ethically objectionable in another way: it turns an arbitrary or conventional sign into a supposedly natural one.

According to Saussure, the linguistic sign is arbitrary: no intrinsic link connects a particular sound-image (signifier) and a particular concept (signified). Yet other types of sign (photographs, for instance) admit a degree of motivation, or analogy, between signifier and signified. What the myth tries to do is to pass off an arbitrary sign as a natural, analogical, one. There is no reason in the nature of things why the Black soldier should serve as a sign of French imperiality: his individual life, recorded in the photograph, has been chosen to purvey a message that could have been transmitted through many other images and that relates not to a natural order of things but to a historical and political situation. As a myth, then, the photograph of him is an arbitrary sign. But, as a photograph, it is a likeness, and in some sense natural (an effect of light rays on film).[11] The arbitrary historical myth thus hides behind the natural analogical photograph. It does so by constructing a deceptive analogy between the message and the image. The message is that 'in the French empire, we're all alike, black and white'; the photograph seems to convey this because, *when he salutes*, the Black soldier looks just like a French one. This introduction of a spurious motivation into a fundamentally arbitrary sign Barthes finds ethically repellent (*MY*, 211–12/136–7). It is the procedure by which the myth seeks to ground political and historical situations, and ideological alignments, in the realm of the natural (*MY*, 215–16/140–1).

How does the general analysis presented in 'Le mythe, aujourd'hui' relate to the particular myth-analyses? Some might object that the notion of a myth as a sign or message taking as its vehicle another message hardly applies in the case of material objects: the new Citroën (*MY*, 150–2/95–7) is a vehicle in the literal sense, not a first-level message. Barthes's later semiology gives an answer to that objection: society inevitably transforms functional objects into signs of their function, so the Citroën DS, as a car, is already a sign before, as a particular model, it acquires the further connotations Barthes analyses.[12] Wrestling, though, on this showing, is not strictly speaking, a myth, according to the terms of Barthes's analysis: for though it seizes upon the literal appearance of a contest to construct something further, a ritual, it emphasizes its own artificiality (its arbitrariness) rather than concealing it, as myth does, behind an appearance of naturalness. It can therefore still be brought within the analysis.

It is one thing to analyse the workings of the myth, another to assess how it is in practice received. There are three possible positions of reception, which can be identified by the semiologist, but which of these are open to the individual subject is not in itself a problem for semiology.[13] The signifier can be viewed as the empty receptacle into which a certain concept is to be poured: this is the position of the myth-producer (for example the newspaper editor or the advertiser) looking to communicate ideas such as 'loony leftists' or 'sophistication'. Or the sign can be broken down into its two component messages, the literal and the mythical one, by the mythologist, who can show how the Black man's salute is appropriated as a symbol of French imperiality (that is, how the myth-producer works). Finally, if the two functions of the mythical signifier are not distinguished and it is apprehended as a seamless whole, we have the perspective of the reader, who simply 'sees' French imperiality *in* the picture. For the sign to persuade, the connection between signifier and signified must appear *natural*, as both the mythologist and the myth-producer know it is not (*MY*, 213–14/138–9).

To read is to be complicit: this is one aspect of the myth's fundamentally aggressive nature, that we cannot help reading it. I think that this is the implication of a shrewd observation by the critic Eve Tavor Bannet.[14] Barthes speaks of the Black soldier as saluting the French flag: in fact, as Bannet points out, there is no flag in the picture, it is simply inferred by Barthes (*MY*, 201/125). We know what the image means, ideologically, but that reading of it is itself a construction. For the image to work as the sign of French imperiality that it undoubtedly is (knowing the politics of *Paris-Match*) the salute must appear as an abstract gesture. And since soldiers do not salute *in vacuo*, the reader postulates the salute as being essentially directed towards the abstract symbol of the flag. For if we could see, say, a white sergeant-major in the picture giving the soldier an order, we might wonder what it was: to peel potatoes, or join a patrol to flush out 'terrorists' from the bush. A picture showing the actual relations of authority in a colonial army would be less suitable for propaganda than one in which the orders seem to come from France herself, symbolized by the imagined flag. The image, then, postulates its imaginary continuation by the viewer in order to work its full mythical effect.

To appear as natural the myth must connect with certain habits of thought so basic to the culture of its presumed recipients that their validity is taken for granted. But the specific ideas and beliefs may be regarded as less significant than the system that produces them: the formal categories that shape the culture's ideas and beliefs in general. We have seen already that what constitutes myth is not content, but form, the combination of two systems of meaning; but the question now is of the forms that that relationship can take, the rules governing the production of a mythical from a literal message. The rules for the production of discourse, or a discourse, are what we mean by rhetoric, so we can call the following the rhetorical figures of myth:

    1. *Tautology*. A thing is defined by itself ('theatre is theatre'). Thus any possibility that its nature is complex, debatable, is excluded, and we can remain snugly inside a world of essences identified with the world of appearance.[15] The same applies to platitudinous statements that are not tautological in the strict sense: 'Athalie is a play by Racine' (*MY*, 96) is a perfectly correct factual statement, but its factual truth serves to verify certain unspoken implications. The maxim is simply a prestigious example of the platitude (*MY*, 242–3/168–9).

    2. *Identification*. Difference, otherness, is reduced to a fundamental identity: Buddhism is 'really' the same as Christianity (*MY*, 164/102). Or, the complementary strategy, it is exoticized, turned into an alien essence (*MY*, 165/103). Thus, in neither case do we have to

understand it: we can either assimilate it or gawp at it (*MY*, 239–40/ 165–6).

3. *Neither-norism.* Conflicts and oppositions can always be sub-limated by weighing up the rival forces and rejecting both in the name of some higher value, which there is no particular need to specify, and which does not commit us to anything (*MY*, 144–6/88–90).

4. *Vaccinations.* An object (an institution or product) is denounced, and the denunciation then undermined, as the alleged shortcomings turn out to be illusory or superficial, transcended by the object in its essence (*MY*, 44–6/45–7).

5. *Transformation of quality into quantity.* The title of this figure alludes to one of the laws of the Hegelian/Marxist dialectic: the transformation of quantity into quality. Mythical thought is indeed profoundly anti-dialectical. It reduces reality to the juxtaposition of two readily computable values (*MY*, 241–2/168): like the (bourgeois) theatre audience that decides whether it is getting its money's worth in virtue of the obvious exertions of the actor (*MY*, 108). The whole of human behaviour, of social and political reality, is reduced to a simple exchange: what you get, or do, you pay for (*MY*, 85). But for the system to be preserved, it is therefore important to get the price right – above all, not to be 'done'. Any form of behaviour that suggests that society is rather more complex and connected than this vision allows for – a strike, for instance, which affects those who think themselves unconcerned by it – has to be denounced as an affront to common sense (*MY*, 134–7).

The *privation of history*, of the history which makes reality intelligible, Barthes lists separately, but it can be seen as a variant of 1 and 2. Thus, to talk about the East without linking it to its history is to fix it in an essence of Orientalness, as the eternal Other of Western civilization ('East is East, and West is West') (*MY*, 163–5/101–3). In a sense all these figures can be reduced to two categories: statements of essence, and statements of balance (the Essences and Libra are the constellations of the mythical zodiac) (*MY*, 238–43/164–9).

Barthes's counter-rhetoric has two main features: the paradox, as we have seen, which denies the tautology ('wrestling is not a sport but a spectacle'), and the concluding *pointe*, the barbed allusion to a larger social and political context that the article (up to that point imitating the message it is dealing with) keeps back for its end.[16] And this context is what I now wish to deal with.

Myth has an *economic* dimension: by simplifying reality, it saves on intellectual effort, and, moreover, what it simplifies reality to is the most basic commercial relationship (at the antipodes of the complex relationships of modern capitalist production) (*MY*, 242/168). It may thus be called a characteristically bourgeois, indeed, by the restriction of outlook it imposes, petty-bourgeois, form. Barthes's hostility to the petty-bourgeois is unwavering, though historically mobile, but in the context of the 1950s it can largely be explained by the belief (right or wrong, but sharpened by the rise of Poujadism) that the petty bourgeoisie are the natural recruits of right-wing irrationalism: in short, fascism (*MY*, 240/166). That myth is predominantly bourgeois might be inferred not only from the bourgeois presuppositions of its rhetorical figures but from the dominance of the bourgeoisie in French society. Myth indeed assists in the process of ex-nomination by which the bourgeoisie conceals its political and social dominance (*MY*, 224–6/149–51). Since anything can be appropriated for mythical ends (*MY*, 194/117–18), the whole of everyday life – social rituals, eating and drinking, clothing – and the institutions we take for granted like the judicial system can be permeated with representations that are tributary to the way in which the bourgeoisie represents the relationships between human beings and the world, to itself and to us (*MY*, 227/152). In virtue of this omnipresence, 'bourgeois norms are lived in experience as the self-evident laws of a natural order' (*MY*, 228/153). The petty bourgeoisie, politically allied to the bourgeoisie proper without sharing its economic status, are particularly affected by this so that they participate imaginatively in institutions and rituals from which their material condition altogether excludes them: the badly paid typist sees herself in the bride at a lavish society wedding (*MY*, 228–9/154; compare *MY*, 47). The consumption of bourgeois representations outside the bourgeoisie produces an illusion of class as non-existent, and thus fosters the rule of the bourgeoisie as a class.

The myth, then, reducing the world to a set of essences, social interaction to so many individual transactions, what is different to what is the same or to what is fundamentally alien, serves to ground the bourgeois world-view in an eternal Nature, a pseudo-Physis as Barthes terms it. Myth is thus not just a message, but a message that is political by depoliticizing (*MY*, 229–31/154–6). It turns history into essence, culture into Nature, and obscures the role of human beings in producing the structures they inhabit and thus their capacity to change them.

One might ask, however, whether all myths function in this way, whether myth is necessarily right-wing. Firstly, the figures of mythical rhetoric seem to be predisposed towards the transmission of the bourgeois world-view. Secondly, although Barthes admits that myths of the Left are possible, he argues that they cannot exert the same force as myths of the Right. They can bear only on a few political notions, and cannot impregnate the whole of daily life like their bourgeois counterparts, nor are they integral to leftist, as they are to bourgeois, political strategy (*MY*, 235/160–1). There is no proletarian culture or ethics to go with proletarian politics (a highly questionable statement): ideologically, Barthes insists, the proletariat is reduced to borrowing from the petty bourgeoisie (*MY*, 226/151). Leftist myths belong in any case to phases where the Left is on the defensive. For the idea of revolution is fundamentally anti-mythical, since so far from depoliticizing, it politicizes everything (*MY*, 234/159–60). What would happen, though, if no revolution took place, but leftist myths did, after all, start to spread? Barthes's later work is a response to what he perceives as that situation.

The mythologist (the analyst, not the creator of myth), is then, a critic of bourgeois reality, but he is not, *qua* mythologist, a revolutionary. His activity is none the less, an authentically political act, both a postulation and an exercise of liberty (*MY*, 244/170). But his is not an easy position to occupy. For he is alienated not only from the world of the consumers of myth (much of the population), but from other forms of behaviour and language in which myth is explicitly or implicitly denied. The myth does not, as we saw, operate directly on the real, but on signs: its language is a metalanguage. But if this is so, then the mythologist, producing language out of an existing metalanguage, is one stage further removed from reality, like the Platonic artist copying a natural world that is itself a copy. At various points in *Mythologies*, Barthes celebrates a different, a direct, relationship between language and reality: the country-dweller's proverbs, unlike the bourgeois aphorism, are linked to a direct appropriation of the world through labour (an element of myth in this picture), the engineer talks of a car not as a mythical image but as a material object with definite properties (*MY*, 242–3/168–9, 246/172). But clearly the mythologist is not in this position: he dissolves objects into myths. Sometimes, Barthes cheats (his own word), reversing this process by writing about substances as such (*MY*, 246–7/172–3), as he had done in his study of the metaphorical world of Michelet.[17]

Finally, the mythologist is not a poet. Instead of searching for some irreducible meaning in the object, he dissolves it into the bearer of a historical concept (a signified) (*MY*, 247/173). In other words, the semiological critique of the ideological sign condemns its practitioner to pay a heavy toll. The tension between the desire to decipher the world and the desire to grapple with its irreducible materiality haunts the work of Barthes to the end. But it is never itself mythified as an *essential* reality, an inevitable component of the human condition. It is seen as the product of a history, an alienated present, that spurs us on to attempt a Utopian reconcilation between the human activity of interpretation and the world it is applied to. Meanwhile, the writing of *Mythologies* itself, its dazzling subversions and paradoxes, its deadpan or hilarious analyses suddenly giving way to eloquent indignation and contempt, survives as itself an embodiment of that reconciliation.[18]

Chapter 1   Myths

1 Strictly speaking, Barthes denies that the myth conceals anything (*MY*, 215/
   140), although some of his analyses involve reminders of truths that the myth
   seems to function so as to make us forget (compare, for example, *MY*, 40/42,
   77/68). I think the point is that the myth does not conceal the underlying
   meaning it transmits: it is not a 'hidden persuader'. But it does conceal that
   meaning's status as a *message*: it conceals the sender (broadly speaking, the
   bourgeoisie).
2 How far this applies to present-day Algeria, I do not know, but to suppress
   the passage would have been to defuse the political charge of Barthes's
   writing here.
3 *Brecht on Theatre*, p. 71.
4 For the general notion of carnival, see Mikhail Bakhtin, *Rabelais and his
   World*, pp. 5–12. I am thinking chiefly of Bakhtin's reference to carnival as a
   liberating suspension or reversal of hierarchies (pp. 10–11). For a powerful
   study of the role of the carnivalesque in Barthes, focusing especially on the
   body, see Ann Jefferson, 'Bodymatters: Self and Other in Bakhtin, Sartre
   and Barthes'.
5 If I give only the French references for most of these passages, this is
   because they do not occur in the English version of *Mythologies*.
6 Ferdinand de Saussure, *Cours de linguistique générale*, p. 33/16. The term
   'semiotics', deriving from the American philosopher Charles Sanders Peirce,
   is now more generally accepted than 'semiology'. I shall, however, use the
   Saussurean term 'semiology', because Barthes remains faithful to its French
   equivalent *sémiologie* throughout his career.
7 Without reading Saussure (which he says he did only in 1956 (*R*, 98; *AS*,
   11/5)) Barthes could have encountered something of his ideas through

other writers. See Annette Lavers, *Roland Barthes: Structuralism and After*, p. 51. This is the best study of the intellectual and cultural background of Barthes's work. According to his biographer Louis-Jean Calvet, however, Barthes read Saussure in Alexandria in 1949–50, at the instigation of A.J. Greimas (*Roland Barthes*, p. 124).

8 I follow the standard practice of enclosing signifiers between oblique strokes (/tree/) and signifieds between chevrons (⟨⟨tree⟩⟩).

9 The terminology Barthes devises to clarify this distinction is potentially misleading, and not resorted to here. Barthes calls the first order of meaning, that on which the mythical meaning is parasitic, the linguistic order (because he wants to identify myth as a language upon language, a metalanguage) (*MY*, 200/124). But the term 'linguistic', is problematic as applied to non-verbal systems: photography is on one level, as Barthes himself later points out, not a language since it does not involve a code (*OO*, 11/5). The final term of the first system is also the first term of the second, mythical, system: the signifier of the mythical sign (*MY*, 202/126). In order to distinguish these two roles, Barthes rebaptizes the original sign the 'meaning', (as the final term of system 1) and the 'form' (as the first term of system 2). As examples of the 'meaning' Barthes cites 'my name is Lion', 'a Black man is saluting the French flag'. These are not signs, however, but signifieds in the first order of meaning: the signs being the sentence *quia ego nominor leo*, and 'a photograph of a Black man saluting the French flag'. Barthes is in fact collapsing the first-order signs into their signifieds.

10 'Imperiality', 'exemplarity': neologisms, of course, which some would condemn as jargon, forgetting that new words are necessitated by the lack of existing names for the things in question and that these concepts cannot be stated in everyday terms because, as concepts, they are absorbed by the receiver of the mythical message without being clearly identified. See *MY*, 206/130.

11 The naturalness of the photograph is discussed on p. 196.

12 See below, p. 78.

13 Similarly Saussure observes that the activity of the speaking subject has to be studied in a number of disciplines which have no place in linguistics except through their relation to language (*Cours*, p. 37/18).

14 Eve Tavor Bannet, *Structuralism and the Logic of Dissent*, p. 54. It will be seen that I dissent from the argument she constructs around this observation, and especially from the suggestion (p. 55) that Barthes is being ironic at the expense of those who refer to 'colonialism' and 'oppressors': his irony is directed at those who attempt such irony and the expression 'so-called' is a quotation from their discourse (*MY*, 201/125).

15 Barthes's critique of tautological discourse may be indebted to the ontology of Sartre. For Sartre the identity-principle (A is A) applies only to the realm of being-in-itself. Human action belongs rather to that of being-for-itself, where being is not what it is, and is what it is not (*L'Etre et le néant*, pp. 90–104). In Sartrean terms, myth reduces free human action to the inevitable unfolding of a Nature credited with the characteristics of being-in-itself.

16 See, for example, *MY*, 40/42, 56/55, 125/84. Barthes himself analyses his own rhetorical technique in *Mythologies* in *RB*, 59–60/55.
17 He discusses, for example, water and oil (*MY*, 83–4), wine and milk (*MY*, 74–7/65–8), wood (*MY*, 60/60–1).
18 The same point is in Roger, *Roland Barthes, roman*, p. 80.

STRUCTURE AND HISTORY IN THE STUDY OF THE FAIRY TALE[*]

Vladimir Propp

0.   The book, *Morphology of the Folktale*, was published in Russian in 1928. At that time it produced two
different reactions. On the one side there were folklorists, ethnographers, and literary critics who welcomed the
book warmly. At the same time, however, others accused
the author of formalism, an accusation that has been repeated over the years even to the present. More than
likely this work would have been forgotten, like so many
others, perhaps to be used only by specialists in the
field, were it not rediscovered shortly after the Second
World War. People began to discuss it at conventions, to
write about it, and eventually it was translated into English. And so the question naturally arises: How to explain
this new-found interest? In the field of the exact sciences some very significant discoveries were being made,
something made possible by the challenge of new and increasingly more accurate methods of research and design.
Efforts at verification through the methods of the exact
sciences were extended even to the humanities. The comparison between structural linguistics and mathematics
extended gradually to other disciplines. One of these was
theoretical poetics. But the notion of art as a system

*Translated from "Struttura e storia nello studio della
favola," pp. 201-227 in *Morfologia della fiaba*, Nuovo
Biblioteca Scientifica Einaudi 13 (Turin: Einaudi) by Hugh
T. McElwain, Rosary College, River Forest, Illinois (see
§§0.3, 0.5, and 0.9 of the Introduction to this issue).
The editors of *Semeia* wish to thank the publisher, Giulio
Einaudi, for permission to translate this article.

of signs, the procedures for formalizing and modelling,
the possibility of using mathematical formulas, were all
anticipated by my book, even though at the time it was
written there was no such complex of concepts and terminology as are taken for granted in science today. So once
again this book became the object of different evaluations.
Some saw it as useful and indeed necessary for more exact
research methodology; others, as had happened previously,
accused the author of formalism, and held that the book
did not furnish any valid information.

1.0   Claude Lévi-Strauss (1960, 1976) is one of those
numbered among the latter group. He is a noted structuralist, and structuralists, too, have often been accused of
formalism. In an effort to put the difference between
structuralism and formalism in proper perspective, Lévi-
Strauss uses *The Morphology of the Folktale* as an example
of formalism. The reader must decide whether or not Lévi-
Strauss proves his point. Yet when one is attacked, the
natural response is to defend oneself. The kind of polemic
that grows out of such arguments and counter-arguments
could prove to be of general scientific interest. This is
the reason I have willingly accepted the kind invitation
of my Italian publisher to respond to Lévi-Strauss' article.
He has thrown down the gauntlet, and I have accepted the
challenge. Thus the readers of *Morphology* will be witness
to our duel, and will support the combatant they consider
the victor, assuming that there is one.

1.1   In our debate, Lévi-Strauss has the rather distinct advantage of being a philosopher, while I am just an
empiricist. I am an empiricist with integrity, however;
one who first and foremost observes facts attentively and
studies them scrupulously and methodically, verifying assumptions and continually examining the situation at every
phase of the reasoning process. The empirical sciences
themselves of course can be of various types. In some
cases the empiricist must limit himself to description, to

pointing out characteristic elements. This is especially
true if the research in question deals with an isolated
fact. Such descriptions are certainly not without scientific value, as long as they are worked out correctly.
But if one describes and studies series of facts and their
interrelationships, then such a description is changed
into a phenomenological discovery or insight, an insight
which is no longer of only limited interest, but is also
open to philosophical analysis. My work, too, gave rise
to such analysis, but it was only vaguely seen in the epigraphs which opened some of the chapters. Lévi-Strauss,
however, is familiar only with the English translation of
my book. Unfortunately the translator took some unwarranted liberties. Since he obviously did not grasp the
purpose of the epigraphs, which indeed at first sight
might not have seemed integral to the main text, he decided they were purely decorative and ruthlessly omitted
them. But these epigraphs were either taken from the
series of works which Goethe gathered under the common
title of *Morphology*, or else from his diaries. They were
all intended to express that about which the main text of
the book remains silent. The highest goal of any science
is to discover laws. Where the pure empiricist sees only
unrelated facts, the philosophical empiricist recognizes
the presence of clear interconnections or laws. I have
singled out such laws in a quite limited area, that is,
for the genre of the fairy tale. Even there, however, it
appeared to me that this discovery might be of broader
significance. The term "morphology" was not taken from
those manuals on botany whose principal thrust is toward
classification, and neither was it taken from treatises on
grammar. It was taken from Goethe who collected under
this general heading writings both on botany and on osteology. Under this heading one discovers in Goethe a novel
approach to the study of the laws that undergird and inter-
penetrate nature, and there is not a single case where
Goethe crosses over from botany to comparative osteology.

We feel no hesitancy in highly recommending this book to
structuralists. But if the young Goethe, imbued with the
spoils of Faust, seated in his dusty laboratory, and surrounded by skeletons, saw there only dust, the mature
Goethe, on the contrary, accustomed to the methods of
exact comparison from the field of natural science, saw
things holistically, saw the overarching scheme that embraced all of nature. In reality there are not two individuals, Goethe the poet and Goethe the scientist. The
Goethe of *Faust*, who strives for knowledge, and Goethe the
naturalist, who has reached it, are one and the same person.

There is a further significance to the epigraphs.
The realms of nature and of man are not isolated from one
another. They share some common laws, laws which can be
studied using similar methods. This idea, then only barely
sketched, now furnishes the basis for those research methods needed in the humanities, and to which we have alluded.
This is one of the reasons structuralists (e.g., Dundes)
have supported my work. At the same time some structuralists did not understand that my objective was not to come
to some very wide generalization, though that precise possibility was latent in the epigraphs, but that my efforts
resulted simply from my profession as a folklorist. And
so Lévi-Strauss, obviously perplexed, twice questions what
might have led me to apply my method to the fairy tale.
Since, as he notes, there must be several causes, he takes
it upon himself to explain them to the reader. One of the
reasons, he suggests, is that since I am not an ethnologist, I do not have available mythological resources and I
am simply unacquainted with them. Furthermore, I have not
even the vaguest notion of the effective relations which
exist between myth and fairy tale (Lévi-Strauss, 1976:129-
30). In short, the fact that I did study the fairy tale
is due to my limited scientific horizon; otherwise I probably would have tested my method not on fairy tales but on
myths.

1.2   I do not want to spend too much time on the
logic of this argument which claims that I dealt with
fairy tales because I was not familiar with myths.   Its
logic in fact escapes me.   But I do not think any scholar
should be kept from moving in one particular direction
just because another is suggested to him.   What seems to
follow from this line of reasoning is that Lévi-Strauss
expects the scholar to find a method and then to search
out some phenomenon to which it can be applied; in my case
I apply it--who knows why--to fairy tales, something that
is of little interest to the philosopher.   But in the scientific field things do not happen that way and certainly
not in my case.   Things work differently in my field.
Russian universities at the time of the Czars did not prepare philologists very well in the area of literary studies.   Popular poetry in particular was completely ignored.
To fill in this gap, at the end of my university studies,
I dedicated myself to study Afanas'ev's well-known collection of Russian folktales.   In one series of fairy tales
whose common subject was the persecution of the stepdaughter, I noticed an interesting fact.   In the fairy
tale called *Gelo* (#52a = #95) the stepmother sends the
stepdaughter to Gelo in the forest.   He tries to let her
freeze to death, but she responds to him with such sweet-
ness and patience that he spares her, rewards her, and
lets her go.   The true daughter of the old woman, on the
other hand, does not stand up under the test and perishes.
In the following fairy tale the stepdaughter does not meet
Gelo in the forest, but rather meets a forest spirit, and
in another fairy tale she meets a bear.   But otherwise it
is the exact same fairy tale.   Gelo, the forest spirit,
and the bear all put her to the test, each rewards her in
his own way, but the plot is identical.   The strange thing
is that nobody noticed this and that Afanas'ev and the
others held that these were really different fairy tales.
It is perfectly clear that Gelo, the forest spirit, and
the bear did the same thing in slightly different ways.

For Afanas'ev these are different fairy tales because different characters appear; it seemed to me, however, that
they are identical ones since the actions of the protago-
nists are the same. All of this began to intrigue me, and
I decided to study other fairy tales from the point of
view of the actions which the characters performed. And
so what resulted was a very simple method for studying the
fairy tale based on the actions which the characters in
them perform, independently of the diversity of characters.
To indicate these actions I coined the term "functions."
This observation concerning fairy tales of the persecuted
stepdaughter was the thread that enabled me to unravel the
whole fabric. I was able to establish that other plots
were also based on the repetition of functions, and that
in the final analysis all fairy tales are based on identical functions, so that all these tales have a monotypical
structure.

1.3   But if the translator has done the reader a dis-
service by leaving out the epigraphs from Goethe, the Russian publisher also betrayed my intention by changing, as
he did, the title of the book. It was originally titled
Morphology of the Fairy Tale. To make the book appeal to
a larger audience, the publisher eliminated the term
"fairy" from the title, and thereby led the reader (and
Lévi-Strauss) to believe erroneously that one would find
in it general laws about the folktale as a literary genre.
A book with my original title would easily have found its
place in a series which would have dealt with *Morphology
of Curse*, *Morphology of Comedy*, *Morphology of Apology*,
etc. But I had no intention of studying all the types of
that varied and complex genre known as the folktale. I
limited my investigation to only one type which was significantly different from all the others, namely, the
fairy tale, and specifically the popular ones. We are
talking, therefore, about specific research dealing with a
particular question in folklore. Whether or not this
method of analyzing narratives based on the functions of

their characters might prove effective not only in the
genre of the fairy tale but also in other folktales and
maybe even in the study of narrative works across world
literature, is another question entirely. One can only
generalize that in each case the concrete results will be
quite different. Thus, for example, formula tales are
built on principles radically different from those used in
fairy tales. The types of formulas on which formula tales
are based can be recognized and determined, but such individual formulas, or schemes, will not correspond in the
least to those of fairy tales. There are nonetheless certain narrative genres which can be analyzed using the same
methods. Lévi-Strauss quotes my statement that my conclusions are not applicable to the tales of Novalis and
Goethe nor in general to fairy tales contrived from literary sources. But then he turns around and indicts me on
the grounds that my conclusions are erroneous in those
cases. Clearly they are not erroneous at all; it is just
that they do not have that universal character which my
distinguished critic would like to attribute to them. My
method is comprehensive, but the conclusions are valid
only for that well-determined type of folklore for which
they were devised, namely, the fairy tale.

2.0   I will not respond to all the accusations Lévi-
Strauss brings against me, but I should like to pick up on
a few of the more significant ones. If these prove to be
without foundation, the others, since they are not only
less important but also in some way contingent on these,
will automatically lose their impact.

2.1   Lévi-Strauss' basic charge is that my work has a
formalist orientation and for that reason alone cannot
offer any valid insights. Precisely what he means by
formalism Lévi-Strauss never clearly defines. He limits
himself to pointing out a few characteristics of formalism
in the course of his treatment of the subject. One of
these characteristics would be that formalists study their

chosen material without historical considerations. Lévi-
Strauss accuses me of such a formalist and ahistorical
approach, but then, seemingly trying to temper his criticism, he informs the reader that I have given up on formalism and on morphological analysis after the publication
of my *Morphology*. I have dedicated myself, he says, to
the historical and comparative study of the relationship
of oral literature (his description of folklore) to myths,
rites, and institutions (Lévi-Strauss, 1976:116). However, he does not tell us precisely to which work of mine
he refers. In my book *Russian Agrarian Holidays* (1963) I
used exactly the same method as in my *Morphology*, and I
managed to establish there that all the principal agrarian
holidays consist of identical elements though organized
differently. Of course this work could not have been
known to Lévi-Strauss, who apparently is referring to my
work *The Historical Roots of the Fairy Tale*, published in
1946 and later translated into Italian. Had he glanced
through this volume, however, he would have been aware
that I began there with the explanation of the theories
developed in my *Morphology* and that there the fairy tale
is defined in relationship not to plot but to composition.
In fact, once I had established the unity of composition
in fairy tales, I could not help but wonder about the reason for this unity. I knew from the beginning that the
reason did not lie in internal formal laws. It would have
to be discovered in the early phases of history, or, as
some people prefer, prehistory, that is, in that stage of
development of society which is properly the object of
ethnography and ethnology. Lévi-Strauss is perfectly correct in his affirmation that morphology is sterile if it
does not take ethnographical data into account, directly
or indirectly ("ethnographic observation": Lévi-Strauss,
1976:141). Precisely for this reason I have not *abandoned*
morphological analysis, but have delved into research on
the historical roots of that system which was revealed to
me in the comparative study of fairy tale plots. My *Morphology* and my *Historical Roots* represent, so to speak,

two parts or two volumes of one comprehensive work. The
latter grows directly out of the former and the former is
the basis of the latter. Lévi-Strauss quotes my assertion
that morphological research goes hand in hand with historical investigation (1976:129), but once again he turns my
quote against me. Insofar as this orientation does not in
fact appear in my *Morphology* he is correct, but he has not
taken sufficiently into account the fact that these words
are expressions of a well-fixed *principle*. They represent, moreover, a promise to attend to this historical
research in the future; they are in their own way a debt
which, even if after many years, I have honestly paid. It
is simply false to write about me as one who is trapped
between a "formalist vision" and an "obsession with historical explanations" (Lévi-Strauss, 1976:130). In point
of fact I move with the most rigorous methodology and the
greatest possible coherence *from* a scientific description
of the phenomena and the facts *to* an explanation of their
historical roots. Unaware of all this, Lévi-Strauss goes
so far as to attribute to me a change of heart which presumably has led me to renounce my formalist illusions and
to dedicate myself to historical research. The fact is
that I do not accept any such conversion, nor do I have
the least remorse of conscience. Lévi-Strauss himself
holds that any historical explanation of fairy tales is
really impossible, "since we know very little about the
prehistoric civilizations where they originated" (1976:
131). He also laments the lack of texts for comparison.
The question, however, does not rest on texts (of which
there are certainly plenty), but on two other factors.
First, that the plots draw their origin from *the life and
practices* of the people and from their respective thought
forms in the early stages of the development of human society; and, second, that the appearance of these plots
responds to historical necessity. It is true that we
still know little about ethnology, but nonetheless global
scholarship has already collected a great quantity of
factual data, and this makes such efforts entirely possible.

2.2   But what really matters are the principles involved and not just their manner of formulation in my
Morphology, even less the vicissitudes of its author himself.   One cannot separate formal from historical research;
nor can one place them in opposition.   In fact, the opposite is true: formal analysis and meticulous systematic
description of the material studied are both the condition
and the premise of historical research, and they represent
simultaneously the first step in the process.   There can
be no basis for objecting to the isolated examination of
individual plots, following the procedures used frequently
by the so-called Finnish school.   By the same token, those
who use this approach cannot perceive any connection between plots, nor can they even suspect the existence or
possibility of such a connection.   This is the characteristic orientation of the formalists to whom the whole appears to be a mechanical conglomerate of heterogeneous
parts.   From this perspective, in the case at hand, the
fairy tale genre is seen as a collection of individual
plots isolated within themselves.   The structuralist, on
the other hand, examines the parts as elements of a whole;
the structuralist sees a whole, a system, which the formalist cannot even discern.   The method elaborated in my
Morphology furnishes the possibility of studying the genre
as a whole, a unity, a system, and of comparing the various plots, rather than dismembering them and considering
them separately, as has been the custom of the Finnish
school.   It seems to me that this school, even acknowledging the value of their approach, might be accused of formalism.   The comparative study of plots opens up broad
historical perspectives.   It is not primarily a question
of individual plots which can be explained historically,
but of a composite system to which they all pertain.   One
discovers the historical interconnections among the plots
and that forms the basis for also studying them separately.

2.3   But the problem of the connection between formal
and historical analysis represents only one dimension of

the question. Another aspect derives from the relationship between form and content and the different methods
for studying them. By formalism one usually means the
study of form independently of content. But for Lévi-
Strauss formalism places form and content in opposition
and in this he is not out of step with present Soviet literary historians. Thus, for example, J. M. Lotman (9-10
and passim), one of the more active representatives of
structuralist literary study, writes that the principal
defect of the so-called "formal method" lies in the fact
that it often leads the researcher to consider literature
as a lumping together of techniques, as a mechanical con-
glomeration. One might also add that, for formalists,
form has independent laws and, particularly, internal laws
of development not subject to the socio-historical context.
According to this approach, development in the field of
literary creation is autonomous, and is determined by the
laws of form.

But if this is what is meant by formalism, my
work, *Morphology of the Folktale*, cannot in any sense be
termed formalist, even if Lévi-Strauss is by no means the
only one who makes this accusation. Not every study dealing with form is formalist, and not every scholar who examines the form of works of oral or figurative art must by
that very fact be a formalist.

2.4   Earlier I cited Lévi-Strauss' comments stating
that my conclusions on the structure of fairy tales were
an illusion, a "formalist vision" (1976:130). We are not
talking here of a passing remark but of a deep-felt conviction of this reviewer that I am the victim of "a subjective illusion" (131). He accuses me of constructing
from several different tales one that never existed, and
one that is "such a vague and general abstraction that
nothing would be learned from it about the objective causes
of a multitude of particular tales" (134). Lévi-Strauss is
right in saying that my abstraction, as he calls the schema
I devised, does not reveal the reason for the variety in

folktales and that only historical research can achieve
this. It is not true, however, that my schema is vague
and represents a pure illusion. This statement by Lévi-
Strauss simply proves that, as far as I can gather, he has
not grasped the absolutely empirical, concrete, and particular character of my research. How could this have
happened? Lévi-Strauss believes that my work itself is
already difficult to understand, but it should be noted
that those who have fixed ideas of their own have difficulty understanding the ideas of others. They do not
understand even that which seems clear and which is devoid
of bias. My research does not fit into Lévi-Strauss'
general preconceptions, and this is one of the reasons for
our misunderstanding. Another reason is my own way of
writing. When I wrote the book I was young, and was then
convinced that it was enough to put forth one's observations or ideas and that people would understand and agree.
Thus I was very concise and used a kind of theorem style
in my writings. I assumed that the development and more
precise demonstration of ideas was not necessary. It was
as though these ideas should be as immediately clear and
intelligible to everybody as they were to me. On this I
was wrong.

        To begin with my own terminology, I must admit
that the term "morphology" was not well chosen. But the
term was very dear to me. I had borrowed it from Goethe,
and I used it not only in a scientific but in a quasi-
philosophical and even a poetic sense. Had I been more
exact, I should not have spoken about "morphology," but
should have adopted a much more limited concept. I might,
for example, have used the word "composition," and then
the book would have been called *The Composition of the
Fairy Tale in Folklore*. But even the word "composition"
would have to be more clearly determined, since it too is
open to various interpretations. How am I using it here?
As noted before, my analysis began with the observation
that in fairy tales different characters perform identical

actions, or, in other words, identical actions can be
executed in quite different ways. We saw the evidence
for this in the group of tales dealing with the persecuted
stepdaughter. Yet this observation is valid not only for
variations on a given plot but also for all plots of the
fairy tale genre. Thus, for example, if the hero leaves
home to look for something which is only to be found far
away, he might seek it astride his enchanted horse, or on
the back of an eagle, or maybe on a flying carpet, or a
flying ship, etc. We will not list here all the possible
examples. It is fairly obvious that in all these cases we
are dealing with the spatial transference of the hero to
the place where the object of his quest is to be found,
but that the ways in which the spatial transference happens may be diverse. We have then significant constants
and significant interchangeable variables. Another example is that of the suitor who is unacceptable either because the princess does not want to marry him or because
her father does not want to grant her to him. Impossible
feats are demanded of him: he must leap from his horse to
her window, or take a bath in boiling water, or resolve
the princess' riddle, or procure a hair of gold from the
king of the seas, etc. To the unthinking listener all
these variations appear completely different, and from his
perspective he is right. But to the careful researcher
this multiplicity reveals a unity that can be determined
logically. In the first series of examples the issue was
the transference to the place of the quest (spatial transference), and in the second the issue was the motive for
assigning difficult tasks. The nature of these tasks is
divergent so that they are interchangeable variables; but
their assignment is the constant. I termed these constant
elements functions of the characters, and the scope of my
research consisted in establishing which functions appear
in fairy tales, in determining if they appear in a limited
number, and in what order they follow one another. In my
work I dealt precisely with the results of this analysis.

The functions turned out to be not very numerous, their
forms manifold, their sequence identical. In sum, one
obtains a picture of surprising regularity.

     I thought that all this was simple enough and
easily understandable, and I still believe so. I did not
take into account, however, the fact that the word "function" has many different senses in all languages, and is
used in mathematics, in medicine, and in philosophy.
Those who are not familiar with all these meanings understood me easily enough. According to my definition of the
term for the research in question, "function" signifies the
action of a particular person from the perspective of the
flow of the narrative. Thus, if the hero leaps from his
horse to the window of the princess, we do not speak about
the function of leaping from a horse (a description acceptable enough outside the narrative progress viewed as
a whole), but about the function of executing a difficult
task, insofar as this is related to the request for the
princess' hand. In the same way, if the hero flies on an
eagle's back to the place where the princess lives, one is
not dealing with the function of flying on an eagle's
back, but rather with that of being transferred to the
place of the search (spatial transference). The word
"function" then is a conventional term which is understood
in my work in this sense and in no other.

     The determination of "functions" is the result
of a specific comparative analysis of the material, and it
is therefore impossible to agree with Lévi-Strauss when he
asserts that these "functions" are established in a completely arbitrary and subjective fashion. "Functions" are
rather the product of comparison, of correlation, of abstraction of a logical structure from thousands of cases.
But Lévi-Strauss understands the term "function" in a
sense completely different from that adopted in my *Morphology*. In demonstrating that the functions are determined arbitrarily, he has recourse to the example of different persons protecting a fruit tree: one will consider

the most important thing to be its function of productivity; another might consider the depth of its roots most
important; for primitive people the most important function of the tree might be to join heaven and earth (the
tree may grow to the sky). From the point of view of this
logic productivity may be defined appropriately as one of
the functions of the fruit tree, but productivity is not
an action, and certainly not the action of a character in
a narrative. But I am concerned precisely with narratives
and the investigation of their specific laws. Lévi-Strauss
attributes to my functions a generalized, abstract sense
which they do not have, and then refutes them. The functions, however, have not been determined arbitrarily.

2.5   I would like now to consider what I mean by composition. I understand composition to be the sequence of
functions as that is dictated by the tale itself. The
scheme that might be abstracted is not an archetype nor is
it the reconstruction of a unique tale from the past (as
my critic seems to think), but something completely different: it is rather the single compositional scheme that
stands at the base of fairy tales. Lévi-Strauss is right,
in fact, on one point: this compositional scheme does not
have real existence. But it becomes real in narration in
very diverse forms. It stands at the basis of the plots
and represents, so to speak, their skeleton. To clarify
this idea somewhat, and to avoid further misunderstanding,
let me exemplify what I intend by plot and composition.
I will state these examples in a concise and somewhat simplified form. Suppose that a dragon steals the king's
daughter. The king seeks help, and the son of a peasant
decides to find her. He sets out on his journey, and
along the way he encounters an old woman who proposes that
he tame a herd of savage horses. He is successful, and
the old woman gives him one of the animals as a gift; the
horse takes him to an island where he finds the kidnapped
princess. The hero slays the dragon, returns home, and
the king rewards him by offering him his daughter's hand.

This is the "plot" of the tale. The "composition" on the
other hand may be delineated as follows: some misfortune
takes place; the hero is asked to help; he goes off on his
quest; along the way he encounters someone who puts him to
the test and then rewards him with some magical agent;
thanks to this magical medium he finds the lost object;
the hero returns and is rewarded. This is the composition
of the tale. It seems clear that an identical composition
can furnish the basis for many plots, and that on the
other hand several plots have basically one identical composition. Composition is the constant factor; plot is the
variable factor. If there were no danger of further misunderstanding in terminology, we might call the structure
of the tale the intertwining of plot and composition. The
composition does not have real existence, just as those
general concepts which are found only in human consciousness do not have real existence in the world of things.
But it is due precisely to these general concepts that we
know the world, understand its laws, and learn to govern
and manage it.

2.60   Before entering into the thick of the problem of
form and content we need to spend a little time on some
preliminary questions.

2.61   In studying the folktale we can note that some
functions (actions of characters) can be conveniently considered as correlates or pairs. For example, charging one
with a difficult task implies its solution; the quest
terminates with the rescue; the battle brings victory; the
disaster with which the tale began is resolved in the end,
and so on. Lévi-Strauss holds that these paired functions
really constitute single functions and are all reducible
to them. If it were a question of logic this might very
well be granted. The battle and the victory constitute in
a way a single unit. But in determining composition these
mechanical associations are not particularly helpful and
in fact produce only a false picture. Those paired functions are performed by different characters: the difficult

task is imposed by one person and is executed by another.
Furthermore, the second half of a paired function may be
either positive or negative. In fairy tales we encounter
both an authentic hero and a false hero: the former exe-
cutes the task and is duly rewarded; the latter does not
succeed and is punished. Between paired functions there
are also inserted intermediate functions. Thus, for example, the kidnapping of the princess ("Villainy": the
first function after the preliminary part) is found at the
beginning of the tale, while her return ("Vaillainy Liqui-
dated") takes place only at the conclusion. However, in
studying the composition, that is, the sequence of functions, the reduction of the paired elements to a single
element would not lead us to an understanding of the laws
which regulate the progress of the action and the development of the plot. It is not possible, therefore, to accept any recommendation subjecting these functions to further logical operations against the very indications of
the material itself.

2.62   For these same reasons I am also forced to reject
another recommendation of Lévi-Strauss. It was very important for me to determine the sequence of the functions. I
found out that the sequence was always the same, and this
has been a very important discovery for the folklorist.
The action of the narrative unfolds in time; the sequence
of functions is therefore chronological. Lévi-Strauss,
however, does not approve of this method of analyzing and
ordering functions. He refers to the sequence I indicated
in alphabetical order by the letters A, B, C, D, etc., and
in place of this chronological series proposes using a
logical system. My critic would like to arrange the functions in a grid with two dimensions, one vertical, the
other horizontal. This distribution is one of the require-
ments of structural analysis, and it was already present
in my *Morphology*, although from a slightly different perspective. It seems that Lévi-Strauss did not consider
carefully enough the appendix at the end of that work

entitled "Materials for a Tabulation of the Tale." The
headings there represent the horizontal reading so that
this is an enlarged version of the compositional schema
indicated in the text of my book by letters. Under these
headings one could insert the text of the fable in detail
and this would give the vertical reading. There is simply
no need to replace this perfectly concrete scheme, drawn
from a comparison of texts, with some other purely abstract
scheme. The difference between my approach and that of my
critic rests on the fact that I extract generalizations
from the material, whereas Lévi-Strauss elaborates on my
generalizations in the abstract. He deplores the fact
that it is not possible to get back to the material from
my abstract schemes. But if he would take any fairy tale
at random and match it against my scheme, he would see
that there is an exact correlation with the material, and
he would come to see firsthand the structural laws of the
fairy tale. Not only that, but by using my scheme as his
point of departure he could make up an infinite number of
fairy tales; and these would be constructed according to
the very laws of the fairy tale itself. Leaving aside
mutually incompatible combinations, one could calculate
mathematically the number of possible ones left. If we
were to call my scheme a model, this model would reproduce
all the constitutive elements (constants) of the fairy tale,
leaving out simultaneously all the elements that are not
constitutive (variables). My model is true to what is
being modelled and is based on the study of the material.
Lévi-Strauss' model, on the contrary, does not correspond
to reality and is based on logical operations not derived
from the concrete material. The abstraction derived from
the material serves to explain it; the abstraction of an
abstraction becomes an end in itself. It has no connection with the material, and one may find that it is in
such contradiction with the data of the real world that it
is ultimately incapable of explaining it. Carrying out
these logical operations completely in the abstract, and

not bothering at all with the material, Lévi-Strauss (who is not interested in fairy tales and does not try to understand them) extracts the functions from their temporal sequence (1976:137-38). Such is not possible for the folklorist since function (act, deed, action), as it is defined in my work, is accomplished in time and cannot be taken out of a temporal context. While on this subject we should remember also that the notions of time, of space, and of number which operate in fairy tales are completely different from those to which we are accustomed and which we tend to consider as absolutes. But this is a particular problem which we cannot go into now. I have alluded to it only because the forced removal of functions from their temporal sequence destroys the fragile thread of the narrative, which, as in the case of an elegant and finely spun spider's web, is destroyed by the slightest touch. But this is yet another reason to arrange functions chronologically, as the narrative itself demands, and not, as Lévi-Strauss would want, according to an achronological schema or "atemporal matrix" (1976:138).

2.63   For the folklorist and the literary historian the central concern is the plot. In Russian the word "fabula," as a literary-historical term, has a well defined meaning: the complex of actions and events which are developed concretely in the course of the narrative. The English translator caught this meaning very well with the word "plot." And it is not pure chance that a German periodical on the art of popular narrative bears the title "Fabula." But for Lévi-Strauss plot is of no interest; he translates it with the word "theme" (1976:117). Evidently he prefers this term since "plot" is a category which makes reference to time, while the word "theme" does not have this characteristic. But no literary scholar will ever accept this substitution. Both the term "plot" and the term "theme" can be understood in very different ways, but can never be used identically or interchangeably. This lack of interest in plot and in narrative appears

likewise in other cases of poor translation. For example,
if the hero meets an old woman (or another character) on
his journey, and she puts him to the test, and gives him
some magical object or agent, this character, in direct
relationship to her function, is defined in my work as the
"donor" and what the hero receives are called by folklorists "magical agents" (*Zaubergaben*). We are dealing here
with a technical term quite suitably translated by the
English expression "donor." But Lévi-Strauss (1960:127)
translated my technical Russian expression as *bienfateur*
(benefactor, benefactress) and this, once again, makes the
term so general and abstract that it loses all meaning.
[*bienfateur* was translated into English as "donor" in
Propp, 1976:121.]

3.   With these digressions out of the way, though
they are required for a better understanding of what follows, we can now enter into the thick of the problem of
form and content. As we have noted already, it is usual
to define formalism as the study of form abstracted from
content. I must admit that I do not understand what that
really means nor do I understand the possibility of its
material application. Perhaps I could understand it if I
knew in any work of art where to look for form and where
to look for content. One can argue endlessly about form
and content as philosophical categories, but the debate
will be sterile if from the beginning the objects of the
discussion are the categories of form and content without
more concrete references to the material in all its many
varieties.

        Following popular aesthetic judgment, the plot
constitutes the content of the work. The content of the
tale of the Firebird consists for the ordinary person in
recounting how the bird flies into the king's garden and
steals the golden apples, and how the prince at the same
time leaves on his search and returns not only with the
firebird but also with a horse and a beautiful bethrothed.

What is important is how things happened. Let us assume
this popular point of view for the moment, and in fact it
is a quite sensible point of view. If plot is considered
as the content, then evidently composition cannot be so
considered. Thus we come logically to the conclusion that
composition must be considered as the form of the work.
From this viewpoint several different contents can be inserted under one form. But we have already affirmed, and
were forced to demonstrate, that composition and plot are
inseparable. Lévi-Strauss himself asserts the same thing:
"Form and content are of the same nature, susceptible to
the same analysis" (1976:131). That is certainly the case,
but let us examine his comment. If form and content are
inseparable, even to the point of being of the same nature,
then an analysis of one necessarily entails an analysis of
the other. What then is the problem with formalism, and
what is my glaring failure when I analyze plot (content)
and composition (form) as an inseparable unit? I realize,
of course, that this notion of form and content is not too
common, and so it is difficult to say whether or not it
can be applied to other types of oral art. Form is generally understood to mean that which pertains to a particular genre, so that one and the same plot may have
various forms, for example, novel, tragedy, movie scenario,
etc. On this point Lévi-Strauss' observation is clearly
confirmed by the efforts to stage narrative pieces or to
adapt them for the screen. Zola's novel emerges as two
quite different pieces in its narrative form and as a
movie; indeed these two versions no longer really have
anything in common. Further, content is generally taken
to mean not the plot, but the idea that shapes the work,
that which the author wished to express, his principles,
his worldview. Numerous efforts have been made to study
and to evaluate the worldview of writers, but in most
cases these studies have a dilletantish character. Tolstoy
(29) used to scoff at such efforts. When asked what he
meant to say in the novel *Anna Karenina*, he answered: "If
I wanted to put into words exactly what I had in mind for

the novel, I would write the same novel over again. And
if the critics finally understood it and summed up in an
appendix everything that I wanted to say, I would congrat-
ulate them." If it is true that form is the expression of
idea in artistic works of sophisticated literacy, it is
even more true in folklore. Here we have laws of formal
composition so rigorous that to ignore them is tantamount
to a most serious error. Following his own political,
social, historical and religious principles, the researcher will impose his personal worldview on fairy tales or
folklore, arguing that they express attitudes either mystical or atheistic, revolutionary or conservative. This
does not of course mean that in folklore the world of
ideas cannot be studied. In fact, the opposite is true.
But the world of ideas ("content") can be analyzed scientifically and objectively only after the formal laws of
artistic production have been clarified. I am in complete
agreement with Lévi-Strauss when he demands both "historical investigation and literary criticism" (1976:141), but
he demands these methods as a *substitute* for what he calls
formal study. Preliminary formal analysis, however, is
the first condition not only of historical investigation,
but also of literary criticism. If my *Morphology* constitutes in a way the first volume of a broader research project, and my *Historical Roots* is the second volume, then a
third could be presented as literary criticism. Only
after the systematic formal study of the fairy tale and
only after determining its historical roots, will it be
possible to analyze objectively and scientifically the
historical development of that world of popular philosophy
and popular morality which represents one of the most interesting and significant components of the fairy tale.
We should be able to see from this perspective a layered
structure, similar to that of geological deposits where
the oldest layers combine with more recent or even present
ones. At this point we could examine all these variable
elements, all these colors, so to speak, since the fairy

tale is a work of art because of plot as well as composition. But to study and grasp all of this presumes a
knowledge of that substructure on which the large variety
within the fairy tale rests.

4.   I cannot answer all of Lévi-Strauss' observations. I would like, however, to focus on a question that
may seem too particular but that does have larger implications. It is the question of the relationship between
myth and fairy tale. For my purposes this is not a problem of major concern, since my research is directed toward
fairy tale and not myth. Lévi-Strauss, however, dwells at
length on the question of myth. This issue is of interest
to him, and it is another area in which he disagrees with
me.
          There is very little material in my book on the
relationship between myth and fairy tale and what is there
is both concise and lacking in proof. I was shortsighted
in expressing my ideas apodictically, but principles lacking proof are not always wrong or inexact. I hold that
myth, as such, and as a historical genre, may be older than
fairy tale. Lévi-Strauss holds the opposite view. It is
impossible here to tackle this problem in all its ramifi-
cations, but we should at least look at some of its dimensions. What precisely is the difference and what are the
similarities between myth and fairy tale from the point of
view of the folklorist? One of the characteristics of the
fairy tale is the fact that it is based on poetic invention and represents a fiction of reality. In most languages "fairy tale" is synonymous with "lie" and "false-
hood." "The fairy tale is over, one can lie no longer,"
is how the Russian narrator concludes his account. Myth,
on the contrary, is a narrative having a sacred character
in whose truth one not only believes but which expresses
the sacred beliefs of a people. The difference between
myth and fairy tale, then, is not a formal difference.
Myths can assume story-form, and the different types can

be studied, even if I did not do so in my book. Lévi-
Strauss holds that "myth and folktale exploit a common
substance" (1976:130), which is perfectly true if by "substance" he understands the unfolding of the narrative or
plot. There are some myths that are built on the same
morphological or compositional system as the fairy tale.
For example, among classical myths we have the myths of
the Argonauts, of Perseus and Andromeda, of Theseus, and
several others. These correspond at times even in some
quite particular details to the compositional system worked
out in *Morphology of the Folktale*. From this perspective
there are some cases in which myth and fairy tale coincide
at the level of form, but this observation cannot in any
sense be universal. A whole series of ancient myths, indeed the majority, have nothing in common with my system,
and this applies even more rigorously to primitive myths.
Cosmogonic myths, myths about the creation and origin of
the world, of animals, of men, and of things have no connection whatever with my morphology of fairy tales; nor
can they be transformed into it. They are based on a completely different morphological system. Such systems are
quite numerous, and mythology has as yet received little
study from this aspect. In those cases in which myth and
fairy tale are based on the same morphological system,
myth is always more ancient than fairy tale. This can be
proved from the history of the plot of Sophocles' *Oedipus*
(Propp, 1944). In Greece this was a myth, but in the
middle ages the plot acquired a sacred and Christian character and its protagonist became the great sinner Judas,
or one of the saints like Gregory, or Andrew of Crete, or
Alban, who through their outstanding virtue were redeemed
from some great sin. But when the hero loses his name,
and the account loses its sacred character, myth and legend
are transformed into fairy tale.

        Lévi-Strauss, however, sees things differently.
He does not believe that myth is more ancient than fairy
tale since, as he states, they can coexist and in fact do

coexist even up to the present: "...in present time, myths
and folktales coexist side by side. One genre cannot then
be held to be a survival of the other" (1976:131). The
example of *Oedipus* shows, however, that in the course of
their historical development plots may shift from one genre
(myth) to another (legend), and from there to a third genre
(fairy tale). Any folklorist will tell you that plots very
often pass from one genre to another, and not infrequently
to an entirely different genre (thus plots of fairy tales
end up as epics, etc.). Yet Lévi-Strauss makes no reference to concrete plots, and prefers to use the words "myth"
and "folktale" in a general sense. He speaks about myth
"in general" and folktale "in general," and thus considers
the genre itself without distinguishing the types and the
plots. This is why he can speak about the coexistence of
myth and folktale up to the present. However, he certainly is not speaking as a historian. One should not consider centuries, but historical periods and their formative
social factors. In studying archaic and primitive peoples
one is led to conclude that all their folklore (and also
their figurative art) has an exclusively sacred or magical
character. Much of what is published in popular magazines,
and sometimes even in scientific journals, as "primitive
fairy tales" has often enough nothing to do with fairy
tales. It is a well known fact, for example, that the so-
called animal fables were told at one time not as fables
but as magical stories or accounts that must have contributed in no small measure to a successful hunt. Material relevant to this observation is abundant. The fairy
tale is later in origin than myth, and there arrives a
moment at which they may effectively coexist, but only in
those cases in which the plots of myths and of fairy tales
are different and pertain to different compositional systems. Classical antiquity was aware of both myths and
fairy tales but their respective plots were different.
The myth of the Argonauts and the fairy tale of the Argonauts cannot exist at the same time for the same people.

Nor can one have a fairy tale about Theseus where the myth
is alive and flourishing, and where a cult to him has been
developed. Finally, with the advanced formative social
factors of the present the existence of myths is now impossible. The role that they performed at one time as the
sacred tradition of the people has now been taken over by
sacred history and ecclesiastical story. Finally, in so-
cialist countries even these last traces of the myths of
sacred tradition are gradually disappearing. In this
sense the problem of the respective age of myth and fable,
and of the possibility or impossibility of their coexist-
ing, cannot be resolved in cursory fashion. One must take
into account the degree of development of the people. It
is essential to know and to understand the morphological
systems, and to know how to distinguish amongst them, if
one is to determine both the similarities and the differences between myth and fairy tale and also to resolve the
problem of their relative age and of the possibility of
their coexistence. The issue is much more complex than
appears to Lévi-Strauss.

5.1   Perhaps it is time now to draw some conclusions
from all this. The philosopher tends to consider as correct those general judgments which correspond to one or
other philosophical system. The scholar meanwhile accepts
as correct those judgments which result from the study of
concrete reality. Although Lévi-Strauss takes issue with
me because my conclusions do not correspond, as he says,
to the nature of things, nonetheless he does not point to
a single specific fairy tale where my conclusions are erroneous; and although such specifics could be most damaging
for the scholar, they are also most useful, appropriate,
and valuable.

5.2   Another very important concern for any scholar
in any specialization is that of method. According to
Lévi-Strauss my method is in error, since the phenomenon
of the transferability of actions from one person to

another, or the persistence of identical actions despite different actors, does not apply exclusively to fairy tales. This observation is indeed correct but instead of undercutting my method it would rather seem to support it. In fact, if in cosmogonic myths a raven, a mink, being it-self, or the anthropomorphic divinity can assume identical roles as founders of the world, myths not only can be but must be studied with the same elaborate methods as fairy tales. The conclusions will differ, of course, and the morphological systems will be very numerous, but the methods will remain the same.

It is very possible that the method used in analyzing narratives according to functions of the char-acters might also prove to be useful for the narrative genres not only of folklore but of literature as well. In any event the methods put forth in my volume (which pre-dated structuralism), as well as the methods of structuralists aspiring to exact and objective study of literature, both have their own limitations. They are possible and even profitable in those cases where one finds oneself faced with the element of repetition on a large scale, as in the case of language and folklore. But when the artistic work in question deals with actions of a unique kind, using exact methods will furnish positive re-sults only when the study of the repeatable elements goes hand in hand with the study of that which is unique, which we have looked upon until now as the manifestation of an incomprehensible miracle. Irrespective of the category into which one places the *Divine Comedy* or the tragedies of Shakespeare, the genius of Dante and of Shakespeare is unique, and is not able to be captured with exact methods alone. And so, if at the beginning of this article we put emphasis on the affinity between the laws studied in the exact sciences and those studied in the humanities, we would like to conclude by pointing out their fundamental and specific difference.

1 Hesiod's Myth of the Races: An Essay in Structural Analysis

Hesiod's poem 'Works and Days' begins with the telling of two myths. After referring briefly to the existence of a double 'Strife' (*Eris*), Hesiod tells the story of Prometheus and Pandora. This myth is immediately followed by another, the myth of the races, which, as Hesiod says, 'crowns' the first. The two myths are linked. Both evoke a time gone by when people lived untroubled by suffering, sickness, and death. Each in its own way accounts for the ills which since that time have become inseparable from the human condition. The myth of Prometheus suggests a moral so clear that Hesiod has no need to expound it. The myth speaks for itself: through the will of Zeus, who, in order to avenge the theft of fire, has hidden man's livelihood from him – that is to say, his food – the human race is condemned to toil. Man is obliged to accept this harsh divine law and obtain no respite from his toil or his suffering. Hesiod draws from the myth of the races a lesson which he addresses in particular to his brother Perses (a sorry wretch), but which is equally appropriate to the mighty on earth, those whose function it is to settle human quarrels through arbitration, in other words, the kings. Hesiod sums up this lesson in the dictum: 'Observe justice, *dike*, do not allow immoderation, *hubris*, to grow.' (2) However, it must be said that if one is content to accept the usual interpretation of the myth, it is hard to see how this instruction can derive from it.

The story tells of the succession of different races who have preceded us on earth, who have in turn appeared and then disappeared. What is there in such a tale to exhort man to Justice? All these races, be they good or bad, were obliged, when the time came, to quit the light of day. And among those races worshipped by people long after they had disappeared beneath the earth, there were some who, while on earth, manifested an appalling degree

247

of hubris. (3)   Furthermore, the order in which the races
appear to follow one upon the other is one of progressive
deterioration.   They are associated with the metals whose
names they respectively bear, and these are arranged in
order from the most precious to the least precious, from
the highest to the lowest.   Gold comes first, then
silver, followed by bronze, and finally iron.   Thus the
myth appears to seek to contrast a divine world whose
order has been unchangeably fixed ever since Zeus's victory with a human world in which disorder gradually establishes itself, until the scales are finally tipped decisively towards injustice, misfortune, and death. (4)   But
this picture of humanity destined to a fatal and irreversible decline seems hardly likely to convince either
Perses or the kings of the virtues of dike and the dangers
of hubris.

This initial difficulty concerning the relationship
between the myth as it appears to us and the significance
that Hesiod attaches to it in his poem is matched by
another which has to do with the structure of the myth
itself.   Hesiod adds a fifth race to the races of gold,
silver, bronze, and iron.   It is the race of heroes which
does not correspond to any particular metal.   Since it is
inserted between the ages of bronze and iron, it upsets
the parallelism between the races and the metals.   Moreover, it interrupts the movement of continuous decline
symbolized by the scale of metals of regularly decreasing
value.   Indeed, the myth makes it quite clear that the
race of heroes is superior to that of bronze which precedes it. (5)

Erwin Rohde noticed this anomaly, and noted that Hesiod
must have had extremely powerful motives to introduce into
the structure an element which was manifestly foreign to
the original myth, particularly when this intrusion
appeared to disrupt its logical pattern. (6)   Rohde
observed that what interests Hesiod most about the heroes
is not their earthly existence but their destiny after
death.   In the case of each of the other races, Hesiod
described on the one hand its life here on earth, and on
the other what became of it once it had left the light of
day.   So it would appear that the myth was serving two
purposes - first, revealing the increasing moral decline
of the human race;   and, second, giving an insight into
the destiny after death of each successive generation.
Although the presence of the heroes appears misplaced from
the point of view of the first aim, it is fully justified
from the point of view of the second.   Where the heroes
are concerned, this subsidiary purpose appears to have
become the principal one.

248

Taking these observations as his starting point, Victor Goldschmidt suggests an interpretation that goes further. (7)   According to this author, the destiny of the metal races after they have disappeared from earthly life is to be 'promoted' to the rank of divine powers.   The individuals of gold and of silver become daemons, *daimones*, after their death.   Those of bronze became the people of the dead in Hades.   Only the heroes do not benefit from a transformation which could only bring them what they already possess: heroes they are, and heroes they stay.   We can, however, see why they are introduced into the myth once we realize that their presence is indispensable if the list of divine beings is to be complete.   According to traditional classification, apart from the *theoi*, gods in other words (of whom no mention is made in the myth) the list consists of the following categories: daemons, heroes, and the dead. (8)   Thus Hesiod would appear to have developed his account of the myth by uniting two different traditions which were no doubt originally independent, and adapting them to each other.   On the one hand, there is the genealogical myth of the races, involving the symbolism of the metals and depicting the moral decline of the human race.   On the other, we have a structural division of the divine world which involved reshaping the original pattern of the myth so as to include the heroes.   In this way the myth of the ages could be seen as the most ancient example of an attempt to reconcile a genetic and a structural point of view.   It is an attempt to make the stages of a temporal succession correspond, term for term, with the elements of a permanent structure. (9)

Goldschmidt's interpretation has the merit of emphasizing the unity and internal coherence of Hesiod's myth of the races.   Whether the myth originally included the race of heroes is a matter of great scholarly controversy. (10) But it is certain that Hesiod rethought the overall mythical theme from the point of view of his own preoccupations. So we must consider the myth as it is presented to us in the context of 'Works and Days', and ask ourselves what, in this form, it means.

On this point one preliminary observation should be made.   So far as Hesiod is concerned one cannot speak of an antinomy between the genetic myth and the structural arrangement.   In mythical thought any genealogy is also at the same time the expression of a structure;   and there is no way to account for a structure other than to present it in the form of a genealogical tale. (11)   The myth of the ages is not, in any respect, an exception to this rule. And the order in which the races follow one another on

earth is not, strictly speaking, chronological.   How
could it be?   Hesiod does not have in mind the idea of a
unique and homogeneous time within which each of the races
has a fixed and definite place.   Each race has its own
time, its own age which expresses its particular character.   This time, just as much as its way of life, its
activities, its qualities, and its defects, defines its
status in contrast to that of the other races. (12)   If
the race of gold is called 'the first', it is not because
it arose one fine day, before the others, in the course of
linear and irreversible time.   On the contrary, if Hesiod
describes it at the beginning of his account, this is
because it embodies virtues - symbolized by gold - which
are at the top of a scale of nontemporal values.   The
succession of the races in time reflects a permanent,
hierarchical order in the universe.   As for the idea of
a continuous and progressive decline, which the commenta-
tors all agree is to be found in the myth, (13) this is
incompatible not only with the episode of the heroes (and
one can hardly suppose that Hesiod did not notice this),
but also with the notion of time which in Hesiod is not
linear but cyclical.   The ages succeed one another to
form a complete cycle, which, once completed, starts all
over again, either in the same order, or, more probably,
as in the Platonic myth in the 'Politicus', in reverse
order, so that cosmic time is unfolded alternately, first
in one direction and then in the other. (14)   Hesiod
laments the fact that he himself belongs to the fifth and
last race, the race of iron, and at that point expresses
the regret that he has not died earlier or *been born
later*. (15)   This remark is incomprehensible in the context of human time that is continuously degenerating, but
it makes perfect sense if we accept that the series of
ages is a recurring renewable cycle, just like the
sequence of the seasons.
   Within the framework of a cycle such as this, even
without taking into account the case of the heroes, the
order in which the races succeed one another does not
appear to follow a progressive decline at all.   The third
race is not 'worse' than the second, and Hesiod never suggests that it is. (16)   In the text, the people of the
silver age are characterized by their mad excesses and
their lack of piety, and the people of bronze by their
acts of immoderation. (17)   What is there in this to
suggest a progressive decline?   There is indeed so little
progression that the race of silver is the only one whose
faults arouse the anger of the gods and which Zeus annihi-
lates as punishment for its lack of piety.   The race of
bronze dies, as do the heroes, fighting in war.   When

Hesiod wishes to make a value judgment between two races
he formulates it explicitly and always in the same way:
he contrasts the two races in terms of dike versus hubris.
He stresses that there is a contrast of this kind in the
first place between the first and second races, and then
again between the third and fourth.   To put it more precisely, in terms of a value judgment the first race is to
the second what the fourth race is to the third.   Hesiod
indeed states that the race of silver is 'very much inferior' to the race of gold on account of its hubris, by
which the race of gold is quite untainted. (18)   He further states that the heroes are 'more just' than the race
of bronze, which is also pledged to hubris. (19)   On the
other hand, he makes no comparative value judgment between
the second and third races.   The race of bronze is simply
described as being 'in no way similar' to the race of
silver. (20)   Thus, so far as the relationships between
the first four races are concerned, the text presents the
following structure: a distinction is made between two
different groups with gold and silver in the one, and
bronze and the heroes in the other.   Each group is divided into two antithetical aspects, one of which is positive and the other negative, and each thus comprises two
associated races, each of which is the necessary counterpart to the other and stands in contrast to it as dike
does to hubris. (21)
    The distinction between the first and second two races
depends, as we shall see, upon the fact that different
functions are involved.   They represent opposed types of
human agents, forms of behaviour, and social and 'psychological' states.   We shall have to be more specific on
these points, but we can note, straight away, one feature
in which they are not symmetrical.   In the first pair the
dominant value is dike, hubris is secondary, treated as
its counterpart.   In the second pair the opposite is
true: the principal consideration is hubris.   Thus while
each of the two pairs has a just and an unjust aspect, it
can be said that, taken together, they are opposed to each
other, just as dike and hubris are.   This explains the
difference between the two sets of races in their fates
after death.   The race of gold and the race of silver
are both promoted, in the strict sense of the term: from
being perishable beings they become daemons.   As in their
existence on earth, so too in the afterlife, the relationship that links them is one of opposition.   The race of
gold becomes epichthonian daemons and the men of silver
hupochthonian daemons, (22) and mortals do 'honour' to
both of them: royal honour, *basileion*, for the race of
gold, and lesser honour for the race of silver, since it

251

is, after all, 'inferior' to the race of gold.   Nevertheless, it is honour for all that, even though it cannot be
justified by virtues or merits, for in their case these do
not exist.   Its only justification can be that the race
of silver belongs to the same category of reality as the
race of gold since it represents the same function, only
in its negative aspect.   The posthumous fate of the races
of bronze and of heroes is quite different.   Neither, as
a race, is promoted.   The race of bronze's destiny cannot
be called a 'promotion', for it is in no way exceptional.
Having died in battle, the people become the 'anonymous'
dead in Hades. (23)   Most of those who make up the race
of heroes share this common fate.   Only a few privileged
persons from this more just race escape the ordinary anonymity of death, and, by the grace of Zeus who rewards them
with this special favour, retain an individual name and
existence in the afterlife.   These few are carried away
to the Island of the Blessed where they live a life free
from all cares. (24)   But they are not in any way venera-
ted or honoured by mortals.   Rohde was right to emphasize
the 'total isolation' of their existence in a world which
seems quite cut off from ours. (25)   Unlike the daemons,
the erstwhile heroes have no power over the living and the
living do not worship them.
These strongly marked parallels show that, in Hesiod's
version of the myth, the race of heroes is not a badly
integrated feature distorting the structure of the myth
but an essential part of it, without which the overall
balance would be upset.   On the other hand, the fifth
race does seem to present a problem.   It introduces a new
dimension, a third category of reality, which, unlike the
other two, does not seem to be divisible into two antithetical aspects, but appears to be presented as a single
race.   However, it is clear from the text that in fact
there is not just *one* age of iron, but rather two types of
human existence, in strict opposition to each other, one
of which acknowledges dike while the other knows only
hubris.   Hesiod lives, in fact, in a world where people
are born young and die when they are old, where there are
'natural' laws (the child resembles the parent), and also
'moral' ones (guests, relations, and oaths should be respected).   It is a world where good and evil are intimate-
ly mixed but counterbalance each other.   Hesiod, however,
foretells the coming of another life, which will be, in
every way, different from the first. (26)   In it people
will be born old with white hair, the child will have
nothing in common with the parent, one will recognize
neither friends nor brothers nor parents nor oaths.
Right will rest upon might alone.   In this world, given

over to disorder and hubris, there will be no good to compensate for suffering.   In the light of this one can see
how the episode of the age of iron, in both its aspects,
can correspond to the preceding themes, so as to complete
the overall structure of the myth.   The first category,
made up of the gold and silver races, was concerned in
particular with the exercise of dike (in the relations of
people with one another and with gods);   the second, the
bronze race and the heroes, was concerned with the manifestation of the physical force and violence linked with
hubris;   the third, the iron age, is related to an ambiguous human world characterized by the coexistence of opposites within it.   Everything good has its evil counterpart: birth implies death;   youth, age;   abundance, toil;
happiness, misfortune.   Dike and hubris, being present
side by side, offer two equally possible options between
which humans must choose.   To this mixed world, which is
that of Hesiod himself, the poet contrasts the terrifying
prospect of a human life where hubris has triumphed
totally, an upside-down world where nothing has survived
but unadulterated disorder and misfortune.

   The cycle of ages would then be completed and time
could do nothing but return in the opposite direction.
In the age of gold everything was order, justice, and joy:
this was the reign of pure dike.   By the end of the
cycle, in the latter part of the age of iron, everything
will be abandoned to disorder, to violence, and to death:
this will be the reign of pure hubris.   From one reign to
the next the succession of the ages does not show a progressive decline.   Instead of a continuous temporal succession of that sort, there are phases which alternate
according to whether they oppose one another or are complementary.   Time does not unfold according to a chronological sequence, but according to the dialectical relationship of a system of antinomies.   We must now indicate
the extent to which this system corresponds to certain
permanent structures in human society and the world of the
gods.

There is no doubt at all that the people of gold are
royal *basileis* and take no part in any form of activity
which falls outside the province of kingship.   Their way
of life is defined, negatively, in two ways: they are unacquainted with war and live at peace, ἥυχοι, (27) which
is unlike the people of bronze and the heroes, who are
dedicated to fighting.   And, second, they know nothing of
labour in the fields, for the earth 'spontaneously' produces countless blessings for them, (28) - this is in contrast to the people of iron, who are dedicated to *ponos*

and are obliged to till the earth to produce their
food. (29)

Gold itself, whose name this race bears, is, as has
been shown, a symbol of royalty. (30)   In Plato's version
of the myth, gold is the distinguishing and qualifying
mark of those, among the different kinds of humans, who
are born to command, archein. (31)   The race of gold
existed in the time when Kronos, ἐμβασίλευεν, ruled in
heaven. (32)   Kronos was a ruler god with associations
with the royal function, and at Olympia, each year at the
spring equinox, a college of priests made sacrifices to
him on the top of Mount Kronos.   These priests were known
as the 'royal ones', basilai. (33)   Finally, the race of
gold enjoys a royal privilege, *basileion geras*, once it
has passed away, for its members are transformed into the
épichthonian daemons. (34)   The expression '*basileion
geras*' acquires its full force when it is pointed out that
in the afterlife these daemons assume the two functions
which, according to the religious conception of royalty,
manifest the beneficent powers of the good king.   As
phulakes, (35) the guardians of mortals, they see to it
that justice is observed while, as *ploutodotai*, the dis-
pensers of riches, they encourage the fertility of the
soil and the increase of the flocks. (36)

Moreover, in Hesiod the same expressions and words used
to describe the people of the ancient race of gold are
equally applied to the just rulers of the contemporary
world.   The people of gold live 'like gods', ὥς θεοί; (37)
and at the beginning of Hesiod's 'Theogony', when the just
king enters the assembly, ready to settle quarrels and
restrain excess by his wise and gentle words, he is hailed
by all as θεὸς ὥς, like a god. (38)   The same picture of
holidays, feasting, and peace amid the abundance generously dispensed by a totally undefiled earth appears
twice. (39)   The first instance is the description of the
happy existence of the race of gold;   the second, that of
the life in the city which flourishes in endless prosperity, under the reign of the just and pious king.   In contrast, when the *basileus* forgets that he is the 'scion of
Zeus', and with no fear of the gods betrays the function
symbolized by his *skeptron*, by straying from the straight
paths of dike through hubris, the city experiences nothing
but calamity, destruction, and famine. (40)   The reason
for this is that close to the kings, mingled among human
beings, thirty thousand invisible immortals are watching,
in the name of Zeus, over the justice and piety of the
rulers.   There is not a single transgression committed by
the kings against dike that is not, sooner or later,
punished through the immortals' intercession.   And among

this myriad of immortals, who are, as the poet tells us in
line 252, ἐπὶ χθονὶ ... φύλακες θνητῶν ἀνθρώπων, we are
bound to recognize the *daimones* of the age of gold who are
described in line 122 as ἐπιχθόνιοι, φύλακες θνητῶν
ἀνθρώπων.

Thus the same portrait of the good ruler is projected
on three different levels at once.   It appears in a mythical past where it represents primitive humanity in the
age of gold;   in contemporary society it is embodied in
the person of the just and pious king;   and in the supernatural world it represents a category of daemons who, in
the name of Zeus, see to it that the royal function is
exercised correctly.

Silver does not possess a specific symbolic meaning of
its own.   It is defined in terms of gold, being like gold
a precious metal, but inferior to it. (41)   Similarly,
the race of silver which is inferior to the race that preceded it exists and is defined only in relation to it.
It is on the same plane as the race of gold, and is its
exact counterpart and opposite.   Pious rule is opposed by
impious rule, and the figure of the king who shows respect
for dike is contrasted with that of the king who has committed himself to hubris.   What seals the doom of the
race of silver is, in effect, their 'mad immoderation',
ὕβριν ἀτάσθαλον, which they cannot avoid either in their
relations between themselves or with the gods. (42)   But
this hubris which characterizes them only applies to the
way they rule.   It has nothing to do with the hubris of
war.   The race of silver, like the race of gold, has no
part in military activities, for these do not concern them
any more than work in the fields.   Their immoderation
operates in an exclusively religious and theological context. (43)   They refuse to sacrifice to the Olympian gods,
and although they may practice *adikia* among themselves, it
is only because they do not wish to recognize the sovereignty of Zeus, the master of dike.   For royalty, it is
natural that hubris should take the form of impiety.
Similarly, in his description of the unjust king, Hesiod
makes it very clear that the reason why this monarch
passes unjust sentences and oppresses people is that he
has no fear of the gods. (44)

Because it is impious, the race of silver is wiped out
by the wrath of Zeus.   As the counterpart of the race of
gold it enjoys comparable honours after its chastisement.
The link, based on function, between the two races is
maintained after death by the parallelism, already
stressed, between the *epichthonians* and *hypochthonians*.
Furthermore, there are also striking analogies between the
race of silver and another group of mythical figures, the

Titans. (45)   They share the same character, the same
function, and the same destiny.   The Titans are the deities of hubris.   The mutilated Ouranos reproaches them
for their mad pride, ἀτασθαλίη, and Hesiod himself calls
them ὑπερθύμοι. (46)   Power is the vocation of these
proud ones.   They aspire to kingship.   They enter into
competition with Zeus for the arche and dunasteia of the
universe. (47)   It is a natural, if not legitimate,
ambition, for the Titans are royal.   Hesychius relates
Τιτάν (Titan) to Τίταξ- meaning 'king' and Τιτήνη meaning
'queen'.   While Zeus and the Olympians represent the
rule of order, the Titans embody the rule of disorder and
hubris.   Once they have been defeated, they must, like
the race of silver, leave the light of day.   They are
hurled far from the heavens, even beyond the surface of
the earth, and they too disappear ὑπὸ χθονός. (48)

Thus the parallelism between the races of gold and of
silver is confirmed by the fact that on each of the three
planes where the image of the just king appears, so too
does that of his double, the king of hubris.   It is confirmed further by the exact correspondence between the
races of gold and silver on the one hand, and between Zeus
and the Titans on the other.   What we find in the account
of the two first stages of mankind is the same structure
as that found in Hesiod's myths concerning sovereign
power.

With the race of bronze we enter a different sphere of
action.   Let us consider how Hesiod himself puts it:
'... a brazen race, sprung from the ash-trees;   and it was
in no way like the silver age, but was terrible and
strong.   They loved the lamentable works of Ares and
deeds of violence.' (49)   One could not state more
clearly that the excesses of the race of bronze do not
bring it closer to, but contrast it with, the race of
silver.   The hubris which characterizes it is exclusively
military, a matter of the warrior's behaviour.   We have
moved from the juridical and religious plane to that of
manifestations of brute force (μεγάλη βίη), physical
energy (χεῖρες ἄαπτοι ... ἐπὶ στιβαροῖσι μέλεσσι), and the
terror (δεινόν ἄπλαστοι) which the warrior inspires.
The people of bronze do nothing but make war.   In their
case there is no mention of the exercise of justice (with
straight or crooked sentences), nor of any worship of the
gods (piety or impiety), just as in the preceding cases
there was no mention of any kind of military activity.
Equally, the race of bronze does not participate in the
activities which characterize the third group, the race of
iron: the people do not eat bread, (50) which would suggest that they know nothing of work on the land and the

growing of cereals. Their death is in line with their
life. They are not destroyed by Zeus but die in war,
falling under the blows they deal each other, overcome 'by
their own arms', in other words, by that physical strength
which is the expression of their essential nature. They
are entitled to no honours: 'terrible though they were',
they pass away into the anonymity of death.

Apart from this explicit information, the author supplies certain symbolical details which complete the picture. First, the reference to bronze has no less precise
a meaning than that of gold. The god Ares himself is
described with the epithet *chalkeos*. (51) The fact is
that bronze, by virtue of certain of its attributes,
appears to be closely linked in Greek religious thought
with the power possessed by the defensive arms of the
warrior. The metallic sheen of the 'flashing bronze',
νώροπα χαλκόν, (52) the sheen from the bronze which sets
the plain alight (53) and which 'goes up to the heavens'
(54) fills the enemy's soul with terror. The sound of
bronze against bronze, the φωνή which reveals its true
nature as living, animated metal, wards off the witchcraft
of the enemy. These defensive arms made of bronze - the
breastplate, helmet, and shield - are complemented in the
panoply of the mythical warrior by some kind of offensive
weapon, a lance, or, even better, a javelin made from
wood. (55) We can be even more precise. The lance is
made of wood that is both extremely supple and at the
same time very hard, the wood of the ash. And the same
word, μελία, is used on some occasions of the javelin
itself and on others of the tree from which it is made.
(56) It is easy to understand why Hesiod said that the
race of bronze came from the ash trees, ἐκ μελιᾶν. (57)
The *meliai*, the nymphs of the trees of war, which themselves reach up to the sky like lances, are constantly
associated in myth with the supernatural beings that represent the warrior. As well as the race of bronze born
from ash trees, we must also mention the giant Talos,
whose entire body is made from bronze. He is the guardian of Crete, and, like Achilles, enjoys a qualified invulnerability over which only Medea's magic wiles can
triumph. Talos too was born from an ash tree. The
band of giants have a direct relationship with the *meliai*
nymphs. Francis Vian (58) has shown that the giants represent a typical military brotherhood, and they too enjoy
a qualified invulnerability. The 'Theogony' tells how
'the great Giants with gleaming armour (made of bronze),
holding long spears (made of ash wood) in their hands and
the Nymphs whom they call Méliae' were born together. (59)
And in the group around the cradle of the infant Zeus of

Crete, alongside the courètes dancing their war dance and clashing their arms and shields to make the bronze ring out, Callimachus still includes the *dyktaiai meliai* whom he calls, significantly, Κυρβάντων ἑτάραι. (60)

The ash trees or the nymphs of the ash trees, from whom the race of bronze was born, also play a role in other accounts of early mortals.   In Argos, Phoroneus, the first man, is descended from a Méliad. (61)   In Thebes, Niobe, the primeval mother, produces seven Méliades, and one may suppose that, as *hetairai* and as wives, they become the female counterparts to the first native men. (62)   These accounts of indigenous origins belong, in most cases, to a body of myths about the role of the warriors which appear to correspond to ritual scenes mimed by a band of young armed warriors.   Vian has emphasized these points in the case of the giants who form ὁ γηγενὴς στρατός, 'the armed band born from the earth', to borrow a phrase from Sophocles. (63)   This band conjures up a picture of lances brandished on the plain, λόγχη πεδιάς, and brute force, θήρειος βία.   The Arcadians,,described as 'those famed for their lances' in the 'Iliad' (64) and as *autochthones hubristai* by the scholiast of Aeschylus's 'Prometheus', (65) claimed descent from a tribe of giants whose chief was Hoplodamos.

The mythical origin of the Thebans was similar.   The Spartans who were their forebears were also *gègeneis* who rose up from the earth, already fully armed, and immediately started to fight against each other.   The story of these Spartans (the word means 'sown') is worth examining more closely.   It illuminates certain details concerning the manner of life and the destiny of the race of bronze.   Once Cadmus had arrived at the place where he was to found Thebes, he sent some of his companions to fetch water at the fountain of Ares which was guarded by a snake. (66)   This snake, which is sometimes represented as one of the *gègeneis* and sometimes as a son of Ares, (67) kills the band of men - whereupon the hero slays the monster.   Acting upon the advice of Athena, he sows its teeth across a plain or *pedion*.   Immediately, fully grown, armed men sprout up and emerge in this field; they are ἄνδρες ἔνοπλοι.   As soon as they are born, they engage in a fight to the death among themselves, and, like the race of bronze, they all perish, except for five survivors who become the ancestors of the Theban aristocracy.   The same ritual pattern is to be found, in a more detailed form, in the myth about Jason at Colchis.   The test that King Aietes imposes upon the hero is a feat of ploughing of a strange kind.   Jason has to go to a field not far from the town, which is called the *pedion* of Ares.   There he

must yoke two monstrous oxen with brazen hooves who belch
forth fire.   He must harness them to a plough and plough
a four-acre field.   In the furrow he has to sow the teeth
of the dragon from which immediately spring a cohort of
armed, fighting giants. (68)   Thanks to a potion Medea
has given him, which makes him temporarily invulnerable,
giving his body and arms a supernatural strength, Jason
emerges triumphant from this feat of ploughing, all of
whose details emphasize its fundamentally military character: it takes place in an uncultivated field, consecrated
to *Ares*; in this field are sown *not the fruits of Demeter
but the teeth of the dragon*; Jason arrives there dressed
not as a peasant but as a warrior, in a breastplate and
with a shield, holding his helmet and his lance;   last, *he
uses his lance as a goad* to control the oxen.   When the
ploughing is done the *gègeneis* spring up from the earth,
like the Spartans.   According to Apollonius Rhodius,

> The plot bristled with stout shields, double-pointed
> spears, and glittering helmets.   The splendour of it
> flashed through the air above.... Indeed this army
> springing from the earth shone out like the full con-
> gregation of the stars piercing the darkness of a murky
> night.

Thanks to Jason's trick of throwing a huge boulder into
their midst, the army's members fall upon and massacre
each other.   This ploughing is a strictly military exploit; it has nothing to do with the fertility of the
soil and has no effect upon its productivity.   Thus it
perhaps helps us to understand one of Hesiod's observations whose paradoxical nature has often been pointed out
although no satisfactory explanation for it has yet been
given.   In line 146 the poet specifies that the race of
bronze 'eats no bread'; a little further on he states
that: 'their armour was of bronze and their houses of
bronze and with bronze they ploughed.' (69)

There seems to be a clear contradiction here.   Why
should they plough the fields if they do not eat wheat?
The difficulty would be removed if the ploughing of the
race of bronze, being likened to that of Jason, was considered as a military ritual and not an agricultural task.
We can support such an interpretation with one final
analogy between the race of bronze and the 'sown ones',
the sons of the furrow.   The Spartans born of the earth
belong, as does the race of bronze, to the race of ash
trees.   They too are ἐκ μελιᾶν.   Indeed, they can be
recognized by the sign of the lance, the distinctive mark
of their race, (70) which is tattooed upon their bodies.
And this sign marks them out as warriors.

There is a difference of value as well as of function

between the lance, a military attribute, and the sceptre,
the symbol of royalty.   Normally the lance is subordinate
to the sceptre.   When this hierarchy is no longer respected, the lance comes to express hubris, just as the
sceptre expresses dike.   Hubris, for the warrior, consists in wishing to recognize nothing but the lance, and
in devoting oneself entirely to it.   This is the case of
Kaineus, the Lapith with a lance, who - like Achilles,
Talos, the giants, and all those who have undergone initiation as warriors - enjoys a qualified invulnerability.
(He can be killed only by being buried beneath a mound of
stones.) (71)   He sticks his lance into the very centre
of the agora, sets up a cult to it, and forces passersby
to worship it as if it were a god. (72)   It is likewise
the case of Parthenopaeus who is a typical incarnation of
warlike hubris: he worships nothing but his lance, rever-
ing it more than a god, and swearing by it. (73)

     The race of bronze is born of the lance, devoted to
Ares, and has no legal or religious function.   It pro-
jects into the past an image of the warrior dedicated to
hubris in the sense that he does not wish to know of anything foreign to his own nature.   But the exclusively
physical violence which is glorified in warlike man cannot
carry him over the threshold of the afterlife.   In Hades
the race of bronze fades away like a wisp of smoke, into
the anonymity of death.   This same element of military
hubris is also to be found embodied in the giants in the
myths of kingship that tell of the struggle for power
among the gods.   After the defeat of the Titans, the
supremacy of the Olympians is assured by their victory
over the giants.   The Titans, who were immortal, were
sent away in chains into the depths of the earth.   But
the giants suffer a different fate.   The gods deny them
their invulnerability and they perish.   For them defeat
means that they will have no share in the privilege of
immortality which is what they covet. (74)   Like the race
of bronze, they share the common fate of mortal beings.
The hierarchy of Zeus, Titans, and giants, corresponds to
the sequence of the first three races.

     The race of heroes is defined in relation to the race
of bronze, as its counterpart in the same sphere of action.
The heroes are warriors; they wage war and die in war.
Far from bringing them closer to the race of silver, the
hubris of the men of bronze sets them further apart.
Conversely, instead of the dike of the heroes setting them
apart from the race of bronze, it in fact associates them
as a pair of opposites.   In effect the race of heroes is
called δικαίοτερον καὶ ἄρειον: it is more just and at the
same time more courageous in battle. (75)   Its dike

concerns the same military function as the hubris of the
race of bronze.   The warrior dedicated by his very nature
to hubris is contrasted with the warrior who is just, and
who, acknowledging his limitations, is willing to submit
to the superior order of dike.   These two antithetical
portraits of the fighter are those which Aeschylus presents in dramatic confrontation in his 'Seven against
Thebes'.   Here a warrior representing hubris, wild and
frenzied, stands before each gate.   Like a giant, each
one expresses impious sarcasms aimed at the sovereign gods
and Zeus.   In each case each one of them is opposed by a
'more just and more courageous' warrior who, since his
ardour in battle is tempered by sôphrosunè, knows how to
respect all things deemed sacred.

The heroes are the embodiments of the just warrior and,
thanks to Zeus's favour, they are transported to the
Island of the Blessed, where, for all eternity, they lead
a life similar to that of the gods.   In the kingship
myths there is one category of supernatural beings which
corresponds exactly with the race of heroes, and in the
hierarchy of divine creatures it occupies the place reserved for the warrior who is the champion of order.   The
reign of the Olympians presupposed a victory over the
giants who represented the military function.   But sovereign power could not exist without force.   The sceptre
is bound to depend upon the lance.   Zeus needs to be constantly accompanied by Kratos and Bia who never leave his
side. (76)   In order to win their victory over the
Titans, the Olympians were obliged to resort to force and
call in 'soldiers' to aid them.   The hundred-armed
(hécatoncheires), who help them to prevail, are, in
effect, warriors similar in every respect to the giants
and the race of bronze.   They are insatiably warlike and
proud of their strength;   and their size and the immeasur-
able power of their arms strike terror on all sides. (77)
They are the embodiment of Kratos and Bia.   According to
Hesiod, (78) the struggle between the Titans and Olympians
had already been going on for ten years.   Victory was undecided between the two royal camps.   But Earth had revealed to Zeus that success would be his if he could win
the help of the hundred-armed, whose aid would be decisive.   Zeus managed to enlist their support.   Before the
final attack, he asked them to unleash their 'great
might', μεγάλην βίην, and their 'unconquerable strength',
χεῖρας ἀάπτους, (79) in battle against the Titans.   But
he also reminded them never to forget to repay the
'friendly kindness' which he had shown them. (80)   On
behalf of his brothers, Cottus, who had been given the
title of ἀμύμων for the occasion, paid homage in his reply

261

to the superior wisdom and understanding (πραπίδες, νόημα, ἐπιφροσύνη) of Zeus. (81)   He undertook to fight the Titans ἀτενεῖ νόῳ καὶ ἐπίφρονι βουλῇ, 'with fixed purpose and wise determination'. (82)   In this episode the hundred-armed are behaving in a way entirely opposed to warlike hubris.   They are subject to Zeus and no longer appear as creatures of pure pride.   The military valour of these φύλακες πιστοὶ Διός, these 'trusty guardians of Zeus', as Hesiod calls them, (83) is henceforth matched by their sôphrosunè.   In order to persuade them to co-operate, and to repay them for their help, Zeus grants the hundred-armed a favour which in certain aspects recalls the one he conceded to the race of heroes when he made them 'demigods', endowed with immortal life on the Island of the Blessed.   On the eve of the decisive battle he offers the hundred-armed nectar and ambrosia, the food of immortality which is the exclusive privilege of the gods. (84)   He thus allows them to accede to a divine status which was not previously theirs.   He confers upon them a full and perfect immortality which they, like the giants, lacked hitherto. (85)   From a political point of view, Zeus's generosity is not entirely disinterested. The function of fighting, which is henceforth to be associated with sovereign power, is now integrated with it instead of being in opposition to it.   Nothing remains to threaten the reign of order.

    There is nothing particularly surprising about the picture of human life in the age of iron.   Hesiod had described it already in the introduction and again in the conclusion to the myth of Prometheus.   The picture is one of disease, old age, and death;   ignorance of what the morrow holds and anxiety for the future;   the existence of Pandora, the woman;   the need to toil.   To us these appear to be disconnected features, but for Hesiod they all form part of a unified picture.   The themes of Prometheus and Pandora are like two panels depicting one and the same story.   It is the story of human wretchedness in the age of iron.   There is the need to toil on the land to provide for one's sustenance and man's need of woman in order to reproduce, to be born and to die, to experience each day both anxiety and hope regarding an uncertain future.   The race of iron leads an existence which is ambiguous and ambivalent.   Zeus willed that for this race good and evil should be not simply intermingled but fused, inseparable.   That is why man cherishes this life of misfortune, just as he surrounds Pandora with love – Pandora, this 'lovable evil' that the gods in their irony saw fit to present to him. (86)   Hesiod indicates quite clearly the origin of all the sufferings endured by the men of

iron - all their trials, wretchedness, sickness, and
anxiety.   It is Pandora.   If she had not raised the lid
of the jar in which all the evils were shut up, humans
would have continued to live as they had hitherto, 'remote
and free from ills and hard toil and heavy sicknesses
which bring the Fates upon them'. (87)   But all these
evils have spread through the world.   Hope, however,
still exists, for life is not all darkness and humans
still find blessings mixed with the evils. (88)   Pandora
seems to be the symbol and expression of this life of mixtures and contrasts.   Hesiod calls her 'the beautiful
evil to be the price for the blessing'. (89)   She is a
terrible scourge introduced among humans, yet she is also
a marvel (thauma) adorned by the gods with attractions and
graces.   She represents an accursed race which man cannot
abide but which he cannot do without.   She is the opposite of man but also his companion.

In her twofold character as woman and earth, (90)
Pandora represents the function of fertility as this is
experienced in the age of iron in the production of food
and the reproduction of life.   There is no longer that
spontaneous abundance which, during the age of gold, made
living creatures and their sustenance spring up from the
soil simply as a result of the rule of justice and nothing
else.   Now it is man who entrusts new life to the woman's
womb, just as it is the farmer who works the land and
makes the cereals grow in it.   All wealth acquired must
be paid for with corresponding effort.   For the race of
iron, earth and woman are both the sources of fertility
and the forces of destruction: they exhaust the energy of
the male, squandering his efforts, 'burning [him] up without a flame, however strong he may be', (91) and deliver-
ing him over to old age and death by 'reaping the toil of
others into their own bellies'. (92)

Hesiod's farmer is plunged into this ambiguous universe.   He must choose between two courses which correspond to the two sorts of eris mentioned at the beginning
of the poem.   The good strife is the one which incites
man to work, urging him not to be sparing in his efforts to
to increase his possessions.   It presupposes that he has
recognized and accepted the harsh law on which life in the
age of iron depends: that there is no happiness or wealth
that has not been paid for in advance by the hard toil of
labour.   In the case of a man whose function is to provide for food, dike consists in total submission to an
order which is not of his creating, and which is imposed
upon him from outside.   For the farmer, respect for dike
lies in dedicating his whole life to toil.   If he does
this, he becomes dear to the immortals;   his barn is
filled with grain. (93)   For him good triumphs over evil.

The other strife is that which incites the farmer to
seek wealth not through toil, but through violence,
deceit, and injustice, tearing him from the work for which
he is made.   This *eris* which 'fosters war and quarrels' (94) represents the introduction into the farmer's
world of the principle of hubris which is connected with
the second sphere of action, that of waging war.   However, the farmer who revolts against the order to which he
is subjected does not on that account become a warrior.
His hubris is not the frenetic zeal which spurs the giants
and the race of bronze to do battle.   It is closer to the
hubris of the race of silver, and is characterized in a
negative way by the absence of all the 'moral and religious' sentiments which rule human lives, in accordance
with the will of the gods.   There is no affection for
guest, friend, or brother;   no gratitude toward parents;
no respect for oaths, justice, or goodness.   This hubris
knows no fear of the gods, nor is it familiar with the
fear that the coward feels when faced with a courageous
man.   This is the hubris which incites the coward to
attack the *areios*, the man more courageous than himself,
and to defeat him, not in fair combat, but with twisted
words and false oaths. (95)
    This picture of the farmer misled by hubris, which is
presented in the age if iron in its decline, is essentially that of a revolt against order;   an upside-down world
where every hierarchy, rule, and value is inverted.   The
contrast with the image of the farmer who is subject to
dike, at the beginning of the age of iron, is complete.
A life of mixtures where good things still compensate for
bad is opposed by a negative universe of deprivation
where all that remains is unadulterated disorder and evil.

In sum, a detailed analysis of the myth from every aspect
confirms and emphasizes the pattern which appeared from
the start to be emerging from the main structure of the
text.   We have here, not five races in chronological succession, arranged in the order of a more or less progressive decline, but rather a threefold construction, each
level being divided into two opposite and complementary
aspects.   The same framework which controls the cycle of
ages also governs the organization of human society and
society in the world of the gods.   The 'past', as presented by the stratification of the races, is built upon the
model of a timeless hierarchy of functions and values.
Thus each pair of ages is defined not only by its position
in the sequence (the first two, the next two, and the last
two), but also by a specific temporal quality which is
closely linked to the type of activity with which it is

associated.   The gold and the silver are ages of vitality, still in their youth.   The bronze age and the heroes
represent an adult life unfamiliar with both youth and
age.   With the iron age we come to an existence which
declines as it becomes older and more exhausted.

Let us undertake a closer examination of these qualitative aspects of the different ages, and of their meaning
in relation to other elements of the myth.   Both the race
of gold and the race of silver are 'young', just as they
are both royal.   But the symbolic meaning of youth is
opposite in the two cases: for the former it is positive
while for the latter it becomes negative.   The race of
gold lives 'forever young' in time, forever new, free from
fatigue, sickness, age, and even death, (96) in a time
still close to that of the gods.   On the other hand, the
race of silver represents the opposite aspect of 'youth',
not the absence of senility, but plain puerility and the
absence of maturity.   A man of silver lives for a hundred
years in the state of a *pais*, clinging to the skirts of
his mother, μέγα νήπιος, like a big baby. (97)   Hardly
has he emerged from childhood and crossed the crucial
point marked by the *metron hèbès*, the threshold of adolescence, than he indulges in a thousand follies and dies
forthwith. (98)   It is true to say that his whole life
amounts to nothing more than an endless childhood and that
the *hèbè* is for him the final point of his existence.
Thus he has no part in *sôphrosunè*, which is the characteristic of maturity and which can even be especially associated with the figure of the *geròn* as opposed to that of
the young man. (99)   Nor does he ever reach the state of
those who, having passed the *metron hèbès*, constitute the
age group of the *hèbòntes*, the *kouroi*, who are subjected
to military discipline. (100)

Hesiod gives us no indication as to how long the lives
of the race of bronze and the heroes last.   All we know
is that they do not have time to grow old: they all die
in battle, in the prime of life.   No mention is made of
their childhoods.   We may conjecture that if Hesiod says
nothing about their childhoods after having spoken at
length about those of the race of silver, the reason is
that the members of the race of bronze do not have childhoods.   In the poem the men appear from the start as
grown men at the height of physical prowess who have never
concerned themselves with anything other than the works of
Ares.   There is a striking analogy here with the myths
about indigenous origins in which the *gegéneis* spring up
from the ground and appear, not as little children who
have just been born and have yet to grow, but as adults
fully grown, armed, and prepared for battle, as ἄνδρες

ἔνοπλοι.   The fact is that the activity of making war is associated with a particular age group, and thus the figure of the fighter is opposed both to the *pais* and to the *gerôn*.   Vian has written the following comment about the giants and it seems to us that it also applies exactly to the race of bronze and the heroes: 'There are neither old men nor infants among them.   From their very birth they are the adults or rather the adolescents that they remain until their death.   Their existence is confined within the narrow limits of one age group.' (101)   The entire life of the race of silver is over before the *hèbè*. The life of the race of bronze and of the heroes begins at the *hèbè*.   Neither group ever experiences old age.

Old age is, on the contrary, a characteristic of the age of iron.   Here life is spent in a continuous ageing. Here are toil, labour, disease, anxiety – all the evils which constantly exhaust a human being and gradually transform that being from a child to a young man, from a young man to an old man, and from an old man to a corpse. This is a doubtful, ambiguous time with the old and the young associated, inextricably linked, the one implying the other, just as good does evil;   life, death;   and dike, hubris.   This time in which the young grow old is opposed, at the end of the age of iron, by a time given over totally to old age.   If men give way to hubris, a day will come when everything that is still young, new, vital, and beautiful will have disappeared from human life: men will be born with their hair already white. (102)   The time of mixed fortune will be succeeded by the reign of pure hubris.   It will be a time when old age and death take over completely.

Thus the features which give the various races their particular temporal quality fit into the same tripartite pattern which we have seen providing a framework for all the elements of the myth.

This pattern recalls, in its main outlines, the tripartite functional classification whose important influence on Indo-European religious thought has been demonstrated by G. Dumezil (whether or not there is a direct link between these two). (103)   The first stage of Hesiod's myth does indeed describe the function of kingship where the king pursues his juridical and religious activities; the second, the military function where the brute force of the warrior imposes a lawless rule;   and the third, the function of fertility and vital foodstuffs which are the special responsibility of the farmer.

This tripartite structure forms the framework within which Hesiod has reinterpreted the myth of the races of metals, and it makes it possible for him to include the

episode of the heroes with perfect coherence.   Thus modified, the story becomes part of a larger body of myth
which it evokes throughout by the subtle yet strict interplay of corresponding relationships at every level.
Because it reflects a classificatory system of general
relevance, the story of the races carries multiple meanings.   It tells of the sequence of the ages of humanity
but at the same time it also symbolizes a whole series of
fundamental aspects of reality.   If this interplay of
symbolic images and connections is translated into our own
language of ideas it can be presented as a diagram which
may be viewed from various angles, where the same structure, regularly repeated, establishes analogical relationships between the different parts.   The series of races,
the different functional roles, the types of actions and
of agents, the age categories, the hierarchy of the gods
in the kingship myths, the hierarchy of human society, the
hierarchy of the supernatural powers other than the *theoi*
- all these different elements that are implied suggest
and complement one another.

While Hesiod's account illustrates particularly neatly
this system of multiple correspondences and overlaid symbolism which is characteristic of the thought processes of
myth, it also presents a new feature.   The material is
organized in a definite pattern of dichotomies, which
dominates the tripartite structure itself and establishes
a tension, within each of its elements, between two
opposed pulls.   This tension between dike and hubris
determines the structure of the myth and the various
planes upon which it operates, and regulates the interplay
of oppositions and affinities.   Not only does it govern
the form of the myth as a whole and give it its general
meaning, but it also gives, in a manner appropriate to
each, a certain element of polarity to each of the three
functional levels.   This is where Hesiod's profound originality lies and this is what makes him a true religious
reformer, comparable in manner and inspiration to certain
prophets of Judaism.

Why is Hesiod so preoccupied with dike and why does it
occupy such a central position in his religious universe?
Why does it assume the form of a powerful goddess, the
daughter of Zeus, honoured and revered by the gods of
Olympus?   The answer to these questions does not emerge
from a structural analysis of the myth but would emerge
from a historical inquiry.   Such an inquiry would aim to
reveal the problems which faced the smallholder in Boeotia
as a result of the changes in social life in about the
seventh century, and which prompted Hesiod to rethink the
substance of the old myths so as to give them new

meaning. (104)   Such an inquiry does not fall within the
scope of the present study.   However, our analysis of the
myth allows us to suggest briefly certain possible lines
of research.

It is noticeable that in Hesiod the figure of the warrior, unlike those of the king and the farmer, has a
purely mythical significance.   There does not seem to be
a place either for the warrior role or for the warrior, as
these are described in the myth, in the world in which
Hesiod and his public live, and which he describes. (105)
The aim of the story of Prometheus, of that of the races,
of the entire poem in fact, is to instruct Perses, who,
like his brother, is a small-scale farmer.   Perses is to
renounce hubris, settle down to work, and stop seeking
lawsuits and picking quarrels with Hesiod. (106)   But
this lesson, addressed by one brother to another, by one
farmer to another, also concerns the basileis in that it
is their duty to settle quarrels and adjudicate lawsuits
justly.   Their sphere of activity is quite different from
that of Perses: their role is not to labour, and Hesiod
does not exhort them to do so.   They must show their respect for dike by pronouncing just verdicts.   To be sure,
the mythical picture of the good ruler, master of fertility, dispenser of all wealth, is a far cry from the kings
who 'devour bribes', (107) whose displeasure Hesiod risks
incurring (and that is no doubt partly why, in Hesiod's
eyes, dike seems already to have left the earth for
heaven). (108)   However, the poet remains convinced that
the way the kings perform their judicial function has
direct repercussions upon the world of the labourer,
either favouring or impeding the abundance of the fruits
of the earth. (109)   There is, then, a connection both
mythical and real between the first and third functions,
between the kings and the labourers.   And Hesiod focuses
his interest upon precisely those problems that concern
both the first and third functions - those that affect
them *both together*. (110)   In this sense there are two
aspects to his message.   It is in itself ambiguous, as is
everything in the age of iron.   It is addressed to the
farmer Perses, at grips with the unproductive earth, with
debts, hunger, and poverty, exhorting him to work hard.
It is also addressed, over Perses's head, to the kings who
live in quite another fashion, in town, spending their
time in the *agora*, and who do not have to work.   The fact
is that Hesiod's world, unlike that of the age of gold, is
a world of mixtures where great and small, nobles - ἐσθλοί
- and humble folk - δειλοί (111) - kings and farmers coexist side by side, but are set in opposition by their
functions.   In this discordant universe help can come

only from dike.   If dike disappears, everything founders
into chaos.   But if dike is respected both by those whose
lives are dedicated to *ponos* and by those who lay down the
law, there will be more blessings than evils;   humanity
will be able to avoid such sufferings as are not inherent
in the mortal condition.

What then is the place of the warrior?   In the picture
that Hesiod draws of the society of his time they no
longer represent a functional category that corresponds to
an existing human reality.   Their only role is in myth,
to explain the presence, in a world of kings and farmers,
of an evil principle: that hubris which is the source of
discord and strife.   It provides an answer to what one
might (anachronistically) call the problem of evil.   What,
after all, is the difference between the justice and fertility which preside over the age of gold and their manifestations in the age of iron, in a world of discord?   In
the age of gold, justice and abundance are 'pure'.   They
do not have counterparts.   Justice exists for its own
sake: there are no quarrels or lawsuits to settle.   Similarly, fertility brings abundance 'automatically', without
any labour being necessary.   The age of gold is unfamiliar with *eris* in all senses.   In contrast, strife is
what characterizes the way of life of the age of iron, or
to be more precise, two contrary forms of strife, the good
and the evil.   Thus dike, whether it be that of the king
or that of the farmer, must always operate *through* one or
the other *eris*.   The dike of the kings consists in settl-
ing quarrels and in arbitrating the disagreements provoked
by the evil *eris*.   The dike of the farmer lies in making
a virtue of *eris*, by directing struggle and competition
away from war to agriculture, so that instead of sowing
ruin they bring forth fertile abundance.

But where does *eris* come from? - what is its origin?
Strife is inevitably associated with hubris and represents
the very essence of the activity of the warrior.   It is
an expression of the innermost nature of the fighter.
And this is the principle, which, 'by increasing wicked
war', presides over the second of the three functional
roles we have discussed.

The myth of the races is thus an example of the way
that mythical thought like that of Hesiod can be both
rigorously systematic and at the same time original.
Hesiod reinterprets the myth of the races of metal within
a tripartite framework.   But he transforms this tripartite structure: by devaluing the warrior activity he
changes it in a way that corresponds with his own religious thought, and by denying it a proper function like
those of the other two roles, makes it the source of evil
and conflict in the universe.

NOTES

1 'Revue de l'histoire des religions' (1960), 21-54.
2 Hesiod 'Works and Days' 213.   On the place and meaning of the two myths in the poem as a whole, cf. Paul
   Mazon, Hésiode: la composition des Travaux et des
   Jours, 'Revue des études anciennes', 14 (1912), 328-
   57.
3 This is the case of the race of silver; cf. l. 143.
4 Cf. Renée Schaerer, 'L'Homme antique et la structure
   du monde intérieur d'Homère à Socrate' (Paris, 1958),
   77-80.
5 'Works' 158.
6 Erwin Rohde, 'Psyche' (8th edn, New York, 1966), 67-
   78.
7 Victor Goldschmidt, Theologia, 'Revue des études
   grecques', 63 (1950), 33-9.
8 On this classification, cf. A. Delatte, 'Études sur
   la littérature pythagoricienne' (Paris, 1915), 48;
   Goldschmidt, Theologia, 30 and ff.
9 Goldschmidt, Theologia, 37, note 1.
10 It is also agreed that the myth originally included
   three or four races.   Cf., however, the reservations
   expressed by Mazon who believes Hesiod's work is entirely original (Hésiode, 339) and those of M.P.
   Nilsson, 'Geschichte der griechischen Religion' 12
   (Munich, 1955), 622.   The themes of an age of gold
   and of successive human races destroyed by the gods
   do indeed appear to have an eastern origin.   On this
   point see the discussion between M.J.G. Griffiths and
   H.C. Baldry, 'Journal of the History of Ideas', 17
   (1956), 109-19, 533-54;   19 (1958), 91-3.
11 In Hesiod's 'Theogony', the genealogies of the gods
   and the cosmological myths provide a basis for the
   organization of the cosmos.   They explain how the
   different cosmic levels (the heavenly, the subterranean, and the earthly worlds) came to be separated,
   and account for the distribution and harmony of the
   various elements that compose the universe.
12 The ages differ not only in respect to how long they
   last; their experience of time, the rhythm of the
   lapse of time, and the direction in which time flows
   are not the same either; cf. below, pp. 20ff.
13 Cf. Friedrich Solmsen, 'Hesiod and Aeschylus' (New
   York, 1949), 83, note. 27.
14 Plato 'Politicus' 296c and ff.   Several features in
   the myth in the 'Politicus' recall the myth of the
   races.
15 Hesiod 'Works' 175.

16 Contrary to Solmsen's claim, when he writes: 'The third generation ... has traveled much farther on the road of *hybris* than the second.' Despite the reference to lines 143-7 there is nothing to substantiate this claim.

17 Compare Hesiod 'Works' 134 ff. and 145-6.

18 Ibid. 127.

19 Ibid. 158.

20 Ibid. 144.

21 E. Meyer noticed the link between the races of gold and silver on the one hand, and the race of bronze and the heroes on the other. But he interpreted it as one of consanguinity, with a process of decline in the first case and improvement in the second; cf. Hesiods Erga und das Gedicht von den fünf Menschengeschlechtern, 'Mélanges Carl Robert' (Berlin, 1910), 131-65.

22 Cf. Hesiod 'Works' 123 and 141: ἐπιχθόνιοι, ὑποχθόνιοι.

23 Ibid. 154: νώνυμνοι.

24 The symmetry between the destinies after death of the men of bronze and the heroes is just as marked as in the case of the men of gold and the men of silver. The men of bronze disappear in death, leaving no name; the heroes live on in the Island of the Blessed, and their names which are celebrated by the poets live on forever in men's memories. The former fade away in night and oblivion while the latter belong to the domain of light and of memory (cf. Pindar 'Olympians' 2, 109 ff.).

25 Rohde, 'Psyche', 77.

26 Cf. Hesiod 'Works' 184: nothing will ever again be as it was in the past, ὡς τὸ πάρος περ.

27 Ibid. 119.

28 Ibid. 118-19; note the expression: αὐτομάτη.

29 Compare the picture of human life in the age of iron, in 176-8, with that presented in the myth of Prometheus in 42-8, and 94-105.

30 Cf. F. Daumas, La valeur de l'or dans la pensée egyptienne, 'Revue de l'histoire des religions', 149 (1956), 1-18; E. Cassin, Le Pesant d'or, 'Rivista degli Studi Orientali', 32 (1957), 3-11. On the correspondences among gold, sun, and king, cf. Pindar 'Olympians' 1.1 ff.

31 Plato 'Republic' 413c ff.

32 Hesiod 'Works' 111.

33 Pausanias 6.20, 1.

34 Hesiod 'Works' 126.

35 Ibid. 123; cf. Callimachus 'Hymn to Zeus' 79-81:

the kings come from Zeus ...; Zeus sets them up as
the 'guardians of the towns'; in Plato ('Republic'
413c ff.), the men of gold who are born to rule are
called '*phulakes*'. The term 'guardian', in Plato,
refers sometimes to the category of men who govern,
in the widest sense, and sometimes, more specifically, to those who are entrusted with the military
function. This specialization is understandable:
the kings are *phulakes* inasmuch as they watch over
their people in the name of Zeus; the warriors
fulfil the same function in the name of the king.

36 Hesiod 'Works' 126. The epichthonian daemons who
are linked with the function of royalty here assume
a role which is normally reserved for female divinities such as the Charites. Now these divinities, on
whom depend the fertility or, alternatively, the
sterility of the earth, are ambivalent powers. In
their white character they manifest themselves as
Charites while in their black they become the Erinyes
(cf. as well as Aeschylus's 'Eumenides', Pausanias
8.34, 1 ff.). The same ambiguity is revealed in the
relationship between the epichthonian daemons and
hypochthonian daemons. They appear to represent the
two aspects, one positive and the other negative, of
the effect of the king on the fertility of the soil.
The powers which can encourage or impede fertility
manifest themselves on two planes. Normally they
operate in the third functional domain (agriculture),
as female divinities, but they also operate on the
first (kingship) in so far as it affects the third,
and here they take the form of male daemons.

37 Hesiod 'Works' 112.

38 Hesiod 'Theogony' 91.

39 Hesiod 'Works' 114 ff., 225 ff.

40 Ibid. 238 ff. The same theme appears in the 'Iliad'
16.386. On the relationship between Zeus, the
skeptron, and the kings 'who hand out justice', cf.
'Iliad' 1.234; 9.98.

41 Cf. Hipponax frg. 38 (O. Masson) = 34-35 (Diehl).
'Father Zeus, king of the gods (θεῶν πάλμυ), why have
you given me no gold, king of silver (ἀργύρου
πάλμυν)?'

42 Hesiod 'Works' 134.

43 Referring to a course of lectures given by G. Dumézil,
at the École des Hautes-etudes, 1946-7, F. Vian
writes, in a note, on the subject of Hesiod's second
race: 'It is characterized by immoderation and
impiety as seen from a theological, not a military
point of view' ('La Guerre des Géants. Le mythe

avant l'époque hellénistique' (Paris, 1952), 183, note 2).

44 Hesiod 'Works' 251.
45 Cf. Mazon, Hesiode, 339, note 3.
46 Hesiod 'Theogony' 209, compare with 'Works' 134 and 'Theogony' 719.
47 Ibid. 881-5; Apollodorus 'The Library' 2.1.
48 Hesiod 'Theogony' 717; cf. also 697.
49 Hesiod 'Works' 144-6.
50 Ibid. 146-7.
51 Cf., for example, Homer 'Iliad' 7.146.
52 Ibid. 2.578; 'Odyssey' 24.467.
53 Homer 'Iliad' 20.156; Euripides 'The Phoenician Women' 110.
54 Homer 'Iliad' 19.362.
55 This 'panoply' is also found in the *palladion* and *tropaion*.
56 Homer 'Iliad' 16.140; 19.361, 390; 22,225; 'Palatine Anthology' 6.52; cf. Hesychius: μελίαι, either δόρατα, trees; or λόγχαι, lances.
57 Hesiod 'Works' 145.
58 Vian, 'La Guerre', especially 280 ff.
59 Hesiod 'Theogony' 185-7.
60 Callimachus 'Hymn to Zeus' 47.
61 Clément 'Stromata' 1.21.
62 Scholiast on Euripides 'The Phoenician Women'.
63 Sophocles 'Trachiniennes' 1058-9.
64 'Iliad' 2.604, 611; 7.134.
65 Scholiast on Aeschylus 'Prometheus' 438.
66 Apollodorus 3.4, 1.
67 Euripides 'The Phoenician Women' 931, 935; Pausanias 9.10, 1.
68 Apollodorus 1. 9, 23; Apollonius Rhodius 'Argonautics' 3.401 ff. and 1026 ff.
69 Hesiod 'Works' 150-1. It does not seem feasible to take this, as some have, to mean: 'they worked in bronze.' Cf. Charles Kerenyi, 'La mythologie des Grecs' (Paris, 1952), 225.
70 Aristotle 'Poetics' 16.1454, B22; Plutarch 'On the Delays of Divine Vengeance' 268; Dio Chrysostom 4.23; Julian 'Speeches' 2.81c.
71 Apollonius Rhodius 'Argonautics' 1.57-64; Apollodorus 'Epitome' 1.22.
72 Scholiast to 'Iliad' 1.264 and to Apollonius Rhodius 'Argonautics' 1.57.
73 Aeschylus 'Sept' 529 ff. Note that this warrior has a name which evokes a young girl (*parthenos*). Kaineus acquired invulnerability when he changed sex; Achilles, the warrior invulnerable except in his heel,

was brought up with girls, and dressed as a girl.
Warrior initiation rites involve transvestism.

74   We know that *Ge* tried to procure for the giants a
pharmakon for immortality, which would protect them
from the attacks of Heracles and the gods; Apollodorus 1.6, 1.

75   Hesiod 'Works' 158.

76   Hesiod 'Theogony' 385 ff.   Note the exact parallelism between the episode of the hundred-armed and that
of Kratos and Bia.   Like the hundred-armed, Kratos
and Bia take the side of Zeus against the Titans, at
the decisive moment.   This ensures victory for the
Olympians, and Kratos and Bia, again like the
hundred-armed, receive as a reward certain 'privileges' which they had not hitherto enjoyed.

77   Compare Hesiod 'Theogony' 149 ff. and 'Works' 145 ff.

78   Hesiod 'Theogony' 617-64.

79   Ibid. 649.

80   Ibid. 651.

81   Ibid. 656-8.

82   Ibid. 661.

83   Ibid. 735.

84   Ibid. 639-40.

85   There are a number of intermediary stages between the
mortality of the 'ephemeral ones' and the immortality
of the gods, in particular the series of beings known
as *macrobioi*, among which must be classed the nymphs
such as the *meliai*, and the giants.

86   Hesiod 'Works' 57-8.

87   Ibid. 90 ff.

88   Ibid. 179.

89   Hesiod 'Theogony' 585.

90   Pandora is the name of a goddess of the earth and
fertility.   Like her double, *Anesidora*, she is represented, in illustrations, emerging from the earth
in accordance with the theme of the *anodos* of a
chthonian and agricultural power.

91   Hesiod 'Works' 705.

92   Hesiod 'Theogony' 599.

93   Hesiod 'Works' 309.

94   Ibid. 14.

95   Ibid. 193-4.

96   Ibid. 113 ff.   Their end resembles sleep more than
death.   The children of the night, Thanatos and
Hypnos, are twins, but opposite twins; cf. Hesiod
'Theogony' 763 ff.: Hypnos is quiet and gentle
toward men, while Thanatos has a heart of iron and an
implacable spirit.

97   Hesiod 'Works' 130-1.

98   Ibid. 132–3.
99   On the positive aspect of the 'old man', as a synonym
     for wisdom and justice, cf. Hesiod 'Theogony' 234–6.
100 Cf. Xenophon 'Constitution of Lacedaemon' 4.1:
     Lycurgus was particularly concerned with the Hebontes
     or kouroi.
101 Vian, 'La Guerre', 280:   'On ne trouve chez eux ni
     vieillards, ni bambins: dès leur naissance ils sont
     des adultes, ou mieux, les adolescents qu'ils
     resteront jusqu'à leur mort.   Leur existence est
     enfermée dans les limites étroites d'une classe
     d'âge.'
102 Hesiod 'Works' 181.
103 G. Dumézil, to whom we showed this article in manu-
     script, points out that in 'Jupiter, Mars, Quirinus'
     (Paris, 1941), he suggested a trifunctional interpre-
     tation of the myth of races.   On page 259 he wrote:
         it seems clear that, just as in the corresponding
         Indian myth, the myth of races in Hesiod assoc-
         iates each of the Ages (or rather each of the three
         'pairs' of Ages) in the course of which humanity
         is renewed only to decline, with a 'functional'
         conception of the differences in the species – the
         three functions being religion, war and labour.
     Subsequently Dumézil came to accept as satisfactory
     the interpretation proposed by Goldschmidt.   (Cf.
     Dumézil, Triades de calamités et triades de délits à
     valeur fonctionelle chez divers peuples indo-
     européens, 'Latomus', 14 (1955), 197, note 3.)   He
     tells us that the present study seems to support and
     confirm his first hypothesis.
104 Cf. Edouard Will, Aux origines du régime foncier
     grec. Homère, Hésiode et l'arrière-plan mycénien,
     'Revue des études anciennes', 59 (1957), 5–50.   This
     contains illuminating remarks concerning the changes
     in the status of the landowner, to which Hesiod's
     work bears witness.   (These modifications include
     the sharing out of the inheritance, the division of
     the land into small plots, the different ways of
     handing on the *kleros*, the problem of debts and of
     obtaining credit, the process whereby the smallholders
     became dispossessed and the powerful seized vacant
     holdings.)   Louis Gernet notes that at the time when
     the term πόλις was introduced, to describe an already
     organized society, the judicial function was trans-
     formed, as can be seen by comparing Homer and Hesiod
     ('Recherches sur le développement de la pensée
     juridique et morale en Grece' (Paris, 1917), 14–15).
105 It is well known that at an early stage in the

development of the city state, the warrior disappeared as a particular social category and also as
a type of man embodying specific virtues.   The
transformation of the warrior of the epics into the
hoplite fighting in a close formation was not only a
revolution in military techniques but was also a
decisive social, religious, and psychological change.
Cf. in particular, Henri Jeanmaire, 'Couroi et
Courètes' (Lille, 1939), 115 ff.

106   On the dispute between the two brothers, the basis
for and the vicissitudes of the lawsuit, cf. B.A.
Groningen, 'Hésiode et Persès' (Amsterdam, 1957).

107   Hesiod 'Works' 264.

108   Gernet writes:

Hesiod's δίκη (as opposed to Homer's more homogeneous δίκη) is multiple and contradictory because it
is in keeping with a new and critical state of
society: δίκη as custom will sometimes be the
force behind the law (189, 192);   δίκη as sentence
is frequently considered to be unjust (39, 219,
221, 262, 264;   cf. 254, 269, 271).   These two
forms of δικη are opposed to divine Δίκη (219-20
and 258 ff.):   in these two passages, Δίκη is the
formal antithesis of the two δίκη ('Recherches',
16).   Cf. also the remarks of the author on the
becoming divine of Αἰδώς in Hesiod 75.

109   Hesiod 'Works' 238 ff.

110   This common interest is made explicit in Aratos's
poem in the passage where, following Hesiod, he gives
an account of the races of metal.   The reign of dike
here appears to be inseparable from agricultural
activity.   The men of gold know nothing of discord
and strife.   For them 'the oxen, the plough and dike
herself who is the dispenser of rightful blessings,
provide for everything in great abundance.'   When
the men of bronze forge the sword of war and crime,
they kill and devour the oxen used for ploughing
('Phenomena' 110 ff).

111   Hesiod 'Works' 214, where the opposition is very
marked.

8. The Black Hunter and the origin of the Athenian *ephebeia*[1]

Pierre Vidal-Naquet (1968, 1979)

To M.I. Finley

> *We have seen nothing;*
> *We are beastly-subtle as the fox for prey,*
> *Like warlike as the wolf for what we eat;*
> *Our valour is to chase what flies . . .*
> Shakespeare, Cymbeline 3.3.39—42

Before, and even more since, the discovery of Aristotle's *Constitution of the Athenians* the Athenian *ephebeia* has been a subject of controversy. This two-year 'military service' is described by Aristotle in chapter 42 of his little treatise. But was it an entirely artificial creation resulting from Lycurgus's policies, as Wilamowitz maintained, or was it rather an extremely ancient — even archaic — institution, of the kind likened by nineteenth-century scholars to the Spartan *krypteia*?

The argument has grown rather stale now, and as a result of the analyses and discoveries of the past thirty years it is easy enough to reach agreement on two points.[2] First, no one would now claim that the *ephebeia* in Lycurgus's time was in every respect an ancient institution: the Athenian politician re-ordered and rationalized whatever existed before his time. Second, everyone would now agree that the *ephebeia* of the fourth century BC had its roots in ancient practices of 'apprenticeship' whose object was to introduce young men to their future rôles as citizens and heads of families — that is, as full members of the community. I need hardly remind the reader of the rôle played by comparative ethnology in the realization of the significance of initiatory rituals in the ancient world: as early as 1913 Henri Jeanmaire based his own work on such studies (1913: 121—50), and only a little later Pierre Roussel commented upon a text of Aristotle (*Constitution of the Athenians* 42.5) in similar terms (1921: 456—60). We know that the ephebe 'cannot go to law either as a defendant or as a plaintiff unless it is a matter of upholding an inheritance, arranging the affairs of an heiress, or a priesthood related to the *genos*'. Aristotle's own explanation is simple: the ephebes must not suffer any distraction from their military service. But this sort of explanation is valid only for Aristotle's own time; Roussel observed, 'the *ephebeia* is much more than a period of military service. It is the period of transition between childhood and

147

complete participation in the life of the society . . . There is so much evidence from other societies, including Sparta in Greece itself, that young people led a life apart for a period of time before their definitive admission into the social group, that one is inclined to see an example of this practice here' (p. 459).

'Definitive admission' meant for the young citizen essentially two things: marriage, and entry into the hoplite phalanx (or later, becoming a sailor in the Athenian navy). So long as these two conditions remained unfulfilled — and the second was especially important in classical Athens — the young man's relation to the *polis* is ambiguous. He both is, and is not, a member.

This ambiguity is strikingly illustrated at the level of topography — remembering that the organization of symbolic space does not always coincide with actual geography. When Aeschines the orator mentions his own ephebic generation (around 370 BC), he says that he served for two years as '*peripolos* of this land' (*On the Embassy* 167) after child-hood. When Plato came to copy the institution of the *ephebeia*, he makes his *agronomoi* circle round his city on the frontiers, first in one direction, then in the other (*Laws* 6, 760b; cf. Vidal-Naquet, 1981) thus taking literally the etymological meaning of *peripolos*, 'one who circles round'. In the fourth century BC the ephebic *peripolos*[3] was normally stationed in the frontier forts: Panacton, Deceleia, Rhamnus and so on. That might perhaps be entirely natural for lightly-armed young men[4] who were only called upon to fight under exceptional circumstances,[5] and would then obviously be used on patrol (which is another possible translation of *peripolos*). And yet these young men are associated with foreigners and with citizens of recent date: Aeschines served as a *peripolos* with young men of his own age and with mercenaries (*On the Embassy* 168); Thucydides mentions *peripoloi* twice, first in association with Plataeans (Athenian citizens of recent date) at a night-ambush near Nisaea in 425 BC (4.67—8), and later he says that the man who murdered Phrynichus in 411 was a *peripolos*, his accomplice being an Argive (8.92.2). Other sources too state that Phrynichus's murderers were foreigners (Lysias, *Against Agoratos* 71; *Sylloge*[3] 108 = Meiggs and Lewis, 1969: 260—3, no. 85).[6]

The same word could then designate both the young men of Athens and foreigners in her service. Both are marginal to the city (though the ephebe's marginality is temporary). But the ephebe's relation to the world of the frontier is complex. As young soldiers, they occupy the frontier-zone of the city which is expressed physically in the ring of fortlets (just as in Crete, where there is epigraphic evidence for a clear-cut distinction between the young men, who occupy the *phrouria*, the *oureia*, the frontier-area, and the full citizens);[7] when they take the

148

oath which makes them full hoplites, they mention the boundary-stones which separate Athens' territory from her neighbours'. But with these stones are associated wheat, barley, vines, olives, fig-trees — in a word, the world of cultivation (Daux, 1965: 78–90; cf. J. and L. Robert, 1966: 362–3 no. 165).

A short discussion of a non-Athenian poetic text may make it easier to understand this. The finest evocation of the duality of the Greek ephebe is no doubt the Jason of Pindar's fourth Pythian ode. Pelias, the old king of Iolcus, was appointed to 'die by the hands of the noble sons of Aeolus or their unrelenting schemes':

ἐξ ἀγαυῶν Αἰολιδᾶν θανέμεν χεί-
ρεσσιν ἢ βουλᾶς ἀκνάμπτοις (72–3 Snell)[8]

He had been warned to beware 'at all costs the man with one sandal' who should pass from 'a lofty retreat' to 'the sunny plain' — 'stranger be he or townsman' (ξεῖνος αἴτ'ὼν ἀστός: 75–7). And indeed Jason comes from afar off where he had been brought up, in wild nature, by Chiron the centaur and his daughters. He is a foreigner, and received as such, but also a citizen, speaking of himself as such to his fellow-citizens: κεδνοὶ πολῖται, φράσσατέ μοι σαφέως (117). He is a qualified ephebe twenty years old, ambiguous, with two javelins, and dressed both in the clothing of Magnesia but also in the leopard-skin of the wild man:

ἐσθὰς δ 'ἀμφοτέρα μιν ἔχεν,
ἅ τε Μαγνήτων ἐπιχώριος ἁρμό –
ζοισα θαητοῖσι γυίοις,
ἀμφὶ δὲ παρδαλέᾳ στέγετο φρίσσοντας ὄμβρους. (79–81)
. . . and a twofold guise was on him.
A tunic of Magnesian fashion fitted close his magnificent limbs,
and across it a panther's hide held off the shivering rains.
(tr. Lattimore)

The hair which the Athenian ephebe cut as a mark of entry into manhood still hangs down his back (82–3).

This prolonged adolescence takes us away from the world of social reality and into the realm of myth. Let us return to Athens, where the ephebe's ambiguity — at the level now of its institutional reality — can be seen as double. As Jules Labarbe saw (1953: 58–94), there were really two ephebic structures: the official *ephebeia*, which was a civic military service, and a more archaic one through which one gained admission to the phratry. Hence the expression *epi dietes hēbēsai*, which means (1) to be an ephebe in the civic sense, that is, to have reached the age of eighteen; and (2), as the literal sense suggests, to have attained the *hēbē*, to have been an ephebe for two years (cf. Labarbe, 1957: 67–75; Pélékidis, 1962: 51–65). Labarbe showed that the first *ephebeia* was marked ritually by the sacrifice of the *koureion* (the young man's long

149

hair) at the age of sixteen. I may add that in one case at least admission to the phratry was not ratified until one year had elapsed from the date of the offering of the hair (*Sylloge*³ 921, lines 27–8 [= Sokolowski, 1969: no. 19, with bibliography — the so-called 'Ruling of the Demotionidae']).

The sacrifice of the hair took place at the time of the *Koureôtis*, the third day of Apatouria, the great festival celebrated by the phratries of the Ionian world, which took place in the month Pyanepsion (September–October). This month was marked by a series of festivals which have been shown, by Jeanmaire in particular (1939), to have been festivals celebrating the return of the young men from the campaigns of the summer. And it was through studying the aetiological myth connected with the Apatouria that I was led to formulate the ideas presented here.

The myth is known from a large number of texts dating from the fifth century BC right down to the Byzantines Michel Psellos and Johannes Tzetzes, who are of course simply resuming older sources. The texts do not for the most part come from the principal ancient works of literature or history; though alluded to by Strabo and Pausanias, it is recounted only by Konon (an extremely obscure Hellenistic mythographer), Polyaenus and Frontinus; otherwise it is a matter of scholiasts' remarks and entries in ancient lexica.[9] In view of the state of the sources, it is hardly possible to define an 'ancient' and more recent versions of the story, and I will therefore try to indicate the most important variants.

The scene is the frontier between Athens and Boeotia: an *eschatia*, mountainous areas that are the 'end' of a city's territory, and whose inhabitants are always at loggerheads with their neighbours over the border. Such places existed on the borders of all Greek states (Robert, 1960: 304–5, esp. 304 n. 4). They were the terrain of hunters and shepherds, frontier zones constantly in dispute. And they were necessary to Greek cities if only for training the young soldiers for war (the ritual nature of which training has been demonstrated by Brelich, 1961; cf. Garlan, 1975: 29–31).

A conflict broke out between the Athenians and the Boeotians. In some versions, over Oenoe and Panacton, in others over the frontier deme Melainai. The fourth-century historian Ephorus (quoted by Harpokration) says that the dispute was *huper tēs Melanias choras*: 'over an area called Melania'. I will observe simply that at Panacton there was an annual sacrifice to mark the Apatouria (*Sylloge*³ 485). The Boeotian king was Xanthos (or Xanthios, or Xanthias), which means 'the fair one'. The Athenian king was Thymoites, the last of the descendants of Theseus. It was agreed to settle the dispute by means of

150

a duel, a *monomachia*. But Thymoites stood down, according to a scholiast on Aristophanes's *Frogs* and another on Aelius Aristeides's *Panathenaicus*, because he was too old. Another warrior came forward and was, according to some versions, promised the succession in return. His name was Melanthos (or Melanthios), 'the black one'. So the Black One was to fight the Fair One.

As they were fighting, Melanthos suddenly cried out, 'Xanthos, you do not play according to the rules (συνθῆκαι) — there is someone at your side!' — and as Xanthos looked round in surprise, Melanthos took his chance and killed him. The sources differ over details of what happened. Polyaenus and Frontinus say it was a ruse pure and simple; Halliday compares it to Tom Sawyer's trick when he cries out 'Look behind you Aunty' and thus escapes the beating she was about to administer (1926: 179). The *Lexica Segueriana* makes Melanthos pray to Zeus *Apatēnōr* (Zeus 'of wiles'). Most mention Dionysus's intervention — Dionysus *Melanaigis*, 'of the black goatskin'; and Plutarch (*Quaestiones conviviales* 6.7.2, 692e) says that Dionysus *Melanaigis* and *Nukterinos* ('of the night') was worshipped at Eleutherae (that is, not far from Panacton).[10] Afterwards, the victor Melanthos became king of Athens.

In every source, the Apatouria is explained by paronomastic etymology. The festival is supposed to commemorate this *apatē* ('wile', 'deception'), whether the inspiration of the deception is ascribed to Dionysus, to Zeus or to Melanthos himself.[11] The sources offer this explanation even though the scholiast on Aristophanes's *Acharnians* 146, as well as the grammarian quoted by the Suda s.v. Ἀπατούρια, knew an explanation which is more or less correct: *Apatouria* = *Homopatoria* (Ὁμοπατόρια). Nowadays we would say that the α of Ἀπατούρια is a copulative: the festival of the Apatouria is the festival of those who have the 'same father' — in other words, the festival of the phratries.

Over the years, there have naturally been many attempts to explain this myth. First of course historically — many such, from Johannes Töpffer's *Attische Genealogie* (1889: 225–41) to Felix Jacoby's great commentary on the Atthidographers, the historians of Attica. We are assured that Melanthos was a historical personage, a Neleid, the father of Codrus who, thanks to another *apatē* (disguising himself as a peasant), managed to get himself killed and thus ensured the safety of Athens in accordance with the oracles' prophecy. Melanthos is also described as the 'ancestor' of the phratry of the Medontidae. Attempts have even been made to pinpoint the story's date — Wilamowitz put it not earlier than 508 BC, because the frontier was only established then (1935–7: 5.1, 22 n. 2). And Jacoby, while not denying the mythical nature of the

151

Pierre Vidal-Naquet

story, envisaged the possibility of a real frontier skirmish (*FGrH* 3 b Supplement 2: 50 [on 323a F 23]).

But it was Hermann Usener who first attempted to provide an overall explanation of the myth.[12] He pointed out that this was a duel between the *Black* and the *Fair*, as a few ancient authors realized: Polyaenus quotes, or invents, an oracle given before the encounter, which runs: τῷ ξάνθῳ τεύξας ὁ μέλας φόνον ἔσχε Μελαίνας 'Having wrought the death of the fair one the black one seized Melainai.' [*Melainai* means 'the black country'.] Usener saw the duel in symbolic terms, as a ritual combat between winter and summer, an interpretation welcomed by, among others, Lewis Farnell (1909: xlvii; 1896–1909: 5.130–1), A.B. Cook (1914–40: 1.689) and Herbert Rose (1961: 131–3).[13] But it fails to explain what needs to be explained: the link between the duel and the festival itself. The same applies to Nilsson when, in a variant of the theory, he suggested that this *agon* ('contest') linked with the worship of Dionysus was one of the earliest forms of tragedy (1951–60a: 1.61–110, 111–16).

Many years later, in *Couroi et Courètes*, Henri Jeanmaire offered an entirely different view (1939: 382–3). He saw the duel between Xanthos and Melanthos as a ritual joust, perhaps followed by a procession, through which a claimant to the throne declared himself master of the territory. The name of Melanthos is replaced in Pausanias 9.5.16 by that of Andropompos ('the Leader of the procession'); and according to Plutarch (*Quaestiones graecae* 13, 294b–c) it was in a similar way — a duel involving a trick almost identical with ours — that Phemius, king of the Aenianians, established his claim to the valley of the Inachus. It also recalls the famous — legendary — battle between Pittakos and Phrynon at the time of the war over Sigeum between Athens and Mytilene (Will, 1955: 381–3).

But to my knowledge only Angelo Brelich has really attempted to explain the possible relationship between this myth and the Apatouria, the festival of the phratries during which the ephebes were received into the phratry after consecrating their hair (1961: 56–9).[14] In particular, he stresses the frequency with which duels between young men take place in frontier-districts and observes that Dionysus (whom he identifies with Dionysus *Melanaigis*) is described sometimes as *hēbōn* ('with his beard starting to grow'). But he fails to push his interpretation much further than this.

For my part, I was struck by three points which require explanation. First, that the story takes place in the frontier region, just as it is to the frontier that the Athenian ephebes are sent, and that in their oath they swear to protect the boundary-stones of their country. The second point is the story's stress on the *apatē*, the trick. Why should the

152

ephebes have been offered a model of behaviour quite contrary to that which they swear in their oath to observe? We have single-handed combat (*monomachia*) and trickery, contrasted with fair hoplite-fighting on even terms. (Let it be noted in passing that the very name Melanthos was probably evocative for a reader of Homer: just as Dolon is the cunning wolf in the *Iliad* (Gernet, 1968b: 154–71) so in the *Odyssey* Melanthios or Melantheus is a treacherous goatherd (17.212, 22.159, 161, 182 etc.) and his sister Melantho is a treacherous servant (18. 321–2). Their father is called Dolios, 'the cunning one'.)[15] Thirdly, I was struck by the stress on black in the story (*melas* (adj.), stem *melan-*). We find the name Melanthos, the location, which in some texts is called Melainai, and Dionysus of the Black Goatskin (*Melanaigis*). And this is not the only occurrence of an association between the Athenian ephebes and the colour black: at least on certain solemn occasions, they wore a black *chlamys* (a short cloak) which was replaced, thanks to the generosity of Herodes Atticus, by a white one in the second century AD.[16]

In his discussion of the inscription which provides us with this last item of information (*IG* II² 3606), Pierre Roussel showed that the black *chlamys* was supposed to commemorate Theseus's forgetfulness: that ephebe of ephebes forgot to change the black sails on his ship for white ones on his return from Crete (after killing the Minotaur). But aetiology is not explanation; and George Thomson understood this black garment as a sign of ritual exclusion (1941: 107). And there is certainly something very peculiar about this predominance of black — we have only to refer, for example, to Gerhard Radke's conscientious catalogue (1936; cf. Moreux, 1967: 237–72) to understand just how startling, indeed shocking, a ritual victory for black might be in a festival celebrating the entry of young men into the community.

It may help to formulate these problems more precisely if I now digress in order to discuss the Spartan *krypteia*, an institution which has often been compared to the Athenian *ephebeia*, and which, though it involved a much smaller number of young men, was indeed parallel to it in some respects. It is well known that we have a very small number of sources for the *krypteia*.[17] But the scholiast on Plato's *Laws* 1, 633b says explicitly that it was a preparation for the military life. And Köchly argued as early as 1835 [following Karl Otfried Müller] that this training was to be compared to that of the Athenian *peripoloi* ([Müller, 1844: 2.302]; Köchly, 1881–2: 1.587–8); a point made even more clearly by Ernst Wachsmuth, who lucidly observed that this military apprenticeship took the special form of a helot-hunt (1846: 1.252; 2.304).[18]

A brilliant article by Henri Jeanmaire (1913: 121–50) elucidated the

153

Pierre Vidal-Naquet

fundamental characteristics of the *krypteia* by means of comparison
with certain African societies: compulsory isolation of certain young
men around the time of puberty; living in the bush; even the killings
of helots — all of these can be paralleled in black Africa, in the
initiation-ceremonies and secret societies of Wolf-men and Panther-men.
But if that is so, what of the military rôle of the *krypteia*? Jeanmaire's
reply was unequivocal: 'the whole of Spartan military history cries out
against the idea of turning the Spartiate hoplite into a tracker in the
bush, clambering over rocks and walls' (p. 142). And he added wryly
that if the *krypteia*, with its camping-out by night in the mountains,
had really been a training for military life at the time of the battle of
Thermopylae (480 BC), Ephialtes's path (by which the Persians surprised the Spartans) would have been discovered and guarded.

To my mind Jeanmaire was both profoundly right and profoundly
wrong. What he failed to understand was that the *krypteia* was by no
means completely unrelated to the life of the hoplite: for *krypteia* and
the hoplite life were symmetrical opposites. If we make a list from what
the sources tell us, we get the following result:

(1) The hoplite is armed to the teeth; the youth in the *krypteia* is
gumnos, which means either that he carried no arms at all (Scholiast
on Plato's *Laws* 1, 633b) or that he had only a dagger (Plutarch,
Life of Lycurgus 28.2).
(2) The member of the *phalanx* is opposed to the youth on his own or
living in a small group.
(3) The fighter in the plain is opposed to the youth who runs wild in
the mountains.
(4) Plato's youth in the *krypteia* did his training in the middle of
winter; the hoplite, according to Thucydides, fought in summer (cf.
καλοκαίρι in Modern Greek).
(5) The trustworthy hoplite cheered on by Tyrtaeus (7th cent. BC) is
opposed to the cunning killer of helots.
(6) The man who fights in the light of day is opposed to the youth who
fights by night.
(7) The Scholiast on Plato's *Laws* says that the youth in the *krypteia*
ate whatever he could find, living from hand to mouth, probably
without ever finding time to have anything cooked; whereas the
hoplite is above all a member of a common mess, the *syssition*.
(8) The members of the *krypteia* stayed in the areas which became, in a
sense, the frontiers of enemy territories — for the Ephors annually
declared war on the helots in a ritual comparable to the Roman
declaration of war by the *Fetiales*.[19] [By contrast, the full hoplites
were obliged to remain, in peacetime, close to their *syssitia*, that is,
close to Sparta itself.]

154

In sum, with the hoplite order (*taxis*) reigns;[20] in the *krypteia* there is nothing but cunning, deception, disorder, irrationality. To borrow Lévi-Strauss's terms, one might say that the hoplite is on the side of Culture, of what is 'cooked', while the *krypteia* is on the side of Nature, of the 'raw', bearing in mind of course that this 'Nature', the side of non-culture, is itself to some degree socially organized.[21] And we might apply this point more widely: for example, in Crete we find *agelai* of young men, which Pierre Chantraine interprets as the 'herds of animals that are driven along' (1956: 32–3), opposed to the *hetaireiai*, the 'brotherhoods' of mature men. And I could go on, but I have said enough to indicate how, by a procedure which Lévi-Strauss would term a logical inversion, the *krypteia* dramatizes the moment when the young élite Spartiate leaves behind him forever his childhood.

In his *Polarity and Analogy* (1966) Geoffrey Lloyd has brilliantly shown how the principle of polarity played a fundamental rôle in the reasoning of Greek thinkers in the Archaic period – indeed I believe that his conclusions could easily be extended to include the Classical period itself: how can we understand Thucydides, for example, without using the notion of polarity?[22] And my intention here, as must already be evident, is to detect evidence of polarities expressed not in book-thinking but in social institutions; and I propose to do that without entering upon the question of whether 'thought' and 'institutions' are the effective consequences of one single entity, the Lévi-Straussian 'human mind'.

I think we may generalize and extend what I have already said in discussing the Spartan *krypteia*: for we must recognize that in Athens, and in many other parts of the Greek world – above all in Sparta and Crete, where very archaic institutions were preserved until well into the Hellenistic period – the transition between childhood and adulthood (the period of marriage and fighting) is dramatized both in ritual and in myth by what we might call the 'law of symmetrical inversion'. Indeed, since the publication of Arnold van Gennep's *The Rites of Passage* in 1909 (van Gennep, 1960), many rituals of status-transition have been analysed in these terms.[23] I may remind the reader, for example, that in Argos young women sported a (false) beard when they got married (Plutarch, *De mulierum virtutibus* 4, 245f); and that in Sparta, when a girl was to be married she 'was handed over to a *numpheutria* who cut off all her hair, dressed her in a man's clothes and shoes, and made her lie down all alone on a mattress in the dark' (Plutarch, *Life of Lycurgus* 15.5). The two cases are quite parallel, as is obvious when we remember that, according to Herodotus (1.82.7) adults in Argos had to be entirely bald, while in Sparta, they had to let their hair grow long. We have here then a kind of double inversion.

155

Pierre Vidal-Naquet

But we must return to Athens, and look again at the festivals connected with the young men's 'return' that are so marked a feature of the month Pyanepsion (September—October). In these festivals the ephebes played an important part; and they are all the more significant for me inasmuch as they also marked the end of the period of 'apprenticeship' — for this was probably the point at which the ephebes took their famous hoplite-oath in the Aglaurion and when they received their arms from the city.

Very shortly after the *Apatouria* occurred the festival known as the *Oschophoria* (held on the seventh day of Pyanepsion).[24] This is a particularly interesting festival because its aetiological myth is concerned precisely with Theseus's return from Crete after killing the Minotaur, and the conflicting emotions he feels — glad because he has been victorious, filled with grief at his father's death (Plutarch, *Life of Theseus* 22.4). And it was precisely this death which the ephebes' black *chlamys* was believed to commemorate.

The traditional sources for the Oschophoria diverge markedly from one another. I do not propose to analyse them exhaustively,[25] but will simply emphasize some points which have sometimes been neglected. First of all an essential rôle in the Oschophoria is played by an outlying *genos* [a group of relatively wealthy families claiming descent from a single ancestor], that of the Salaminians who had moved to Attica. It was this *genos* in particular which provided the youths (*neaniai*) who carried the vine-branches complete with bunches of grapes (*ōschoi*) — who were in consequence called *ōschophoroi*.[26] Secondly, the first event of the festival was a procession (*parapompē*) from Athens to the shrine of Athena Skiras at Phaleron. Now the word *skiron* means 'lime' and so 'badlands'; and Felix Jacoby has shown that the names *Skiras*, *Skiros* and *Skiron* were generally given to outlying districts which either were, or had been at some time in the past, frontier-areas.[27] Thus 'Skira' is another name for the offshore island of Salamis; Skiron is a village on the old boundary between Athens and Eleusis, and so on. The procession to the shrine of Athena Skiras was made up of boys (*paides*) led by two boys *disguised as girls* carrying the *ōschoi*; these boys are referred to as *paides amphithaleis*.[28] Plutarch explains the transvestism by saying that among the seven maidens whom Theseus took with him to Crete there were two boys disguised as girls.[29] I cannot here venture to tackle the very complex problems presented by the festivals connected with Athena Skiras: the sources are so confused that it is hard to tell which of the various festivals they refer to. I will simply point out that Athena Skiras seems to have been linked significantly with the custom of dressing-up: it is during her festival that Praxagora and her friends decide in Aristophanes's *The Assembly of Women* to dress up

156

as men and wear false beards (and it so happens that one of the characters has a husband who is a Salaminian [18—25, 38]).[30] Plutarch, *Life of Solon* 8, gives two versions of how the Athenians seized Salamis (otherwise known as Skiras) from the Megarians; and in one of them the beardless young men disguise themselves as women. And he says that a festival was established on the promontory Skiradion after the seizure (though he links its details to the second story, which, though involving a deception, contains no transvestism) (9.4).

Besides the procession and the boys' transvestism, the Oschophoria featured a race (*agōn, hamilla*) between ephebes carrying *ōschoi*. Most of our information about this is derived from Proclus's *Chrestomathia*.[31] The course ran from the temple of Dionysus to Phaleron. The competitors were either two representatives from each of the ten tribes, each pair running separately; or else twenty youths, two from each tribe, all running against each other. The victor drank the 'fivefold cup', a mixture of oil, wine, honey, cheese and flour. After the ceremonies at Phaleron, and in particular the rituals of seclusion and the *deipnophoria* ('food-carrying'), there were libations, followed by a revel (*kōmos*) which brought the participants back to Athens. It is evident from Plutarch (*Life of Theseus* 22.3) that this revel was accompanied by a herald, and that the return journey too was explained by reference to Theseus's return from Crete (he was supposed to have stopped at Phaleron in order to sacrifice). In the story, Theseus's herald precedes him with the news of success, and discovers the death of Aegeus, which he reports to Theseus, who is still outside Athens. Theseus's party then entered Athens loudly lamenting, but still the bearers of happy news. And for this reason, says Plutarch, it is not the herald himself who is crowned at the Oschophoria, but his staff (*kērukeion*); and cries of joy, 'Eleleu', alternated with keening, 'iou, iou', in commemoration of Aegeus's death.[32]

The structure of the Oschophoria is thus marked by a series of oppositions. The most blatant is that between male and female, which is clear in the procession itself (boys dressed as girls versus the youths), but also in the contrast between the procession (boys dressed as girls) and the race (*dromos*) between the ephebes (the race of course is nothing if not virile: in Crete, the *dromeus* is a mature man (Willetts, 1955: 11—14), and in Lato, in particular, the word for leaving the *agela* to become a man is 'running out' (ἐγδραμεῖν: *IC* 1.16 [Lato], 5.21); according to Aristophanes of Byzantium an *apodromos* was a young boy not yet allowed to take part in the public races).[33] The race during the Oschophoria is indeed exactly parallel to the *staphulodromia* during the Spartan festival of the *Carneia*, which was also a festival of the phratries: it was a race in which five unmarried young men ran

157

against each other (Harrison, 1927: 234 cf. 321). Thirdly, joy is opposed to grief, as is shown by Plutarch's *Life of Theseus* 22.3 — which has been considered, wrongly I think, to be a later interpretation.

It is well known that in archaic Greek societies, as well as in other societies, dressing up as a woman, as in the procession at the Oschophoria, was a means of dramatizing the fact that a young man had reached the age of virility and marriage. The classic example in Greek mythology is the story of Achilles on Skyros (Jeanmaire, 1939: 354—5; Delcourt, 1961: 1—16; cf. Bettelheim, 1962: 109—21). But it can be demonstrated that it is not the *kind* of disguise which is important, rather the *contrast* which it underscores. The opposition between light and dark for example is no less significant: young men not yet adult are known sometimes to have been called *skotioi* ('of the dark': Scholiast on Euripides, *Alcestis* 989); the *neaniai* ('youths') of the Oschophoria are called *eskiatraphēmenoi*, 'brought up in the dark' (Plutarch, *Life of Theseus* 23.2; Proclus, *Chrestomathia* 89 [p. 56 Severyns]).[34] Both Malla and Dreros in Crete seem to have held ceremonies of admission to the adult age-classes, which involved ritual nudity before the conferring of hoplite arms. The young men are called *azōstoi*, which Hesychius defines as 'those who are without arms'. At Dreros they were called *panazōstoi* and *egduomenoi*, 'those who have no clothes' — the latter term occurs also at Malla.[35] There was likewise at Phaestus a festival called the *Ekdysia* ('Clothes off'): the aetiology here is a story about a girl who turned into a boy — which forms a link between the two sets *boy : girl* and *naked : armed* (Antoninus Liberalis, *Metamorphoses* 17 [Leukippos]; cf. Papathomopoulos, 1968: 109—10; Willetts, 1962: 175—8).

It is perhaps worth noting finally that the sexual inversion of any young man about to become an adult is quite clearly related to these facts: it is enough to mention Ephorus's well-known story about the rape (*harpagē*) of a young Cretan boy, who is taken by his lover into the country (of course!) for two months, for a life of relaxation and *hunting*. It is on his return to the town that he receives the arms which make him a hoplite (*FGrH* 70 F 149 [from Strabo 10.4.21: 483C]).

I come now to the theme of the hunt, which appears in the title of this paper, and which I still have to explain and, if possible, justify. Pierre Chantraine has noted (1956: 40—65) that hunting is linked fundamentally with the *agros* in Greece, the land which lies beyond the cultivated area, that is, with the *eschatiai*, the borderlands of Greek cities. Plato calls his ephebe, the person who defends the frontier area, an *agronomos* (*Laws* 6, 760e—761a). More generally, hunting was so normal for heroes, whom the ephebes emulated, that F. Orth

158

remarked that 'heroes are hunters and hunters heroes' (1914: 559).[36] In a sense, hunting is firmly on the side of the wild, the 'raw', of night;[37] and the skills employed in the Spartan *krypteia* were those of hunting. But only in a sense: we have to make certain distinctions.

My starting-point is a well-known text on education, from the end of Plato's section on education in the *Laws* (7, 822d—824a). Using the method demonstrated in the *Sophist*, Plato introduces here a whole series of distinctions. Each time he speaks of a left side, the side of evil, and a right side, that of good. Fishing depends upon the use of nets: it therefore falls squarely on the left. One ought then to restrict oneself to the hunt and the capture of quadrupeds (θήρευσίς τε καὶ ἄγρα: 824a). Here too, though, he makes a distinction: one is not allowed to hunt by night with nets and traps. All that seems to be permissible is that type of hunting which conforms to the ethos of the horseman and the hoplite: coursing the animal, or killing it with a lance — both of them kinds of hunting which involve the use of one's bare hands (though bird-catching is tolerated *en agrois*, 'beyond the area of cultivation'). 'But as for the man who hunts by night, the *nuktereutēs*, with only nets and traps, let no man allow him to hunt anywhere' (824b).

When faced with a text of this kind, we must of course allow for Plato's dichotomizing method, and for his moralizing tone. Perhaps we should allow for a similar tone when Pindar describes Achilles killing deer without dogs, and without guile or nets, but simply by running faster than they (*Nemean* 3.51—2) — even though it reminds us of the Cretan *dromeus*. But there are several texts which draw a contrast between two types of hunting: adult hunting, where the spear is used rather than the net, and which takes place by daylight, sometimes in a group, and which is in keeping with the hoplite ethos; opposed to it is hunting by night, a 'black hunt' based on the use of the net. The heroic prototype of the group-hunt is of course the hunt of the famous black Calydonian boar. Now it has been observed that 'the use of nets is not a feature of pictorial representations of the Calydonian boar hunt' — any more than it is of the literary accounts (Chantraine, 1956: 65, quoting La Coste-Messelière, 1936: 130—52 [though Immerwahr, 1885: 52—4 points out that this feature does occur on Roman representations of the hunt on sarcophagi; and see now Koch, 1975. Ed.]). And for this reason: the Calydonian boar hunt is a hunt involving the adult heroes of Greece. Likewise, Hegesandros reports a Macedonian custom whereby no man could dine reclining until he had killed a boar without the aid of net or snare (Athenaeus, *Deipnosophistae* 1.31, 18a). Poor Cassander had to wait until he was thirty-five before he could enjoy this privilege — distinguished hunter though he was. We may put the point slightly differently: unless he had accomplished some signal exploit a young

159

man could not be a full participant in the communal meals which were a feature of so many archaic or marginal societies.

Two Spartan customs neatly illustrate how integral hunting was to the hoplite ethos. According to Plutarch (*Life of Lycurgus* 12.4), any-one who took part in the communal meals had to present the table with the choicest parts of his sacrifice, or if he had been hunting, with part of the bag. One was allowed to dine at home if the sacrifice or hunt had finished late, but the others had to come along too (τοὺς δ᾿ ἄλλους ἔδει παρεῖναι). And Xenophon informs us that hunting dogs and horses were common property; while any food left in the mess after dinner had to be kept in a special place for any hunters who were delayed (*Constitution of the Lacedaemonians* 6.3–4).

By contrast with these heroic and communal exploits, hunting by oneself and with nets seems often to be typical of the adolescent. This is indicated by many texts, though it is true that many are late. According to Oppian, *Cynegetica* 2.25, it was Hippolytus, the prototype of the youth who is unmarried and who refuses to marry, who invented the hunting-net. In the story of young Philios, the first task imposed on him was to kill a lion ἄνευ σιδήρου, 'without an iron weapon'. And he slew it not with a net, but with a typical trick (*apatē*) — he made it drunk (Antoninus Liberalis, *Metamorphoses* 12). And Brelich has emphasized the interest of an odd passage in Xenophon's *Cynegeticus* (2.3), where he defines the hunt as characteristic of the transition from childhood to adolescence and adds: 'the hunter who uses a net must love his art, must be of the Greek tongue and be about twenty years old'. It is in such terms perhaps that one might explain why on the Chigi Vase in the Villa Giulia in Rome there is a line of men creeping through the undergrowth, over against the line of horsemen and the line of hoplites (the Chigi Vase is of course Late-Corinthian). And it is by reference to the same oppositions that we can understand why Nestor has two different initiations into the art of war in the *Iliad*, first as a young man, lightly-armed, taking part in a cattle-raid at night, and then as a heavy-armed adult (*Iliad* 11.670–762, with the decisive discussion of Bravo, 1979).

But I want to argue that the essential evidence for the rôle of the hunt in the various stages of a young Greek male's life is provided by a figure whom it is high time that I dealt with: the Black Hunter, Melanion.

> Let me tell you a little story
> I heard when I was a boy
> How
> There once was a youth [νεανίσκος] called Melanion, who
> Was so appalled at the prospect of women he flew
> To the mountains rather than marry.[38]
> And he hunted hares

160

And he set his snares
With his dog there,
And never came back for anyone!
(Aristophanes, *Lysistrata* 781–96, tr. Dickinson)

Melanion appears here as an ephebe, but a sort of ephebe manqué –
a kind of Hippolytus in fact, as Wilamowitz saw clearly in his commentary (1927: 169–70). If we looked no further than this chorus, we
should have here a version of the widespread myth of the gloomy soli-
tary hunter who is either a misogynist or who tries to insult Artemis,
and who, in either case, flouts the social rules. It is the well-known type
of the hunter Orion – who was indeed, according to Oppian, *Cynegetica*
2.28–9, the inventor of hunting by night.

But look further we must. Putting the story of Melanion back into
its mythical context, we can bracket it with the story of a young girl,
the Arcadian Atalanta, who was a huntress and who excelled in running.[39] Their legend is set near a frontier mountain, Mount Parthenion,
between the Argolid and Arcadia. Pausanias (8.6.4) says that the
nearest village was called Melangeia. Like Melanion, Atalanta was
brought up in the mountains, suckled by a bear (Artemis's animal).
Euripides (frg. 510 Nauck²) characterizes her as μίσημα Κυπρίδος,
'hated by Aphrodite' – a social failing parallel to Melanion's. Theognis
(1291–4) describes her as 'the blonde Atalanta who strides over the
mountain peaks, fleeing from the desire of marriage'. For Hesiod she is
the 'light-footed Atalanta' (frg. 73.2, 76.5, 76.20 Merkelbach–West) –
the maiden who escapes from the Centaurs' attempts to rape her
(Apollodorus, *Bibliotheca* 3.9.2). Aelian knows of her only that she was
a virgin (*Variae historiae* 13.1) – just as all that is known of Melanion
in Aristophanes's chorus is that he refuses to marry. In Apollodorus's
well-known version, she comes home and challenges any comer to a
race, stipulating that it shall be an armed race. She thus trespasses on
male preserves twice-over. Xenophon says that Melanion won her hand
thanks to his skills as a hunter (*Cynegeticus* 1.7); but a widespread
mythological tradition (for example, Apollodorus) had it that Melanion
beats Atalanta and wins her for his wife by means of an *apate* of a
feminine kind – dropping Aphrodite's three golden apples, one at a
time. Both of them were depicted on Cypselus's chest at Olympia
(Pausanias 5.19.2). During that period of their lives which was more or
less unexceptionable, they both took part in the Calydonian boar hunt:
they appear together for example on the 'François vase', Atalanta all
light in colour, Melanion all black (in keeping with pictorial con-
vention); and a white hound is about to spring on the black boar. They
had a son, whose name, significantly enough, was Parthenopaeus.[40]
And once again they violated sexual rules by having intercourse in a

161

Pierre Vidal-Naquet

shrine sacred to Zeus or Cybele, the Mother of the Gods. And then they were transformed into lions, because, it is said, lions are unable to have sexual intercourse.[41]

The Athenian ephebe is in a sense the true heir of the Black Hunter. The Black Hunter is, as I have observed, an ephebe manqué, an ephebe who may fail at every turn.[42] And many Attic vases depict a young ephebe setting off with his hound: perhaps they do indeed, in their own way, represent the young man on the threshold of adult life.

It is time to draw this paper to a close. In historical terms, the ephebe in Archaic and Classical Greece was a pre-hoplite. By virtue of this, in the symbolic enactments which are the rites of passage, he was an anti-hoplite: sometimes a girl, sometimes a cunning hunter, sometimes black. It is not in the least surprising that a myth like that of Melanthos should have been considered a model for the ephebe.[43] And at the technical level, the ephebe is a light-armed soldier, an anti-hoplite who ensured the perpetuation, often quite unseen, of a mode of fighting which is both pre- and anti-hoplite, and which reappears into the light of day (and of history) during the Peloponnesian War and in the fourth century BC.[44] Creature of the frontier-area, of the *eschatia*, he guarantees in his hoplite-oath[45] to protect the boundary stones of his country, and with them, the cultivated fields, the wheat, barley, olive-trees, vines and figs.

We might extend this study of the *ephebeia* to a consideration of the rôle of the warrior in Greek mythology. Long before the introduction of hoplite warfare into Greece and Rome, the warrior's function in Indo-European society was twofold. On one side was order, which later led to the development of the *phalanx* and the legion; and on the other disorder and the exploits of the individual (cf. Dumézil, 1958: 57–8). As Georges Dumézil has stressed, these personal exploits, through which the young warriors won recognition, derived from their *furor*, *lussa*, *celeritas*, *menos*, from their fighting spirit; but the exploits of the Irish Cúchulainn, which made his return-journey from the frontier-zone so difficult and dangerous, were also tricks.[46] And in just the same way it is by a trick, in Livy's account, that Publius Horatius defeated the three Curiatii (1.25.7–12). There is a striking parallel in Herodotus's story of the battle between 300 young Spartans and 300 young Argives in the frontier area of Thyreatis (1.68) [after which Othryadēs, the sole Spartan survivor, set up a trophy while the two surviving Argives returned to Argos with the news of victory; both sides could thus legitimately claim to have won. Ed.]. Young Horatius may thus be distant cousin to the Black Hunter.

162

8. The Black Hunter and the origin of the Athenian 'ephebeia'

1 This is a considerably revised version of the original article. I have taken account of several points which have been made to me, especially by O. Picard, and of the criticisms of Maxwell-Stuart, 1970: 113—16.

2 For the controversy, see Wilamowitz-Moellendorff, 1893: 1.193—4; Robert, 1938: 297—307; Jeanmaire, 1939; Pélékidis, 1962 (with full bibliography); Marrou, 1956: 36—45, 105—12, 186—9. Reinmuth, 1971: 123—38 has shown from the inscriptions that the *ephebeia* existed in 361 BC, considerably before the period of Lycurgus's domination of Athenian political life. To be sure, the

254

date of the inscription which Reinmuth relies on has been questioned by Mitchell, 1975: 233–43; but the scholar who found the stone, M. Mitsos, was in a position to defend Reinmuth (cf. J. and L. Robert, 1976: no. 194). And most important of all, Philippe Gauthier has shown decisively in his discussion of Xenophon, *Ways and Means* 4.51–2 (which had not hitherto been adduced in the debate) both that the *ephebeia* antedates Lycurgus – the *Ways and Means* was written in 355 BC – and that, prior to Lycurgus, it was not a duty imposed upon all young male citizens (1976: 190–5).

3 On *peripoloi* generally in the Greek world, see Robert, 1955: 283–92; we may add two recent items from Acarnania and Epirus: cf. J. and L. Robert, 1973: nos. 229 and 260.

4 Xenophon, *Ways and Means* 4.52 thus uses the verb *peltazein* rather than *hopliteuein*, the *peltē* being a light shield [and *hopliteuein* referring to the performance of military service equipped with heavy hoplite armour, especially the shield, *hoplon*. Ed.] : cf. Gauthier, 1976: 192–3.

5 Young men were only used to fight under exceptional circumstances, and so are normally specifically mentioned: note the episode in the first Peloponnesian War, a battle against Megara involving the *neōtatoi* (the young men not normally called up) and the *presbutatoi* (the older men no longer normally called up): cf. Thucydides 1.105.4 and Lysias, *Oration* 2.50–3, with Loraux, 1980a.

6 I am not here concerned with the mutual inconsistencies of these passages.

7 See *IC* 1.9 (Dreros), 1.126–7; and for *oureuō* = 'be a young soldier in the frontier forts', van Effenterre, 1948b: 1033–4. Thucydides 5.41.2 reproduced in Bengtson, 1962: 124–5, no. 192) offers a clear-cut, official distinction between the frontier areas and the territory proper of Argos and Sparta.

8 The text sets formal combat against stratagem, an opposition whose significance is discussed below.

9 Here is a list – assuredly incomplete – of the 'sources' (a quite inadequate term, as will at once be realized, for most of these texts): Hellanicus, *FGrH* 4 F 125 = 323a F 23 (= Scholiast T on Plato, *Symposium* 208d) with Jacoby's commentary; Ephorus, *FGrH* 70 F 22 (= Harpokration, s.v. ἀπατούρια [1, pp. 42–3 Dindorf]); Konon, *Diēgēseis* in *FGrH* 26 F 1, 39 (Μέλανθος); Strabo 9.1.7 (393C); Frontinus, *Stratagemata* 2.5.41; Frontinus, *Stratagemata* 1.19; Justin 2.6.16–21; Pausanias 2.18.8–9; 9.5.16; Eusebius, *Chronicon* p. 56 (ed. Schoene); John of Antioch, in *FHG* 4, p. 539 § 19; Proclus, *in Timaeum* 21b (1.88.11–90.12 Diehl); Nonnus of Panopolis, *Dionysiaka* 27.301–7; Michael Apostolius, s.v. ἀπιὼν ἐς Ἀπατούρια in *Corp. paroemiogr. gr.*, edd. Leutsch and Schneidewin, 2, p. 294; Michael Psellus, *De Actionum nominibus* 40 (= Migne, *PG* 122, cols. 1017d–20a); Joh. Tztetzes, *Commentarium in Aristophanis Ranas* 798a (4.3, pp. 907–9 Koster); Lycophron, *Alexandra* 767 with scholia (ed. Scheer); *Etymologicon Magnum* s.v. ἀπατούρια (cols. 336–7 Gaisford), and s.v. κουρεῶτις (1522–3 Gaisford); *Lexica Segueriana* s.v. ἀπατούρια (in Bekker, *Anecdota graeca* 1, pp. 416–17); Scholiast on Aelius Aristeides, 1 (*Panathenaikos*) 118.20 (3, pp. 111–12 Dindorf); Scholiast on Aristophanes, *Acharnians* 146 (p. 7 Dübner), and *Peace* 890 (p. 315 Dübner); Suda, s.v. ἀπατούρια (1, no. 2940 Adler); s.v. Μέλανθος (3, no. 458 Adler); s.v. μέλαν (3, no. 451 Adler); s.v. Ξάνθος (3, no. 8 Adler); George Syncellus in *FHG* 4, p. 539. These sources have recently been assembled and discussed by Fernandez Nieto, 1975: 2.15–20 (no. 3).

10 [This is not quite accurate: Plutarch, who is here discussing wine and its uses, makes one of his characters say: σὺ δ' (i.e. his interlocutor, Niger) ἀξιοῖς τοῦ νυκτερινοῦ καὶ μελαναίγιδος ἐμφορεῖσθαι, 'But you want us to fill up on [wine] "dark as night and sable-skinned" ', which seems to be a cult-title of Dionysus;

255

but V.-N.'s general point remains valid, cf. Suda s.v. Μέλαν (3, p. 350 no. 451 Adler); Konon in *FGrH* 26 F 1 § 39 lines 27—30. Ed.]

11 There is here more than a mere etymological play on words. As Pauline Schmitt informs me, there was according to Pausanias 2.33.7, on the island of Sphaeria near Troezen, a temple of Athena Apatouria, which played an important part in the initiation of young girls. The 'original' *apatē* (deception) is the union of Poseidon and Aethra, mother of Theseus; see Schmitt, 1977: 1059—73.

12 Usener, 1912—13a: 4.292—7, following a suggestion by Maass, 1889: 805 n. 13; see also Usener, 1912—13b: 4.437—47.

13 Farnell's theory was very like Nilsson's (1951—60a: 1.61—110, 111—16), which of course he did not know.

14 Marie Delcourt's remarks in 1965: 18 are completely unfounded, being based upon mistaken facts.

15 Dolios himself is a sympathetic figure: *Odyssey* 24.222—5, 387—90, 397—411 [and at least some of his sons, apparently. Ed.]. Annie Schnapp has discussed this theme of *dolos*—Dolon in a forthcoming article.

16 This point has been challenged by Maxwell-Stuart, 1970: 113—16. He tries to minimize the significance of Philostratus, *Lives of the Sophists* 2.550, according to which the ephebes wore in assembly and in public processions a black *chlamys*. His criticism does not carry conviction because, although he is familiar with Roussel's article (1941: 163—5) — which to my mind is decisive — he persists in thinking that *IG* II² 1132 (honorific inscription for Herodes Atticus) refers to Herodes's father, Claudius Atticus, whose vow Herodes was fulfilling. But Roussel showed that the text in fact refers to Theseus: it says 'the son of Aegeus much to his dismay forgetting his father . . . ' (λήθην πατρὸς ὠκεώμενος | Αἰγείδεω: 20). Moreover, there is no way of showing that this inscription refers to the mysteries of Eleusis. On the other hand, I have taken account of two important points by Maxwell-Stuart, and removed a reference to Xenophon, *Hellenica* 1.7.8 (which I interpreted wrongly) and the evidence of the vases (which I misrepresented).

17 See Plato's *Laws* 1, 633b and the relevant, and very important, scholia on it; Heracleides of Pontus in *FHG* 2, p. 210; Plutarch, *Life of Lycurgus* 28; note too Plutarch, *Life of Cleomenes* 28, which mentions one Damoteles, who was in Cleomenes's army the head of the *krypteia* (that is, in charge of ambushes) [cf. Köchly, 1881—2: 1.586—7. Ed.].

18 It would be diverting to compare these 'military' interpretations in the nineteenth century with the liberal, not to say Louis-Philippian, one of Henri Wallon, the 'father of the Republic', for whom the *krypteia* was essentially a police-operation.

19 Plutarch, *Life of Lycurgus* 28.4 (quoting Aristotle). For a defence of the seriousness of this tradition, see Finley, 1975b: 165 with n. 9; 176—7.

20 At the level of ideology, of course; the actual social organization of the Spartiate hoplite-body is more complicated than this, as Nicole Loraux reminds me (see Loraux, 1977: 105—20).

21 See Lévi-Strauss, 1966b: 19—30, and, more generally, 1970, with Yalman, 1967: 71—89; also Jaulin, 1967: 40—119, 141—71 (the astonishing account of the author's 'initiation' by a tribe in Chad), and Dumézil, 1968: 63—5 (on another type of opposition between the 'naked' and the 'heavily-armed' warrior).

22 Rational decision (*gnōmē*) is for Thucydides the opposite of fortune (*tychē*); discourse the opposite of action, just as the hot is the opposite of the cold or the dry of the wet in Milesian cosmological thinking.

23 On the concept of inversion, one could quote the whole of Lévi-Strauss's work; see also Pembroke's important paper, 1967: 1—35.

256

24 On the Oschophoria, see Mommsen, 1898: 36, 278—82; Rutgers van der Loeff, 1915: 404—15; Deubner, 1932: 142—6; Severyns, 1938: 2.243—54; Jeanmaire, 1939: 346—7, 524, 588; Jacoby, *FGrH* 3 b 1: 285—304; 3 b 2: 193—223; Faure, 1964: 170—2.

25 The entire literary tradition on the Oschophoria and Skira is printed in Jacoby, *FGrH* 3 b 1 (Supplement): 286—9 in his commentary upon some of the most important passages (Philochorus, 328 F 14—16). The only significant inscription relevant to the Oschophoria is that belonging to 363 BC which gives us the record of an agreement between the two segments of the Salaminian *genos* which had been in dispute (first published, with a full commentary, by W.S. Ferguson, 1938: 1—74; conveniently reprinted in Sokolowski, 1962: 49—54, no. 19).

26 See Sokolowski, 1962: 50, line 49. The same *genos* provided two female *deipnophoroi* ('food-carriers') who brought food to the young people 'shut away' during the seclusion ceremonies in Phaleron; cf. Nilsson, 1951—60e: 2.731—41.

27 Jacoby, *FGrH* 3 b 2 (Supplement): 200—3. The sanctuary of Athena Skiras is said to be 'outside the city' (ἐξ τῆς πόλεως): *Etymologicon Magnum* p. 717. 28 [= Jacoby, *FGrH* 3 b 1 (Supplement): 287 no. 7. Ed.].

28 *Amphithalēs* has two meanings: 'a child with both parents alive'; and 'one who cuts and handles green branches or twigs in rituals or processions': see Robert, 1940: 509—19.

29 See Plutarch, *Life of Theseus* 23.3—4, quoting the Atthidographer Demon [*c.* 300 BC]; Proclus, *Chrestomathia* 88—91 (pp. 56—7 Severyns) [= Photius, *Bibliotheca* 239].

30 These points seem to have gone unnoticed.

31 Proclus, *Chrestomathia* 91—2 (p. 57 Severyns): εἴπετο δὲ τοῖς νεανίαις ὁ χορὸς καὶ ᾗδε τὰ μέλη. ἐξ ἐκάστης δὲ φυλῆς ἔφηβοι διημιλλῶντο πρὸς ἀλλήλους δρόμῳ ('the chorus followed the young men [the procession with the two boys dressed as girls V.-N.] and sang the songs; ephebes from each tribe competed against each other in a running race'); see also the scholiast on Nicander of Colophon, *Alexipharmaka* 109 [p. 36 Ábel and Vári: ὠσχοφόροι δὲ λέγονται Ἀθήνῃσι παῖδες ἀμφιθαλεῖς ἀμιλλώμενοι κατὰ φυλάς, οἱ λαμβάνοντες κλήματα ἀμπέλου ἐκ τοῦ ἱεροῦ τοῦ Διονύσου ἔτρεχον εἰς τὸ τῆς Σκιράδος Ἀθηνᾶς ἱερόν: 'Oschophoroi means at Athens boys who carried sacred branches and who competed by tribes; they ran with vine-branches from the temple of Dionysus to the temple of Athena Skiras.' Ed.]. The inscription of the Salaminioi, quoted above, apparently alludes to this competition (*hamillos*) in lines 61—2 (Sokolowski, 1962: 51): τὸ δὲ πρόθυμα τοῦ ἀμίλλου ἐν μέρει ἑκατέρους κατάρχεσθαι: 'Each party (i.e. the two segments of the Salaminian *genos* whose dispute is here resolved) shall perform in turn the sacrifice which precedes the contest' [cf. Ferguson, 1938: 37. Ed.].

The literary tradition is hopelessly confused, since the sources seem to mix up at least four festivals, the Oschophoria, the Skira, the Skiraphoria and the Thesmophoria. The first and last of these took place in the month Pyanepsion (September—October) and the Thesmophoria was confined to married women. But what about the Skira? Aristodemus of Thebes, a late hellenistic Boeotian writer, assigned the ephebic race, which I have assigned to the Oschophoria on the authority of Proclus, to the festival of the Skira, which was connected with Athena Skiras, just as the Oschophoria was (*FGrH* 383 F 9, from Athenaeus, *Deipnosophistae* 11, 495e). The scholiast to Aristophanes, *Ecclesiazusae* 18 (p. 315 Dübner) says that the Skira was a June festival (12 Skirophorion). If so, it is impossible to suppose that the youths carried *óschoi*, bunches of ripe grapes. I cannot therefore agree with Jacoby when he writes: 'Our tradition is perfectly clear: the procession is attested for the Oschophoria, the race for

257

the Skiraphoria' (or the Skira, perhaps); and then clarifies this 'tradition' by arguing that part of Proclus's text is interpolated (*FGrH* 3 b 1 (Supplement), commentary on 328 F 14–16). Additional support for my interpretation is provided by the existence at Sparta of a ritual race very close to that described by our sources, linked to a festival of the phratries (the Carneia), and in which the runners carry bunches of grapes in just the same way (see p. 157 below).

On the Skira, see Dow and Healey, 1965: 16–17, 33, 39–41, 44, revising and commenting upon *IG* II² 1363 (though the book must be used with caution: cf. J. and L. Robert, 1967: 481–2 [no. 217] and the authors they cite, especially Jean Pouilloux and Georges Roux).

[V.-N.'s comments on Jacoby here are surely justified; but I do not think we can be certain that the parallel between the Oschophoria and the Staphulodromia in Sparta was quite as exact as he argues. The only source which states categorically that the ephebes who ran in the race carried *oschoi* is the Scholiast on Nicander of Colophon in the passage I have translated above. Proclus himself says only that it was the two young men dressed as girls who carried vine-branches and grapes: τοῦ χοροῦ δὲ δύο νεανίαι κατὰ γυναῖκας ἐστολισμένοι κλῆμα τ᾽ ἀμπέλου κομίζοντες μεστὸν εὐθαλῶν βοτρύων: 'two young men from the chorus, dressed as women and carrying a vine-branch covered with fat grapes . . . '. In view of the much greater circumstantiality of this passage, and section 92, it seems easier to suppose that it is the scholiast on Nicander which has compressed a fuller account to the point of confusion, or muddled a procession in the Oschophoria involving (1) two young men carrying vine-branches and (2) a race between *ephebes* with a similar one in the Skiraphoria, when the grapes were just starting to set. In this connection, it is instructive that this scholiast thought that *ôschê* meant simply 'a vine branch', and by extension the branch of any tree, thus missing the point stressed, for example, by Proclus, and by the *Etymologicon Magnum* 619.32 Gaisford, that the branch carried ripe bunches of grapes. Ed.]

32 See also Aristodemus of Thebes, *FGrH* 383 F 9 and Proclus, *Chrestomathia* 91–2 (p. 57 Severyns).

33 '(They call the ephebes) *apodromoi* in Crete because they do not yet take part in the running races': ἐν . . . Κρήτῃ, ἀποδρόμους, διὰ τὸ μηδέπω τῶν κοινῶν δρόμων μετέχειν: Eustathius, *Commentarius in Hom. Odyss.* 8,247 [p. 1592. 58], quoted by Willetts, 1955: 11 n. 8.

34 It will be recalled that there were festivals, such as the *Pannychis* during the Athenian Panathenaia, from which all but the young were excluded, and which were held at night (cf. Euripides, *Heracleidae* 780–3); note too the ritual mentioned by Herodotus 3.48, discussed by Schmitt, 1979: 226–7.

35 See *IC* 1,9 (Dreros), 1.11–12; 98–100 (p. 85); 1,19 (Mallos), 1.17–18, with Guarducci's commentary on pp. 87, 232; cf. Schwyzer, 1928: 237–48 and van Effenterre, 1937: 330–2.

36 The main work on hunting in classical Greece remains Otto Manns, 1888: 7–38; 1889: 3–20; 1890: 3–21. There is some information to be gleaned from Aymard, 1951 (mostly about Roman hunting), and cf. Brelich, 1958: index, s.v. Caccia. When this article was first published, I did not know Kerenyi, 1952: 131–42, which raises a number of the problems discussed here. See now also Schnapp, 1973 (still unpublished); Brelich, 1969: 198–9; and Pleket, 1969: 281–98, which is thought-provoking.

37 In the well-known opposition between hoplite and archer in Euripides's *Herakles*, the archer is rejected, since he hunts wild animals (153–8).

38 ['To the mountains' translates ἀφίκετ᾽ ἐς ἐρεμίαν, | κἀν τοῖς ὄρεσιν ᾤκει: 'he went to the wild land, and dwelt in the mountains' (lines 786–7). Ed.]

39 The literary texts concerning Atalanta are given, for example, by Immerwahr,

258

1885: 1–28. Bowra, 1950: 52–69, though devoted to Swinburne's poem *Atalanta*, is suggestive; but the fundamental discussion is now Arrigoni, 1977; cf. Detienne, 1979a: 27–34, 40–2, 44–51. On the episode of the apples, see Trumpf, 1960: 20.

40 'A half-child man' (ἀνδρόπαις ἀνήρ), says Aeschylus, *Seven against Thebes* 533; the very name, Parthenopaeus, means 'with a face like a girl's'.

41 Apollodorus, *Bibliotheca* 3.9.2; Ovid, *Metamorphoses* 10.560–607; *Vatican Mythographer* 1.39 (ed. Mai); Hyginus, *Fabulae* 185; Servius *in Vergil. Aeneid.* 3.113. The sources differ concerning the name of Atalanta's husband.

42 This type of figure in myth should be compared with the whole range of those who refuse transition. That is a subject which has not yet been explored.

43 Starting from here, I have tried to show that one can interpret Sophocles's *Philoctetes* in terms of the *ephebeia* (1972: 161–84) (see n. 27, p. 261 below).

44 Xenophon's work on war and hunting reveals this modification of the hoplite tradition extraordinarily well. Many sentences – for instance those which advise the training of youths and older men for war by the practice of hunting – have a polemical significance which has hardly been noticed.

45 This is as far as I go along with the remarks of Pleket, 1969: 294 on the ephebe as a hoplite-in-the-making. On the ephebic oath as a hoplite oath, see Siewert, 1977: 102–11.

46 See Dumézil, 1942: 37; 1956: 23; and more generally, Vian, 1968: 53–68. In the properly Roman context, several studies by J.-P. Morel have thrown new light on the rôle of the *iuventus* (the age-class of young men) in the age-class structure: cf. 1969: 526–35; 1976: 663–83.

259

ANOTHER SHOWDOWN AT THE CLEFT WAY: AN INQUIRY INTO CLASSICISTS' CRITICISM OF LÉVI-STRAUSS' MYTH ANALYSIS

Within the last three decades classicists seem to have developed an Oedipus complex. Ever since the appearance of Claude Lévi-Strauss' seminal essay, "The Structural Study of Myth," in 1955, in which he performed a brief structural analysis of the Oedipus myth *exempli gratia*, many classical scholars have been both fascinated and dismayed.[1] Time and again they have returned to this essay, laying out Lévi-Strauss' little chart of mythemes, summarizing his methodology, and then picking apart his analysis: "The conclusion is clear: the proposed schema is flawed at every point and cannot be accepted." [2] Lévi-Strauss' brand of structuralism has been labeled as "arbitrary", as "the last resort of idealism", and dubiously hailed as "the one method for dealing with even the unintelligible, the absurd," as perhaps "the final game of nihilism".[3] He stands accused of scientism, of ingenuity, of reducing society to a machine, of "finding the harmony but losing the melody", of having no method, of being an anthropologist.[4] Kirk, who mentions the essay only in a footnote to an extended treatment of Lévi-Strauss' myth analysis, dismisses it as "interesting but erratic", disdainfully "prefer[ring] to say no more about it." [5] Even his admirers have had their misgivings about his treatment of the Oedipus story. Detienne observes that the myth carved up and reorganized as though it were its own relational context ". . .thus. . .became subject to the ingenuity and caprice of the model's constructor." [6] Edmund Leach, the anthropologist classicists often cite as Lévi-Strauss' cicerone, ruefully notes, "Those who think all this is vaguely reminiscent of an argument from *Alice Through*

[1] C. Lévi-Strauss, "The Structural Study of Myth", in *Myth: A Symposium*, ed. T. A. Sebeok (Bloomington 1955) 81-106; revised for *Structural Anthropology*, trans. C. Jacobson and B. Grundfest (Garden City, NY 1968) 205-31.

[2] J. Dee, "Lévi-Strauss at the Theban Gates," *CW* 72 (1979) 257-61, at 260.

[3] W. Burkert, *Structure and History in Greek Mythology and Ritual* (Berkeley and Los Angeles 1979) 1-226, at 13-14.

[4] Scientism: Burkert (note 3, above); ingenuity: Detienne (this note, below); "losing the melody": B. Nathorst, *Stockholm Studies in Comparative Religion* 9 (1969) 51; society as a machine: G. S. Kirk, *The Nature of Greek Myths* (Harmondsworth 1974) 81; lacking in method. Burkert (note 3, above) 11: J. A. Barnes, "Time Flies Like an Arrow," *Man*, n.s. 6 (1971) 537-52; arbitrariness: M. Detienne, *Dionysos Slain*, trans. M. Muellner and L. Muellner (Baltimore and London 1979) 1-130, at 3; Dee (note 2, above) 259, 260; C. Lévi-Strauss (himself!) (note 1, above) *Structural Anthropology* 230; anthropologist: G. S. Kirk, *Myth and Its Meaning and Functions in Ancient and Other Cultures* (Berkeley and Los Angeles 1974) 45; M. I. Finley, "Anthropology and the Classics", in *The Use and Abuse of History* (New York 1975) 107-12.

[5] G. S. Kirk (note 4, above) *Myth and Its Meaning*, 83, n. 46.

[6] M. Detienne (note 4, above) 7.

the Looking Glass will not be far wrong," and concludes, "such methods cannot show us the truth; they only lead into a world where all things are possible and nothing sure." [7] Peradotto confesses to being scandalized that Lévi-Strauss failed to apply in his Oedipus analysis his explanation of how myths work to overcome cultural paradoxes: "replac[ing] two unmediatable oppositions by two equivalent or analogous terms which admit a third one as a mediator." [8] He then calls for a syntagmatic reading of the myths of a "hot" culture like the Greeks' because it is less aprioristic, less deductive, and less subjective than the method used with Oedipus (95).

The list of critics and criticisms could be lengthened, but the issue should by now be apparent. This early essay on "The Structural Study of Myth," rather than the four massive volumes of *Mythologiques*, has become for many classicists the focus of the debate on the value and suitability of a structuralist approach to myth. Indeed, many classicists know of Lévi-Strauss' work or of structuralism in general only through this essay or through criticisms of it such as those above. But many of these criticisms are incorrect, or at best misleading, and they deserve to be set aright, not least of all because this particular essay serves for so many classicists as the exemplar of Lévi-Strauss' structural study of myth. In particular, Lévi-Strauss' treatment of the Oedipus myth has unplumbed resources. Careful philological investigation brings to light information that confirms and supports rather startlingly Lévi-Strauss' undoubtedly sketchy treatment. In other words, his analytical model has impressive explanatory power not only because it illuminates aspects of the myth that otherwise seem obscure, irrelevant, or contradictory, but also because it predicts verifying data for his analysis of the Oedipus myth: that is, it guides us in the proper search for such confirmatory data which Lévi-Strauss may have presupposed, even if he did not know they existed.

To provide a convenient framework for making that case and setting out the data, the present paper has been written as a reply to a recent assault on Lévi-Strauss' handling of the myth. James Dee's "Lévi-Strauss at the Theban Gates" provides a useful focus for two reasons.[9] First, it sums up either explicitly or implicitly most classicists' complaints about Lévi-Strauss' myth analysis. Secondly, Dee brandishes philology as his principal weapon to slay the structuralist dragon, while it is precisely philology, I believe, that will validate Lévi-Strauss' contribution.

There are three main thrusts to Dee's criticism of Lévi-Strauss' essay. First, he challenges the underlying meaning of lameness that Lévi-Strauss claimed for the names of Labdakos, Laïos, and Oedipus. For Lévi-Strauss lameness is a mythological characteristic of autochthons, and hence these names are a code to indicate in this myth "the persistence of the autochthonous origin of man" (91). Secondly, Dee insists that the

---

[7] E. Leach, *Claude Lévi-Strauss* (New York 1970) 66.

[8] J. Peradotto, "Oedipus and Erichthonius: Some Observations on Paradigmatic and Syntagmatic Order," *Arethusa* 10 (1977) 85-101, at 91.

[9] Note 2, above.

narrative sequence of the myth, in structuralist terms the "syntagmatic chain", determines the myth's meaning: e.g., ". . .the arbitrary assignment of meaning to a fragment of myth without considering its function as part of a series of events leads to a serious misreading" (259), or ". . .the consequences of the act are vital" (260). In this, of course, he means to rebut Lévi-Strauss' view that the meaning of a myth is found by analysis of paradigmatic events or relationships without regard for their chronological sequence in the narrative. Finally, Dee charges Lévi-Strauss with perhaps the gravest sin a non-classicist can commit when he ventures to write on the ancient world: "*arbitrarily* impos[ing] on story fragments. . .*values other than those of the Greeks*" (260) [italics mine].

In fact, Dee admits that the name Oedipus did mean to the ancient Greeks "swollen foot" on account of the pin that bound the infant's ankles when he was abandoned, in some versions, on Mt. Kithairon. As well he might, for the ancients clearly understood the name in this way (e.g., Eur. *Phoen.* 26-27; Apoll. 3.5.7; Paus. 10.5.3; Diod. Sic. 4.64.1; Nik. Dam. *FGrHist* 90 F8). Nor is the case any less strong for Labdakos meaning lame, although Dee attempts to impugn the notion. However, Herodotos's comment (5.92.2B) on the lame (*chôlê*) daughter of the Bakkhiad Amphion at Korinth (*Amphiôni. . .ginetai thugatêr chôlên: ounoma de hoiên Labda*) makes it clear the girl was named Labda *because* she was lame (here *de* is equivalent to *oun*: cf. Denniston 170). That is, the letter form of *labda* was a pictograph of lameness (*Et. Mag.* 199, s.v. *blaisos*). Since it is a characteristic of myth that later versions or variants reduplicate key aspects of the story for emphasis, it is not a valid objection that because the letter form *labda* was not introduced into Greece until the ninth or eighth century B.C., Labdakos is a late and hence unreliable addition to the myth. In fact, it is at least ironic that scholars who themselves privilege literary—and thus comparatively late—versions of the myth should insist that structuralist analysis rely on materials of the greatest antiquity or risk being faulted. For in myth, as most nonstructuralists would admit, age does not confer authenticity. A myth remains a myth as long as it is felt as such, sometimes over many centuries, undergoing many permutations. Thus, in understanding the myth *per se*, as separate from the text that is its vehicle, it is immaterial whether Oedipus was abandoned on Mt. Kithairon or set adrift in a chest (schol. Eur. *Phoen.* 26, 28; Hyg. *Fab.* 66); the underlying theme is constant, i.e., the parent's abandonment of the child, which in Lévi-Strauss' analysis could be generalized to yet a higher level of abstraction, the undervaluing of blood relations. In this way, Labdakos as the nomenclature of lameness and hence the signifier of autochthony, though called "late", may be viewed as the surviving permutation of some ur-mytheme now lost that contained the same information. In any case, even Dee grudgingly admits Labdakos is connected with lameness.

It is the etymology of Laïos, Oedipus's father's name, as left-sided (and hence as "lame" and thus autochthonous) that Dee successfully attacks. Linguistically, *laios* (pre-homeric **laiwos*), "left-sided", has nothing to do with Laïos. But Laïos' putative autochthony is not so easily denied. There is good reason to believe that Laïos' name means "stone-man" and is to be connected with a well known myth of autochthonous origins. Apollodoros (1.7.2) tells how Deukalion and Pyrrha after the flood created a new human race by casting stones over their shoulders. He concludes, "Hence people (*laoi*) were metaphorically so-called from the fact that a stone (*lithos*) is a *laas*." This etymology was in fact quite old. There was a play on these words, for instance, in Homer (*Il.* 24.611): *laous de lithous poiêse Kroniôn*. Here, the children of Niobe, slain by Apollo and Artemis, lay unburied for nine days because Zeus had turned the people to stone, including Niobe who remained perma-nently petrified on Mt. Sipylos. Niobe was of course connected with the house of Kadmos because she was married to Amphion, a descendant of Chthonios, one of the autochthonous Spartoi (Apoll. 3.5.5-6). Thus, this portion of the myth represents a simple transformation, in Lévi-Strauss' sense, of the process of autochthonous generation: instead of stones turning into people, people turn into stones. The Deukalion and Pyrrha myth itself was certainly viable in classical times as Pindar, *Ol.* 9 (43-46) makes clear:

> Deukalion and Pyrrha, coming down from Mt. Parnassos, founded their house at the first, and without sexual intercourse (*ater eunas*) established as their countrymen (*homodamon*) a stone generation (*lithinon gonon*), and they were called people (*laoi*).

Clearly, this is a myth of autochthony, where sexual intercourse is de-nied, in favor of reproduction on a vegetal metaphor: men spring from stones sown in the earth.[10] Thus the offspring are described as *homo-damon*, literally, of the same *dêmos*, because *dêmos* is, as Benveniste has pointed out, "a territorial. . .concept" (*not* one of blood kinship), which "designates both a division of land and the people who inhabit it."[11] The Theban paradigm for this myth is, of course, Kadmos' sowing of the dragon's teeth from which came the Spartoi, the "sown" men. The scholiast to Pindar, furthermore, explains the passage thus:

> Epicharmos says people are so called from the fact that stones (*lithoi*) are *laes*. Philochoros, from Kekrops, for this man wishing the race of the Athenians to increase, ordered them to take stones (*lithous*) and cast them into their midst, from which he perceived they were twenty thousand. Accordingly, he says the masses were called (*laoi*) from Kekrops. (Philochoros *FGrHist* 328 F95).

Kekrops was, of course, an Athenian autochthon himself, half-man and half-snake, and his method of increasing Athens' population that of autochthony.[12] The significance of these texts is that they explain the ori-

[10] On the vegetal metaphor, cf. C. Lévi-Strauss (note 1, above) 92; cf. the birth of Erich-thonios (Eur. *Phoen.* 267): *eblasten ek gês*.
[11] É. Benveniste, *Indo-European Language and Society*, trans. E. Palmer (London 1973) 371.
[12] On Kekrops's autochthony and his herpetic characteristics cf. Apoll. 3.14.1; Arist. *Vesp.* 438 and schol. ad loc.; Eur. *Ion* 1163 ff.; schol. *Plut.* 773; D.S. 1.28.7.; Hermipp.

gins of a race of men specifically known as autochthonous through the same folk etymology, that people (*laoi*) have their beginnings as stones (*laes*) sown in the earth. Thus, it is possible that the name of Oedipus' father, Laïos, is connected with this etymology.

That is, Laïos could be construed as deriving from the adjective that is formed from the stem **law-* and the suffix *-io-*, the latter denoting that which belongs or pertains to. Such a formation would account for the spelling of the name Laïos, a trisyllable with a long *a*: when the digamma ("*w*") dropped out of Greek, its force was still felt, and the *a* and *i* were not diphthongized. The difficulty is that the only attested Greek adjective from *laas* is *lainos*, composed of the stem **law-* and the adjectival suffix *-ino-*, which indicates the material of composition (in this case, "made of stone"). Thus, the conjectural etymology, though enticing, seems a dead end. Or, stated another way, if Laïos is a stone-man, why was he not named Laïnos? The solution to this difficulty lies in the difference in what the adjectival suffixes denote at a more abstract level: those in *-io-* are classificatory and conceptual; those in *-ino-*, descriptive and specific.[13] Thus, Laïos would be so called because his name *classified* him as an autochthon, while Laïnos would have meant he was quite specifically "of stone" and not flesh and blood. That Laïnos is an appropriate name because it classifies turns out to fit very well Lévi-Strauss' analysis of how certain cultures use their taxonomies of concrete items in the world around them as *bonnes à penser*, as "goods to think with".[14] That is, in the language of the myth Laïos is the concrete classifier for the abstract concept "born from one". But outside of the specialized language, such a word, *laïos*, would have no function, and hence it does not otherwise occur in Greek. Finally, as some have pointed out, the name is also derivable from *laos* (pre-Homeric **lawos*), and hence the play on the words *laas/laos* is not inconceivable here too. As the Greeks were obviously well acquainted with this play, specifically in the context of myths of autochthony, a context that has a paradigm in Kadmos' sowing of the dragon's teeth, the autochthony of Laïos in Greek mythology has a high probability. Of Lévi-Strauss one may say that although the etymological basis of his original claim for Laïos' autochthony was erroneous, the explanatory power of his method is vindicated: on the hypothesis that Laïos should have the "same" meaning as Labdakos and Oedipus, careful investigation turns up data that substantiate the conjecture.

Finally, Dee is right that Lévi-Strauss neglected to include Kadmos' sowing of the dragon's teeth in his fourth column (assertion of autochthony). But that was an oversight, not a fault in method or theory. To probe a little further, Laïos was credited with inventing homosexuality by raping Pelops' son, Chrysippos (Peisander *FGrHist* 16 F10; Ael. *NA* 6.15; *VH* 13.5); in any case, the rape was a well known part of the myth

POxy 1367; Suidas s.v. *Kekrops*, s.v. *Prometheus*, s.v. *drakaulos*; Plut. *Mor.* 551E-F; Charax *FGrHist* 103 F39; Athen. 555D; Just. 2.6.7; Kastor *FGrHist* 250 F4.

13 Benveniste (note 11, above) 219.

14 C. Lévi-Strauss, *The Savage Mind*, trans. G. Weidenfeld (Chicago 1966) 35-108.

(Apoll. 3.5.5). This aspect of the myth verifies Lévi-Strauss' analysis, for in his view the failure of autochthony is that, unlike sexual union, it is *per se* sterile, non-reproductive. Homosexuality is the same, and hence it is not surprising that Laïos' problem that brings him to consult the Delphic oracle is his failure to have children, that is, his sterility.[15] Thus, had Lévi-Strauss cared to dig deeper into the tradition, he would have uncovered even further information to support his claims.

Indeed, were we to consider the entire myth, going as far back, say, as Inachos and Io, clearly the same mythical cell as that of Agenor and Europe, or collaterally tracing the stories of Kadmos' various descendants, many more items could be assigned to Lévi-Strauss' chart. Still more would be added, if all the *variants* of these related stories were considered. Of course, such a procedure entails the question of what precisely constitutes a myth. That is a moot question which will receive further attention below. But it is worth pointing out right away that there is little or no justification for selecting, as is often done, one version as the "authentic" account or for conflating discrepant variations into an internally consistent narrative. Such a technique for myth study is doomed to failure because it is the method of history, which pretends to reconstitute a unique reality that theoretically at least should have a single most accurate accounting: "was eigentlich gewesen". Myths, however, do not refer to events that happened; hence, there is no external reality against which they can be read and found in line or else wanting.[16] In fact, it is a well known contribution of Lévi-Strauss' theory that it posits the myth to be the summation of all its variations, even the most contradictory or superficially unrelated. This technique relieves us of the unwelcome burden of arbitrarily choosing a "correct" account and discarding or undervaluing the rest. In other words, it enriches rather than impoverishes our data base. In fact, what we find is that, far from being confusing contradictions, a myth's variants turn out to be transformations of each other, that is, in some important sense, the same myth. A small example, directly related to the central story of Oedipus himself, provides an instructive illustration.

Edmund Leach pointed out in his critique of Lévi-Strauss that the story of Phaidra and Hippolytos ". . .is very close to being the inverse of the Oidipous story".[17] In fact, the two stories are merely transformations of each other, that is, they are different versions of the same myth. In the Oedipus story the son unwittingly slays his father (patricide) and sleeps

[15] It is worth noting that such sterility is precisely the reason why Aegeus, scion of Athens' autochthonous line, consulted the Delphic oracle: Apoll. 3.15.6; Plut. *Thes*. 3.3.

[16] That is, myths do not mirror or reflect reality, especially unique events. In some cases inverting or denying real situations, in other rearranging their relationships, they form a *bricolage*. Cf. the remarks of Lévi-Strauss in *La Geste d'Asdiwal* (conveniently available in C. N. J. Mann's translation in *The Structural Study of Myth and Totemism*, ed. E. R. Leach (London 1967) 29-30): "The myth is certainly related to given (empirical) facts, but not as a *representation* of them. The relationship is of a dialectic kind, and the institutions described in the myths can be the very opposite of the real institutions." On this same point, cf. Detienne (note 4, above) 15 f.

[17] Leach (note 7, above) 80.

with his mother (incest). In the other, the (step-)mother fails to sleep with the son (failed incest), and upon her false accusation, the father kills his son (filicide), in both cases, wittingly. By a few transformational rules, changing the roles of father and son and of mother and son in their respective interactions, alternating the success or failure of incest and the actor's knowledge about their relations, one story can be turned into the other. Neither is in fact logically prior, that is, the main story of which the other is the variant. Both are equal, because just as Myth₁ (Oedipus) can be turned into Myth₂ (Hippolytos) by a set of rules, so Myth₂ can be turned into Myth₁, by applying an inversion of the rule set, 1/R. The theme, that of "Potiphar's Wife" (*Genesis* 39), is well known of course and has many instances in Greek mythology, e.g., the stories of Bellerophon and Sthenoboia, of Peleus and Astydameia, and so on.[18] What one might expect, of course, is that, if it is correct that these other stories are transformations of the Oedipus myth, there should possibly have been such a transformation in the tradition of the Oedipus myth itself.

And there was. A little known account exists that Oedipus remarried after the suicide of Iokaste, and that his second or third wife was Astymedousa, daughter of Sthenelos (Pherekydes *FGrHist* 3 F95).[19] The scholion A to *Il.* 4.736 (cf. also Eustath. *ad loc.*) notes the curious story:

> After Oedipus lost Iokaste he took as his next wife Astymedousa who falsely accused his children of trying to rape her. Enraged, he placed a curse on them to receive the land as a bloody inheritance (*di' haimatos paralabein tên chôran*).

This account has a structure identical to the story of Hippolytos and Phaidra, including the father's curse that insures his sons' deaths. What is significant about this tradition is that Lévi-Strauss' theory of the transformationality of myths *predicts* its possible existence. It is just this power of prediction, that Laïos ought somehow to be marked as autochthonous, or that the central mythical cell of the Oedipus story should exist in such a transformation, that makes Lévi-Strauss' particular claims for this myth and his more general method of analysis worthy of being taken seriously.

Our investigation so far brings us logically to a consideration of another of Dee's criticisms, that Lévi-Strauss assigns arbitrary meanings to the mythemes he selects:

> . . .Lévi-Strauss' assertion that the two great monster-slayings represent a denial of autochthony is merely arbitrary. Greek mythology is after all full of monster-killings. The dragon. . .has at least the

---

[18] Bellerophon: *Il.* 6.155-195; Apoll. 2.3.2; Hyg. *Fab.* 67; *Astr.* 2.18. Peleus: Apoll. 3.13.3; Pind. *Nem.* 4.57-64 (cf. schol. ad loc.) and 5.26-32; schol. Arist. *Nub.* 1063; schol. Apoll. Rhod. *Arg.* 1.224. Cf. also the story of Phoinix: Apoll. 2.13.8; *Il.* 9.437-84; schol. ad *Il.* 9.448; schol. Plato *Legg.* 931B. For a convenient (though popularizing) collection in English translation of parallel tales from around the world and especially the ancient Near East see J. D. Yohannan, *Joseph and Potiphar's Wife in World Literature* (New York 1968), esp. 305-08 (for a bibliography for the ancient world).

[19] Cf. Paus. 9.5.11; Peisandros *FGrHist* 16 F10.

virtue of being chthonic in nature, but the Sphinx has no obvious connections with autochthony or its denial. (259)

It is hard to understand just why Dee believes this assignment is arbitrary. Surely, he can't think that autochthony (or its denial) is unimportant in Greek mythology, regardless of what method we use to analyze the myths. Just to examine the myths of Attika turns up a large brood of autochthons: Erechtheus, Erichthonios, Kekrops, Amphiktyon, and Kranaos. Not only are some of these names clearly derived from *chthôn* (earth), they are actually equivalent in meaning to *autochthôn*. As Nilsson pointed out long ago, Erechtheus and Erichthonios are probably doublets of each other, their names deriving from *eri* (an intensifier) and *chthôn*.[20] What's more, a number of Attic autochthons are specifically depicted as half-serpent or related to snakes in some important way.[21] They are all literally born from the earth, some sprouting like vegetables. Erichthonios was such a product (Paus. 1.2.6; 1.14.6; Harp. s.v. *autochthones*). Indeed, Ion asked of Kreousa (still ignorant of his identity) in Euripides' play of that name, "Did your father's father and ancestor spring from the earth?"; the verb used is *eblasten* (267), the word properly used of plants (*LSJ*, s.v. *blastanô*). Kreousa's reply is also worth considering:

Kr.: Yes, Erichthonios. . .
Ion: And did Athena in fact receive him from the earth?
Kr.: Into her virgin hands (*parthenous ge cheiras*), although she did not give him birth. (268-270)

This exchange refers to the myth in which Hephaistos attempted to rape Athena, but failed, so that he managed to ejaculate only on her leg. Thereupon she wiped the semen off and threw the rag on the ground, from which Erichthonios was instantaneously born (Apoll. 3.14.6; cf. the variant in Amelesagoras *FGr Hist* 330 F1). It is worth noting that the myth emphasizes three points: 1) *coitus interruptus*, or the *failure* of sexual reproduction; 2) Athena's virginity; and 3) Erichthonios' birth from the soil.[22] Such a mythical cell happens to fit Lévi-Strauss' interpretative dichotomy between sexual reproduction and vegetal growth, between blood kinship and autochthony: where the failure of intercourse is reinforced by Athena's virginity, an insistent virginity that thwarts sexu-

[20] M. P. Nilsson, *The Mycenaean Origin of Greek Mythology* (Berkeley and Los Angeles 1932) 162.
[21] For Kekrops, see note 12, above. In some myths Erichthonios is part snake: schol. Plato *Tim.* 23D; *Et. Mag.* 371, s.v. *Erechtheus*; Serv. ad Virg. *Georg.* 3.113; Hyg. *Fab.* 166; *Astron.* 2.13; in others, fully a snake: Hyg. *Astron.* 2.13; Tertull. *Spect.* 9; Phil. *Apoll.* 7.24; Paus. 1.24.7. His birth is connected with snakes: Amelesagoras *FGrHist* 330 F1; Apoll. 3.14.6; Eur. *Ion* 20 ff., 267-274, 1426 ff.; Paus. 1.18.2; Hyg. *Fab.* 166; *Astron.* 2.13; Fulg. 2.14; Lact. *Div. Instit.* 1.17. Further on Erichthonios's autochthony, cf. Eur. *Ion* 737, 999-1000, 1466. Kranaos is also described as an autochthon: Apoll. 3.14.5.
[22] In this interpretation of the myth's significance (the *failure* of autochthony) I differ from Peradotto (note 8, above), esp. 93-95, who has claimed Erichthonios *mediates* "the old autochthony contradiction" by being both autochthonous and the result of bisexual reproduction. My detailed reasons for this disagreement will appear in a subsequent study.

al contact and results in autochthonous creation, for here quite literally Hephaistos' seed is cast upon the earth (metaphorically expressed in other myths by the dragon's teeth of Kadmos or Kekrops' and Deukalion and Pyrrha's stones). Given evidence like this, whatever we are to say of autochthony's significance in Greek mythology, it is hardly a notion imposed from outside the culture. Indeed, in classical Athens the claim to autochthonous origins for the Athenian people was widespread.[23]

The Thebans, of course, are autochthons too. Not only did the ancients explicitly say so (e.g., Hellanikos *FGrHist* 323a F27 = Harp. s.v. *autochthones*), but their myths assert it. Echion and Chthonios, two of the Spartoi who grew from the dragon's teeth Kadmos sowed in the earth, are each progenitors of the ruling line of Thebes. Both are ancestors of Oedipus. Specifically, to be sure, Dee directs his objections to the putative autochthony of the Sphinx and the dragon son of Ares. As he grants that dragons are chthonic, and since snakes are integral features of autochthony myths in ancient Greece, nothing further need be said here. But about the Sphinx Dee is flatly wrong: she is explicitly connected with autochthony. In some versions of the myth the Sphinx is the half-human (virgin) and half-animal offspring of Echidna and Orthos or Typhon (Apoll. 3.5.8; Hes. *Theog.* 326-329). Echidna herself was a monster, half-virgin and half-snake (Hes. *Theog.*, ibid.), the progeny of Earth (*Gê*) and Tartaros. So too is the Sphinx sometimes described as half-virgin and half-snake, e.g., Peisander *FGrHist* 16 F10.2: *tên ouran echousan drakainês*. She is likewise so depicted in certain ancient artwork.[24] More specifically, Euripides describes her as chthonic, as born from the earth, in his *Phoinissai*:

> You came, you came,
> O winged thing, earth's offspring (*gas locheuma*),
> Child of Echidna of the underworld,
> Seizer of Kadmeians. (1018-1021)

> Would that that winged virgin, mountain monster, had not come,
> Earth's misfortune,
> With Sphinx's most unmusical music. . .
> Offspring that Hades from beneath the earth
> Sends against Kadmeians. (806-811)

In this connection, the Sphinx's virginity that is so often emphasized is worth a comment: as in the case of Erichthonios and Athena, here virginity denies sexual reproduction and hence is a characteristic of

---

[23] The *loci* are too numerous to mention here in entirety. See for instance, Hdt. 7.161; Th. 2.36.1; Dem. 60.8; Hyp. 6.7; Arist. *Lysis.* 1082; *Agri.* F 110K; Eur. *Herakl.* 69, 826-827; Lykourg. *in Leoc.* (=Plut. *Mor.* 60D-E); Eur. *Ion* 29, 589 ff.; Arist. *Vesp.* 1076; Th. 1.2.5; Lys. 2.17; Plato, *Menex.* 237B; Isok. *de Pace* 49; *Paneg.* 24, 63; *Panath.* 124-125. See also E. Ermatinger, *Die attische Autochthonensage bis auf Euripides* (diss. Zürich/Berlin 1897); O. Schroeder, *De laudibus Athenarum a poetis tragicis et ab oratoribus epidicticis excultis* (diss. Göttingen 1914) 5-9.

[24] W. H. Roscher, *Ausfürliches Lexicon der griechischen und römischen Mythologie*, repr. (Hildesheim 1965) 4.1365.

autochthony. Finally, there is much in the tradition to ascribe auto-chthony to the Sphinx, and Lévi-Strauss' ascription is hardly arbi-trary: it can be verified by concrete texts. As in the earlier cases we con-sidered, such philological verification points to the theory's predictive power. While Lévi-Strauss may not have known of these particular texts, the interpretative paradigm he has placed over the myth both forecasts and locates the Sphinx's autochthony, anticipating the confirming data of philology.

Dee's third major criticism is in essence an attack on the paradigmatic method, based upon the *a priori* assumption that myths as stories convey their meaning linearly or syntagmatically: "Recognition of the nexus of *act* and *consequences* is essential in judging the attitudes which are to be found in and through Greek mythology." [25] Such a position is not so na-ive as it might at first appear. In fact, it is implicitly compounded with three other (unexpressed but operative) critical stances of dubious validi-ty: 1) identification of a myth with the text or texts that convey it; 2) privileging of certain texts containing the myth based on their literariness or their authors' reputations; 3) psychologism or the mimetic fallacy, that the characters of a myth are personalities with hopes, fears, motiva-tions, and intentions. While these assumptions still enjoy great populari-ty in classical scholarship, they are not verities inherent in literature itself but are rather constituents of a literary-critical model for interpreting texts. As many critics inveigh against Lévi-Strauss' method as "artifi-cial" and "contrived", it is worth pointing out that there is no such thing as a naive or natural reading of a text or myth: the meaning these are seen to convey depends ultimately on the critical assumptions, many of them covert or unexpressed, which the reader brings with him.

As noted earlier, a decided methodological advantage of Lévi-Strauss' treatment of mythology is that it provides a means for dealing with a great multiplicity of contradictory variants of the same myth. Tradi-tionally, classicists have employed one of two methods when confronted with the inevitable proliferation of mythical variants: either to privilege one text (or a related group of texts) as the "correct" or true version of the myth from which all others fall away, or else to conflate all the varia-tions, banishing those details or aspects which would contradict the re-constructed exemplar. Both of these techniques are essentially those of history. Every modern history of ancient Greece, for instance, is a con-flation, the careful selection and arrangement into a seamless narrative from an anarchic universe of contradictory sources. Usually, too, for given periods, one ancient historian by virtue of his *auctoritas* is privileged, seen as providing the true account against which all other in-formation must be sceptically weighed. Yet the dangers of this approach occasionally—and acutely—come to light. In a well known case, Thucy-dides reports the Athenians put two generals, Glaukon Leagrou and Andokides Leogorou, in charge of the squadron of ships sent to Kerkyra in 433 B.C. (1.51.4). But an inscription of the squadron's expenses men-

25 Dee (note 2, above) 261.

tions three commanders, Glaukon, Metagenes, and Drakonti[des] (*IG* 1²
295 = Meiggs & Lewis 61). This embarrassing contradiction of a historian who has been accorded virtual infallibility has provoked a blizzard of
explanations, a daggered text, and textual emendations, all designed to
rescue Thucydides from the possibility of having been just plain wrong.[26]
Of course, with history there is a rationale for this method: history is
referential. Ultimately, it is supposed to refer to actual people, things,
and events. But such a method cannot possibly apply to myth for the
simple reason that the people, things, and events in a myth never existed
or occurred. With such a criterion lacking, there is no epistemological
justification for making one version of a myth more canonical than
another. Notwithstanding, this is the approach of many classicists. G. S.
Kirk, for instance, ruefully notes that the great writers of classical Greece
almost always dealt with one small aspect of a myth, while it was the
"prosaic" encyclopedists of the Greco-Roman era who preserved myths
in the greatest extent. Yet he is not deterred from privileging the accounts
of Homer, Pindar, or Sophokles for their "charm" and resorting to the
mythographers only when necessary.[27] In such a treatment there is a
fundamental misunderstanding of the difference between a myth and the
various texts that instantiate it, the very difference between *langue* and
parole that Lévi-Strauss borrowed from Saussure and was so careful to
note as crucial in myth study.[28] Just as language has an identity separate
from specific speech acts or written texts and can and must be analyzed
as such, so too with myth. Presumably, no scholar would make the mistake of treating the Greek of a Sophoklean play as the Greek language itself or of turning the Greek in that text into the model against which all
other texts should be found in conformity or else wanting. Neither
should we do the same with a myth that appears in such a text. If that is
so, then even the lowliest scholion, the most turgid handbook account,
or the obscurest reference in an Atticist lexicon assumes equal importance with the most sublime literary sources as a vehicle in the transmission of a myth.

Indeed, that the myth itself is something quite distinct from the versions that instantiate it becomes quite clear from our sources. Thus, to
cite just a couple of examples, different reasons are alleged for the curse
Oedipus laid on his sons Eteokles and Polyneikes, and different accounts
exist of Oedipus' fate after his incest was discovered. In the case of Oedipus' curse, there is a version that his sons earned their father's wrath
when they refused to help him when he was being forced into exile
(Apoll. 3.5.9); another that their step-mother Astymedousa falsely ac-

[26] For a discussion of the problem and the scholarship cf. A. W. Gomme, *Historical
Commentary on Thucydides* (Oxford 1956) 1.188-90; and F. Jacoby, comm. to Hellanikos
FGrHist 323a F24.

[27] G. S. Kirk (note 4, above), *Nature. . .*14-15; and *Myth and Its Meaning. . .*where he
ridicules the principle that 'a myth is made up of its variants' as "quite fantastic." Yet Kirk
offers no solution to the very serious problem his rejection of this principle poses: what are
we to do with all these variants?

[28] Lévi-Strauss (note 1, above) 84-85. A useful explanation of these concepts and their
implications is provided by J. Culler, *Structuralist Poetics* (Ithaca 1975) 8-16.

cused them of rape (schol. A *Il.* 4.376; Eustath. ad loc.); another, that they had given their father the wrong portion of a sacrificial animal (schol. Soph. *OC* 1375; Zen. *Cent.* 5.43, citing the *Thebaid*); yet another, that they set the royal silver before him against his express wishes (Athen. 465E = 11.14); finally, that they had imprisoned him (Eur. *Phoin.* 66). The same proliferation of versions is apparent for Oedipus' fate. Some relate, as we've just seen, that he was imprisoned or forced into exile by his sons. Sophokles's *Oedipus at Colonus* has it that it was Kreon who forced Oedipus into exile. Homer apparently knew of none of these outcomes, and in the *Iliad* (23.678-680) and the *Odyssey* (11.271-280) Oedipus continued to rule in Thebes. What is to be made of such variations? In such cases, the causal nexus, as Dee puts it, becomes confounded: the supposed intentionality of the actor shifts. What is the consequence of a certain act, if the consequences keep changing with different versions of the myth? What is in Oedipus' mind, if the causes of his curse constantly change along with our sources? Under such circumstances, it becomes impossible to set up a sequence of events for a myth whose meaning is ruled by the notion of cause and effect, because the causes keep changing as do the effects.

In place of such a narrative analysis, whose major principle can be little more than *post hoc ergo propter hoc*, and which constantly breaks down before the kaleidoscopic profusion of mythical variants, Lévi-Strauss has substituted paradigmatic analysis. In this view, as is well known, the myth conveys its various messages not through narrative but through the semantic oppositions of its component mythemes. Now it is certainly debatable whether the number of such categories Lévi-Strauss has selected is adequate to the myth's complexity, or whether his simple homology tells us all a myth has to say:

> The inability to connect two kinds of relationships is overcome (or rather replaced) by the positive statement that contradictory relationships are identical inasmuch as they are both self-contradictory in a similar way.[29]

But it is no just criticism of this procedure to describe it as "abstract [ing] parts of narratives and treat[ing] them as if they conveyed meaning independently of their context," as Dee does.[30] For in Lévi-Strauss' paradigmatic reading of a myth, its component parts *only* have meaning in terms of their logical relations with each other. In such a reading, context is all, both the logical context of the myth's structure and the cultural context from which it comes.

---

[29] Lévi-Strauss (note 1, above) 91. This homological function has come under criticism from a variety of directions. Cf. Culler (note 28, above) 42-43; A. J. Greimas, "The Interpretation of Myth: Theory and Practice," in *Structural Analysis of Oral Tradition*, ed. P. Maranda and E. K. Maranda (Philadelphia 1971) 81-121; F. Jameson, *Prison House of Language* (Princeton 1972) 113-20; J. J. Lizka, "Elements of a Semiotic Theory of Myth," presented orally at the Semiotics Society of America meeting, Nashville, October 1981.

[30] Dee (note 2, above) 260.

Perhaps what Dee objects to is Lévi-Strauss' identification of auto-chthony and kinship relations as the main semantic categories of the Oedipus myth. The question then becomes, on what basis can Lévi-Strauss justify his selection of these categories or claim to see them correctly represented in the myth? Autochthony has already been discussed in some detail. That discussion, which is in fact brief, given the bulk and clear cultural importance of the data that still survive, should make obvious that autochthony was a topic of great concern to the Greeks, appearing extensively in their mythology. As regards bisexual reproduction, one need only peruse the *Bibliotheka* of Apollodoros, or any other mythological source, to see the astounding emphasis put upon sexual relations in Greek mythology. The same may be said for kinship relations: there is a clear fascination with genealogy, with marriage alliance and descent.[31] Indeed, one could well say that such concerns not only permeate Greek mythology, they dominate it: they constitute its conceptual frame and its mode of explication. Indeed, the very fact that from our mythographic sources we can construct the most elaborate and exquisitely detailed genealogies for beings who never lived, for lineages that never existed, should be ample indication that marriage, kinship, and descent were of supreme importance in Greek mythology. No culture invests such energy in the construction of fabulous genealogies, if these are not somehow intrinsic expressions of that culture's deepest concerns. Proof of such intense interest in mythical genealogy, if proof be needed, is provided not only by the Greco-Roman encyclopedists, but also, *inter alia*, by the fragments of the fourteen authors from the fifth and fourth centuries B.C. whom Jacoby has collected in *FGrHist* 1-14. Surely, then, it is no will-o'-the-wisp to posit kinship as a principal issue of Greek mythology in general, and of the Oedipus myth in particular. In sum, kinship relations are not arbitrarily imposed as categories upon the myth without regard for context, as Dee charges.

To be sure, what is unusual about Lévi-Strauss' handling of this material is that he does not give it a syntagmatic analysis, that is, does not interpret it according to the rules of historical narrative by seeing significance in "the act and its consequences." In this regard, his paradigmatic analysis seems to violate the myth's surface structure. For what gives form to these myths is genealogy. It provides not only the framework of the narrative but also brings with it the implicit code of history, differentiating 'before' from 'after', postulating 'cause' and 'effect', accounting for succession, and providing a continuum along which to plot change and development. But the reason that a linear, historical, or "cause and effect" reading of such myths will not work is that the frame that gives them structure is after all *pseudo*-genealogy: there were no real causes, nor any real effects. Therefore, it is no wonder that myths show such a profusion of contradictory variants. What is constant about the myths, on the other hand, are their repetitions, their similarities, their redundancies. For explaining them the paradigmatic method is very useful. It provides a technique and a rationale for comparing those similari-

---

[31] As Peradotto (note 8, above) 88-89 has also observed.

ties or their oppositions in order to uncover the myth's message. It is striking and somewhat puzzling that this aspect of Lévi-Strauss' myth analysis has caused such criticism, since it is not unlike the procedure of very traditional thematic studies.

In particular, the paradigmatic method is useful for dealing with the totality of a myth's variants or its seemingly bizarre details that on the surface appear to have little to do with the myth's more obvious story. What are we to make after all of the Delphic oracle's injunction to Kadmos to stop seeking his errant sister Europe, to follow a cow instead, slay it when it stops and found a city on that spot?[32] What are we to make of Kadmos' slaying of the snake that guarded the spring of Ares, or of his transformation into a snake?[33] To call these fabulous embroideries explains nothing. The question is after all, what do they mean? More specifically, why cows and snakes? A syntagmatic reading does not tell us much. But if these mythemes are looked at as paradigms in a larger context, they gain in significance. As Leach pointed out long ago, the errant cow may signify the errant daughter, the daughter who leaves her agnatic family. And hence it is an instance of the undervaluing of blood relations, or, conversely, an instance of the overvaluing of affine relations.[34] Accordingly, in such an analysis the wandering Europe is a paradigm of the wandering Io (who indeed is metamorphosed into a cow), so that these two genealogically distant 'events' in the myth are to be related, while Kadmos' slaying of the errant cow substituted for Europe itself becomes categorized as the undervaluing of blood relations. Furthermore, this explanation makes some sense of the apparent absurdity in the related myth of Amphitryon's winning of Alkmene. Alkmene refuses marriage with Amphitryon until he recovers for her father the cows stolen by the Taphians. These Amphitryon regains by seducing Komaitho, daughter of the Taphian king Pterelaos, who makes her father vulnerable by cutting the single hair on his head: Komaitho's betrayal of her father is, upon such an analysis, the undervaluing of her blood ties and the overvaluing of a relationship with another man. This mythical cell is no more than paradigmatically repeated when Amphitryon slays Elektryon, his bride-to-be's father, by hitting him with a club he threw at a runaway cow from the herd of recovered cattle he was bringing back from the Taphians.[35] This otherwise silly and seemingly gratuitous murder now gains significance within a larger framework. A similar

[32] Apoll. 3.4.1; Paus. 9.12.1; 9.19.4; schol. Eur. *Phoen.* 638; schol. Aisch. *Sept.* 486; schol. *Il.* 2.494; Hyg. *Fab.* 178; Plut. *Sulla* 17.5; Nonn. *Dion.* 4.299; *Et. Mag.* s.v. *Mykalessos*; Hellanikos *FGrHist* 4 F51.

[33] Apoll. 3.4.1; Eur. *Phoen.* 930 ff.; Paus. 9.10.5; schol. Soph. *Ant.* 126. Kadmos's transformation: Eur. *Bacch.* 1530 f.; Apoll. Rhod. *Argon.* 4.516 ff.; Dion. Perieg. *Orb. Descrip.* 390 ff.; Eustath. ad 391; Strabo 1.2.39; 7.7.8; Paus. 9.5.3; Athen. 462B; Steph. Byz. s.v. *Dyrrachion*; Hyg. *Fab.* 6. Nonnos said that Kadmos and Harmonia were turned into *stone* serpents (*Dionys.* 14.126-129; 16.367-369), a double indication of autochthony; this account is related to that of the rocks of Kadmos and Harmonia (Dion. Perieg. *Orb. Descrip.* 390; Skylax *Periplus* 24).

[34] Leach (note 7, above) 77.

[35] Apoll. 2.4.5-6; Tzetzes *Lyc.* 932; schol. *Il.* 14.323; Hes. *Scut.* 11-45, 79-82; Paus. 9.11.1.

analysis can be employed for the herpetic Kadmos. Like Oedipus, Kadmos both instantiates and denies autochthony. It is a key feature of this paradigmatic method that it collapses the apparent history or time-extension of myth to a synchronous moment. Thus, it is not a problem, as it must be upon a syntagmatic reading, that Io and Europe are separated by five generations, or that chronologically Kadmos' slaying of the dragon is considerably prior to his metamorphosis. In a paradigmatic reading, time contracts to a single instant, and its events are to be read simultaneously. It is effectively the same simultaneity that variants of a mytheme or a mythical cell show. For example, the five distinct accounts of Oedipus's curse upon his sons can be overlaid and seen as conveying the same message: the undervaluation of kinship (above, pp. 347-48).

The basic goal of this paper has been to defend the integrity of Lévi-Strauss' treatment of myth as a method. It cannot be dismissed as Johnson did with Berkeley's idealism by kicking a boulder, stubbing his toe, and crying out, "I refute it *thus.*" What makes Lévi-Strauss' analysis of the Oedipus myth important and worthy of serious inquiry is ultimately its utility, that it provides a means to deal economically with the multifarious versions of the myth, with its surface contradictions, with its otherwise trivial and inexplicable, but naggingly insistent, details. What makes it viable is its power to explain rationally and systematically these aspects of myth that are so often ignored. What lends it credibility, finally, is its power to predict, to alert us to the possible survival of confirming data and to tell us where and how to search for that data. In this task philology can become the partner of structuralism and need no longer be its foe.

Wayne State University   K. R. WALTERS
CW 77.6 (1984)

THE HEAD AND THE LOINS:
LÉVI-STRAUSS AND BEYOND

R. G. WILLIS

University of Edinburgh

This article examines, in a central African context, the relation between myth and social organisation. This is a question which has been raised implicitly but acutely by the recent work of Lévi-Strauss (1964). The development of the analytical exposition of Amerindian mythology in *Le cru et le cuit* strongly suggests that the structural solidity for the analyst of mythological thought varies inversely with its distance from ethnographical reality: the more remote its connexion with observable social facts, the more substantial it can be shown to be, and vice versa. By contrast, this article attempts to show how the analysis of mythological thought, which is intrinsically paradoxical and elusive, *can* be accommodated within the normal parameters of social anthropological investigation. The subject is a myth collected among the Fipa of south-west Tanzania.

Myth and myth-makers

The Fipa are a Bantu people fairly distantly related linguistically to the Bemba. They inhabit a high, rolling and largely treeless plateau near the south end of Lake Tanganyika, which forms the western boundary of their country; another lake, Rukwa, marks the easterly limit of Fipa territory. The people live in compact village settlements and numbered 86,462 at the last census in 1957. In the middle of the Fipa plateau there is a mountain called Itweelele which is the centre of a small kingdom (or chiefdom) about four miles in diameter called Milansi; this tiny kingdom is supposed to be the oldest and original source of authority in Ufipa (the name given to the land of the Fipa). Traditionally Ufipa was further divided into two kingdoms ruled by rival but related dynasties called Twa; these two kingdoms, Nkansi and Lyangalile, are supposed to have been one in the earliest days. The origin of Twa power and its relation to the aboriginal kingdom of Milansi form the subject of the myth to be considered.

The story appears several times in early writings of the colonial period about the Fipa—an indication of its central importance as an embodiment of the Fipa sense of their own identity. I collected a number of different versions of this key myth, some of the variations in which corresponded to the differing, and sometimes opposed, political interests of focal groups in Fipa society (Willis 1964); all versions, however, possessed the same common structure, which is typified in the following (translated) text which I collected in 1964 from an illiterate old man:

> There were once three sisters who came from a far country in search of somewhere to settle. They reached Ufipa from the east and went round the western part of the country. After walking for a long time they at length reached a hillock and they said to themselves, 'Let us rest here'. One of the women sat down on a rock, another on the ground and a third was holding a red fruit called *isuku*. The one who was holding the fruit *isuku* became known

315

as the Child of Isuku, the one who was sitting on the ground was called Earth-Person and the one who sat on the rock as the Child of the Stone.

Meanwhile the king of Milansi said one day to his wife: 'Something is going to happen to us before long. If certain strange people come here be sure not to give them my royal stool, even if they say, "Give it to us". If you do they will take away our kingdom.'

Soon afterwards he went into the wilderness to hunt, spending the night out there. The three women meanwhile had arrived at the place called Kanda,[1] where even today you can see their footprints. Not long afterwards they arrived at Itweelele mountain, the home of the king of the Fipa. There they were met by the queen, his wife, and they said to her, 'Give us stools so that we may sit down.'

The queen took out one stool and the leader of the three women passed it on to her younger sister; she then produced another and the leader passed it on to her elder sister, saying, 'I don't want that one but the king's own stool: bring it to me.'

The queen refused. Then the strange woman entered the hut herself and finally overbore the queen so that she was obliged to surrender the royal stool. Taking it, the stranger said, 'This country is mine: may the people live long.' Then the three sisters sat down.

Meanwhile the king, where he was in the wilderness, heard a buzzing noise in his ears and knew it meant that the long-awaited strangers had arrived. Straight away he returned to the royal village, and when he reached it he met the three sisters. They greeted one another with all courtesy, then the king went inside his hut with his wife.

'O wife, what did I tell you?' he said. 'Did I not warn you against giving my royal stool to the strangers? Now they have taken the kingdom from us.'

Next morning the three regal sisters said to the king, 'Let us go to the top of the mountain, so that you may show us the limits of your domain.' Now it happened that the king had allowed his under-arm hair to grow very long, and, when they reached the summit, he felt ashamed of exhibiting it to the three women. So he kept his arm low, and said, 'My country ends just there.'

'Why, his country extends only as far as the mountain!' the three women said, and their leader stood erect and pointed, saying, 'My rule extends from Lake Tanganyika in the west to Lake Rukwa in the east; and from Unyamwanga in the south to Lyamfipa [an escarpment at the northern end of the Fipa plateau] in the north!'

So it was that the rule of the Twa began in Ufipa; and the king of Milansi remained as priest of Itweelele, the sacred mountain.

This is a moving and a tragic tale. Considered purely as a story, as entertainment (which is why Fipa like to tell and hear it) it is effective for much the same reasons that *Hamlet* and *Cinderella* are effective as stories: because its form is psychologically arresting and satisfying. In the Fipa myth an initial situation of conflict is brought to a climax (and note how artfully the tension is prolonged and heightened during the episode with the stools); the inevitable moment of triumph and tragedy occurs when the strange and majestic woman asserts her claim to sovereignty over the country of Fipa, in a way that (as we know already) must compel acceptance by the established king: she performs the symbolic act of sitting on the royal stool of Milansi.

So the Twaci (the feminine form of Twa) have conquered. What happens now? Here the story surprises us with an unexpected 'twist': the king returns, sees and knows he has lost, in spite of all his efforts to avoid such a consummation—and he accepts his fate with calm and dignity, royally in fact.[2] In his defeat, the king establishes his *moral superiority* over the aggressive intruders, a superiority which is given formal recognition later in the Twa acceptance of the permanent rule of the king and his line over Milansi and the sacred mountain of Itweelele, and his perpetual priesthood. This surprising development recreates, on another and higher plane, the initial situation of opposition and tension between Milansi and Twa.

316

The final episode, the ascent of the mountain and the demarcation of the two, territorially unequal, kingdoms of Milansi and the Twa, introduces a new affective element into the story—that of comedy: like us, Fipa find the incident of the under-arm hair amusing. In this episode too, the king gives further evidence of his social self-control: his sense of shame (*insoni*) over his inappropriate growth of hair leads him to sacrifice a claim he might still have made to a wider territorial sovereignty, for the story implies that Milansi's domain originally embraced the whole country. The final irony is that the king himself, by his own action, effectively cedes the land of Fipa to the strangers, at the same time as he, seemingly, makes a claim to the central core of his old kingdom—a claim which is almost contemptuously granted by the Twaci women, interested as they are in real power.

In thus summarising and interpreting the story, we have encountered its most obvious structural characteristic, one which it shares with most, if not all, members of the genus 'story': an initial situation, in which two basic elements or factors are brought into relation, unfolds, as it were in spiral form, through successive stages of crisis, partial resolution, renewed crisis, and final reformulation. The con-cluding resolution contains latent ambiguities (Did the king really mean to give away the country or does it still belong to him? Did the Twaci recognition of Milansi's authority over the sacred mountain mean that the Twa think of the king of Milansi as their superior? Or is Milansi really Twa territory and the king there as a political dependant? etc.) which gives the effect of continuing the dialectical 'spiral' indefinitely, and accounts for the story's 'timeless' quality.

Obviously too, the existence of contradictions which the narrative appears to resolve but succeeds only in transforming into new and latent contradictions, relates to the function of the story as what Malinowski (1948: 120) called a 'socio-logical charter'—a retrospective justification and validation for an existing and rather complex social order, in which there is inherent and fundamental inner conflict.

This article is principally concerned to reveal and analyse the configuration of opposed, complementary and associated ideas and values which Fipa see as con-tained in the basic situation of the sovereignty myth: the relation of Milansi and Twa. Through what I call its 'conceptual-affective structure', itself formed from the basic 'bricks' of mythological thought—sets of binary discriminations—the myth, I shall argue, both reflects and maintains the formal similarity of two apparently disparate dimensions of Fipa society: sovereignty and descent.

To begin with, let us return to the manifest subject of the myth, the kingdoms of Milansi and the Twa. These two foci of Fipa concepts and values are linked in a relation of complementary opposition which inheres in the fact that they represent two qualitatively different and incommensurate kinds of sovereignty (ritual and political, respectively); that nevertheless they are interdependent (the Twa derive their legitimacy, their right to rule, from Milansi; Milansi in turn depends upon Twa power, on the ability of the Twa administrative-military apparatus to main-tain Ufipa as a political entity); and that both terms, Milansi and Twa, have attributes implying superiority *and* inferiority vis-à-vis the other: Milansi is the ritual superior of the Twa, but its political and territorial inferior; Milansi is the senior kingdom, but strength, in the form of organised coercive force, is all on the side of the Twa.

The more important concepts associated with the Milansi-Twa relation, and their differential value-loading, are summarised in the following diagram, in which a double-headed arrow represents a relation of complementary opposition and 'plus' and 'minus' signs represent relative values:

$$
\begin{aligned}
\text{MILANSI} &\longleftrightarrow \text{TWA} \\
\text{Ritual authority } (+) &\longleftrightarrow \text{Ritual dependency } (-) \\
\text{Political dependency } (-) &\longleftrightarrow \text{Political supremacy } (+) \\
\text{Seniority } (+) &\longleftrightarrow \text{Juniority } (-) \\
\text{Lack of power } (-) &\longleftrightarrow \text{Possession of power } (+)
\end{aligned}
$$

More abstractly, the opposition and combination of differentially-valued concepts in the Milansi-Twa relation could be represented as follows:

$$
\left\{
\begin{array}{l}
+ \longleftrightarrow - \\
- \longleftrightarrow +
\end{array}
\right\}
$$

These conceptual oppositions are entirely explicit in the minds of all Fipa who concern themselves with such matters. Thus the reigning king of Nkansi, the northern and larger of the two Twa 'states', said to me of the king of Milansi, 'He is our priest'. At the same time he objected to my referring to the latter personage by the title 'Mwcene', implying political sovereignty, and said he should be called ¡WakuMilansi, 'the one of Milansi', on the model of titles given to subordinate administrators in the Twa kingdoms. For his part, the present king of Milansi, Catakwa Mauto, told me that the whole of Ufipa was 'his' country, and the Twa ultimately derived their authority from him.

Descent: 'head' and 'loins'

If we now turn from the Fipa conceptual scheme of sovereignty to another social dimension, that of descent,[3] we encounter a further system of ideas. It will be argued that there is a formal similarity amounting to structural congruence between this idea-system and that associated with sovereignty.

Fipa conceptualise descent, experienced as a complex of consanguineal, marital and affinal relations, in terms of two composite symbols: 'head' (*unntwe*) and 'loins' (*unnsana*). At the most abstract level, 'head' stands for the organising and controlling function or aspect of the most inclusive Fipa descent group or category, the *uluko*, with its elected chief, the *umweenekasi*, and its network of reciprocal rights and duties binding members together; the symbol 'head' evokes the *uluko* as a formal and continuing entity.[4] The symbol 'loins', at a similarly abstract level, evokes for Fipa the *uluko* in its regenerative and developmental capacities and functions: the descent group as a changing entity, in reciprocal relationship, through exchange of women and bridewealth, with the world outside it.

Less abstractly, 'head' is associated with masculinity or maleness, patrilineality, paternity, intellect and authority and 'loins' with femininity or femaleness, matrilineality, maternity, sexuality and reproduction. In terms of social categories, and consistently with these abstract associations, 'head' denotes patrilateral relatives and 'loins' denotes matrilateral relatives; these are ego-centred categories.[5]

At the most concrete level, the two symbols refer, as the English terms used to translate them imply, to distinct and separate regions or parts of the human body.

The literal meaning of *unntwe* is 'head', in the physiological sense; but although I translate *unnsana* as 'loins', this is not an exact equivalent. Physiologically *unnsana* refers to the lower abdomen and lower back in both men and women; it adjoins, though it does not include, the genital regions in both sexes. Even so the word *unnsana* has marked sexual associations for Fipa, probably because complete control of the muscles of this region is considered a prerequisite of erotic maturity; it is the object of a style of ventral dancing called *imiteete*, which is taught to pubescent girls and which boys imitate, to facilitate such control.[6]

'Head' and 'loins' then are foci for sets of ideas from markedly different areas and levels of experience within the world of Fipa descent: they are what Turner calls 'dominant symbols' (1964: 35, 50).

But not only do these two symbols separately focus and englobe clusters of ideas, but these ideas are themselves polarised in oppositional pairs analogously to the relation of complementary opposition between the 'dominant' or 'key' symbols, 'head' and 'loins'. Some of these concepts have already been mentioned. They include, for example, 'maleness' ('head'), which is opposed to 'femaleness' ('loins'), 'intellect' ('head') opposed to 'sexuality' ('loins') and 'authority' ('head') opposed to 'reproduction' ('loins'); from the latter opposition (authority versus reproduction) is derived that between 'seniority' ('head') and 'juniority' ('loins'). To the first terms in all these pairs Fipa give a relatively higher value, so that this cluster of concepts can be represented in the following way:

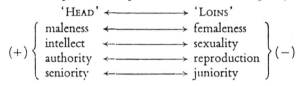

But this is far from being the whole story. In another cluster of polarised concepts associated respectively with 'head' and 'loins' the relative value-loading is reversed. For, as Fipa see it, 'weight', 'numbers', 'strength' and 'fellowship' are associated with *unnsana*, 'loins'; and 'lightness', 'fewness', 'weakness' and 'constraint' are the corresponding attributes of *unntwe*, 'head'. A well known Fipa proverb says, 'The loins are heavy, the head is light' (*Uk'unnsana kwanwama, uk'unntwe kwapepela*): it is the women who come into the descent group, the *unnsana* side, Fipa say, who make the *uluko* strong. Another proverb contrasts the 'meat' associated with 'loins' with its entire lack on the 'head' side: in the huts of his mother and her siblings a man can expect food and friendship while the father and his siblings are supposed to be far less forthcoming.[7] To the father's sister (*imaangu seenje*) is attributed a power of lethal cursing over her brother's children.

We thus have a further cluster of conceptual pairs associated with the dominant symbols 'head' and 'loins' and which is relatively valued in the opposite sense from the first cluster:

The complementary opposition of the dominant symbols 'head' and 'loins' is thus characterised by a contrary valuation of some of the most important pairs of subordinate and associated concepts. From our consideration of the meaning for Fipa of the descent-based symbolism of 'head' and 'loins' there thus emerges a picture of a conceptual-affective structure which could be most abstractly represented as follows:

$$\left\{ \begin{array}{l} + \longleftrightarrow - \\ - \longleftrightarrow + \end{array} \right\}$$

This is the same representation as that derived from our analysis of the manifest meaning of the sovereignty myth.

Explicit and implicit patterns

Empiricist critics of structural analysis in anthropology often raise the question—frequently with justice, no doubt—of how far the 'pattern' elicited in any particular case reflects the thinking of the people being analysed; coupled with this question there is usually the implication that the 'structure' supposedly revealed is, to a greater or lesser extent, a creation of the analyst, who has arbitrarily imposed an order of his own on the ethnographical material. This accusation lurks behind the charge of 'formalism' frequently levelled against Lévi-Strauss (cf. Yalman 1967). In dealing with the Fipa material I have sought, on purely methodological grounds,[8] to avoid this pitfall for the unwary structuralist: as far as the main argument is concerned, I have confined myself to sets of complementary oppositions which are perfectly explicit in Fipa thinking. Having made what I hope can be accepted as a *prima facie* case for the existence of a structural congruence between the idea-systems associated respectively with sovereignty and with descent, I feel the more justified in going on to strengthen that case with evidence from less clearly formulated areas of Fipa thought.

In dealing with this material, a regularity of another kind emerges: a conceptual opposition that is implicit in one dimension—sovereignty or descent—is always explicit in the other, as in the following examples.

1. Male(ness)—female(ness). This complementary opposition is explicit in the descent context. A Fipa who is asked for his descent name 'on the head side' (*uk'unntwe*) will reply with a name he inherits from his father and which is transmitted patrilineally; asked for his name 'on the loins side' (*uk'unnsana*), he will mention one of another category of names which he inherits from his mother.[9] But the same opposition is also implicit at the level of sovereignty: the dynasty of Milansi was founded by a *man*, while the Twa trace their origin to a *woman*.[10] The intrinsic maleness of Milansi may be seen in the fact that all the rulers recorded in oral tradition and including the present incumbent have been men, whereas women, as well as men, have at various times ruled in the two Twa kingdoms of Nkansi and Lyangalile.

2. Up—down. This relation is explicit, as a fact of geography, in the political dimension. Milansi, the royal village of the kingdom of the same name, is and always has been—according to tradition—situated on the slopes of Itweelele, the sacred mountain. The royal villages of the Twa, on the other hand, have always

been situated at one point or another on the Fipa plateau—never on a mountain. That is to say, Milansi is recognised by Fipa as being 'up' or 'high', in relation to the centres of Twa power, which are 'down' or 'low'. An analogous relation is implicit in Fipa conceptualisation of the principles of descent and derives from the physiological model of the two symbolic terms, 'head' and 'loins': in the human body, in its normal erect posture, 'head' is 'up' or 'high' and 'loins' are 'down' or 'low'.

3. Fixed—moving. Here again the oppositional relation is explicit between Milansi and the Twa. The royal village of Milansi is and always has been geographically fixed; but the location of Twa royal villages, up to the colonial period, was frequently changing—Twa rulers sometimes changed the site of their capitals several times during the course of a single reign.[11] Again an analogous relation is implicit in the context of descent and inheres in the fact that Fipa marriage is predominantly virilocal: it is men, the 'head' side in descent terms, who stay put, while women, the 'loins' side, move.[12]

Myths and 'mythical thinking'

Although Lévi-Strauss has so much to tell us about myths, he does not explicitly define the concept 'myth'. Instead, he seems to proffer an implied 'operational' definition, which would take some such form as: 'myths are linguistic phenomena characterised by a multi-dimensional structure of binary oppositions; separate myths can be shown by analysis to form transformation groups in which constituent elements and oppositions in different myths are reciprocally complementary'. It is also characteristic of myth and 'mythical thinking', according to Lévi-Strauss, that the number of structural dimensions in any myth, and the number of myths in a transformation group, are in principle unlimited: in this way myths produced by societies widely separated in space (and presumably also, in time) can be shown to be related, and to illuminate one another.[13]

On these terms, and without committing ourselves at this stage on the 'logical status' (Yalman 1967: 86) of Lévi-Strauss's analytical framework, the thinking of the Fipa would appear to conform well enough to the Lévi-Straussian formalisation of the 'mythical'. The two idea-systems considered in this article, the first derived from analysis of the sovereignty myth, and the second from analysis of Fipa notions about descent, can be shown, by following standard Lévi-Straussian procedure, to form a single 'transformation group'.

To begin with, certain elements—oppositional pairs—in these two systems are common to both: e.g., seniority versus juniority; and up versus down. Other pairs in the two idea-systems, Milansi-Twa and 'head'-'loins' appear on analysis to be analogues of one another and therefore capable of reciprocal transformation, thus:

System 1	*System* 2
Milansi	'head'
ritual authority ⇌	authority—intellect
territorial inferiority ⇌	'lightness'
weakness ⇌	'fewness'

System 1   *System 2*

Twa   'loins'

political power (= proliferation of offices)[14] ⟷ sexuality—reproduction

territorial superiority ⟷ 'heaviness'

strength ⟷ 'numbers'

Moreover, if we now return to our point of departure, the Fipa sovereignty myth, it can be seen to be rich in clues and references to an underlying system of binary discriminations in the best Lévi-Straussian tradition. Thus the version given here associates a fruit called *isuku* with one of the Twaci women, who is called Mwaana Kasuku (*isuku* and *Kasuku* are derived from the Fipa word for 'redness', *ukasuke*). Ethnographical evidence shows that the colours red and white are symbolically significant for Fipa. The Twa rulers of the country were traditionally buried in a red ox-skin; and red, being associated with blood, was a symbol of war and violence: men painted red marks on their faces before going into battle. Red is therefore particularly appropriate as the colour of the Twaci women (in some versions of the myth they are themselves said to have been of reddish hue), the bringers of change and war to the originally simple and peaceful land of the Fipa.

The colour white, on the other hand, is symbolic of spiritual power for Fipa and hence appropriate to Milansi, the ritual capital of Ufipa. In another sense white is appropriate to Milansi as the guardian of peace, as opposed to the turbulent Twa.[15] In the sphere of descent, spiritual authority is also attributed to the *umweenekasi*, the head of the *uluko*, whose duty it is to mediate with the ancestral spirits on behalf of his group.

Returning to the myth again, another of the Twaci women is called Earth-Person (*Unnsi*); this association of Twa with the earth naturally suggests to anyone acquainted with the Lévi-Straussian idiom that Milansi might, by way of opposition, be associated with the sky: and sure enough, Fipa tradition says that Milansi 'fell with the earth' from the sky at the beginning of time (Willis 1964)—and the same is said of the first king of Milansi, Ntatakwa. In similar vein, the name of the third Twaci woman, 'Child of the Stone', could be seen as belonging to the same oppositional group, with 'stone' as metonymous for 'earth'.

Perhaps enough has now been said to indicate that Fipa notions about sovereignty and descent belong to a wider cosmological pattern of dualistic classification and opposition which is *the same kind of pattern* as that which Lévi-Strauss has sought to reveal elsewhere in the 'primitive' world.[16] This kind of 'mythical' thinking, as Lévi-Strauss has said (1964: *passim*), has the characteristic of appearing to the analyst as 'unending': always revealing new dimensions, new series of oppositions. Such thought, in this case among the Fipa, admits of no exhaustive or conclusive exposition; but this same characteristic, once recognised, points to the existence within the basic oppositional forms of Fipa thought of more abstruse cognitive potentialities than we have yet indicated. Thus I would argue that in the opposed concepts of Milansi and Twa, 'head' and 'loins', there are contained, partly latent and partly explicit, notions of complementary duality akin to those which have exercised the minds of philosophers and theologians through the ages: such as the ideas of 'being and becoming', 'transcendent and contingent' and 'continuity and change'. The name 'Milansi', briefly translated, means 'the eternal village'—an implied contrast with the transitory settlements of the Twa.[17] A similar opposition of ideas of continuity and fixity, on the one hand, and of movement and change on the other, is associated with the opposed symbols 'head' and 'loins'. In their most basic thought categories Fipa thus unite in complementary opposition the ideas of society as a continuing entity, and therefore in some sense unchanging, and as the subject of historical mutation.

The time has now come however to leave these rarified and irremediably hypothetical heights and consider more closely the nature of mythological thought and, within the Fipa context, the central question of its relation to more substantial aspects of the social order.

Thought in aural cultures

It seems to me that in his analysis of the structure of mythological thought Lévi-Strauss has formalised the experience of every fieldworker who has gained some intimacy with the thought-forms of a pre-literate society. In what McLuhan calls 'aural' (or sometimes 'oral') cultures thought is integral, it entertains contradictions (which can be resolved only by conversion into other contradictions, as in *La geste d'Asdiwal*), it has no centre and no boundaries (Stearn 1967: 52). The apparent 'centre' of Lévi-Strauss's exposition of Amerindian mythology in *Le cru et le cuit*—the 'myth of reference'—has been arbitrarily chosen, as the author admits, for the purpose of the argument (Lévi-Strauss 1964: 10). The subsequent arrangement of the material is in a sense no less arbitrary, based as it is on the working-out of an elaborate analogy with the structure of music. But this unexpected approach, in which a few basic themes in the repertoire of Amerindian mythology are repetitively explored and developed, is palpably in harmony with the spirit of mythological thinking: it works. The book is itself fashioned in the shape of a gigantic myth—as Lévi-Strauss says, 'in spiral form' ('*en spirale*') (1964: 12).[18]

Some part of the as-yet-unassimilated significance of this experiment in controlled *participation mystique*, I would suggest, derives from the fact that every myth is an allegory of the field experience, just as the inner life of the fieldworker is necessarily mythical. For an 'observer'—the word is itself indicative of cultural bias—from a 'visual' culture to immerse himself in what McLuhan calls an integral, 'ear' culture is to suffer a profound disorientation. He enters a world of apparent contradictions which are resolvable, it seems, only and always in an inappropriate context, at another 'level': the 'resolution' is thus always provisional, always dissolving into other contradictions, which are equivocally resolved in similar manner. Yet from the first the contradictions are *felt*, rather than *seen*, to form a pattern which is regular even, or rather especially, in its very discontinuities. This is why Lévi-Strauss has chosen music, which is structure apprehended through the ear instead of the eye, to represent the spirit of mythological thought.

It is not surprising that the edifice Lévi-Strauss has constructed in *Le cru et le cuit* escapes the empirical constraints which he initially seeks to place upon it, emphasising '. . . la position centrale de nos mythes, et leur adhérence aux contours essentiels de l'organisation sociale et politique' (1964: 63).

But just as, for the fieldworker, a true rendering of indigenous thought involves abandoning the neat categories of social compartmentalisation he had brought with him, so in mythical analysis, 'chaque matrice de significations renvoie à une autre matrice, chaque mythe à d'autres mythes' (1964: 346). And the brilliant work of synthesis represented by *Le cru et le cuit* is achieved at the cost of jettisoning sociological correlates in favour of 'the human spirit' (*l'esprit*) as the ultimate point of reference: '... l'unique réponse que suggère ce livre est que les mythes signifient l'esprit, qui les élabore au moyen du monde dont il fait lui-même partie. Ainsi peuvent être simultanément engendrés, les mythes eux-mêmes par l'esprit qui les cause, et par les mythes, une image du monde déjà inscrite dans l'architecture de l'esprit' (1964: 346).

This is not a position which suggests possibilities of practical and theoretical advance—at least in social anthropology. It opens an enormous gulf between social thought—the collective representations of a vast culture area—and social action, the institutions to which these thought-forms must in some way correspond. The question that arises is: can mythological thought, which is endlessly dualistic, elaborate the more complex conceptual structures appropriate to systems of social relations?

One way in which this *might* be done is suggested by an earlier work of Lévi-Strauss, his *La geste d'Asdiwal* (1958), in which the myth goes through successive oppositional transformations at various levels—geographical, economic, sociological and cosmological. All these oppositions are, according to Lévi-Strauss's interpretation of the Asdiwal myth, reflections of a basic social contradiction inherent in the custom of matrilateral cross-cousin marriage among the Tsimshian Indians. This theory, which has been subjected to some criticism, is essentially speculative and unverifiable.[19] As a solution to the problem of the relation between mythological thought and social organisation it is unsatisfactory. The Fipa example, on the other hand, points to a way in which dualistic ideas can be combined so as to form, as it were, a higher order of conceptual organisation which will be appropriate to the complexity of its social referents.

If we now return to the Fipa sovereignty myth, we see that its manifest meaning relates to a system of ideas and values which, though of considerable complexity, is contained within the complementary opposition of two 'key' terms, 'Milansi' and 'Twa'. We have also drawn attention to the existence of another system of ideas and values in the universe of descent, derived from and contained within the complementary opposition of the dominant symbols 'head' and 'loins'; and we have argued that there is a structural congruence between these two conceptual-affective systems. If this latter point is conceded, the sovereignty myth becomes not merely a 'charter', in Malinowski's sense, for the relation between the kingdoms of Milansi and the Twa, but is also, at another level, an allegory of the world of descent, as Fipa experience it. The myth has meaning at different cognitive levels in two apparently unrelated dimensions of Fipa society. The first meaning (concerning the relation between ritual and political sovereignty) is overt and manifest; the second meaning, in terms of descent, is latent; both meanings, it must be presumed, contribute to the significance for Fipa of the sovereignty myth.

The interpretation of the Fipa sovereignty myth put forward in this paper does not preclude its analysis in terms of a system of binary discriminations in the standard Lévi-Straussian manner; indeed the assumption, already made explicit, is that the myth is basically structured in accordance with such a system. But the central significance of the myth for Fipa, it is argued, is its embodiment, at different cognitive levels, of what I have called 'conceptual-affective' structures which directly reflect social organisation. In these structures clusters of ideas, which are opposed on the model of englobing 'key' oppositions, are themselves divided into opposed sub-clusters or sub-sets—vertically, as it were—by a contrary value-loading. The following diagram (fig. 1) attempts to convey some of the complexity of this conceptual-affective system. In it a single arrow (→) represents the operation of logical or empirical (or logico-empirical) transformation;[20] a double arrow (←→) represents the complementary opposition of two concepts; a plus or a minus sign indicates the relative value given to the concepts enclosed within the round brackets; square brackets enclose the two idea-systems; and the sign ≡ indicates structural congruence between them.

The actual situation is a good deal more complex than this. The diagram shows only a few of the more important, and entirely explicit, oppositional concepts associated with the two pairs of key ideas; a more comprehensive representation would have to indicate the theoretically infinite number of oppositional pairs which *could* be derived from the key oppositions and, in doing so, it would also be desirable to indicate another variable quantity—the relative explicitness or otherwise of all these ideas in Fipa thinking. The diagram may be incomplete in another way, since other idea-systems may exist, structurally congruent with those related to sovereignty and descent, in other dimensions of Fipa society: this article describes two which I have been able to isolate and analyse.[21]

The approach to mythical analysis attempted in this article is in a sense opposite to that exemplified in Lévi-Strauss's recent work (1964). Where Lévi-Strauss *begins* 'at the most concrete level ... in the heart of a population' (1964: 9) and ends amidst 'the architecture of the spirit' (346), this approach begins with the myth, veiled as it is in primal music and mystery, and works towards the socially concrete, in terms of identifiable institutions and systems of relations.[22]

Further reflection suggests that these two approaches, and others too, may all be necessary, or at least desirable: the demonstration that myth, and myths, can be understood in terms of a system of binary discriminations does not exhaust the possibilities of structural analysis, as Burridge has pointed out (1967). For if, on the one hand, the implication of the Lévi-Straussian procedure and precedent is that the full meaning of, for example, the Fipa myth can emerge only when it is examined in the course of an analysis ranging over the whole corpus of Bantu mythology, on the other hand the method results in and operates through an intractable paradox. The synoptic approach exemplified in *Le cru et le cuit*, in which Lévi-Strauss has taken the entire mythical heritage of the Amerindians for his province, achieves astonishing coherence and complexity—but at the price of severing virtually all links with the solid ground of ethnography. In following so faithfully the spirit of mythological thought, Lévi-Strauss has been obliged, in the manner of that thought itself, to elude the straightforward categories of everyday tribal life for the elliptical linkages of *participation mystique* (Lévy-Bruhl). It has been Lévi-Strauss's achievement to discover a rigorous logical pattern, a paradoxically abstract 'science of the concrete', behind these seemingly random juxtapositions.[23]

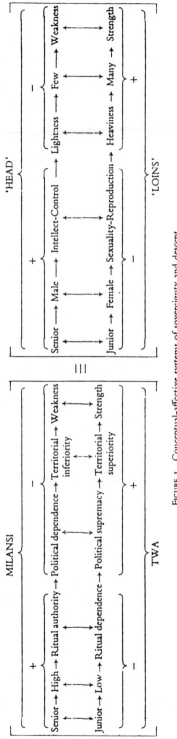

FIGURE I. Conceptual-affective systems of sovereignty and descent.

The object of the more recent work of Lévi-Strauss, it seems to me, has not been to elaborate any kind of empirically verifiable 'map' of mythological thought, but to demonstrate, through sympathetic and uninhibited participation in *la pensée sauvage*, the vastness and richness of the territory yet to be explored by social anthropology. Reading *Le cru et le cuit*, in particular, is like inhabiting the mind of some super-ethnographer as he undergoes a field experience ranging through seemingly limitless expanses of time and space.

These portentous 'field notes' are a notable challenge to the assumptions of particularistic and relativistic empiricism. But they will remain theoretically barren unless translated, like all such information, into the common language of social anthropology. What is needed to complement the synoptic labours of Lévi-Strauss and to begin the complex task of incorporating the immense new territory he has prospected into the body of our discipline, is not less structuralism but more —at the 'grass-roots' level of ethnography. In this article I have tried to indicate, in the context of my own fieldwork, how such an approach could be made. Structuralist and obviously 'Lévi-Straussian' in inspiration, it is also empirically-oriented, since it relates to 'concrete' social institutions.

Summary

In conclusion, the following assumptions and hypotheses seem to arise from or be suggested by, the arguments in this article.

1. Thought in pre-literate or 'aural' cultures is characterised by what Lévy-Bruhl called *participation mystique*, Lévi-Strauss has described in terms of an 'un-ending' series of conceptual oppositions, resolutions and transformations, and McLuhan has most recently called 'a total field of simultaneous relations, without centre or margin' (Stearn 1967: 52).

2. 'Myths' and 'mythological thinking' are, *at a certain level of analysis* (which has become almost synonymous with the name of Lévi-Strauss) alike insofar as they are composed of formally similar systems of oppositions and 'participations' (or 'binary discriminations').

3. But, according to the evidence adduced in this article, 'myths' are also *particular* in that they relate, through what I have called their conceptual-affective structure, or structures, to one or more organisational aspects of the society that produced them. This conclusion, or hypothesis, if found to be generally true by comparison with other societies, would have at least one significant consequence: it would restrict the anthropological use of the term 'myth', which in the work of Lévi-Strauss seems indistinguishable from the wider category of 'story', to oral forms exhibiting the necessary structural characteristics.

4. Conceptual-affective systems, or structures, in the sense the term has been used here, are aspects of social institutions and systems of relations. They are made out of the basic mythological 'bricks' of oppositions and participations and their relatively greater complexity is explained by the presence of an affective, 'value' component which results in cross-cutting internal oppositions of clusters of concepts within the total system. In a 'myth' all the major constituent elements of such structures (value-loaded ideas) are directly or symbolically embodied.

It is precisely the affective element in mythological thought, on which Lévy-Bruhl particularly insisted (1949: 167-9), that evaporates during the course of an

2—M.

overall analysis of *Le cru et le cuit* dimensions, leaving a passionless structure of remote and mathematical beauty: the 'music' takes on form, but loses its emotional content, which can be derived only from communication with human beings—the 'field' situation.[24]

5. Analysis of the Fipa material has suggested that a single myth can include, and relate to, more than one conceptual-affective structure—because these structures, though aspects of institutions and systems of relations which are 'disparate' to conventional analysis, are in fact, like the numberless versions of the myth itself, formally congruent. The evidence presented here suggests that the central Fipa myth is a 'sociological charter' of a depth and comprehensiveness which might well have surprised Malinowski, and that the language of the charter is a sort of ultra-Lévi-Straussian one.

NOTES

My first stay in 1962–4 among the Fipa was financed by the Emslie Horniman Anthropological Scholarship Fund; a second visit in 1966 was made possible through a grant from the Wenner-Gren Foundation for Anthropological Research.

[1] I was told that there is a place on the Lake Tanganyika shore of this name, which comes from a verb meaning 'to press down with the foot'.

[2] The behaviour of the king of Milansi in this story epitomises the Fipa ideal of manly conduct. On the one hand the king is personally courageous, as evidenced by his lone hunting expedition into the wilderness; on the other hand, when it comes to social relations, as in his approach to the usurping strangers and even to his wife who has, though against her will, betrayed him, he exhibits a gentle courtesy (*ukoonde*). This latter quality entails a mastery over his emotions, and particularly his aggressive impulses, which is for the outsider a notable characteristic of the Fipa male.

[3] Or more precisely, 'descent and kinship'. To avoid being unduly cumbersome, the term 'descent' is to be understood in this article as including the notions of 'kinship' (and 'affinity').

[4] Among the Fipa there is no direct association between descent and territory: cultivation rights go with village residence. The members of any single *uluko* are typically distributed between a number of villages and they (i.e., the senior, principally male, members) meet together as a group fairly infrequently, and usually only when a question of inheritance or succession has to be decided.

[5] Fipa have no formalised, ancestor-oriented rule of descent, such as patrilineality or bilineality; instead, descent groups select, or emphasise, common descent through both or mixed lines on an *ad hoc* basis.

[6] The Oxford English Dictionary gives one meaning of 'loins' as 'the part or parts of a human being or quadruped, situated on both sides of the vertebral column, between the false ribs and the hip-bone' (1961, 6, 405). This corresponds quite well to the region of the human body denoted by *unnsana*. One difficulty is that figuratively *unnsana* connotes female reproductive potential whereas the Biblical associations of 'loins' are with male generative powers; but if this difference of sexual implication is borne in mind, 'loins' appears to me to be preferable as a rendering of *unnsana* to the sexually neutral 'flank' or 'waist'.

[7] This proverb ('*Uk'unnsana kuli nyama, uk'unntwe—ee, weene!*') is of course also a pun: the loins are a 'meaty' part of the body as opposed to the head, which is most obviously without 'meat'. It may be that the equivocal significance of the symbolic terms 'head' and 'loins' has had an unconscious 'feedback' effect on Fipa notions of physiology: for instance, I have heard Fipa say that the heart (*umweeso*) is 'your own' while the head 'is just something on top'.

[8] In principle I see no reason why a territory, that of the 'unconscious', in which linguists, for example, operate without noticeable inhibitions, should be taboo for social anthropologists.

[9] Fipa have two categories of descent name. The first category has four members and these descend patrilineally; the second category has 26 members and these are inherited matrilineally.

[10] Though this woman is nameless in the version of the myth I have quoted, other versions give a variety of names: Unnda, Mwati and Mami Tende. The name of the first king of Milansi is usually said to have been Ntatakwa ('the unnamed one'); he is said to have been the first man in the world.

11 The main purpose of these movements, as in other preliterate African states (e.g. Buganda) was to maintain the central power over a geographically wide area and to counteract the centrifugal tendencies which arose in peripheral regions.

12 Of 187 marriages recorded in various parts of Ufipa, 139 (90 per cent. of the total sample) were virilocal and 18 (10 per cent.) were uxorilocal.

13 Cf. Lévi-Strauss (1964: 13–14): 'Il n'existe pas de terme véritable à l'analyse mythique, pas d'unité secrète qu'on puisse saisir au bout du travail de décomposition. Les thèmes se dédoublent à l'infini . . . La divergence des séquences et des thèmes est un attribut fondamental de la pensée mythique . . . Comme les rites, les mythes sont *in-terminables.*' .

On the meaning of 'myth' and 'mythical thinking', Lévi-Strauss deliberately casts his net wide:

'Nous rejetons, en effet, les opinions trop hâtives sur ce qui est mythique et ce qui ne l'est pas, et revendiquons pour notre usage toute manifestation de l'activité mentale ou sociale des populations étudiées, dont il apparaîtra en cours d'analyse qu'elle permet de compléter le mythe ou de l'éclairer . . .' (1964: 12).

14 As in other 'patrimonial' (Weber) systems of government, Twa power was manifested in a multitude of royal office-holders and title-holders, together with a relatively numerous class of officials with specific administrative duties. Milansi, in contrast, had no 'administrative staff'.

15 The peaceful and peace-making role of the Milansi kingship is a recurrent motif in Fipa oral tradition (cf. Willis 1964).

16 It seems hardly necessary to point out that the apparent generality of dualistic thinking does not imply that the opposed ideas, or the important symbolic oppositions, are the same in all societies. Among the Fipa, for example, the opposition of 'right' and 'left', though found in some specialised contexts, is not of general importance; certainly the idea of the superiority of 'right' over 'left', which apparently forms the keystone of the symbolic thinking of many societies, is not explicit for Fipa. Similarly the symbolic opposition of 'hot' and 'cold', which is so essential in the thought and behaviour of the Bemba (to whom the Fipa are linguistically quite close) does not occur in Fipa thought.

17 An earlier guess that 'Milansi' meant 'swallow the country' (Willis 1964) has proved to be erroneous. I have since learnt that the name is a combination of the stem of the verb *uku-laanda*, 'to go on and on' and *unnsi*, 'village'.

18 McLuhan uses the same 'spiral' image to describe the mode of thought he sees as typical of 'oral' cultures':

'The Hebrew and Eastern mode of thought tackles problem and resolution, at the outset of a discussion, in a way typical of oral societies in general. The entire message is then traced and retraced, again and again, on the rounds of a concentric spiral with seeming redundancy' (1964: 26).

19 Cf. the detailed comments by Douglas (1967), who finds this interpretation 'far-fetched'. In his more recent work it would seem that Lévi-Strauss has abandoned this search for a centre, or ultimate basis, in myth—an approach which, if one follows McLuhan, could itself be seen as reflecting an unconscious bias of Western 'visual' man.

20 The connexion between ritual authority and political dependence is an observable fact for Fipa, as is the association between maleness and seniority; on a more abstract plane of accepted ideas, the same is true of the association between intellect and 'lightness' and sexuality-and-reproduction and 'heaviness' (cf. the proverb quoted above). The connexions between 'senior' and 'high' and 'junior' and 'low' are both logical and conventional, while those between territorial inferiority and weakness and 'many' and 'strength' are primarily logical but also matters of fact and experience.

21 Some of these idea-systems and their correlated social institutions may have been partially or wholly destroyed in the changes of the colonial and post-colonial era. Thus the pre-colonial Fipa village was structured on lines which suggest parallels with the opposed attributes of ritual and political sovereignty and the opposed principles of descent: in it overall authority belonged to the headman (*umweene nnsi*), who was also the chief priest of the village and sacrificed on behalf of the whole community. Responsibility for public order and particularly the suppression of sexual offences, including the public use of obscene language, was in the hands of an elder *woman* magistrate, called ¡*Wakwiifatila*. She was assisted by a squad of men, whom she could call on to arrest trouble-makers. The headman, apparently, had no such powers of physical coercion, suggesting a parallel with Milansi ('male' and lacking coercive power) and Twa ('female' and with such power).

Although most Fipa villages still have an ¡*Wakwiifatila*, such of her powers as were deemed proper have been long ago assumed by the Native Courts. Old-established thought-and-action patterns sometimes die hard, however, it may be that the prominent part played by Fipa women in a recent anti-sorcery movement in Ufipa (Willis in press) and the surprising air of legitimacy which seems to have surrounded their activities, can be explained, partially at least, by reference to traditional norms.

[22] In his critical appreciation of Lévi-Strauss, Burridge (1967) seems to advocate a similar approach to myth to that attempted in this paper, when he calls for analysis based on content rather than form.

[23] Lévy-Bruhl himself, in his last years, seems to have been aware of the possibilities of order in the apparent chaos of *participations*, as these words from *Les carnets* suggest:

'... Etudier en quoi la participation consiste dans ces divers cas, comment elle se présente, ce que peut être, dans ces complexes, la part de l'abstraction (quelle sorte d'abstraction?) des *patterns* ou schèmes ...' (1949: 88).

[24] Cf. the recent comments of Fortes on the consequences of Lévi-Straussian structuralism: 'By isolating the classifying, categorising and communication functions of totemic institutions, Lévi-Strauss illuminates a fundamental aspect of the syndrome. But it is at the cost of neutralizing the actor. No wonder, then, that we functionalists and Lévi-Strauss and his followers seem to be talking past one another. For we and they are looking at the configuration of actor, action and cultural materials of action from opposite sides. For us, language is verbal custom: for them, all custom is transposed language' (1967: 9).

By contrast with Fortes, who seems to assume that the two approaches he mentions, though perhaps complementary, are operationally incompatible, the approach to mythical analysis in this article attempts to include the actor oriented element of 'value' within an objective, structuralist framework.

REFERENCES

Burridge, K. O. L. 1967. Lévi-Strauss and myth. In *The structural study of myth and totemism* (ed.) E. R. Leach (Ass. social Anthrop. Monogr. 5). London: Tavistock.

Douglas, M. 1967. The meaning of myth. In *The structural study of myth and totemism* (ed.) E. R. Leach (Ass. social Anthrop. Monogr. 5). London: Tavistock.

Fortes, M. 1967. Totem and taboo. *Proc. R. anthrop. Inst.* 1966, 5–22.

Leach, E. R. 1967. Introduction: In *The structural study of myth and totemism.* (ed.) E. R. Leach (Ass. social Anthrop. Monogr. 5). London: Tavistock.

Lévi-Strauss, C. 1955. The structural study of myth. *J. Am. Folkl.* **28**, 428–44.

——— 1958. La geste d'Asdiwal. *Annu. Éc. Hautes Étud. Sci. relig.* 1958/9, 3–43.

——— 1962. *La pensée sauvage.* Paris: Plon.

——— 1964. *Mythologiques: le cru et le cuit.* Paris: Plon.

Lévy-Bruhl, L. 1949. *Les carnets de Lucien Lévy-Bruhl.* Paris: Plon.

McLuhan, M. 1964. *Understanding media: the extensions of man.* London: Routledge & Kegan Paul.

Malinowski, B. 1948. Myth in primitive psychology. In *Magic, science and religion and other essays.* Glencoe, Ill.: Free Press.

Stearn, G. E. 1967. Conversations with McLuhan. *Encounter* **28**, 50–8.

Turner, V. W. 1964. Symbols in Ndembu ritual. In *Closed systems and open minds: the limits of naïvety in social anthropology* (ed.) M. Gluckman. London: Manchester Univ. Press.

Weber, M. 1947. *The theory of social and economic organization.* New York: Free Press of Glencoe.

Willis, R. G. 1964. Traditional history and social structure in Ufipa. *Africa* **34**, 340–52.

——— in press. Kamcape: an anti-sorcery movement in south-west Tanzania. *Africa.*

Yalman, N. 1967. The raw: the cooked :: nature: culture. In *The structural study of myth and totemism* (ed.) E. R. Leach (Ass. social Anthrop. Monogr. 5). London: Tavistock.

ACKNOWLEDGMENTS

Barthes, Roland. "Myth Today." In Roland Barthes, *Mythologies* (trans. Annette Lavers) (New York: Hill and Wang, 1972): 109–37. Reprinted with the permission of Farrar, Straus & Giroux, Inc.

Douglas, Mary. "The Meaning of Myth, with Special Reference to 'La Geste d'Asdiwal'." In Edmund Leach, ed., *The Structural Study of Myth and Totemism* (London: Tavistock, 1967): 49–69. Reprinted with the permission of Routledge.

Dumézil, Georges. "The Archaic Triad: The Documents." In Georges Dumézil, *Archaic Roman Religion,* Vol. 1 (Chicago: University of Chicago Press, 1970): 141–47. Reprinted with the permission of University of Chicago Press and Editions Payot.

Dumézil, Georges. "Interpretation: The Three Functions." In Georges Dumézil, *Archaic Roman Religion,* Vol. 1 (Chicago: University of Chicago Press, 1970): 148–75. Reprinted with the permission of University of Chicago Press and Editions Payot.

Leach, Edmund. "Lévi-Strauss in the Garden of Eden: An Examination of Some Recent Developments in the Analysis of Myth." *Transactions of the New York Academy of Sciences,* Series 2, 23 (February 1961): 386–96. Reprinted with the permission of the New York Academy of Sciences.

Levin, Isidor. "Vladimir Propp: An Evaluation on His Seventieth Birthday." *Journal of the Folklore Institute* 4 (June 1967): 32–49. Reprinted with the permission of the *Journal of Folklore Research.*

Lévi-Strauss, Claude. "The Structural Study of Myth." *Journal of American Folklore* 68 (October-December 1955): 428–44. Reprinted with the permission of the American Folklore Society. Not for further reproduction.

Lévi-Strauss, Claude. "The Story of Asdiwal." In Edmund Leach, ed., *The Structural Study of Myth and Totemism* (London: Tavistock, 1967): 1–47. Reprinted with the permission of Routledge.

Littleton, C. Scott. "The Comparative Indo-European Mythology of Georges Dumézil." *Journal of the Folklore Institute* 1 (December 1964): 147–66. Reprinted with the permission of the *Journal of Folklore Research*.

Moriarty, Michael. "Myths." In Michael Moriarty, *Roland Barthes* (Stanford: Stanford University Press, 1991): 19–30, 212–14. Reprinted with the permission of Stanford University Press and Polity Press.

Propp, Vladimir. "Structure and History in the Study of the Fairy Tale." *Semeia* 10 (1978): 57–83. Reprinted with the permission of Scholars Press.

Vernant, Jean-Pierre. "Hesiod's Myth of the Races: An Essay in Structural Analysis." In Jean-Pierre Vernant, *Myth and Thought among the Greeks* (London & Boston: Routledge and Kegan Paul, 1983): 3–32. Reprinted with the permission of Harvester Wheatsheaf.

Vidal-Naquet, Pierre. "The Black Hunter and the Origin of the Athenian *Ephebeia*." In R.L. Gordon, ed., *Myth, Religion and Society* (Cambridge: Cambridge University Press, 1981): 147–62, 254–59. Reprinted with the permission of Cambridge University Press.

Walters, K.R. "Another Showdown at the Cleft Way: An Inquiry into Classicists' Criticism of Lévi-Strauss' Myth Analysis." *Classical World* 77 (July-August 1984): 337–51. Reprinted with the permission of the Classical Association of the Atlantic States.

Willis, R.G. "The Head and the Loins: Lévi-Strauss and Beyond." *Man,* n.s., 2 (December 1967): 519–34. Reprinted with the permission of the Royal Anthropological Institute of Great Britain & Ireland.